Cross–Cultural Training and Teamwork in Healthcare

Simona Vasilache
Bucharest University of Economic Studies, Romania

A volume in the Advances in Healthcare
Information Systems and Administration
(AHISA) Book Series

Medical Information Science
REFERENCE
An Imprint of IGI Global

KH

Managing Director:	Lindsay Johnston
Production Manager:	Jennifer Yoder
Development Editor:	Allyson Gard
Acquisitions Editor:	Kayla Wolfe
Typesetter:	Christina Henning
Cover Design:	Jason Mull

Published in the United States of America by
Medical Information Science Reference (an imprint of IGI Global)
701 E. Chocolate Avenue
Hershey PA 17033
Tel: 717-533-8845
Fax: 717-533-8661
E-mail: cust@igi-global.com
Web site: http://www.igi-global.com

Library of Congress Cataloging-in-Publication Data

Cross-cultural training and teamwork in healthcare / Simona Vasilache, editor.
     pages cm
  Summary: "This book explores the complex relationships between patients, physicians, and nurses with different cultural backgrounds, integrating theoretical and empirical perspectives on medical teamwork"-- Provided by publisher.
  Includes bibliographical references and index.
  ISBN 978-1-4666-4325-3 (hardcover) -- ISBN 978-1-4666-4326-0 (ebook) -- ISBN 978-1-4666-4327-7 (print & perpetual access) 1. Transcultural medical care. 2. Cultural competence. 3. Cross-cultural orientation. I. Vasilache, Simona, 1982- editor of compilation.
  RA418.5.T73C77 2014
  610.7306'9--dc23
                                    2013012287

This book is published in the IGI Global book series Advances in Healthcare Information Systems and Administration (AHISA) (ISSN: 2328-1243; eISSN: 2328-126X)

British Cataloguing in Publication Data
A Cataloguing in Publication record for this book is available from the British Library.

For electronic access to this publication, please contact: eresources@igi-global.com.

2/23/16

Advances in Healthcare Information Systems and Administration (AHISA) Book Series

ISSN: 2328-1243
EISSN: 2328-126X

MISSION

The **Advances in Healthcare Information Systems and Administration (AHISA) Book Series** aims to provide a channel for international researchers to progress the field of study on technology and its implications on healthcare and health information systems. With the growing focus on healthcare and the importance of enhancing this industry to tend to the expanding population, the book series seeks to accelerate the awareness of technological advancements of health information systems and expand awareness and implementation.

Driven by advancing technologies and their clinical applications, the emerging field of health information systems and informatics is still searching for coherent directing frameworks to advance health care and clinical practices and research. Conducting research in these areas is both promising and challenging due to a host of factors, including rapidly evolving technologies and their application complexity. At the same time, organizational issues, including technology adoption, diffusion and acceptance as well as cost benefits and cost effectiveness of advancing health information systems and informatics applications as innovative forms of investment in healthcare are gaining attention as well. **AHISA** addresses these concepts and critical issues.

COVERAGE

- Clinical Decision Support Design, Development and Implementation
- E-Health and M-Health
- IT Applications in Physical Therapeutic Treatments
- IT Security and Privacy Issues
- Management of Emerging Health Care Technologies
- Pharmaceutical and Home Healthcare Informatics
- Rehabilitative Technologies
- Role of Informatics Specialists
- Telemedicine
- Virtual Health Technologies

IGI Global is currently accepting manuscripts for publication within this series. To submit a proposal for a volume in this series, please contact our Acquisition Editors at Acquisitions@igi-global.com or visit: http://www.igi-global.com/publish/.

Titles in this Series

For a list of additional titles in this series, please visit: www.igi-global.com

Advancing Medical Practice through Technology Applications for Healthcare Delivery, Management, and Quality
Joel J.P.C. Rodrigues (Instituto de Telecomunicações, University of Beira Interior, Portugal)
Medical Information Science Reference • copyright 2014 • 361pp • H/C (ISBN: 9781466646193) • US $245.00
(our price)

Research Perspectives on the Role of Informatics in Health Policy and Management
Christo El Morr (York University, Canada)
Medical Information Science Reference • copyright 2014 • 323pp • H/C (ISBN: 9781466643215) • US $245.00
(our price)

Cross-Cultural Training and Teamwork in Healthcare
Simona Vasilache (Academy of Economic Studies, Romania)
Medical Information Science Reference • copyright 2014 • 326pp • H/C (ISBN: 9781466643253) • US $245.00
(our price)

Serious Games for Healthcare Applications and Implications
Sylvester Arnab (Coventry University, UK) Ian Dunwell (Coventry University, UK) and Kurt Debattista (University of Warwick, UK)
Medical Information Science Reference • copyright 2013 • 370pp • H/C (ISBN: 9781466619036) • US $245.00
(our price)

Telemedicine and E-Health Services, Policies, and Applications Advancements and Developments
Joel J. P. C. Rodrigues (Instituto de Telecomunicações, University of Beira Interior, Portugal) Isabel de la Torre Díez (University of Valladolid, Spain) and Beatriz Sainz de Abajo (University of Valladolid, Spain)
Medical Information Science Reference • copyright 2012 • 572pp • H/C (ISBN: 9781466608887) • US $245.00
(our price)

E-Healthcare Systems and Wireless Communications Current and Future Challenges
Mohamed K. Watfa (University of Wollongong, UAE)
Medical Information Science Reference • copyright 2012 • 462pp • H/C (ISBN: 9781613501238) • US $245.00
(our price)

Human-Centered Design of E-Health Technologies Concepts, Methods and Applications
Martina Ziefle (RWTH Aachen University, Germany) and Carsten Röcker (RWTH Aachen University, Germany)
Medical Information Science Reference • copyright 2011 • 426pp • H/C (ISBN: 9781609601775) • US $245.00
(our price)

www.igi-global.com

701 E. Chocolate Ave., Hershey, PA 17033
Order online at www.igi-global.com or call 717-533-8845 x100
To place a standing order for titles released in this series, contact: cust@igi-global.com
Mon-Fri 8:00 am - 5:00 pm (est) or fax 24 hours a day 717-533-8661

Table of Contents

Detailed Table of Contents

Section 1
Cross-Cultural Training

Chapter 1

Simona Vasilache, Bucharest University of Economic Studies, Romania
Alina Mihaela Dima, Bucharest University of Economic Studies, Romania

The chapter discusses the possibility for European education to convergence in the Bologna framework by studying the literature dedicated to educational policies in leading academic journals. Using a content analysis methodology, the qualitative research aims to highlight the key topics and research concerns of academics in European higher education and to correlate their research focuses, which are being promoted and implemented in European universities as effective policy. The results may serve as guidelines for both policy makers and executives in higher education, as well as for broader categories of stakeholders.

Chapter 2

Simona Agoston, Bucharest University of Economic Studies, Romania
Katja Lasch, German Academic Exchange Service, Romania

The chapter discusses the internationalization process of Romanian universities against a background of increasing multiculturalism. The authors collect and analyze data related to the flows of international students and staff in Romanian universities, as well as measures taken to promote student and staff circulation and to attract candidates from abroad. The conclusions of the study point to the fact that not only do Romanian universities do too little to become attractive to foreign students but due to a chronic lack of accurate data they also do not really know where they stand as to be able to improve. The present research attempted, thus, to advance knowledge about the status quo and to promote strategies for improvement.

Chapter 3

The chapter discusses, comparatively, funding mechanisms for universities in Europe and advances potential ways for their harmonization in the framework of their Bologna convergence. The findings of the research suggest that, while there is a European-level shift to performance-based funding and quantitative indicators tend to say that European HE funding systems are to a certain degree convergent, qualitative analysis indicates that the outcomes are still divergent and more efforts have to be put into really bringing these systems to a common ground.

Section 2
Cross-Cultural Teamwork

Chapter 4

The chapter discusses the specificities of organizational culture in healthcare environments, taking into account general managerial theories and their suitability to particular professional settings. The challenges of teamwork and the things to be particularly considered by decision-makers in the healthcare system are discussed and critically analyzed.

Chapter 5

The chapter discusses, on research-based findings, the particularities of culture in hospitals, in a cross-cultural perspective with a particular focus on the Polish case. The findings of the study point to the fact that exterior factors and perceptions have a decisive impact on the patient evaluation of the hospital experience, so hospitals should dedicate some of their efforts to improving organizational culture and its perceived effects on patients.

Chapter 6

This chapter sets out to analyze the problem of defining the concept of organizational culture as well as models and typologies used in reference materials. It presents various issues of organizational culture: paradigms of organizational culture, definitions of organizational culture, and two-dimensional typologies of organizational culture. The single-dimensional classifications present the following dichotomies: 1) weak culture – strong culture, 2) positive culture – negative culture, 3) pragmatic culture – bureaucratic culture, 4) introvert culture – extrovert culture, 5) conservative culture – innovative culture, 6) hierarchic culture – egalitarian culture, 7) individualist culture – collectivist culture. Furthermore, this chapter includes: multidimensional typologies of organizational culture, corporate identity – alternative approach to organizational culture and relations between culture, and structure, strategy, and organization setting. Moreover, based on the quality pilot study, it strives to explain peculiarity of this concept in relation to Polish hospitals. Results of pilot studies of organizational cultures of hospitals in Poland relate to four hospitals in Lodz Province.

The chapter reviews the clash between personal and organizational culture in multicultural settings, advancing ways to mediate between the two and to apply proper strategies in order to establish sound interpersonal relations while not losing sight of the general objectives of the business organization.

Chapter 8

The chapter discusses the marketing strategies of private Romanian healthcare clinics from a communication perspective, advancing methods to improve customer outreach. The study puts together data from the private medical services market and comparatively analyzes the marketing strategies, making recommendations towards the optimal cost-benefit mix.

The chapter provides an overview of the changes suffered by the secondary and higher education systems in the communism to post-communism transition and discusses the transformation of the teaching methods and the impact of these transformations. Most teachers aspire to make critical thinking the main objective of their instruction; most of them do not realize that to develop as thinkers students must pass through stages of development in critical thinking. The conclusions point to the fact that most teachers are unaware of the levels of intellectual development that students go through as they improve as thinkers. The research shows that significant gains in the intellectual quality of student work will not be achieved if teachers do not recognize that skilled critical thinking develops only if properly cultivated and only through predictable stages.

Chapter 10
Internal Communication in EU Project Management in Bucharest University of

The present research underlines the importance of communication within an organization among its main stakeholders and its influence on the external market. It passes through explaining the communication in all fields and domains, creating an overview of the institutional communication, and why it is considered difficult to effectively propagate within a large institution. In addition, the internal communication and information and research so far conducted is analyzed with respect to the findings and lessons learned. In addition, it is important to know and understand how the internal communication evolved during years and which were the main approaches identified throughout the organizations. The case study aims to evaluate the level of information and the efficiency and effectiveness of the internal communication process within Bucharest University of Economic Studies with respect to its projects developed and financed through European funds in the last six years. The study is mainly run through the help of the questionnaire that was addressed to teachers and students within the faculty and has also the purpose to help improve the related communication in the foreseeable future based on the relevant findings.

Preface

This collection of viewpoints on cross-cultural training and teamwork serves at least two purposes: to point out the variety of ways in which training and teamwork take place across cultures in sensitive areas like education and healthcare and to make available the state of the art in the works of the researchers devoted to the domain.

The book is structured in two sections: the first one, comprising the introductory three chapters, discusses the transformation of education in Romania, as a framework for all researches on healthcare and teamwork having Eastern Europe as a setting. Thus, this section sets the background for the second one, which is dedicated to teamwork, with a particular focus on healthcare premises.

The first chapter discusses the possibility for European education to convergence in the Bologna framework by studying the literature dedicated to educational policies in leading academic journals. Using a content analysis methodology, the qualitative research aims to highlight the key topics and research concerns of academics in European higher education and to correlate their research focuses, which are being promoted and implemented in European universities as effective policy. The results may serve as guidelines for both policy makers and executives in higher education, as well as for broader categories of stakeholders.

The second chapter discusses the internationalization process of Romanian universities against a background of increasing multiculturalism. The authors collect and analyze data related to the flows of international students and staff in Romanian universities, as well as measures taken to promote student and staff circulation and to attract candidates from abroad. The conclusions of the study point to the fact that not only do Romanian universities do too little to become attractive to foreign students but due to a chronic lack of accurate data they also do not really know where they stand as to be able to improve. The present research attempted, thus, to advance knowledge about the status quo and to promote strategies for improvement.

To conclude the first section of the book, the third chapter discusses, comparatively, funding mechanisms for universities in Europe and advances potential ways for their harmonization in the framework of their Bologna convergence. The findings of the research suggest that, while there is a European-level shift to performance-based funding and quantitative indicators tend to say that European HE funding systems are to a certain degree convergent, qualitative analysis indicates that the outcomes are still divergent and more efforts have to be put into really bringing these systems to a common ground.

The second section starts with a transition chapter, which links cross-cultural issues with inside hospital teamwork. The fourth chapter discusses the specificities of organizational culture in healthcare environments, taking into account general managerial theories and their suitability to particular professional settings. The challenges of teamwork and the things to be particularly considered by decision-makers in the healthcare system are discussed and critically analyzed.

The fifth chapter discusses, on research-based findings, the particularities of culture in hospitals, in a cross-cultural perspective with a particular focus on the Polish case. The findings of the study point to the fact that exterior factors and perceptions have a decisive impact on the patient evaluation of the hospital experience, so hospitals should dedicate some of their efforts to improving organizational culture and its perceived effects on patients.

The sixth chapter attempts to analyze the problem of defining the concept of organizational culture as well as models and typologies used in reference materials. Moreover, based on the quality pilot study, it strives to explain peculiarity of this concept in relation to Polish hospitals.

Next, the seventh chapter reviews the clash between personal and organizational culture in multicultural settings, advancing ways to mediate between the two and to apply proper strategies in order to establish sound interpersonal relations while not losing sight of the general objectives of the business organization.

The eighth chapter discusses the marketing strategies of private Romanian healthcare clinics from a communication perspective, advancing methods to improve customer outreach. The study puts together data from the private medical services market and comparatively analyzes the marketing strategies, making recommendations towards the optimal cost-benefit mix.

The ninth chapter links again with education, in an attempt to round up the approach. The chapter provides an overview of the changes suffered by the secondary and higher education systems in the communism to post-communism transition and discusses the transformation of the teaching methods and the impact of these transformations. Most teachers aspire to make critical thinking the main objective of their instruction; most of them do not realize that to develop as thinkers students must pass through stages of development in critical thinking. The conclusions point to the fact that most teachers are unaware of the levels of intellectual development that students go through as they improve as thinkers. The research shows that significant gains in the intellectual quality of student work will not be achieved if teachers do not recognize that skilled critical thinking develops only if properly cultivated and only through predictable stages.

The tenth chapter underlines the importance of communication within an organization among its main stakeholders and its influence on the external market. It passes through explaining the communication in all fields and domains, creating an overview of the institutional communication, and why it is considered difficult to effectively propagate within a large institution. In addition, the internal communication and information and research so far conducted is analyzed with respect to the findings and lessons learned. In addition, it is important to know and understand how the internal communication evolved during years and which were the main approaches identified throughout the organizations. The case study aims to evaluate the level of information and the efficiency and effectiveness of the internal communication process within Bucharest University of Economic Studies with respect to its projects developed and financed through

European funds in the last six years. The study is mainly run through the help of the questionnaire that was addressed to teachers and students within the faculty and has also the purpose to help improve the related communication in the foreseeable future based on the relevant findings.

Thus, the book assures a fair balance between training-related and healthcare-focused topics, as well as an equilibrium between chapters employing quantitative methods and chapters relying on qualitative or discursive techniques for defending their point.

Given its focus on Eastern Europe, an area which, after the fall of communism more than two decades ago, experienced dramatic shifts in its educational and medical systems and controversies that are not properly healed today, the book may provide useful insights into a domain that remains highly controversial and, at the same time, highly attractive for both professionals and the general public.

Simona Vasilache
Bucharest University of Economic Studies, Romania

Section 1
Cross-Cultural Training

Chapter 1
Comparative Analysis of Educational Policies Research

Simona Vasilache
Bucharest University of Economic Studies, Romania

Alina Mihaela Dima
Bucharest University of Economic Studies, Romania

ABSTRACT

The chapter discusses the possibility for European education to convergence in the Bologna framework by studying the literature dedicated to educational policies in leading academic journals. Using a content analysis methodology, the qualitative research aims to highlight the key topics and research concerns of academics in European higher education and to correlate their research focuses, which are being promoted and implemented in European universities as effective policy. The results may serve as guidelines for both policy makers and executives in higher education, as well as for broader categories of stakeholders.

EDUCATION IN A NEW EUROPE: A CONVERGENCE PERSPECTIVE

It's twenty years since *Comparative Education Review* has published a special issue on *Education in a changing Europe*. The editorial essay, signed by Erwin Epstein, Elizabeth Sherman Swing, and François Orivel, has the title we partly borrowed: *Education in a New Europe*. The centripetal tendencies of Western Europe, the second, post-communist, educational revolution of the Eastern Europe, privileging centrifugal moves, are, as stated by the three guest editors, constituents of the European model of the 1990s. Still, the picture had more to offer, even at that time, than this Manichaeism between convergence and divergence. National and ethnic groups,

DOI: 10.4018/978-1-4666-4325-3.ch001

migrants and their heirs hinder the ideal of unity in education. In other words, the issue of identity and the intellectual reflection of it are intimately connected with the future of education. Considering this context, the problems raised by the editorial essay and by the special issue as a whole are the frailty of a European dimension in education (that "learning to be European", as the quoted authors phrase it) and the persistence of national identities.

A legitimate question to ask, two decades after, is whether these problems are still lurking today, from behind the convergent education ideal. It is obvious that the European Community sets moving targets. The 2010 horizon of the Lisbon strategy is recently replaced by New Europe 2020, whose first objective, *smart growth*, retunes the former strategic aim: "an economy based on knowledge and innovation". Not the strongest in the world, but taking as pillars these two outcomes of the educational system, and of higher education in particular. According to the recent study by Eurydice, *Focus on Higher Education in Europe 2010. The impact of the Bologna process*, the most well-known initiative in educational convergence across Europe was a success story. The next moves to be taken are increased quality and accessibility – enrolling around 40% of the respective age group in universities, as compared to less than one third presently, according to Androulla Vassiliou, Commissioner responsible for Education, Culture, Multilingualism and Youth.

That would, theoretically, put an end to the researches dedicated to the effects of the Bologna process, given that its main targets are attained. Still, critics say that goals may be anytime reported as accomplished, given that they are vague. *The Chronicle of Higher Education* notes, in September 2010, that *As Europe's Higher Education Systems try*

to work in concert, notes of discord remain. The core concern of the article is that, more than one decade after the process was started, there is still debate on measurement issues (e.g., how to measure mobility?), which are essential to defining and benchmarking goals. This is one of this chapter's concerns.

Another issue raised by the higher education officials interviewed by *The Chronicle* (as Siegbert Wuttig, responsible of a DAAD – German Academic Exchange Service – department) is that transformations having little to do, in fact, with Bologna are associated with this process. The world of universities is obviously changing, but how much of it can be really traced back to Bologna? This is why a valid system of indicators is needed, to separate random correlations from changes having a causal link with the Bologna provisions. A former education expert in the European commission, David Coyne, takes the criticism even farther, claiming that politicians have a pompieristic approach, with an inflation of communiqués on the success of the process, when, in fact, little real progress has been made. Or, in professor Ulrich Schollwöck's (2001) words, "the discrepancy between the political rhetoric of excellence and the situation right at the battleline". He also points to the perception, rather widespread inside the system, that *something is rotten* if so many reforms are needed, in a short interval of time.

A conclusion which may be drawn from here is that, being time-bound, the Bologna process is bound to be successful, at least declaratively. After 2010, the European higher education system should move on to the next level. Still, in *Higher Education Review*, Helmut de Rudder (2010) asks: *Mission accomplished? Which mission?* The vagueness of goals is reframed.

It may be seen that the situation, as compared to twenty years ago, is more puzzled today, despite the existence of (more or less) clear targets. Taking into account the risk of doing things for the sake of having them done, specific to post-communist societies, and the risk of overdoing things (for instance, the excesses of Bologna in Germany), one has to explore and exploit the enormous amount of national variation carried by the higher education systems. Measurement tools going beyond superficial resemblances, systems of indicators capturing as much as possible of the cultural roots of a multi-century institution ("Humboldt is dead… long live Humboldt") are, presently, to our opinion, essential to assessing the benefits of the process and correcting its drawbacks.

Taking a convergence viewpoint, which claims that the process is possible, but it is naturally slower than advertised, and intertwined with concurrent processes affecting the higher education market (e.g, the diversification of funding schemes, or social repositioning towards universities) we investigate, in parallel, the most general level of involvement in education, that of policies, and the "battlefield" of academic reflection on policies, in the form of reviewed articles published over the last decade. Is there a common ground, or are researchers themselves connected to the 'global fate' of the system prophesized by the Bologna, and actively influencing it is the main concern of our study.

EDUCATIONAL POLICIES IN EUROPE

Educational policies, sometimes also called educational *philosophies*, have been, under various forms, a constant research concern. Almost every school of thought proposed a vision about *school, education*, and followed certain objectives and results of the investment in education. School has evolved from "merchants of wisdom" in classical-era Greece, perhaps the first teachers *by profession*, and the first who stressed the importance of systematic education on the completion of successful people, to more centralized, more institutionalized forms. Sophists' purpose, namely that of teaching their disciples to handle any situation (with all the controversies that have resulted from this), was maintained, however, as an axis of educational policies, being found until today, in the concept of *flexible professional*. Thus, education, never leaving this ambition of completeness (*de omne re scibili* was the motto of the comprehensive humanistic education), but having to deal with the pressing need of more specialization has evolved between two poles: a relational pole, represented by the master-disciple duo, and a structural pole, represented by the school institution, be it called *academy, university* or *college*.

The first pole presumes a very particular type of policy, that of rules and limits which arise in a relationship. To what extent, from a few of such privileged relationships can be created a system, possibly a mass education, is a question that goes beyond the scope of this research. We may rather speak, in case of a highly-relational education (because, otherwise, any kind of education is or should be also relational, not just institutional), of niches, of exceptions difficult to be inserted and reproduced on a large scale. We will focus, therefore, on the institutional pole, and on the interactions between the education institution and on state and supra-state systems which decide its present and for which it decides the future. We focused our research on that sector of the system where its influence is greatest, as social representativeness, economic, political and cultural involvement, etc.: the universities. The route that they take goes from divergence to convergence; from the desire to individualize to the desire to harmonize their curriculum, and to facilitate the movement of students and teachers. In a 2006 article published in *The Journal of Higher Education*, John C. Scott analyzes the university's mission, from the first universities in the Middle Ages to postmodernism, from the emphasis put on education, to the orientation on city problems and involvement in research, or in public service.

Traditionally, universities have not been regarded as organizations. Researchers referred to them using either the word of institutions, meaning structures that fulfill an important social role (Readings, 1996), like that of founding (lat. *instituere*), or the concept of the community of equals (having the nineteenth-century German college as a model, with only horizontal relationships), whose members were selected to officiate the social ceremony. The liberal philosophy of modernism, which made the universities the subcontractors of the nation-state, institutions that propagate its values and make its people grow, suffered, post-2000, a pronounced decline. The corporate university (Aronowitz, 2000) makes its presence felt not only in the form of private organizations that provide highly specialized education and addresses almost exclusively the mastering of certain skills (so called McDonald's universities), but also with the help of the willingness of old-fashioned universities to mimic management and marketing practices of for-profit companies. To use the words of Lyotard (2004), the university of culture has been replaced by the university of excellence, in which the only

form of legitimation is performing under the pressure of the academic capitalism (Clegg and Steel, 2002), which requires it to become competitive by delivering knowledge to the market: knowledge, as an institutional asset vital for the economic production is and will continue to be subject of a major interest - perhaps the largest - in the global competition for power (Lyotard, 2004). Academic tribes (Becher and Trowler, 2001), inherited from the collegiate model of the university, cannot survive as specialized autarchies, in a society which, as Campbell already said years ago, is looking to form mosaics of uniqueness. Given these circumstances, universities must become more intelligent (Forest, 2002), seeking to maximize both profits and prestige (Strober, 2006).

However, in this shift from institutions to organizations, to which known management models can be applied, universities retain some features that make them idiosyncratic in the spectrum of organizations. In a systematic presentation, these are:

Multiplicity of Stakeholders: Universities have moved from the status of autonomous communities to that of organizations with interest holders (Neave, 2002), which means that their management no longer focuses solely on what is going on inside the university, but must also face the external pressures. The intern-extern opposition is doubled by a public-private opposition, which could be widening in the near future. Also, the diversity of the fields of study generates multiple oppositions between universities, because, although they do not offer similar specializations, they must be compared, because each wants to occupy the best possible place on the market. Because a university now has many more interest holders than a business of the same size, its goals are vaguely defined - the university tries to be everything to everyone and objectives it chooses seem, therefore, ambiguous, because the university must deal with a large load of uncertainty and potential conflictual situations (Baldridge et al., 2000). On one hand, this situation arises because universities produce public goods, and this, according to Samuelson (1954), are, by their nature, less well defined than private goods. On the other hand, as stated by Bourdieu and Johnson (1993) universities are at the same time positioned and able to take a position. The views expressed by governments or supranational bodies position them, but, in turn, they also position themselves in the field of symbolic forces, seeking to influence the rankings and achieve greater market share, placing themselves conveniently compared to holders of interests.

Problematic Hierachies: Although universities tend to behave like medium or large organizations, regarding their managerial and marketing decisions, the possibility of hiring or firing their managers is much more limited. Moreover, there is no clear distinction between technical and institutional levels of the hierarchy (Birnbaum, 1988). The teaching staff, dealing with the technical problems of teaching and learning, includes also members from the governing structures of the university, which take part in developing policies and strategies in the university (the University Senate, for example) and beyond (Ministry of Education, Parliament, etc..), which leads to overlapping that are not always in the interest of the university, especially when there are conflicts between academic interests (investing in excellence) and administrative interests (reducing costs, increasing taxes, dissolution of entrance exams to attract more students). The specificity of the universities requires from the university leaders in

depth knowledge of the system from within, because managerial experience gained in a certain type of university is inapplicable for another type (if, for example, we compare a technical university with a vocational one). The public-private mix further complicates decision-making in universities - there are universities which are financed mainly from private sources, and which tend to apply a policy of the supplier-customer type, and others dependent on state funding. Also, public and private universities are competing for the same human resources. These reasons lead to discrepancies between what the universities state as their vision, mission and what they actually implement. Universities from developing countries basically follow some global institutional scenarios, which say what a university should be (Krücken, 2006). Thus, in the missions of Romanian universities we find words borrowed from the missions of famous universities in Western Europe or America, which does not mean that the realities are comparable. In fact, managing a university according to its real mission, in the socio-economic and cultural environment in which it exists, is much more complicated than the simple adherence to a model of success.

Professional Bureaucracies: Mintzberg (1979) defined them as inflexible structures that produce standardized results (in the case of universities, concepts and skills), but cannot get out of their patterns to adjust to new requirements. The so-called pigeonholing process (and it is no coincidence that the niches for correspondence, in the university departments, have this name), specializing in narrow and non-communicating fields corresponds to learning in a single step, as defined by Argyris (1999): an expert diagnoses a problem that must be resolved, and then applies an algorithm. Trying to make it out of this structure puts him in a weak position, that of not to being an expert, but an apprentice, which is an unacceptable situation in the logic of professional bureaucracy. However, strict specialization does not ensure performance, because it limits the possibility of comparing with others. Interdisciplinary remains a goal, although, besides the advantage of the wider area of knowledge, it has the disadvantage of increasing the risk of just knowing something about everything. The transformation of university structures and patterns to adapt to new business paradigms (Clark, 1998) implies, according to Brunsson and Sahlin-Andersson (2000), three levels: the construction of identity (*who are we*? Introduceţi text sau o adresă de site web sau traduceţi un document. Hence the organizational objective of being special), the construction of the hierarchy (the transition from control to coordination, involvement in joint projects and building a common vision, capturing, on another level, the essence of the collegiate model) and the construction of rationality, which implies finding the means through which the university can become accountable for its work in the audit society (Power, 2000). In fact, the university remains autonomous only if it can prove that it obtains the outcomes desired by society. This is the contemporary form of the social contract: the university receives its independence, on the condition to provide its society with what it asks. All these idiosyncrasies represent challenges for the university management, especially seen in the case of Romania, in the context of transition from communism to post-communism, from centralized economy to market economy and from national legislations to supranational, European regulations and standards of excellence. This triple transition transforms Romanian universities into organizations that must face a very uncertain future and a present marked by claims and equally large challenges. The system of educational policies which we propose to study represents the buffer zone between the external challenges, internal conflicts, and the projection of the idea of University at various social, economic and cultural levels.

There are, in educational policies, a number of weaknesses. Among them we can mention: the tendency to homogenize the system, to standardize it in order to serve the interests of some exclusive groups, limiting access to education. In other words, from the education for those who deserve we move towards an education for those who can afford it. On the other hand, the university system distances and isolates from the rest of society, speaking a language of its own. Third, and finally held, the Romanian universities depend on state funding and the curriculum is determined nationally, centralization which severely limits the business initiatives.

Given the mentioned developments and weaknesses of educational policies, it becomes obvious why this sub-theme requires an approach based entirely on the recent scientific literature, endeavor which we will undertake in the following sub-section.

Research Methodology

Starting from the above assumption, that educational policies represent a key theme for the project, we analyzed the articles devoted to educational policies during the period January 1, 2006 - December 1, 2010, published in the main databases (EBSCO, Emerald Management Extra, Science Direct, ProQuest, Sage Journals Online, SCOPUS, SpringerLink) and ISI Web of Knowledge.

The period chosen for review is consistent with the current meaning of recent literature dedicated to this domain and the selected databases correspond to mainstream publications. The database search was based on key words, and the repeated results were excluded. Also, we excluded ISI journals that are also found in the analyzed databases. The search was limited to results that refer to Europe, even if the publication was not necessarily a European one.

The relative frequency of the articles which discuss educational policies in Europe encountered in the selected databases, within the time allocated (the report refers to the total number of articles on topics of education) is:

- 3,15% for ISI Web of Knowledge
- 4,02% for SCOPUS
- 10,14% for ProQuest
- 12,3% for SpringerLink
- 15,2% for Science Direct
- 22,7% for Emerald Management Extra
- 23,1% for EBSCO
- 24,6% for Sage Journals Online

There is a marked presence of articles devoted to education policies in databases specialized on social themes. The low frequency in the ISI database can be explained by the small number of ISI journals exclusively devoted to educational issues in Europe (two, European Journal of Education and the European Journal of Teacher Education, plus two magazines devoted to comparative research in education - Comparative Education and Comparative Education Review - from 150 journals specialized on education) and also by the small number of "generalist" magazines in which such broader approaches could find their place: only two, Education Finance and Policy and Journal of Education Policy are specifically focused on policies, to them adding titles such as Journal of Higher Education, Studies in Higher Education, Review of Higher Education. The vast majority of magazines are oriented towards niche-areas,

either geographically - Asia, America, developing countries, either in terms of target topics: teacher training, management education, economics education, etc.

For each of the two categories, ISI journals, respectively journals included in international databases, we formed two groups, one main group and a control group, the latter consisting of highly specialized journals on educational policies in order to give us the possibility to compare general trends in research with the specialized trends.

We chose a sample of 15 magazines (10% of the total ISI journals devoted to education), divided into five specialized journals on education policy /education in Europe, and 10 magazines with a broader theme.

For ISI journals, the two groups are presented in Table 1.

We used the sample size for journals included in international databases, considering more useful to have two samples of compa-

Table 1. Main group and the control group for ISI journals

Main Group	Control Group
Educational Research Review	International Journal of Educational Administration and Policy
Education + Training	Higher Education Policy
Quality Assurance in Education	Journal of Educational Administration
Higher Education, Skills and Work-based learning	International Journal of Sustainability in Higher Education
Issues in Education	Educational Administration Quarterly
Journal of Diversity in Higher Education	International Journal of Educational Management
Quality in Higher Education	
International Journal for Academic Development	
Current issues in education	

rable sizes, than to make up a sample starting from the 1538 magazines with educational topics included in databases, which would have greatly complicated the research. The two groups are presented in Table 2.

Upon completion of this conceptual map, eight research areas resulted, including 78 research topics, reflecting the variety of approaches regarding educational policies, necessarily inter-related with issues of social and economic research. Reforms in education cannot be understood and evaluated outside their economic and social impact. In a 2010 article from *Higher Education,* Argentin and Triventi discuss the relationship between institutional reforms, inequality in education and unequal opportunities on the Italian labor market. Educational reforms stimulated by accession to the Bologna process on the one hand, which led to a vertical differentiation of a university system rather uniform until the early 2000s, and labor market reforms, on the other hand, *Legge Treu*, from 1997, which facilitated the access of young people in the

Table 2. Main group and control group for BDI indexed journals

Main Group	Control Group
Assessment & Evaluation in Higher Education	Education Finance and Policy
Education as Change	Journal of Education Policy
Higher Education	European Journal of Education
Higher Education Research and Development	Comparative Education
History of Education	Comparative Education Review
Journal of Higher Education	
Oxford Review of Education	
Perspectives in Education	
Research in Higher Education	
Studies in Higher Education	

labor market, and *Riforma Biaggi,* from 2003, which stressed the labor market flexibility, in the aspirants sector, have influenced the dynamics of social inequality. Several candidates have access to the Bologna first cycle, but, starting from the second cycle which gives them a better insertion in the labor market upon graduation, the candidates whose parents have graduated college are privileged. However, these influences, the authors conclude, are short-term oriented and confined to a narrow social categories, which demonstrates that the transition to Bologna system still has a small impact on the option to attend college, to continue and to position oneself in some way in the labor market.

Barone and Ortiz (2010) expose the risks of over-education in European universities. Inflation of diplomas leads to devaluation of their qualifications and poor social recognition of graduates. The two researchers analyze over-education in eight European countries, Spain, Italy, Austria, Germany, Czech Republic, Netherlands, Norway and Finland. Over-education is, according to the authors, the lack of certain job-specific skills, in other words, training in theory, without practical adherence. Research results have shown that the risks are disproportionately distributed in the countries considered. Thus, in Germany, Austria, Czech Republic, Italy, this risk is not present, due to national policies that control the increasing number of graduates. In Norway, Finland, Netherlands, the proliferation of universities is more pronounced, but the evolution of the labor market in these countries justifies the need for skilled labor. However, some graduates may end up in jobs that require soft skills rather than highly specific skills and, as many of them are in the public sector, the authors consider the situation a compromise between the state and universities, the former recovering over-qualified officers trained by the universities. Finally, Spain is an example of a European country in which over-education is a mass phenomenon. In the authors' vision, in the next years other countries, such as Britain, will be exposed to the risk.

In this context of separation of university training from the real needs of the labor market, it is seen the need of partnerships with industry or community environment. Abramo, d'Angelo and Di Costa (2010) discuss university-industry cooperation as a priority of developed national politics (OECD, 2007). Innovation in universities should, according to D'Este and Patel (2007), target this axis of collaboration with industry and of use of the research results in the latter's advantage. Public-private partnerships are, in the authors' vision, the main way in which the junction between academic research and industrial research takes place. The relation of innovation in universities, and the use of these innovations in the industry with regional development is also analyzed (Fingleton and L□pez-Bazo, 2006), showing that accelerating growth in a region has an influence on neighboring regions, contributing to the long-distance spread of innovation. More important, however, than geographical proximity is the quality of research that a university undertakes (Abramo et al, 2009). However, collaboration cannot be achieved if the directions of the university research are not converging with the directions of development of the industry in an area relatively accessible to collaboration. Thus, we can distinguish two types of policies: policies at the macro level, concerning the reforms of the education system, of the labor market, of macroeconomic climate from a given region, and university policies that determine the orientation of the university towards a specific research area and the focus on teaching or scientific activities, or a combination of the two.

Of course, the two types of policies interfere. However, from the table that we built based on research areas and research themes outlined in the body of articles reviewed, there is a prevalence of approaches dedicated to macro policies, less influenced by the university, as individuality. Even in the field of entrepreneurial universities, it is noted that only one subject (*teachers' professional roles and identities*) is intrinsic for the universities - and not even this in full, the professional identity being determined by the interaction with external factors - the others being driven by decision-making structures from outside the university.

Is the university a victim of the changes in the world that is a part of? 30 years ago, Cohen (1973), inclined to say yes, the university being caught between students' pressure and external intrusions. The situation doesn't seem to have changed much in recent approaches found in specialty publications. We took into consideration the research areas less covered in research papers published in ISI journals, which show an even more pronounced orientation towards social and economic context, towards issues related to integration of different cultures, the dialogue of universities with the industry organizations in their field and with national governments and supranational bodies, such as UNESCO.

There is a concentration of approaches around a smaller number of subjects, indicating a greater convergence of views expressed by researchers. Niche areas, such as non-formal education or themes representative for developing countries in Central and Eastern Europe, which combine various educational policies copied from developed countries (Hoppers, 2009), can be encountered in the range of approaches.

The results of the bibliographic research, after the content analysis, can be found in the following sub-section.

Results and Discussions

The hierarchy of ISI journals, both those in the control group and those from the main group, which is made according to the frequency of articles dealing with educational policies, and which reports the total number of articles in the group during the period under review, is presented in Table 3.

A gap can be noticed between the journals with a relatively large number of articles devoted to educational and the other journals in each group. Also, the frequency of articles devoted to educational policies in the control group is significantly higher than in the journals that formed the core group, which validates the choice of groups.

The ranking of the top ten research topics of ISI journals is presented in Table 4.

The hierarchy of journals indexed in IDB is more homogeneous, confirming the picture of concentration inferred by the conceptual map of research areas and themes. There is a greater density of articles in journals devoted to educational policies at the top of the hierarchy, especially in the control group, which validates the choice of the two groups.

The hierarchy for the journals indexed in the international databases is presented in Table 5.

Although the number of research themes identified is relatively high, there is a concentration around a few main concerns, which in general correspond to the issues on the public agenda. More than one-tenth of the articles discuss the issues of higher education financing, while public-private partnerships also distance themselves from the rest of the hierarchy. The problem is funding is encountered

Table 3. The hierarchy of journals indexed ISI

	Journal	# articles	% articles
Main Group	Research in Higher Education	31	23
	Higher Education Research and Development	22	17
	Assessment & Evaluation in Higher Education	17	13
	Higher Education	13	10
	Perspectives in Education	11	8
	Journal of Higher Education	11	8
	Studies in Higher Education	8	6
	Oxford Review of Education	7	5
	Education as Change	6	5
	History of Education	6	5
	Total	**132**	**100**
Control Group	Journal of Education Policy	71	40
	Education Finance and Policy	44	25
	European Journal of Education	33	19
	Comparative Education	29	16
	Total	**177**	**100**

Table 4. The hierarchy of the main research topics in ISI journals

	Journal	# articles	% articles
Main Group	Educational Research Review	35	26
	Issues in Education	27	20
	Current issues in education	18	13
	Educational Review	12	9
	Quality Assurance in Education	11	8
	Journal of Diversity in Higher Education	11	8
	Quality in Higher Education	7	5
	International Journal for Academic Development	6	4
	Education + Training	5	4
	Higher Education, Skills and Work-based learning	4	3
	Total	**136**	**100**
Control Group	Higher Education Policy	80	39
	Journal of Educational Administration	51	25
	International Journal of Educational Administration and Policy	42	21
	International Journal of Sustainability in Higher Education	31	15
	Total	**204**	**100**

Table 5. The hierarchy of topics in the journals indexed IDB

Research Topics	# articles	% articles
Education reform	23	6.7
Access to education	21	6.1
Investing in education	20	5.8
Fundraising	17	7.0
Human capital costs	15	4.4
Performance indicators	15	4.4
University efficiency	10	2.9
Insertion on the market	8	2.4
Flexible curriculum	6	1.8
Bricolage in creating policies	5	1.5

in the form of discussions about the costs of education at university level. The internationalization strategies are addressed tangentially, and they rather stand for a market orientation in the university, once the general framework of inter-university mobility in Europe was created. Overall, the themes identified as principal occupy approximately 40% of the research agenda of the ISI journals selected in this study.

In the case of the journals indexed in the international databases the hierarchy of the principal research topics is presented in Table 6.

Table 6. The hierarchy of the main research themes in IDB indexed journals

Research topic	# articles	% articles
Financing of higher education	34	11.0
Public-private partnerships	23	7.4
Education reform	17	5.5
Quality assurance	14	4.5
University tops	8	2.6
Performance indicators	5	1.6
Excellence in research	5	1.6
The transition from education to labor market	4	1.3
Schooling costs	3	0.9
Internationalization strategies	3	0.9

One can notice the same relative clustering in the case of the main themes addressed in journals indexed IDB. Also, the tendency is to quantify educational policies, to evaluate their impact in terms of cost, investment, and efficiency indicators. More general themes, or specific themes to certain areas (e.g. for countries in transition) occur in the second half of the hierarchy.

Both analyses took into account the main group of journals, as well as the control group.

The frequency distribution by year, both for the ISI journals and for IDB journals is shown in Figures 1 and 2.

One can notice the same relative clustering in the case of the main themes addressed in journals indexed IDB. Also, the tendency is to quantify educational policies, to evaluate their impact in terms of cost, investment, and efficiency indicators. More general themes, or specific themes to certain areas (e.g. for countries in transition) occur in the second half of the hierarchy.

Both analyses took into account the main group of journals, as well as the control group.

It can be noted that the trend is upward, if we take into account the fact that 2010 is incomplete. Also, one should bear in mind the normal metabolism of scientific articles, which makes it possible for an article written in a year to be published next year or even two years after. On average, however, the interest in educational policies, reflected in ISI journals, remains strong.

Figure 1. The evolution of the number of articles published in ISI journals

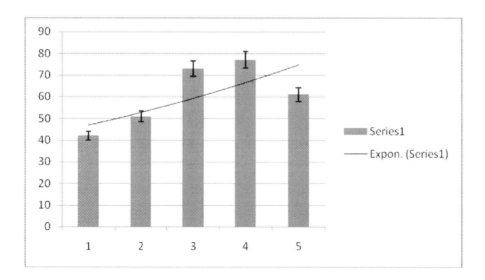

Figure 2. The evolution of the articles published in IDB journals

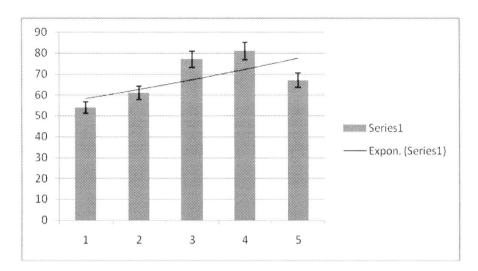

It can be seen that the two trends are similar, the difference being in the volume of articles published, the number being greater for the IDB journals due to an easier and faster access to publication. We therefore assume that this second trend better estimates the real dynamics of research in educational policy, being closer to the actual moment of start of the research process.

CONCLUSION

Between January 1, 2006 and December 1, 2010, the issue of educational policy has been discussed in 644 articles, indexed both IDB and ISI, included in our research. Out of these, 376 articles were published in specialized journals considered educational policies, and 268 articles in journals with a more general view of education. A comparison between the main group of journals and the control group for each category, showed a greater concentration of articles in specialized journals. In general, the articles are topic-oriented towards the funding of higher education, costs and efficiency indicators. The trend that is depicted refers to the movement of the educational policies to a measurable, quantifiable area, with the help of functions and efficiency indicators.

In our opinion, the orientation towards indicators at the expense of broader approaches leads to an excessive professionalization and a narrowing of the field, which excludes social dialogue and availability of these issues on the agenda of public debate.

ACKNOWLEDGEMENT

This work was supported by CNCSIS-UE-FISCCDI, project PNII-RU-TE_351/2010.

REFERENCES

Abramo, G., D'Angelo, C., & Di Costa, F. (2010). Citations versus journal impact factor as proxy of quality: Could the latter ever be preferable? *Scientometrics, 84*(3), 821–833. doi:10.1007/s11192-010-0200-1

Abramo, G., D'angelo, C., Di Costa, F., & Solazzi, M. (2009). University-industry collaboration in Italy: A bibliometric examination. *Technovation, 29*(6/7), 498–507. doi:10.1016/j.technovation.2008.11.003

Argentin, G., & Triventi, M. (2010). Social inequalities and labour market in a period of institutional reforms: Italy 1992-2007. *Higher Education, 61*(3), 309–323. doi:10.1007/s10734-010-9379-6

Argyris, C. (1999). *On organizational learning* (2nd ed.). Oxford, UK: Oxford University Press.

Aronowitz, S. (2000). *The knowledge factory: Dismantling the corporate university and creating true higher learning*. Boston: Beacon Press.

Baldridge, J.V., Julius, D.J., & Pfeffer, J. (2000). Power failure in administrative environments. *Academic Leadership, 11*(1).

Barone, C., & Ortiz, L. (2010). *Over-education among European university graduates* (DEMOSOC Working Paper 2010/33). Departament of Political Science & Sociology, University of Pompeu Fabra.

Becher, T., & Trowler, P. (2001). *Academic tribes and territories*. Buckingham, UK: Open University Press.

Birnbaum, R. (1988). *How colleges work: The cybernetics of academic organization and leadership*. San Francisco, CA: Jossey-Bass.

Bourdieu, P., & Johnson, R. (1993). *The field of cultural production: Essays on art and literature*. New York: Columbia University Press.

Brunsson, N., & Sahlin-Andersson, K. (2000). Constructing organizations: The example of public sector reform. *Organization Studies, 21*(4), 721–746. doi:10.1177/0170840600214003

Clark, B. R. (1998). Creating entrepreneurial universities: Organizational pathways of transformation. *Higher Education, 38*(3), 373–374.

Clegg, S., & Steel, J. (2002). The emperor's new clothes: Globalisation and e-learning. *British Journal of Sociology of Education, 24*(1), 39–53. doi:10.1080/01425690301914

Cohen, A. M. (Ed.). (1973). *Toward a professional faculty*. San Francisco: Jossey-Bass.

D'Este, P., & Patel, P. (2007). University-industry linkages in the UK: What are the factors determining the variety of interactions with industry? *Research Policy, 36*(9), 1295–1313. doi:10.1016/j.respol.2007.05.002

de Rudder, H. (2010). Mission accomplished? Which mission? The Bologna process – A view from Germany. *Higher Education, 43*(1), 3–20.

Fingleton, B., & López-Bazo, G. (2006). Empirical growth models with spatial effects. *Papers in Regional Science, 85*(2), 177–198. doi:10.1111/j.1435-5957.2006.00074.x

Forest, J. F. J. (2002). *Higher education in the United States: an encyclopedia.* ABC-CLIO Publishers.

Hoppers, C. (2009). Education, culture and society in a globalizing world: Implications for comparative and international education. *Compare: A Journal of Comparative Education, 39*(5), 601–614. doi:10.1080/03057920903125628

Krücken, G. (2006). Innovationsmythen in Politik und Gesselschaft. In *Kluges entscheiden: Disziplinäre grundlagen und interdisziplinäre verknüpfungen.* Tübingen: Mohr Siebeck.

Lyotard, J.-F. (2004). Anamnesis: Of the visible. *Theory, Culture & Society, 21*(1), 107–119. doi:10.1177/0263276404040483

Mintzberg, H. (1979). *The structuring of organizations: A synthesis of the research.* Englewood Cliffs, NJ: Prentice-Hall.

Neave, G. (2002). Anything goes: Or: How the accommodation of Europe's universities to European integration integrates an inspiring number of contradictions. *Tertiary Education and Management, 8*(3), 178–191. doi:10.108 0/13583883.2002.9967078

OECD. (2007). *Education at a glance 2007.* Paris: OECD.

Power, M. (2000). The audit society - Second thoughts. *International Journal of Auditing, 4*(1), 111–119. doi:10.1111/1099-1123.00306

Readings, B. (1996). *The university in ruins.* Cambridge, MA: Harvard University Press.

Samuelson, P. A. (1954). The pure theory of public expenditure. *The Review of Economics and Statistics, 36,* 387–389. doi:10.2307/1925895

Scott, J. C. (2006). The mission of the university: Medieval to postmodern transformations. *The Journal of Higher Education, 77*(1), 1–39. doi:10.1353/jhe.2006.0007

Strober, M. (2006). Habits of the mind: Challenges for multidisciplinary engagement. *Social Epistemology, 20*(3/4), 315–331. doi:10.1080/02691720600847324

Chapter 2
Multiculturalism and Internationalization of Romanian Universities

Simona Agoston
Bucharest University of Economic Studies, Romania

Katja Lasch
German Academic Exchange Service, Romania

ABSTRACT

The chapter discusses the internationalization process of Romanian universities against a background of increasing multiculturalism. The authors collect and analyze data related to the flows of international students and staff in Romanian universities, as well as measures taken to promote student and staff circulation and to attract candidates from abroad. The conclusions of the study point to the fact that not only do Romanian universities do too little to become attractive to foreign students but due to a chronic lack of accurate data they also do not really know where they stand as to be able to improve. The present research attempted, thus, to advance knowledge about the status quo and to promote strategies for improvement.

INTRODUCTION

The academic paradigm with regards to management and leadership and more specifically internationalization and multiculturalism of universities is facing major challenges. These challenges are triggered mainly by external factors such as economic, socio-political and technological complexity, a higher level of academic mobility in the last decades, and the phenomenon of globalization which exerts a significant impact on various academic

DOI: 10.4018/978-1-4666-4325-3.ch002

dimensions and calls for the reorganization and adaptation of Higher Education Institutions (HEI).

One of the most prominent voices in the field of academic systems, German researcher Ulrich Teichler (1996, 2004, 2010), states that at a certain moment one or two major research topics capture and even monopolize the interest of the academic community. Therefore, it can be observed that at the beginning of '80s the research field of tertiary education is dominated by studies analyzing the increasingly important role and mission of universities within the global society and academic management with a focus on identifying financing opportunities. In their "golden age" the aforementioned topics graced the headlines of many specialized conferences and journals in this field of research. In the same decade many scientific journals dedicated to the study of different aspects of university education were established. From the beginning of the `90s the topic of the internationalization of the universities started to raise the attention of more and more researchers. Nowadays the debate regarding the internationalization strategies are still ongoing; however they evolved towards the comparative analysis of academic globalization or regionalization with a focus on the cross cultural dimension.

Teichler (2004) argues that higher education has never been "more international" than today and that this process will be even more accelerated in the future. On the one hand, even in the past, when physical boundaries between countries were still playing a decisive role, universities were perceived as very international when compared to other organizations. This is primarily due to the universal dimension of knowledge and appreciation granted by the members of the university to intrinsic and cosmopolitan values. It is also due to more pragmatic factors such as the educational market which is essentially a reputational market and the prestige of a university is based, to a considerable extent, on its international reputation, on the mobility of the students and faculty, on the research projects carried out in mixed teams etc. On the other hand, we might add that universities have never been more "multicultural" than today. This fact is due to the increase in student and staff mobility, joint research projects, joint academic programs, all largely due to the increased mobility of people in general, which also transform the academic environment in a multicultural milieu.

This paper aims to analyze the Romanian academic market from two complementary perspectives: the degree of its multiculturalism considering the beneficiaries of educational services and the degree of internationalization of the Romanian universities. We base our research on the assumption that between the two dimensions, multiculturalism and internationalization, there is a positive, direct and reciprocal relation: the higher the level of multiculturalism, the greater the degree of internationalization and vice versa. This paper is divided into three main parts, which link the theoretical and empirical research and the macroeconomic with the microeconomic analysis. In the first part of the paper we analyze the concepts of academic multiculturalism and internationalization from a theoretical perspective. Further on we focus on the Romanian academic market, whose particularities are critically analyzed by means of some key indicators recommended in the scientific literature, while a great emphasis lies on the student and teacher exchange and the framework offered by the Romanian Government. Next we shift the perspective from the macroeconomic analysis to the microeconomic one by using surveys to research the issues of multiculturalism and internationalization in some of the most representative higher education institutions in Romania.

ACADEMIC INTERNATIONALIZATION AND MULTICULTURALISM

Despite the numerous debates and papers written on the topic of internationalization of universities, this subject has not reached yet its conceptual boundaries and there is no universally accepted definition of this phenomenon (Kehm and Teichler, 2007). In the attempt to study the dynamics and set the conceptual limits of the phenomenon of "internationalization of higher education institutions" two distinct approaches were identified (Marginson and van der Wende, 2009; van der Wende, 2010):

- The first approach focuses on increasing international visibility by organizing international programs which involve cross-border partners, mobility for students, teachers and researchers, double degree programs, joint research projects, language courses focused on developing cross cultural competencies, etc.
- The second approach refers to the universalization, globalization and internationalization of the essence and of the basic functions of higher education. However, this phenomenon is more complex, going beyond the implementation of solely certain cross-border mobilities or an institutional partnership between two or more universities.

Obviously, policy makers at national and institutional levels focused so far mainly on the first approach, the visible and pragmatic one; the second approach has a more philosophical character, whose essence is more difficult to capture and to substantiate.

Internationalization of higher education represents the process of integrating intercultural and international dimensions in teaching, research and administrative services in a university (Knight, 2004). Teichler (2009) and Bartell (2003) state that internationalization is generally defined as an increase of cross border activities. In a more advanced stage of internationalization, we encounter the phenomenon of multiculturalism in universities with the student and teaching population but also the content of the curricula. Academic internationalization and multiculturalism are two phenomena which cannot be separated, they come along with the globalization of today's society.

Conscious of the need to integrate international trends within strategic thinking, universities have developed various internationalization strategies, which were summarized in four main categories by Knight (1999, 2008), as shown in Table 1.

The manner in which all these elements are combined together with the selection of one or more areas of focus determine the institution's strategy. As such, while some universities tend to focus on academic programs and extracurricular activities with an emphasis on the multicultural dimension of the student and teachers communities (Mahrous and Ahmed, 2010; Hanson, 2010; Dixon, 2006), others may choose to invest more in the development of research activities and common research projects (Lunn, 2008; Naidoo, 2009). Moreover, some may decide that a home-based internationalization process is the preferred one, where all internationalization activities take place in the home country by relying mainly on international exchanges, while others may conclude that it is preferable to open a subsidiary in another country so as to consolidate the position in the region and respond to the increased demand (Naidoo, 2009).

Table 1. Internationalization strategies

Dimension	Types of Activities/Instruments
Academic programs	• student mobility programs (incoming and outgoing) • foreign languages classes • internationalized curriculum • internships abroad • international students on campus • double degree programs • study programs in languages of international circulation • intercultural training programs (e.g. orientation week for foreign students, classes to learn the language of the respective country etc.) • exchange programs for the faculty's members (teaching and auxiliary staff) • fellowships for professors
Research activities and common research projects	• participation in international research programs • organizing international lectures and seminars • articles and working papers published in famous international journals • programs for PhD students exchange and young researchers • concluding research partnerships with international institutions and companies frm abroad
International relations and services	• university programs that provide support to equivalent institutions in emerging countries • partnerships with NGOs in other countries • strategic partnerships with universities abroad • development of campuses in other countries • on-line and distance courses • gaining membership and active participation in international academic consortia and associations • alumni development programs in other countries
Extracurricular activities	• international student associations and clubs • international and intercultural events organized by the university and hosted in its campus • relationships with different ethnic and cultural groups • international summer schools

Source: Adapted from Knight, 1999, 2008

According to Davies' matrix of approaches towards internationalization (Davies, 2001) the following four basic strategies for internationalization in higher education institutions can be identified:

- **Ad-Hoc – Marginal:** Few actions are engaged towards internationalization and there is no clarity regarding the decision making process and its outcomes;
- **Systematic – Marginal:** There are few activities supporting the process, but they are effectively and efficiently organized and the decisions taken are transparent;
- **Ad-Hoc – Central:** The internationalization process may be sustained by a high level of activity, but with no clear vision or understanding of the notions involved, and characterized by an impromptu nature;
- **Systematic – Central:** Actions towards internationalization are engaged across a wide range of the institution's activities in an integrated and coherent manner, triggering reinforcement reciprocity between them. The international mission has an unambiguous character and is sustained by specific policies and supporting procedures.

Studies about intercultural education reveal two dimensions: the formal education, which is delivered within the subjects included in the curriculum, such as cross cultural management, language courses, civilization and history, etc. and the informal education which can be achieved only by direct contact and interaction with ambassadors of other cultures. This interaction can occur either at the home university by fostering a larger share of foreign students and teaching staff or by an exchange program abroad (UNESCO, 2006). Cultural identity is not an *a priori* defined construct, but rather an ongoing process, which is determined by internal and external societal factors. One of the key elements within this process is represented by the confrontation with other human beings, while the own culture identity emerges and is better highlighted when compared with the other ones (Burke, 2009; Lasch, 2011).

Both internationalization and multiculturalism represent a great challenge that Romanian universities have to overcome by developing appropriate policies and instruments. Modern universities in general and Romanian universities in particular have developed their academic culture in a national context. They are financed mainly from national funds and they are a symbol of the nation state (Enders, 2004). Even though Romania had a remarkable share of foreign students during the communist regime, the system did not foster social interaction between Romanian and foreign students and did not provide cross-cultural education. Therefore, compared to other European universities, in Romania the multicultural elements were underrepresented, as the overwhelming majority of students, teachers and researchers had a uniform ethnic, racial, religious and cultural background. Along with the fall of the communist regime and the opening of the Romanian society to new horizons,

the myth of the "monocultural" society and education was abolished and the decision makers and educators started to become aware of the necessity of intercultural education and enforcement of intercultural dialogue within education institutions.[1]

STATE OF ART REGARDING INTERNATIONALIZATION AND MULTICULTURALISM OF THE ROMANIAN ACADEMIC MARKET

Student mobility represents one of the key indicators in the exploration of the level of internationalization of Romanian HEIs. Data such as number of students from abroad, countries and regions of origin but also the net flow of inbound and outbound mobility rates offer important clues for the assessment of Romania's attractiveness as a study destination. The flow of international students is a consequence of both national and institutional strategies and of the individual decisions of students (Altbach et al., 2009).

Romania is not a new player within the international higher education market as it achieved remarkable results in recruiting international students in the 1970s. In the 1970s the Ceausist regime struggled to attract foreign students with the goal of earning hard currency. There were offered educational packages particularly tailored to other communist countries but also for Asian and African states, which were willing to send young people to Romania in order to obtain an academic qualification. They would pay tuition fees to the Romanian government for these services.

By 1981 the number of foreign students at Romanian HEIs reached its climax with 16,962 students enrolled: nearly 9% of the entire student population at that time. At the beginning of the 1980's Romania ranked among the top 15 providers of university education worldwide (Nicolescu et al., 2009).

In the 1990's the number of foreign students in Romania started to decline, falling to just 13,279 persons in 1999. The development over the last decade shows that the number of incoming students has been stable, but still relatively low. While the number of students in Romanian universities increased significantly, the absolute number of foreign students remained relatively constant. Therefore, the inbound mobility rate decreased from 3.25% in 1999 to 0.94% in 2009. Not only has Romania lost its top position from the 1980's but is currently lagging behind the world average (2%). Even compared to other Central and Eastern European countries such as Bulgaria (3.4%), Hungary (3.6%) and the Czech Republic (7.34%), Romania registers modest results. Within the last decade the number of outgoing Romanian students far exceeds the number of incoming foreign students. This situation is in line with a general development trend which emerged of late in Eastern Europe (See Figure 1) (UNESCO Institute for Statistics, 2012).

While the number of international mobile students worldwide more than doubled between 1999 and 2009, the number of students coming to Romania has remained relatively stable (UNESCO Institute for Statistics, 2009). This means that the Romanian HEI's did not capitalize on the ascending trend and favorable international atmosphere.

Regarding the countries of origin of the foreign students enrolled in Romania, Europe remains the leading region, although over the last ten years countries from Asia and Africa gained importance (See Figure 2).

This evolution means a diversification of the international student community in Romania. The ERASMUS statistics also confirm this trend. Romania joined the ERASMUS program in 1997 and international exchange based on bilateral contacts between HEIs started in 1998. The figures indicate that the ERASMUS program has been a success story for Romania. As the numbers illustrate, the decision to access the Bologna area and to implement the required tools that facilitate the recognition of studies such as the European Credit Transfer System (ECTS) and the Diploma Supplement represented a milestone for the development of international mobility of students and teaching staff (Wells, 2011, p.157). Between 2000/2001 and 2009/2010 more than 30,000 Romanians received an ERASMUS scholarship. In the same period of time Romania hosted over 7,000 students from institutions in other ERASMUS member

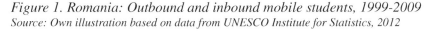

Figure 1. Romania: Outbound and inbound mobile students, 1999-2009
Source: Own illustration based on data from UNESCO Institute for Statistics, 2012

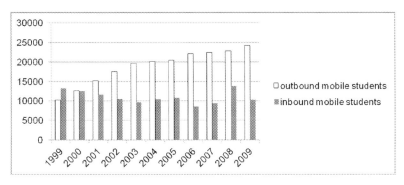

Figure 2. Regions of origin for the foreign students enrolled in Romania, 1999-2009
Source: Own illustration based on data from UNESCO Institute for Statistics, 2012

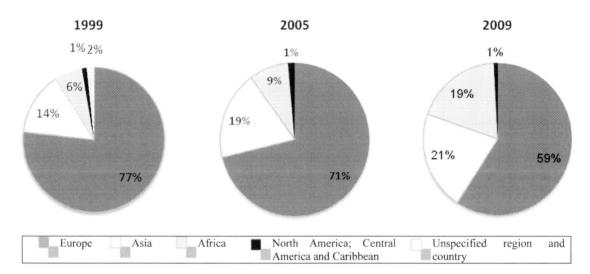

states. Data show that in the academic year 2009/2010 the number of outgoing ERASMUS students was 2.8 times larger than the number of incoming ERASMUS students. Despite this imbalanced ratio, one can note a significant improvement compared to 1998/1999 when the ratio was 10.77(See Figure 3) (European Commission, 2001, 2012a).

In the academic year 1998/1999 Romanian HEIs hosted students from 12 out of 24 ERASMUS member states. In 2009/2010 23 out of 30 countries participating in the ERASMUS program sent students to Romania. Most of the inbound ERASMUS students come from France, Italy, Portugal and Spain (European Commission, 2001, 2012b).We can observe a strong cultural link between Romania and the aforementioned countries, based on a similar Latin cultural background also emphasized by shared linguistic roots. It should be also mentioned that a long tradition of academic exchange between Romania and France exists, and can be traced back to the

Figure 3. ERASMUS statistics in Romania, 1998-2010
Source: Own illustration based on data from European Commission 2001, 2012a

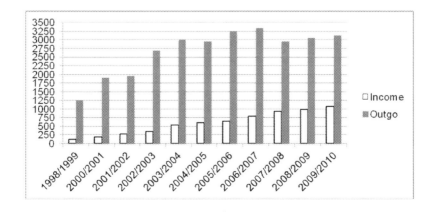

18th century. As shown in the following figure, surprisingly it is Germany and not Great Britain which serves as the main non-Latin exchange partner. This can be explained by the strong cultural links between the two countries developed over the modern history (the German minority from Transylvania and Banat played a major role in bridging the two cultures), but also by the broad offering of programs taught in the German language at Romanian universities and the large number of joint programs with German HEIs (See Figure 4).

Although Romania hosted students from over 110 countries in 2009, a look at the top 10 reveals that the exchange activity is centralized around a small number of states, as displayed in the Table 2.

The high number of Moldavians can be explained by several factors. Romania is an attractive study destination for Moldavians students as they study in their mother tongue and can gain a degree recognized in Europe. Besides that, the Romanian government fosters the exchange by a generous scholarship

Figure 4. ERASMUS incoming students in Romania by country of origin, 2009/2010
Source: Own illustration based on data from European Commission, 2012b

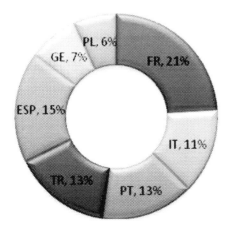

offer which targets both high school students and students enrolled in HEIs. So far Romania has offered more than 1,150 scholarships annually for Moldavian citizens who attend various academic programs. These scholarships holders are assigned to various state universities throughout Romania (Ministerul Educatiei, 2011). Apart from this, the number of students from Tunisia increased significantly in recent years. Romanian HEIs offer study programs in French and English which attract students especially in the field of medicine, engineering and economics. The presence of Israel and Italy in the top 10 can be explained by the large number of Romanians who immigrated to these countries and whose children might return to Romania to pursue an academic degree.

Within the last 25 years the concept of internationalization has become a central topic not just for HEIs, but also for national governments (de Wit, 2010). The establishment of state financed agencies like Campus France (1998) in France and Universidad.es (2007) in Spain as well as the establishment of the consortium GATE Germany within the German Academic Exchange Service (DAAD) reflects the effort on national level to support HEIs in their internationalization process and to attract students and academics to these countries. The EU funded project „Building capacities of East-Central Europe national agencies to promote Higher Education outside the EU", which aimed at improving the internationalization strategies in Hungary, Czech Republic and Slovakia shows that the topic has also become a relevant issue for Eastern Europe too (Building capacities, 2008).

But what are the initiatives undertaken in Romania on the national and institutional level in order to attract international mobile students? At the national level, Romania has

Table 2. Top 10 countries of origin for foreign students in Romania, 1999- 2009

	1999			2005			2009		
1	Moldova	4029	30%	Moldova	4834	45%	Moldova	3389	33%
2	Greece	3978	30%	Greece	759	7%	Tunisia	1058	10%
3	Israel	590	4%	Ukraine	605	6%	Israel	612	6%
4	Ukraine	463	3%	Israel	592	5%	Greece	567	5%
5	Albania	410	3%	Tunisia	414	4%	Italy	408	4%
6	Morocco	300	2%	Albania	359	3%	Germany	260	3%
7	Bulgaria	290	2%	The Former Yugoslav Rep. of Macedonia	357	3%	Morocco	258	2%
8	Germany	278	2%	India	271	3%	Mauritius	222	2%
9	Serbia and Montenegro	240	2%	Germany	231	2%	Bulgaria	216	2%
10	Pakistan	204	2%	Syrian Arab Republic	99	1%	Sweden	212	2%

Source: Own illustration based on data from UNESCO Institute for Statistics, 2012

not yet developed a coherent internationalization strategy, even though within the last two years the Romanian government has undertaken different steps in order to foster the internationalization of Romanian HEIs.

An October 2008 Bologna Report states that the recruitment of foreign students from European Higher Education Area (EHEA) and non EHEA countries represents a major issue for Romanian Universities (Korka, 2009) with the overall goal of increasing the competitiveness of the Romanian HEIs. Therefore „a strategy aiming at improving dissemination of information on higher education opportunities in Romanian universities, learning conditions and advantages is currently under examination in the Ministry of Education, Research and Youth and will be presented to the Rectors' Conference" (Korka, 2009, p. 32).

Following the aforementioned statement, in 2009 the Ministry of Education, Research and Youth set up an International Students Department (ISD) which has been working since of June 15th, 2009 within the Ministry (Government Decision Nr. 51, 2009). The main goals of this department are:

- To promote Romania's academic image overseas and to increase the number of foreign students;
- To support the HEIs in their effort to promote their educational offerings at the international level;
- To develop advertising materials and to participate at educational fairs in order to inform the audience about the Romanian educational system;
- To facilitate the application process for foreign students.

As first concrete steps, the site study-in-romania.ro was launched and a guide for international students was published. Unfortunately the site is not up to date and basic information is missing. There is no data available regarding the support of HEIs in their internationalization..

Besides the aforementioned policies the Romanian state is currently offering a small number of scholarships (85) for students from all over the world and also places students from outside the EU within the Romanian education system based on bilateral agreements (Ministerul Afacerilor Externe, 2011). Furthermore, the new education law adopted in 2011 lays the groundwork for more international developments in the universities. For example, it eases the employment of foreign citizens within the Romanian HEIs (Legea Educatiei, 2011).

Over the last few years several steps have been undertaken in order to facilitate and foster the internationalization of Romanian HEIs. The recent statements indicate that on a central level the internationalization has become an important issue. Following the trends in other countries, further central measures are expected to be taken in the coming years.

SURVEY BASED RESEARCH REGARDING INTERNATIONALIZATION AND MULTICULTURALISM OF ROMANIAN UNIVERSITIES

In the next section we aim at shifting the perspective regarding the academic internationalization and multiculturalism in Romania from the macroeconomic to the microeconomic level, which is researched through the use of surveys.

A questionnaire was developed by the authors and was distributed online to the main Universities of Romania. Despite the fact that both authors are professionally active in the academic environment and maintain strong relations with the representatives of the international relations offices, to whom this questionnaire was addressed, the response rate was modest, at less than 25%. Therefore this outcome does not indicate the reluctance of the approached personnel to answer the questions, but the lack of information at university level, and consequently the lack

of capacity to provide the data required in the questionnaire. Seven valid questionnaires were submitted and analyzed from the main public universities in Romania: University of Bucharest, Polytechnic University Bucharest, Academy of Economic Studies of Bucharest, University "Alexandru Ioan Cuza" of Iasi, University of Pitesti, University "Stefan cel Mare" of Suceava, University "Lucian Blaga" of Sibiu. Even if not a large number of responses were collected and the results are not statistically representative, we consider the aforementioned universities relevant for our study as they cover a wide range of academic institutions: large, middle and small sized universities both from the capital city Bucharest as well as from other smaller university cities throughout Romania.

The questionnaire comprises 15 questions, both opened- and closed-ended ones which cover the two main areas of interest for the present study: multiculturalism and the degree of internationalization.

The first question analyzes the intercultural milieu of the surveyed universities, by comparing the number of foreign students (ERASMUS and non ERASMUS) and the number of students belonging to other ethnic groups/minorities/diaspora with the total student population. We can state that no correlation was observed between the size of the university or the geographical location and the number of students with an international or different ethnical background. The share of international students and students belonging to other ethnic groups/minorities/diaspora ranges between 4.07% from the total student population (University "Alexandru Ioan Cuza" of Iasi) and 1.46% (University "Lucian Blaga" of Sibiu). The average is 2.41%, a figure which is considerably higher than the national average computed in 2009 of 0.94%. Considering the fact that the only common characteristic of the researched university is the fact that they are public universities, we may conclude that the degree of multiculturalism/internationalization of public universities in Romania exceeds that of private universities, which in turn decreases the average rate at the national level. This situation can be explained by the fact that the Ministry of Education allocates special funds for the academic formation of students belonging to other ethnos/minorities or to the Romanian diaspora who plan to study in public universities in Romania. Therefore these candidates are inclined to apply for a place in the public universities.

Analyzing the data obtained we observe that, by far, the most international and multicultural out of the three academic cycles (Bachelor, Master, Phd) is the Bachelor program, followed by the Phd program and lastly by the Master program.

Regarding the ethnic background we observe that the share of representatives of other ethnos/minorities is very small, ranging between 0% and 1.17% of the total student population. This can be explained by the fact that the most important ethnos is Romania is represented by the Roma population. In general not many Roma obtain a high school degree and the dropout rate is very high among them. As a consequence not many of them get the chance to be involved in tertiary education. Furthermore, those who succeed to enter HEIs tend to not declare their ethnos. Other large minorities in Romania are the Hungarians and Germans who live in Transylvania but just one university from Transylvania is represented in our research, namely University "Lucian Blaga" of Sibiu.

Romanians from diaspora represent between 0% and 10.2% of the total student population. The percentage of long term for-

eign students (non Erasmus), ranging between 1.59% and 6.37% is greater than the number of ERASMUS incoming students, ranging between 0.36% and 1.36%.

The top ranked country of origin of the long term foreign students is by far the Republic of Moldova, reflecting the effort of Romanian authorities to support the students from this country with special career development programs, aimed at fostering the relation between the two countries. The top ranked countries of origin for the ERASMUS students are Spain, Portugal, Italy and France. This result is in accordance with the figures obtained at the national level, which place the incoming ERASMUS students from Latin countries on top positions.

Regarding the multicultural dimension of the surveyed universities it can be observed that, despite the small numbers of other ethnics/minorities, all the universities offer lectures and other activities aimed at cultivating and supporting the respect for socio-cultural diversity. These activities facilitate the attainment of intercultural skills and promote the socio-cultural dialog between the parties involved in the educational process. In all of the universities represented in our research, these initiatives take place on a regular basis. Although the figures are rather modest, we can observe a positive trend in this respect which indicates that this type of initiative is still in an early stage. However, these positive developments are also emphasized by the fact that no discriminatory actions have been reported so far in any of the universities we researched.

In the main university in Transylvania- the most multicultural region of Romania-, University Babes-Bolyai from Cluj Napoca (which did not provide data for this study, but which was analyzed due to the important role it plays in the region) degree programs are offered in the minorities' language: 94 study programs in Hungarian and 19 study programs in German. We should note the fact that in Romania 73 study programs take place in the German language. This puts Romania on the top spot in Europe for the number of degree programs offered in German (DAAD Informationszentrum Bukarest, 2010).

The second part of the questionnaire assesses the level of internationalization at the universities from different perspectives: the number of foreign students, the number of foreign professors, accessibility of the programs (measured by the programs taught in foreign languages), joint programs, as well as the initiatives undertaken in order to increase the visibility of the university at international level (promotional strategies) and the structure and services offered by the university's international office.

Regarding the number of foreign professors who teach at the sampled universities the figures illustrate a very domestic environment: in five out of seven universities the rate of foreign professors compared to the total teaching staff is less 5%, while in just 2 universities ("University "Alexandru Ioan Cuza" of Iasi and University "Lucian Blaga" of Sibiu) their

rate is between 6-25%. Therefore, probably due to the looser ties and easier bureaucratic administrative procedures, the middle sized universities are more dynamic from this perspective than the larger ones. At University "Lucian Blaga" of Sibiu this situation can be explained by the relations with representatives of the German minority who emigrated to Germany and are a professionally active in the German academic environment.

Table 3 depicts the study programs offered in foreign languages and the double degree programs. The distinction was made between studies of foreign languages (e.g. German or English philology, language and literature studies, etc.) and other studies in foreign languages (e.g. Business Administration in Foreign languages, European Study in Foreign Languages, Engineering in Foreign Languages, etc.).

An overall positive trend is observed regarding internationalization through developing programs in foreign language, which can be found at over 70% of the universities. All big universities offer programs in foreign languages and also joint programs for double degrees with partner universities from abroad. All of the programs in foreign languages are taught in English, French and German, while

Table 3. Study programs in foreign languages and joint programs

University	Language and Literature	Other Programs in Foreign Languages	Double Degree Programs
Academy of Economic Studies of Bucharest	-	X	X
Polytechnic University Bucharest	-	X	X
University Bucharest	X	X	X
University "Alexandru Ioan Cuza" of Iasi	X	X	X
University "Lucian Blaga" of Sibiu	X	-	-
University of Pitesti	X	X	-
University "Stefan cel Mare" of Suceava	X	-	-

Source: Own illustration based on the results of the survey

most of the joint programs are at the Master's level and are conducted solely by the major Romanian universities together with universities from France, Germany and the Netherlands[2]. Even if not included in the present survey, the University Babes-Bolyai of Cluj-Napoca can be presented as a best practice model regarding the double degree programs: just at Bachelor's level there are five joint programs with German universities: Economic Studies, History, German Studies, European Studies and Biology.

In order to assess the access to the study programs for foreign students we have also researched the websites of the universities. Just 28% of the universities have the entire site and the enclosed links translated into English, while the rest have the site just partially translated and are difficult to follow for a foreign applicant.

The insufficient level of translation of the university websites indicates that they are not fully aware of the necessity of attracting foreign students and the programs in foreign languages might be rather designed for Romanian students who want to study in a foreign language. However, it can be still concluded that Romanian universities have made the first steps towards drawing foreign students by facilitating their access to studies.

Regarding the promotional strategies aimed at increasing the international visibility of universities, the survey results reveal the fact that all universities have formulated a promotional strategy and employ the main promotional instruments. All universities with the exception of University of Pitesti present their study offerings at international fairs, although in big universities such as the Academy of Economic Studies of Bucharest and University of Bucharest the participation in fairs decreased over the last two academic years due to the cost-cutting policies imple-

mented in the Romanian public institutions during the recent period of crisis. All of the researched universities designed promotional materials such as marketing brochures, flyers in foreign languages, etc. However, when having a closer look at these materials, it can be stated that some of them do lack important information for the students and there is room for improvement in the future. The main competitive advantages of the universities are not properly highlighted, this outcome emphasizing also the lack of clarity and coherence when presenting the main reasons for a foreign student to study at the respective university. The reasons listed are - with some exceptions - very general, are not tailored to the university profile and indicate a poor reflection on their own competitive advantages and a fuzzy strategy regarding internationalization. Over 85% of the universities declare that visits abroad are conducted in order to advertise the university. However, we suspect confusion at the university level between the special targeted promotional visits abroad and the informal meetings and presentations hold by various members of the university when travelling abroad for different academic purposes. None of the universities researched either hired a specialized agency for their promotion abroad nor used the services of various international websites for study. The classical promotional toolkit is employed, as none of the universities indicated a new instrument of promotion. This suggests so far the limited innovation and creative capacity in this respect.

All of the universities have a specialized department for international affairs, with full time employees, indicating the beginning of professionalization of services for foreign students. The number of employees in the international departments ranges between 3 employees at University "Stefan cel Mare" of Suceava, and 9 employees and 3 interns at University "Alexandru Ioan Cuza" of Iasi. In general, these employees are also in charge of the European Programs like ERASMUS. Surprisingly there is no relation between the size of the university and the capacity of the international office: large universities such as Polytechnic University Bucharest and University of Bucharest have only 4 employees who work within the department, while smaller universities such as University "Lucian Blaga" of Sibiu or University of Pitesti have 6 and 5 employees respectively.

Regarding the services offered to foreign students, in more than a half of the universities a Romanian tutor, responsible for helping the foreign student to understand the administrative system and to settle in the new environment, is assigned to each foreign student. Just 3 universities organize an orientation week, which help foreign students familiarize themselves with the new study environment. All of the universities offer support in finding accommodation and also offer Romanian language courses. Therefore, it can be concluded that all universities offer the basic support services for foreign students and some of them have already stepped into a new phase of development, by offering more sophisticated services such as Romanian buddies and an orientation week.

Regarding the tuition fee policies, the citizens of the European Union obey the same rules as the Romanians (the best candidates can obtained a study place financed by the public budget, while the other ones have to pay a tuition fee), while for other nationals a different policy applies. All of the universities follow the recommendation of the Ministry of Education regarding the level of tuition fees for non EU citizens. Thus, for the Bachelor program, the tuition fee/month varies between 220-270 Euro depending on the specialization,

with the exception of University of Pitesti where it can reach 420 Euro and University "Lucian Blaga" of Sibiu where it can reach 320 Euro. For Master and PhD degrees the tuition fees are slightly higher, averaging 250 Euro/month and 280 Euro/month, respectively. The tuition is small compared to other countries, which makes Romania an attractive study destination especially for African and Asian students.

CONCLUSION

In the last two decades the topic of internationalization of HEIs has gained an increasing importance as have the theoretical research and the practical policies employed by universities. The present study reveals that Romania follows the international trend but did not take full advantage of the increasing international mobility of students. At the moment, the share of international students in Romania lags behind the world average as well as the level of other Eastern European countries. While the number of outgoing students more than doubled since 1999, the number of incoming students has remained stable, so that Romania is a "donor country" on the global education market. As there is a positive correlation between internationalization and multiculturalism, we can state that both dimensions are not fully developed in Romania. However, universities are aware of the importance of multicultural education in a globalized world and despite the low level of multiculturalism in Romania – as determined by the small numbers of foreign students - there are lectures offered which foster these skills such as Civilization, Foreign Languages, Cross Cultural Management, etc.

Analyzing the results obtained from the surveys conducted in the universities and the national data, we can conclude that multicultural aspects in Romanian universities are defined by three main factors, which are related to the country of origin of foreign students: the language –which attracts students from Latin countries-, historical ties – in the case of the German speaking countries and similar cultural backgrounds and common historical roots- in the case of Moldavians.

The most important measures of the Romanian government which fostered internationalization have been the scholarship program for citizens of the Republic of Moldova and the accession to the Bologna area. Over the last five years there has been evidence that the Romanian state is aware of the importance of a national strategy for internationalization. Despite some notable first steps, such as the establishment of an international students department within the Ministry of Education, financial constraints have prevented a concrete national strategy from being developed or implemented yet. Thus, according to Davies' matrix of approaches towards internationalization, on a macro level Romania's strategy could be classified as Ad-hoc Marginal.

The research done at micro level, namely at the university level shows that internationalization is not neglected either. The HEIs use a broad set of instruments such as student exchange programs, double degree programs, partnerships with universities abroad, research stays for PhD candidates and summer schools, therefore covering the four dimension of internationalization described by Knight. The fact that all universities participating at the survey have an international office dealing with the incoming and outgoing students and teaching staff, and at the same time being responsible for the relationships with foreign universities, shows a certain degree of professionalization of the international activities. But there is still a lot of room for improvement as is revealed by the analysis of homepages and promotional materials. It seems that Romanian HEIs are quite dynamic with their international activities, but they miss a well-defined vision and strategy. Therefore, within Davies' matrix we would classify them as institutions with an Ad-hoc Central strategy.

It can be stated that the existing structures such as the study programs in foreign languages, the numerous partnerships with foreign universities and the involvement in international research projects provide a solid foundation to cope with the ongoing process of internationalization of education. But in order to have a better performance it would be necessary to develop and implement an integrative strategy, taking into account the existing opportunities and strengths.

While conducting the research for the present paper, it became clear that the information is not centrally collected and consequently there is a huge lack of data at the national and even at the university level regarding various aggregated key indicators such as international students, students with other ethnic background, international research projects etc. Therefore, we consider that the present study brings an important contribution regarding data aggregation and presentation in a structured way. On the other hand side, in order to develop a strategy either on the national or the local level, the first step would be to develop a detailed analysis of the status quo. With this paper, we sought to start this analysis and thereby trigger further similar initiatives.

ACKNOWLEDGMENT

This work was supported by CNCSIS-UE-FISCSU, project PN II-RU-TE_351/2010.

REFERENCES

Agoston, S., & Dima, A. (2012). Trends and strategies within the process of academic internationalization. *Management & Marketing*, *7*(1), 43–57.

Altbach, P., Reisberg, L., & Rumble, L. (2009). *Trends in global higher education: Tracking an academic revolution: Executive summary*. Paper presented at the UNESCO 2009 World Conference on Higher Education. Paris, France.

Bartell, M. (2003). Internationalization of universities: A university culture-based framework. *Higher Education*, *45*, 43–70. doi:10.1023/A:1021225514599

Building Capacities of East-Central Europe National Agencies to Promote Higher Education outside the EU: Project Overview. (2008), Retrieved from http://www.highereducation-promotion.eu/web/overview.html

Burke, P. (2009). *Identity theory*. New York: Academic Press. doi:10.1093/acprof:oso/9780195388275.001.0001

Davies, J. L. (2001). The emergence of entrepreneurial cultures in European universities. *Higher Education Management*, *12*, 25–43.

De Wit, H. (2010). *Internationalization of higher education in Europe and its assessment, trends and issues*. Den Haag, The Netherlands: Academic Press.

Dima, A., & Agoston, S. (2011). Internationalization of universities, reflections on the past and future perspectives. In *Proceedings of the 6th International Conference Business Excellence*, (vol. 1, pp. 177-182). Academic Press.

Dixon, M. (2006). Globalisation and international higher education: Contested positioning. *Journal of Studies in International Education*, *10*(4), 319–333. doi:10.1177/1028315306287789

Educaţiei, M. Cercetării, Tineretului şi Sportului. (2011). *Metodologia de scolarizare a cetăţenilor de origine etnică română din Republica Moldova, din alte state învecinate şi a etnicilor români cu domiciliul stabil în străinătate în învăţământul din România, în anul şcolar/universitar 2011–2012*. Retrieved from http://www.edu.ro/index.php/articles/proiecte_acte_norm/15217

Enders, J. (2004). Higher education, internationalization, and the nation-state: Recent developments and challenges to governance theory. *Higher Education*, *47*, 361–382. doi:10.1023/B:HIGH.0000016461.98676.30

European Commission. (2001). *Abschlussbericht der kommission uber die umsetzung des programms sokrates 1995-1999*. Retrieved from http://ec.europa.eu/dgs/education_culture/evalreports/education/2001/sociexpost/soc1xpCOM_de.pdf

European Commission. (2012a). *ERASMUS statistics Romania*. Retrieved from http://ec.europa.eu/education/erasmus/doc/stat/0910/countries/romania_en.pdf

European Commission. (2012b). *Outgoing and incoming ERASMUS student mobility for studies in 2009/2010*. Retrieved from http://ec.europa.eu/education/erasmus/doc/stat/0910/students.pdf

Florea, S., & Wells, P. J. (2012). *Higher education in Romania*. Bucharest, Romania: Cepes.

Hanson, L. (2010). Global citizenship, global health, and the internationalization of curriculum: A study of transformative potential. *Journal of Studies in International Education, 14*(1), 70–88. doi:10.1177/1028315308323207

Informationszentrum Bukarest, D. A. A. D. (2010). *Deutschsprachige studiengänge an hochschulen in Rumänien*. Bucharest, Romania: DAAD.

Kehm, B., & Teichler, U. (2007). Research on internationalization in higher education. *Journal of Studies in International Education, 11*(4), 260–273. doi:10.1177/1028315307303534

Knight, J. (1999). *Internationalization of higher education in OECD, quality and internationalization in higher education*. Paris: OECD.

Knight, J. (2004). Internationalization remodeled: Definition, approaches, and rationales. *Journal of Studies in International Education, 8*(1), 5–31. doi:10.1177/1028315303260832

Knight, J. (2008). *Higher education in turmoil: The changing world of internationalization*. Rotterdam, The Netherlands: Sense Publishers.

Korka, M. (2009). *Bologna process: Report Romania 2008*. Retrieved from http://bologna.ro/a/upfolders/National_Report_Romania_2009.pdf

Lasch, K. (2011). *Teorii ale identitatii, natiunii si ale nationalismului. Referat stiintific in cadrul cercetarii doctorale Problema identitatii nationale a moldovenilor din Basarabia la inceputul secolului al XX-lea*. Universitatea Babes-Bolyai, Cluj Napoca.

Lunn, J. (2008). Global perspectives in higher education: Taking the agenda forward in the United Kingdom. *Journal of Studies in International Education, 12*(3), 231–254. doi:10.1177/1028315307308332

Mahrous, A., & Ahmed, A. (2010). A cross-cultural investigation of students' perceptions of the effectiveness of pedagogical tools the Middle East, the United Kingdom, and the United States. *Journal of Studies in International Education, 14*(3), 289–386. doi:10.1177/1028315309334738

Marginson, S., & van der Wende, M. (2009). The new global landscape of nations and institutions. In Higher education to 2030, vol. 2: Globalisation. Paris: OECD.

Ministerul Afacerilor Externe. (2011). *Burse oferite cetăţenilor străini de statul român prin MAE*. Retrieved from http://www.mae.ro/node/1794

Naidoo, V. (2009). Transnational higher education: A stock take of current activity. *Journal of Studies in International Education, 13*(3), 310–330. doi:10.1177/1028315308317938

Nicolescu, L., Pricopie, R., & Popescu, A. (2009). Country differences in the internationalization of higher education – How can countries lagging behind diminish the gap. *Review of International Comparative Management, 10*(5), 976–989.

Romanian Government. (2009). *Government decision nr. 51 regarding the structure and function of the ministry of education, research and innovation*. Retrieved from http://www.edu.ro/index.php/articles/12645

Romaniei, P. (2011). *Legea educatiei natio-nale (Monitorul Oficial Nr.18/2011)*. Author.

Teichler, U. (1996). Comparative higher education: Potentials and limits. *Higher Education, 32*(4), 431–465. doi:10.1007/BF00133257

Teichler, U. (2004). The changing debate on internationalization of higher education. *Higher Education, 48*, 5–26. doi:10.1023/B:HIGH.0000033771.69078.41

Teichler, U. (2009). Internationalization of higher education: European experiences. *Asia Pacific Education Review, 10*(1), 93–106. doi:10.1007/s12564-009-9002-7

Teichler, U. (2010). Internationalization as a challenge for higher education. *Europe Tertiary Education and Management, 5*(1), 5–23. doi:10.1080/13583883.1999.9966978

UNESCO. (2006). *UNESCO guidelines on intercultural education*. Paris: UNESCO.

UNESCO Institute for Statistics. (2009). *Global education digest- Comparing education statistics across the world*. Paris: UNESCO.

UNESCO Institute for Statistics. (2012). *Global education digest data base*. Retrieved from www.uis.unesco.org/education

Van der Wende, M. (2010). Internationaliza-tion of higher education. In *International encyclopedia of education* (Vol. 4, pp. 540–545). Oxford, UK: Elsevier. doi:10.1016/B978-0-08-044894-7.00836-8

ENDNOTES

[1] The theoretical part of the article is based mainly on the prior research conducted by the authors and released in other articles, such as Agoston, S., Dima, A. (2012) Trends and strategies within the process of academic internationalization, Management & Marketing, Vol.7, No.1, ISSN 1842-0206, pp.43-57 and Dima, A., Agoston, S. (2011) Internationalization of universities, reflections on the past and future perspectives, Proceedings of the 6th International Conference Business Excellence, Braşov, 14-15 October 2011, Vol 1, ISBN 978-973-598-939-2, pp. 177-182.

[2] Many of the Dutch universities have programs in English and lately they have been very open for partnerships with Romanian universities. Also many Romanian students are accepted to study in the Netherlands.

Chapter 3
Harmonization of the Funding Mechanisms in European Universities

Alina Mihaela Dima
Bucharest University of Economic Studies, Romania

Ramona Cantaragiu
University of Bucharest, Romania

ABSTRACT

The chapter discusses, comparatively, funding mechanisms for universities in Europe and advances potential ways for their harmonization in the framework of their Bologna convergence. The findings of the research suggest that, while there is a European-level shift to performance-based funding and quantitative indicators tend to say that European HE funding systems are to a certain degree convergent, qualitative analysis indicates that the outcomes are still divergent and more efforts have to be put into really bringing these systems to a common ground.

INTRODUCTION

Traditionally, higher education has been considered a public good and universities have been financed from public sources. However, during the last few decades two major trends have been challenging this position, forcing public universities to become more financially

state-independent. One of the trends regards the increase in the cost of education brought about by the massification of higher education and the rising costs of human resources (pension costs etc.) (Estermann & Pruvot, 2011). On the other hand, public funding is no longer able to satisfy the increasing demands of the educational sector which is in direct

DOI: 10.4018/978-1-4666-4325-3.ch003

competition with other public priorities such as health, national security etc. which are facing the same cost inflation. Especially after the 2008 financial crisis, governments have decided to decrease the levels of investment in higher education, forcing universities to seek alternative means of funding. Thus, today's universities are struggling to find alternative sources of financing, in the context of changing educational laws that have as a desired outcome the placement of the burden of funding on the institution side.

Concerning the European Higher Education Area (EHEA), since March 2000, the European Council decided that one of the goals of the EU should be to become "the most competitive and dynamic knowledge-based economy in the world, capable of sustaining economic growth with more and better jobs and greater social cohesion". It is clear that education is the main pillar for achieving this ambitious position and, thus, the council also required member states to increase their investments in education and for these investments to be based more on the output of the higher education institutions. However, the council also emphasized that this is not a matter of concern just for governments and that institutions themselves have to become more market oriented and search new alternative streams of income.

The search of new funding alternatives has led many to deplore the current state of European higher education which they consider to have turned its back on traditional values of quality and selectivity and to have embraced the ones of capitalism: massification, focus on cost reduction and obeying universal standards of quality, most of them which translate poorly to the educational sector. We can talk about a financial fragility of higher education institutions, borrowing the term from Johnstone (2009), which uses it to refer to

the institution (or in a macro sense, the higher educational system of a state or country) that is constantly on the edge of having to compromise its chosen mission or fundamental institutional character because of the inability to consistently raise enough revenue or shed enough expenditures—year after year—to maintain this mission and character. (p.1)

According to the author, the underlying cause that inevitably leads to worldwide financial fragility of all the higher education institutions and educational systems is the natural trajectory of costs, or necessary expenditures, that tends to outpace the natural trajectory of revenues. The explanation behind this phenomenon lies in the fact that certain sectors, as the educational one, cannot profit from substituting capital for labor or from outsourcing to regions where the cost of production factors is lower, leading these sectors to become productivity immune (Baumol & Bowen, 1966).

In spite the fact that it faces many challenges, the tertiary educational sector is viewed as a major driver of economic development (Altbach, et al., 2009), and thus there is increased pressure to perform, meaning to provide equal access for all and high quality teaching, priorities which are incompatible with the difficult conditions in which these institutions have to exist. At the EHEA level, the higher education institutions have to become competitive on a global level and they have to produce graduates that will contribute to the economic development of the EU and the rest of the non-EU countries.

But all is not negative with regards to the financial fragility, as Kwiek (2006a) cites this income diversification impulse as a source of positive change in the educational sector: "financial diversification of an institution is also healthy academically" (p. 3) because it pushes the institution towards entrepreneurial-ism, it punishes failure and passivity and it turns its attention to those activities that have a direct impact on societal good.

AIM OF THE STUDY, METHODOLOGY AND LIMITATIONS

The present study intends to analyze the main trends in higher education financing in the EHEA in order to establish if between its member states we can talk about a convergence in practices and outcomes or a divergence. We will analyze the sources of funding, putting an accent on their proportions in the total educational revenues, the mechanisms through which higher education institutions are able to access these revenues and the total spending on education, considered as per student cost.

The first part of the study looks at the structure of the tertiary system, presenting the types of higher education institutions recognized in each country, the proportion of public to private enrollment and the degree to which both types of institutions are governed by the same laws. This section will act as an introduction to our discussion regarding the funding mechanisms by representing a background onto which we can build certain hypotheses, but also by reminding us that financial statistics usually hide the fact that the reality of higher education is very diverse with respect to its constituent institutions, ways in which these are regarded by society and the role they play inside each member state.

The second part of the present chapter analyses the type of financing available for higher education institutions, putting an emphasis on the external and internal sources of funding and their evolution in time. We also take a look at other financial indicators such as financing per student, expenditure of households and other private institutions and assess their correlation with financial growth indicators such as GDP per capita and investments in research and development (as percentage of GDP). As we present these data we will have in mind to map the main evolution undergone by the funding mechanisms in the EHEA and to establish whether we can talk of a common direction in which all member states are heading or each country has its own path.

The European Higher Education Area (EHEA) brings together 47 states some of which are part of the European Union and some which are from the Asian continent such as the Russian Federation and Azerbaijan according to the official Bologna Process website

Due to the geographic extent of the area, we can expect to find wide discrepancies between educational and public interest principles that lead to differences in the funding mechanisms for the higher education sector. This increases the difficulty of conducting a comparative study, and leads us to put an emphasis on the quantitative aspects (both financial and non-financial), leaving out the qualitative ones such as the quality of teaching, attitudes towards higher education etc.

Moreover, we do not have financial and non-financial data regarding all the 47 members gathered by only one organization, which would ensure their comparability. In the present chapter, we will make comparisons between countries based on two sources of data: Eurostat and the OECD Education Database. From the beginning, we must acknowledge that one important limitation of the present study is the absence of comparable data for all the EHEA members regarding their higher education financing practices.

THE STRUCTURE OF THE HIGHER EDUCATION SYSTEMS IN THE EHEA

Before beginning the analysis of the structure of the national higher educational systems of each member of the EHEA, we should first take a look at the complexity of each system and discuss separately those countries which have a very straightforward higher education sector. In countries such Andorra (1 state university), Iceland (7 public institutions and 1 private university), Liechtenstein (3 private institutions), Luxembourg (3 private universities), Malta (1 state university), Montenegro (1 state university) and the Former Yugoslav Republic of Macedonia (3 state universities and 1 private university), there is a national law regarding the functioning of tertiary institutions and there seem to be less problems regarding the funding mechanisms and no competition among institutions regarding the allocation of these funds.

However, although the internal institutions face no major problems, the entire educational system, due to its limited number of institutions, depends on agreements with neighboring countries that receive some of the students into their tertiary education system. For example, Liechtenstein has contractual arrangements with Switzerland, Austria and Baden-Württemberg (Tübingen), allowing students free entry to the universities in these countries. In return for the free access, Liechtenstein pays a fee for every student that studies abroad, and this, in turn, limits the available budget for national institutions.

Another exception is represented by the Holy See, whose educational system is made of 181 institutions spread all over the world, which are classified in two groups: ecclesiastical universities and faculties and catholic universities, colleges and other institutions of higher learning, These institutions have to obey the national laws of the country of residence as well as the governing documents enforced by the Holy See.

Institutional diversity is one of the key elements of debate in recent discussions about educational policies in Europe and it is regarded by many as a viable means through which the EHEA can achieve its desired goals of becoming competitive in a knowledge-based world and focusing on the needs of students and various other stakeholders. Institutional diversity can be analyzed from many angles, as we can look at the types of institutions, at their mission and goals, degree of autonomy or funding mechanisms. Although all angles bring in valuable information, after having thoroughly analyzed the tertiary sector in five European countries, Reichter (2009) concludes that the available funding mechanisms are those that lead to institutional diversity, more than the degree of autonomy or the typology imposed by law. Following this opinion, the next part of the study will discuss the classification into public and private higher educational institutions in the EHEA, with a view to discuss the proportions held by each category in the total number of students enrolled in the tertiary educational sector and the possible opportunities and threats that might arise from those proportions for public institutions that are seeking to differentiate their financing sources.

The role of private institutions in the higher education sector in countries of Western Europe is marginal at best, considering that countries such as Germany, France, Italy, Austria and the United Kingdom have insignificant private sectors, whereas private sectors represent a rapidly developing segment of education in Central and Eastern European countries, as concluded by Tomusk (2004).

Most EHEA countries have a strong public sector, many of them only recently having started developing their private sector. Greece and the United Kingdom are the only two countries (excluding the smaller countries already discussed) in which all higher education institutions are state run, thus not allowing for the existence of private institutions. Another 12 countries have only a small private sector that covers less than 10% of the educational needs of students and another 12 countries in which the private sector's percentage out of total higher education enrollment varies between 10 and 20%.

The private higher education sector is the fastest growing worldwide, but, according to Altbach et al. (2009), this "sector is 'demand absorbing', offering access to students who might not be qualified for the public institutions or who cannot be accommodated in the other universities because of overcrowding" (p. 56) (See Table 1). Consequently, there should be no real competition between private and public higher institutions, as they cater to different needs and also have different sources of financing, although in some countries the private sector receives subsidies from the public budget.

The existence of a strong private sector, as in such countries as the Netherlands, Cyprus and Belgium, where it accounts for more than 50% of the total enrolments in the tertiary sector could, first of all, impose a business-type model for the public institutions as well, providing them with valuable insights and knowhow regarding the differentiation of financing sources. As Kwiek (2006b) states talking about private higher education institutions in Central and Eastern European countries:

Often private institutions monitor the labor market, open career centers for their graduates, and introduce explicit internal quality assurance mechanisms. Many follow market mechanisms in their functioning as business units, use public relations and marketing tools to have significant portions of local, regional, or national educational "markets", and finally prepare their graduates for living and working in market realities. They have also exerted huge impact on academicians themselves. (p.123)

Moreover, it could alleviate the burden placed on the public budget by the educational sector as a whole, leaving more funding to be accessible to public institutions. The empirical research in the European higher education domain appears to sustain our assumptions. For example, in the total budget of public institutions in countries where the private sector accounts for at least 15% percent of the total sector, the share of operational grants from public authorities is lower than in the other countries (62.81% compared to 67.43%) and the share of third party funding is higher (23.81% compared to 19.13%).

An argument that makes us look more doubtful at the direct impact of the existence of private higher education institutions onto the whole national system of education is represented by the fact that, at first sight, old members of EU have a larger share of private to total enrollment (41.95% on average) than the members admitted in 2004 and 2007 (with an average of 33.66%), the difference in the share of operational grants from the public authorities for public universities is almost insignificant, implying that there is a threshold for the private/total education above which the results are the same, and we have set it at 15%. However, on further investigation, we discover that the domain in which the two types of members differ is the share of third party funding for public universities, which

Table 1. Public and private shares in higher education in the EHEA

Country	Private % of Total Higher Education Enrollment	Year	Share of Operational grant from Public Authorities (%) for Public Universities in 2008	Share of Third Party Funding (%) for Public Universities in 2008
Netherlands	69.9	2002	60	28
Cyprus	66.6	2005/6	80	5
Belgium	55.4	2006	45/50	50/45
Poland	34.1	2007	71	7
Romania	33.8	2007	70	5
Latvia	31.9	2007/8	50	35
Armenia	26.6	2004	-	-
Portugal	25.9	2004/5	60	30
Iceland	22.9	2005	65	35
Moldova	20.0	2003	-	-
Georgia	19.2	2003	-	-
Estonia	18.0	2008/9	48	39
FYR Macedonia	17.9	2007/8	-	-
Bulgaria	17.6	2008/9	55	25
France	16.6	2006	87	8
Russia	14.9	2004	-	-
Azerbaijan	14.4	2003	-	-
Hungary	13.6	2006/7	70	5
Norway	13.4	2006/7	75	25
Albania	12.0	-	-	-
Ukraine	12.0	2003	-	-
Croatia	11.3	2008	70	0
Finland	10.5	2006	65	35
Slovak Republic	9.8	2006	94	5
Spain	9.6	2001	76	3
Czech Republic	8.9	2004	75	20
Lithuania	8.5	2005/6	65	10
Sweden	7.3	2003	88	12
Italy	7.2	2006	65	23
Ireland	7.0	2004	40	25
Turkey	5.8	2005/6	57	39
Germany	4.9	2008/9	n/a	n/a
Austria	4.4	2006	78	16
Slovenia	2.6	2007/8	50	25
Denmark	1.9	2006	73	25
Greece	0	2008/9	n/a	n/a
United Kingdom	0	2006	38	38

Source: Data available on http://www.albany.edu/dept/eaps/prophe/data/international.html

is on average 50% higher in the old members than in the newly admitted countries (29% to 19.33%), fact which points to the idea that there are other underlying factors influencing the educational sector as well, such as the country's economic, political, and, especially, business environment.

Moreover, after comparing private and public higher education institutions included in the EUEREK study, Kwiek (2006a) discovered that private institutions are less entrepreneurial than public ones, having difficulties with accessing research funding, and relying heavily on student fees, thus competing for students and not knowledge creation and research with the other higher education institutions. Also, having a diversified funding base does not seem to be academically healthy for private institutions:

Separate units are rarely rewarded (or punished) for their entrepreneurialism and rarely act as separate business units, as is often the case with most successful public entrepreneurial universities. They do not seem to have incentive policies to support their staff in seeking non-core source of income – the income other than student fees. They do not have access to government funds – but also most often do not have access to government agencies as sources of third-stream income, private organized sources (such as business firms, philanthropic foundations etc.) and do not use policies to support university-generated income (p. 14).

Thus reality may urge us to renounce our views of similarity between the two sectors, to regard with caution the proponents of "friendship", cooperation and harmony between the private and public sector and to search for complementarities, diversity and pluralistic development. As Levy (2006) suggests, the number of private institutions is not enough for an analysis of their impact on the educational sector, we have to take into consideration that private higher education stands for a very diverse sector which is mostly concerned with promoting particular interests, whereas "the public higher education sector typically makes a grand claim to pursuing a national development vision, a unified vision, often planned and implying a certain degree of standardization and quality" (p. 10), but a more in-depth analysis in beyond the scope of the present chapter.

FUNDING MECHANISM OF HIGHER EDUCATION IN THE EHEA

Higher education institutions can obtain funding either from the public budget or from private sources, through tuition fees from households and research contracts and donations from private institutions. The intended result of the current educational policies, either at national or international level, is to increase the proportion of private funding with a view of alleviating the burden placed on the governmental resources by the increased cost of education. In the following paragraphs we will present the three main sources of financing for the tertiary sector (public budget, household income, private investment) with the view to measure their contribution to the total expenditure on higher education in each member state and to compare the mechanisms through which a higher education institution is able to access the funds provided by each source.

To begin with, a significant number of the EHEA member states have adopted differentiated funding strategies for their research components and core activities. As such, HEIs may have the public budget as a resource for the latter, while sourcing its research activities mainly with private investments. This enables the institutions to leverage on the financial resources diversification possibilities and create more innovative, complex strategies to help them adapt to and remain competitive in the increasingly globalized education sector.

In that sense, for the university research activities Auranen and Nieminen (2010) have identified as main internal sources of funding the governmental core funding (if the organization has the authority to decide its allocation and use within itself) and the university's assets, and public (grants from public funding agencies, and contracts with the public administration) and private exter-

nal funding, as potential external financing sources (Auranen and Nieminen, 2010). Data reveals that the state budget is the main source of financing of higher education in the EHEA, providing for up to 90% of the total expenditure in countries such as Norway, Finland, Sweden. However, there are also countries in which government expenditure accounts for only half of the total, such as in the United Kingdom (50%), Slovak Republic (65%) and Italy (66%). Table 2 shows the proportion of the two categories of funding (public and private) for a group of 18 EHEA countries using data from the OECD. We have to keep in mind that low government expenditure has to be balanced either by a high household investment and/or by high levels of private investments and that in most cases, the burden

Table 2. Total, government and private expenditure for higher education in 2007

Country	Government Expenditure	Private Expenditure	Total Expenditure	Government Expenditure (% total)
Norway	49,061	860	49,921	98
Finland	3,327.34	126.06	3,453.4	96
Sweden	54,137	4,934	59,071	92
Austria	4,056.47	529.95	4,586.42	88
Ireland	2,169.94	318.85	2,488.79	87
Germany	27,684.9	5,750.11	33,435.01	83
Belgium	4,375.26	938.49	5,313.75	82
France	23,238.8	5,211.4	28,450.2	82
Slovenia	418.28	95.61	513.89	81
Spain	10,461.27	2,540.39	13,001.66	80
Estonia	2,606	675	3,281	79
Denmark	38,663.7	11,908.5	5,0572.2	76
Netherlands	8,243.99	2,667.1	10,911.09	76
Poland	10,990.3	4,901.5	15,891.8	69
Czech Republic	37,878.4	18,162.86	56,041.26	68
Italy	11,718.58	6,081.56	17,800.14	66
Slovak Republic	14,621.65	7,800.4	22,422.05	65
United Kingdom	12,603.1	12,574.77	25,177.87	50

Source: OECD Education Database, available at stats.oecd.org

is placed on the shoulders of the students and their families and not on those of companies.

Conversely, the higher the proportion of public funding, the more significant can be the state's influence upon the general and financing strategies and development of the HEIs. Depending on the similarities between the countries' specific policies and higher education perspectives regarding the possible funding solutions, and the shares and incentives associated with them, a series of convergent patterns may emerge or not (Auranen and Nieminen, 2010).

As shown in Table 2, although the state is the main provide and it has all the legal and monetary mechanism at its disposal to create a competitive environment for its higher education institutions, the financial data indicate that it is not allocating enough funds with respect to EHEA policies and recommendations.

The evolution of public expenditure analyzed as a percent of the GDP shows a certain migration towards the interval of 1-2% of the GDP, where most of the countries were found in 2001. The countries which were having higher than 2% of the GDP expenditures in 2001-2002 (as Denmark, Norway, Sweden and Finland) have introduced policy changes that have lowered their public contributions below the 2% mark, an exception being represented by Denmark, which is still at 2.29% probably due to the fact that it started with the highest proportion of the GDP, 2.71% in 2001.

The countries situated below the 1% mark in 2001 tended to move inside the above mentioned interval, with the exception of Liechtenstein which started with 0.35% of the national GDP invested in education and managed to reduce to half the percent by 2007. As a result of this trend, in 2008, only seven countries out of the 21 for which we have available data presented in Table 3 were just below

the 1% line, the average public expenditure on education being 1.25%. This is not totally in accordance with the EHEA recommendations of spending at least 2% of the GDP on higher education, the European average appearing to be heading towards a 1.5%.

The most striking find resulted when we compared the percentage of GDP allocated to higher education and the number of students enrolled into the tertiary sector and the data showed a significant low negative correlation between the two (Pearson coefficient = -0.184, sig. = 0.005). Compared to the GDP per capita, the percentage allocated to tertiary education showed a low positive correlation (Pearson coefficient = 0.304, sig. = 0.000) which implies that an improvement in the overall economic environment will result in a higher percentage of the GDP being reoriented towards higher education, which in turn, will help boost the economy and thus lead to a continuous improvement in the welfare of the society as a whole.

Public Funding

As varied are the proportions, the mechanisms for public funding differ as well. We can distinguish between four different approaches: negotiation, incremental, formula funding and contract funding (Eurydice, 2007). As one of the priorities of the EHEA is to increase performance-based funding, many countries have shifted from an incremental funding to formula-based financing, some even adding a contract funding mechanism on top of formulae. The data provided in Table 4 clearly indicate that the most prevalent form of financing higher education institution is based on a combination of a funding formula, research funding, and performance contracts.

Table 3. Total public expenditure on education as % of GDP, at tertiary level of education (ISCED 5-6)

GEO/TIME	2008	2007	2006	2005	2004	2003	2002	2001
Belgium	1.38	1.31	1.32	1.29	1.29	1.31	1.32	1.34
Bulgaria	0.89	0.68	0.73	0.76	0.80	0.83	0.83	0.82
Czech Republic	0.97	1.07	1.23	0.89	0.94	0.94	0.86	0.79
Denmark	:	2.29	2.26	2.38	2.51	2.50	2.70	2.71
Germany	:	1.14	1.11	1.14	1.16	1.19	1.16	1.10
Estonia	1.13	1.07	0.91	0.92	0.86	1.02	1.08	1.03
Ireland	:	1.14	1.14	1.11	1.10	1.09	1.19	1.22
Greece	:	:	:	1.46	1.32	1.10	1.16	1.07
Spain	1.07	0.99	0.95	0.95	0.97	0.99	0.97	0.97
France	1.24	1.23	1.20	1.19	1.21	1.23	1.22	1.21
Italy	0.84	0.76	0.77	0.76	0.77	0.78	0.85	0.80
Cyprus	1.85	1.61	1.65	1.58	1.48	1.55	1.38	1.14
Latvia	0.99	0.93	0.91	0.88	0.68	0.74	0.85	0.89
Lithuania	1.04	1.01	1.00	1.03	1.06	1.00	1.40	1.33
Hungary	1.02	1.03	1.04	1.03	1.01	1.22	1.23	1.08
Malta	1.06	0.95	:	1.07	0.53	0.81	0.90	0.88
Netherlands	1.52	1.45	1.50	1.47	1.45	1.42	1.34	1.36
Austria	:	1.50	1.48	1.49	1.44	1.31	1.29	1.37
Poland	:	0.93	0.96	1.19	1.15	1.02	1.05	1.04
Portugal	0.95	1.20	1.00	0.98	0.83	1.00	0.95	1.03
Romania	:	1.12	:	0.81	0.70	0.68	0.70	0.78
Slovenia	1.22	1.21	1.23	1.25	1.31	1.30	1.27	1.28
Slovakia	0.77	0.79	0.90	0.81	0.98	0.85	0.87	0.82
Finland	1.90	1.85	1.96	2.01	2.07	2.06	2.02	1.99
Sweden	1.82	1.77	1.84	1.92	2.04	2.11	2.10	2.00
United Kingdom	:	0.94	1.10	1.20	0.99	1.04	1.05	0.79
Iceland	1.49	1.39	1.36	1.45	1.39	1.33	1.25	1.07
Liechtenstein	:	0.17	0.19	0.20	0.34	0.32	0.35	:
Norway	2.08	2.16	2.07	2.27	2.40	2.29	2.08	1.84
Switzerland	:	1.32	1.45	1.48	1.65	1.62	1.39	1.25
Croatia	0.95	0.81	0.88	0.76	0.71	0.73	0.59	:
Turkey	:	:	0.91	:	0.87	0.96	0.95	0.87

Source: OECD Education Database, available at stats.oecd.org

In order to understand the underlying motivations of the funding mechanisms we can guide our discussion based on the two questions proposed by Jongbloed and Koelman (2000): what is funded by the government and how is it funded. The first question refers to the input/output orientation of the funding, while the second relates to the competition

Table 4. Public funding for the institutions of public higher education - mechanisms

	BE¹	BG	CZ	DK	EE	IE	EL	FR	IT	CY	LV	LT	LU
Negotiation of the budget with the funding body on the basis of a budget project submitted by the entity	●	●				●	●			●			●
The budget is established by the funding body on the basis of prior costs				●			●		●				
Funding formula	●	●	●	●	●	●	●	●	●		●	●	
Performance contracts based on strategic objectives	●		●	●			●	●					●
Contracts based on a given number of professional graduates					●						●		
Funding for certain research awarded by tender procedure	●	●	●	●	●	●	●	●	●	●	●	●	:

	HU	MT	AT	PL	PT	SI	SK	FI	SE	UK	IS	LI	NO
Negotiation of the budget with the funding body on the basis of a budget project submitted by the entity		●			●	●							
The budget is established by the funding body on the basis of prior costs				●							●		●
Funding formula	●		●	●	●	●	●	●	●	●	●	●	●
Performance contracts based on strategic objectives			●		●		●	●			●		
Contracts based on a given number of professional graduates													
Funding for certain research awarded by tender procedure	●	●	●	●	●	●	●	●	●	●	●	●	●

● The mechanism is applied: Data not available
Source: Adapted from Eurydice (2007)

implied by the funding mechanism, or as Kaiser et al. (2001) have termed it, the supply/demand side orientation of funding.

As such, there can be identified four main funding strategies (Figure 1) that can be pursued depending on the input/output and centralization/decentralization approaches considered: budget oriented, program oriented, student centered and supply driven (Frolich et al, 2010).

Thus, by regarding the funding mechanisms from the perspective of the second question the focus will have to shift towards who influences the number of students that attend a particular higher education institution. According to Miroiu and Aligica (2002) we can talk about demand-side funding if the students have the ability to influence the budget the higher education institution receives through their choice of programme. If the public au-

Figure 1. The four-quadrant funding model
Source: Adapted from Frolich et al (2010)

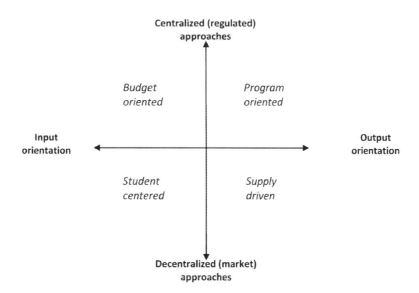

thorities set the number of students that can enroll in a particular institution then there is supply-side funding (Frolich et al, 2010). The authors conclude that most European countries cannot be classified as being demand-side oriented. Thus, it will be more fruitful to focus our presentation of the funding mechanisms on the axis informed by the first question, the input-output orientation.

Traditionally, higher education was financed based on input factors, but in the past decades there were various debates on the role of the two types of criteria. As a result, it has been accepted that input-based funding does not provide the right incentives for educational performance and that output criteria are more likely to induce an increase in the efficiency of the higher education system (Miroiu and Aligica, 2002). According to Estermann and Pruvot (2011), most European higher education institutions receive direct public funding through block grants which are computed on a variety of bases: historical data, input factors (number of students, staff, square meters etc.)

or output factors (success rate, publications, research contracts). On average, funding systems are based on a combination of input and output factors, the resulting formula covering a share of the total public funding that varies greatly among countries (around 25% in Switzerland, 40% in Denmark and 65% in Latvia). For example, in France, 80% of the block grant is linked to the number of students and academic staff with publishing activities and the other 20% is based on performance with 5% for teaching and 15% for research, evaluated on the basis of student success rates and future student employability.

The most used performance indicator or output factor is the one referring to the number of students who graduate and this is especially true in the case of the Czech Republic, Austria and Italy. Other indicators that are used consist of the number of credits the accumulated during their studies or the number of students who comply with the standard study time (Gherghina et al., 2010). These indicators are more likely to act as a stimulus for increased effectiveness of the educational system, but they might not be the best in promoting quality instead of volume. For example, basing the funding formula on the number of graduates might induce certain higher education institutions to reduce the requirements for passing exams and set lower standards for their students in order to allow them to graduate as easily as possible and this would lead to a systemic quality problem. This could be prevent through the use of external quality audits, but this only increases the cost of education and thus the system might spiral again into a funding crisis. The factors used in the formula-based financing can also greatly affect the orientation of the universities' activities as it happens with the Research Assessment Exercise in England that forced higher education institutions to seek partnerships with international companies rather than local ones.

Current trends in EHEA countries such as Norway, Denmark and Portugal indicate a shift toward a rather supply driven and student oriented approach, from the program or budget oriented ones. Even though the funding systems of these countries differ, their funding strategies reflected through their policies and actions display a convergence towards a more decentralized, market driven approach. Main similarities include the use of a formula funding system for teaching, offering incentives for development and change, greater focus on quality, as well as on the students' needs and requirements, an increased degree of internationalization, and greater competitiveness through improved efficiency, effectiveness and transparency. A great influence upon the internal resource allocation within HEIs have the criteria and methods based on which these institutions obtain their funding. Any changes in the latter

can trigger considerable modifications to the allotment established between the supporting and main academic activities, and to their overall content and quality (Frolich et al, 2010). This happens due to the perceiving of these funds as various possibilities to maintain the status quo or to accede to different potential opportunities that they would like to pursue, but do not have the necessary resources. While some effects may have a positive impact upon the quality of education in these institutions and bring them closer to attaining their goals, others may exert a negative influence placing them farther away from the core values of the knowledge based society. In the case of Portugal, for example, with a primary national objective to increase the number of students in higher education and an input-based funding system (centered on the number of enrolled students), HEIs will focus all their efforts in attracting as many students as possible. The issue lies in the efficiency, effectiveness and ethics of the methods they are willing to employ to maximize their input. Investing in the development of the university's brand equity and marketing strategy or in providing better, superior quality services may lead to a sustainable growth in the sector along with a positive effect on society. However, should these institutions try to achieve their targets in numerical terms only, through an artificial growth in the number of students enrolled (by double counting, etc.) or by setting very low admission requirements that could jeopardize the effectiveness and efficiency of the educational process, the ultimate and real goal of the country will be pushed farther on, and the effects will become exactly the opposite of the desired ones (Frolich et al, 2010).

Thus, it can be observed how the HEIs that are mostly public-funded have had their goals and strategies linked indirectly with the national ones through the funding criteria and methods. While in rather homogenous areas in terms of political, social and economical interests, this factor leads to convergence, in-between other member states of EHEA this may determine a higher degree of divergence. However, as the trends suggest a move towards a decentralized, self-sufficient funding system for these institutions, this influence may be reduced in the future.

We have mentioned the fact that besides the formula funding, higher education institutions can also be awarded funds through direct competition related to research projects. In many EHEA countries there have been established public organisms responsible for establishing which institutions should receive grants for their research proposals, besides the core funding they obtain based on the formula. In general, this type of funding is regarded as being more directly linked to a qualitative increase in the productivity of the educational system and there is a tendency to increase its share in the total financing scheme of higher education institutions. For example, in countries such as Sweden, Denmark, United Kingdom and Belgium the share of competitive research grants is higher than 20% in the total revenue received by higher education institutions, and even in the countries where it is lower, Italy and Spain, it still represents at least 10% (Aghion et al., 2008).

Sustaining further the transition towards an output focused funding, performance based funding systems (PRFSs) are designed to reward performing institutions and encourage the non-performing ones in engaging in similar behavior. The broad reason invoked for the implementation of fourteen such evaluation systems for funding since 2010 is that through their interlinking nature, universities influence greatly research performance, innovation and education, having a direct and major influence upon achieving sustainable economical development within the new, enlarged global context. In addition, as a response to the shift from the industrial era to the knowledge based one, governments have also focused on implementing the new public management reforms that focus on tackling a common set of political, economic, social and institutional challenges through aiming at higher quality, excellence, accountability and transparency in research, as well as creating a common framework for comparing and assessing performance and ensure competitiveness at HEIs' level. Kettl identifies the following several major directions addressed through this approach: increasing productivity (the same resources awarded are awarded based on output performance), replacing command-and-control systems with a market oriented approach through decentralization (increased institution autonomy) and the creation of a more competitive environment, stronger service orientation (focusing activities and establishing objectives in relation with the citizens' needs), formulating policies and enhancing accountability by concentrating on and rewarding the outcomes, instead of the inputs (Hicks, 2012). Moreover, PRFSs play an important part in the marketing strategy adopted by each HEI through the brand building opportunities it creates due to the increased comparability potential, prestige association and hierarchy creation within the sector. This further develops their role as excellence drivers for a nation's educational system and sets a favorable background for a common framework of evaluating and fund granting in HE.

Private Funding

In most countries, households contribute the highest proportion of the private income raised by universities by paying tuition and administrative fees. However, as Table 5 shows, in the EHEA there are countries, such as Austria, Germany and the Czech Republic, in which higher education institution do not rely so heavily on household expenditures. The level of student financial contribution directly depends on the level of the tuition and administrative fees and these vary greatly at the EHEA level. In some countries, such as Norway, there are no student contributions, in other (Denmark and Sweden) they are applicable only to some students (such as those coming from non-EU/EHEA states) or are very low (France). At the other end of the spectrum, we encounter countries such as United Kingdom where almost 42% of the total expenditure on higher education comes from households, Poland with 31%, and the Slovak Republic with 25%.

Although tuition fees represent the primary private source of funding for higher education institutions, each country's legislation allows other private sources of financing for academic institutions as well. These range from philanthropy (gifts that are used in order to pay for nonrecurring expenses, such as non-current asset investment represented by buildings, equipment and funding of academic positions), fundraising or auxiliary services and entrepreneurial activities (student boarding, cafeterias, bookstores or corporate sponsorship for private research).

Table 5. Private expenditure on higher education in 2007

Country	Private Expenditure	Household Expenditure	Household Expenditure (% private)
Denmark	11908.5	11908.57	100
Norway	860	860	100
Poland	4901.5	4901.5	100
Estonia	675	619	92
Ireland	318.85	270.33	85
United Kingdom	12574.77	10576.18	84
Italy	6081.56	4990.34	82
Spain	2540.39	2003.5	79
Belgium	938.49	726.17	77
France	5211.4	3895.6	75
Slovenia	95.61	69.72	73
Slovak Republic	7800.4	5496.72	70
Netherlands	2667.1	1625.1	61
Austria	529.95	205.67	39
Germany	5750.11	1850.28	32
Czech Republic	18162.86	4736.1	26
Finland	126.06	N/A	N/A
Sweden	4934	N/A	N/A

Source: OECD Education Database, available at stats.oecd.org.

Before going into further details, we have tried to establish the general trend in regards to private sources of income, basing our analysis on the data available from OECD for the years 2000-2007. Looking at the dynamics of the private expenditure contribution to the total higher education expenditure we were able to construct three categories of countries:

- Countries that did not experience any change, with a stable proportion of private expenditure in the total revenues: Belgium, France, Iceland, Italy, Slovenia;
- Countries that have experienced only mild modifications (a percentage change between 10 and 50%): Austria, Estonia, Germany, Spain and Sweden (under 20%) and Czech Republic, Denmark, Finland, Greece, Ireland, Norway (over 20%);
- Countries that have experienced strong modifications (over 50% change): Poland, Portugal, Slovak Republic, Turkey, United Kingdom.

Concerning the direction of change, we can state that there exists a general tendency towards increasing the proportion of private funds in the total funding available for higher education, as only 10 countries out of the 22 analyzed have experienced a drop in the percentage and, out of these, five were included in the stable category and the other five in the category regarding only mild modifications. Moreover, the countries which have experienced the greatest changes have all shifted towards majoring the proportion of private funding, probably as a result of policy changes in regards to the introduction or modification of the quantum of tuition taxes.

The findings of the Center for Higher Education Policy Studies (CHEPS) support our claims, their Funding Reform report from 2008 citing 14 European countries in which there was a share of at least 25% of revenues from third party funds and they conclude that this is a major improvement since 1995 when there were only six such countries.

Tuition Fees

In general, public authorities are responsible for setting the tuition fees (Estermann and Pruvot, 2011), in some cases either deciding solely on the matter or forbidding tuition fees altogether. However, the trend is towards negotiating the fees at university level and differentiating them among student populations, be it via academic level (Bachelor, Master, Doctorate) or according to the terms of study (full time/part-time, on campus/distance-learning, national/international etc.).

In approximately two thirds of countries, higher education institutions (HEIs) may collect tuition fees from students enrolled for a first qualification. In Estonia, Latvia, Lithuania, Hungary and Romania, this only concerns students who are not subsidized by the state. In the French Community of Belgium, Bulgaria, Spain, France, the Netherlands, Austria, Slovakia and the United Kingdom (Scotland), the amounts of tuition fees are determined by the central education authorities. In the other countries where tuition fees exist for a first qualification, HEIs may determine the amount within the limits defined by the same authorities. In approximately ten countries, either there is no possibility at all to ask students to pay tuition fees, or the possibility is limited to certain part-time courses, students enrolled in a second qualification, courses not included in the study program, situations in which a student has exceeded the normal length of studies etc.

Considering the shift towards a principle of cost-sharing of the educational costs and the increased inability of government budgets to cover the total cost of education, households and especially students are likely to become an important source of additional revenues for universities. Their ability to bear some of the costs related to higher education depends on the possibility of deferring actual payment until they finish their studies and become employed and this is done through the help of student loans which are becoming increasingly popular at the EHEA level. According to Johnstone (2009), student loans are available in the United Kingdom, the Netherlands, and Scandinavia, while France, Italy, Russia and many more do not offer this kind of financial support for students. In the case of UK, the government has also introduced a delayed fee payment scheme, payable post qualification, after reaching a £15,000 annual salary level, as a response to the potential threat of creating a tiered higher education system offering or denying access to people based on their social status and background, as a consequence of the increase in the upper limiting value restricting the maximum amount to be charged as a tuition fee. In this way, risk adverse people would feel more comfortable in enrolling in HE, even though the accumulated debt will be significantly higher, due to the perceived financial safety net offered by the authorities (Maringe et al, 2009).

Another similar tool employed in UK and with great potential to be implemented in other European countries as well, is represented by the human capital contracts (HCCs). Complementing the income-contingent loans (ICLs) solution, these instruments come in aid to the individuals with heterogeneous lifetime incomes and a rather lower income level expectancy for their chosen profession for a longer time, addressing the risk associated with the investment in a different manner. Research estimates that for an investment of €5,000 the cost would extent to a lifetime (24-65 years of age) income cost of 0.47% in Germany and 0.78% in Belgium showing significant advantages over the traditional borrowing instruments. Moreover, in both ICL's and HCC's cases the main gain lies behind the possibility to spread the risk among a wider and diverse pool of incomes (Vandenberghe and Debande, 2008). Encouragement of participation is thus essential to the efficiency and effectiveness of these systems and to the success of such a funding scheme for HEIs. Del Rey and Racionero (2010) suggest three possible means through which the state can achieve this: through subsidies from non-students to students (tax subsidy system), from successful to unsuccessful students (risk-pooling system, such as ICLs) or both (risk sharing system).

Nonetheless, the case of the cancellation of the US ICL Yale project illustrates the need for both approaches, as similar student reactions could be triggered to the idea of having the financial burden of their educational investments laid upon their career decisions, in any of the EHEA member states. US students have found this solution as potentially restrictive in terms of their choice regarding the organization to work for. Some might have wanted to be part of social projects or NGOs or small organizations, or even start a business of their own, but due to the fact that in all cases their income would have been lower than the limit provided, their choices were altered in a rather binding manner to the corporate environment, the sole to be able to provide the conditions to support their financial burden. This is supported also by the fact that only in the case of those neutral to risk, optimal participation is attained, whereas in the case of the risk averse ones participation may be insufficient, excessive or optimal, depending greatly on the degree of risk aversion for each individual. Moreover, in the case of an ability based funding scheme such as this, the students with higher ability and probability of success were found to perceive the cost of financing their studies through these instruments as higher and potentially opt out (Del Rey and Racionero, 2010). Another alternative, the HCC, was created in order to provide the future HE student with the opportunity to apply based only on his future profession choice and the estimation of the average percentage of their forecasted income, to determine the period of time (usually up to ten years) to repay the loan (Bornstein, 2011).

However, while this tool seems to ease the students' financial burden effect upon their future career choices, it does pose an information asymmetry problem. Students might as well conceal their true professional intentions in order to obtain better loan conditions. Still, as Vandenberghe and Debande (2008) remark they remain viable tools in achieving a positive vertical ethical result in terms of granting opportunities and equal chances to students belonging to different social backgrounds.

Expenditure per Student

Before drawing any conclusion about the changes that have marked the funding mechanisms of the EHEA member, we must also analyze their impact at the level of funding allotted per each student. It is a well accepted fact that in order to have higher education institutions perform well in the Shanghai rating,

a country has to devote a generous proportion of its GDP to the tertiary sector. In a previous section we have seen that the proportion of public investment in the higher education system is lower than the European standards, but that measure does not take into account the number of students the system caters to. Thus, in this section we will analyze the evolution of the spending per student as an indicator of the impact of funding reforms and a basis for discussing whether the inclination towards financial indicators is appropriate for the achievement of a converging European higher education area.

Based on the data presented in Table 6, we can see that the annual expenditure per student has increased in all the countries analyzed, and this is supported by the fact that expenses with faculty salaries, teaching loads, class sizes, equipment and library have risen due to the inflation which we have mentioned in the introduction of this chapter. The increase in the expenditure does not seem to reflect a change in educational policy or a greater interest in financing the higher education system, but only an increase driven by the inflationary prices in each country from the EHEA and we base our statement on the argument that there are no sharp increases from year to year, with the exception of Bulgaria, whose expenditure per student has increased by 24% after its 2007 EU accession. Thus, any change in the funding mechanism has not have a major impact on the level of spending per student and these have been quite stable in the period 2004 to 2008.

The stability of the yearly expenditure per student allows us to group the countries in three main cluster based on this financial indicator. The first cluster contains those member states whose expenditure per student gravitates around 4,781.3 EUR PPS/ student.

Table 6. Annual expenditure on public and private educational institutions per student in EUR PPS, at tertiary level of education (ISCED 5-6), based on full-time equivalents

GEO/TIME	2008	2007	2006	2005	2004
Belgium	11766.2	11208.9	10972.2	10008.8	9623.2
Bulgaria	4763.3	3837.3	3861.8	3568.3	3610.6
Czech Republic	6483.2	6825.1	7708.1	5599.5	5584.5
Denmark	:	13689.3	12933.7	12422.8	12822.2
Germany	:	11491.8	10865.7	10603.4	10117.8
Estonia	4450.7	4339.1	3341.7	3287.1	:
Ireland	:	10501.4	9763.9	8876.8	8511.0
Greece	:	:	:	5049.7	4706.0
Spain	10362.5	10432.3	9328.5	8480.4	7872.8
France	11117.7	10618.8	9613.5	9201.7	8872.3
Italy	7326.2	7210.9	7026.1	6758.3	6416.9
Cyprus	10014..3	8922.5	9577.6	8685.4	7344.0
Latvia	4951.1	4543.9	3810.7	3678.4	2931.6
Lithuania	4823.2	4652.3	4014.9	3758.4	3686.1
Luxembourg	:	:	:	:	:
Hungary	:	:	5033.2	5296.7	5536.4
Malta	9603.5	8689.0	:	9128.4	5808.2
Netherlands	13512.1	13276.0	12687.9	12627.7	12386.9
Austria	:	13133.4	12923.9	12503.8	11893.2
Poland	:	3811.8	3605.3	4742.3	3716.5
Portugal	7307.1	7939.8	7209.4	6391.0	4652.3
Romania	:	:	:	2375.8	:
Slovenia	6441.0	5955.1	6509.9	7033.2	6243.0
Slovakia	5089.3	4768.8	5038.6	4885.7	5486.4
Finland	11965.4	11278.6	10721.0	10352.7	10527.2
Sweden	15556.5	15265.2	14125.6	13164.1	13777.8
United Kingdom	:	13015.5	13052.4	12196.3	9389.3

Source: http://epp.eurostat.ec.europa.eu/portal/page/portal/statistics/search_database.

We will call the countries which have never left the cluster they belonged to in 2004 as core countries. The core countries for cluster one belong to the group of new members of the European Union, meaning those states which have entered the union in 2004 and 2007: Bulgaria, Lithuania, Latvia, Slovakia, Estonia, and Poland. Two of the new EU members belong to this group but have had short transition periods to other groups: Czech Republic (up in 2006) and Slovenia (up in 2005). We strongly believe that Hungary, Romania and Greece could be included in this cluster also, but we do not have recent data on which to base our assumption.

The second cluster refers to those countries in which the expenditure per student each year is around 9,088.7 EUR PPS. There are only three core countries for this group: Spain, Cyprus and Ireland, and two more countries which have experienced transition periods: France (up in 2008), Malta (down in 2004) currently belong to this cluster as well. This is a transition group for countries which are heading towards the final cluster, which is centered around 12,741.7 EUR PPS/student. Four countries represent the core of this grouping: Netherlands, Sweden, Denmark, Austria, and the United Kingdom which has advanced from cluster 2 to cluster 3 in 2005.

On the whole, the clusters formed by looking at the expenditure per student are fairly stable, especially the ones that represent the two extreme points. 13 countries spent 0 years outside their initial cluster, 5 countries (CZ, SI, MT, UK, FR) spent only one year outside their main cluster, only 4 countries (FI, BE, IT, PT) spent two years outside their main cluster and for the remaining 5 countries (HU, GR, DE, RO) we do not have enough data. Italy and Portugal were in the first cluster in 2004-2005 and then moved to the second cluster in 2006 where they remained until 2008. The same thing happened to Belgium, only with respect to clusters two and three. Finland advanced to cluster three in 2007, the same as Germany. With respect to the whole analysis, we can say that countries are moving along from cluster to cluster as their spending on higher education increases, but the difference among them seem insurmountable and we must ask ourselves if there is any basis for requiring all the member states of the EHEA to invest the same proportion of their GDP in education. As Jongbloed (2008) states "there is no uniform production technology in higher education" (p. 11) and the vast discrepancies between the clusters we have constructed might not also reflect a discrepancy at the level of the educational outcomes, meaning that the students from the countries belonging to cluster 1 may be as equally well prepared as those students from countries that invest three times the amount of funding in education.

The situation might seem dire as we look at the three clusters and imagine that consistency in the levels of spending for education in the EHEA will take decades to achieve, if ever possible, but, as Jongbloed (2008) goes on to say:

Funding then can only be informed by a cost analysis but never be fully based on it. [...] An analysis of the cost per student in different higher education institutions will be affected (or distorted) because of particular historical reasons (such as past decisions to open specialized study lines or study methods) and – more importantly – because of inefficiencies. Some (maybe even all) universities may simply waste resources and incur an unduly high cost. Other universities may argue that their costs are high because of the high quality education that they provide. (p. 12)

Thus, we must not look only at what it is spent per higher education as a whole, or per student, we must not take into consideration if it comes from the state budget, from household income or from companies, but we must focus our attention upon the ways in which the funding is used and what are the outcomes it helps achieve.

CONCLUSION

Throughout this chapter we have analyzed the shift towards performance based funding that has taken place in all members of the EHEA. In the member states, higher education institutions still receive most of their funding through governmental channels, but these are more oriented towards encouraging performance than before. However, performance is still measured by taking into consideration input factors (e.g. number of enrolled students, number of teaching staff, square meters) and not enough output factors probably due to the fact that there are no primary data sources regarding the outcomes of higher education. But this has received critiques since 1988 by Stiglitz who called it "allocative" inefficiency (maximizing inputs and outputs). And the European directives seem to fit this category as well, as they require each country to invest more of its GDP in education, an input factor, without stressing what the outcomes of that investment should be. This is a double edged factor that should be carefully considered by policy makers in order to reduce the risks of negative effects upon the quality and integrity of the educational processes and system as a whole. There are large discrepancies between the sums invested in education among the members of the EHEA, but this does not necessarily reflect a disproportion in their tertiary sectors' performance.

We have also seen that the contribution of private funding is becoming more and more important and that the students are the new agents on the shoulders of whom the financing of higher education might fall. But we have also noticed that there still are numerous states in which these students cannot benefit from any mechanism of delaying the payment of their studies until they are able to do it themselves. Thus, we have to conclude that the numbers that we have presented in this chapter are just one part of the whole story and that, based on these figures, we can argue that there is a level of convergence of funding mechanisms in the EHEA, but the qualitative aspects seem to indicate that, in fact, we are also dealing with a divergence in outcomes, but this will be seen in future years and will remain to be analyzed by future studies.

ACKNOWLEDGMENT

This work was supported by CNCSIS-UEFISCDI, project PN II-RU-TE-351-2010.

REFERENCES

Aghion, P., Dewatripont, M., Hoxby, C., Mas-Colell, A., & Sapir, A. (2008). *Higher aspirations: An agenda for reforming European universities*. Brussels: Bruegel Blueprint Series.

Altbach, P. G., Reisberg, L., & Rumbley, L. E. (2009). *Trends in global higher education: Tracking an academic revolution*. Paris: UNESCO.

Auranen, O., & Nieminen, M. (2010). University research funding and publication performance—An international comparison. *Research Policy, 39*, 822–834. doi:10.1016/j.respol.2010.03.003

Baumol, W. J., & William, G. B. (1966). *Performing arts: The economic dilemma*. New York: The Twentieth Century Fund.

Bornstein, D. (2011). A way to pay for college, with dividends. *New York Times Opininator*. Retrieved from http://opinionator.blogs.nytimes.com/2011/06/02/a-way-to-pay-for-college-with-dividends

Del Rey, E., & Recionero, M. (2010). Financing schemes for higher education. *European Journal of Political Economy, 26*, 104–113. doi:10.1016/j.ejpoleco.2009.09.002

Estermann, T., & Pruvot, B. E. (2011). *Financially sustainable universities II – European universities diversifying income streams*. EUA Publications. Retrieved from http://www.eua.be/Pubs/Financially_Sustainable_Universities_II.pdf

Eurydice. (2007). *Key data on higher education in Europe*. Brussels: Eurydice.

Frolich, N., Schmidt, E. K., & Rosa, M. J. (2010). Funding systems for higher education and their impacts on institutional strategies and academia. *International Journal of Educational Management, 24*(1), 7–21. doi:10.1108/09513541011013015

Gherghina, R., Nicolae, F., & Mocanu, M. (2010). Comparative research on the correlation of the quantum to public funding for the public institutions of higher education and the institution's performance within the European Union member states. *Management & Marketing Challenges for Knowledge Society, 5*(3), 103–118.

Hicks, D. (2012). Performance-based university research funding systems. *Research Policy, 41*, 251–261. doi:10.1016/j.respol.2011.09.007

Johnstone, D. B. (2009). An international perspective on the financial fragility of higher education institutions and systems. In *Turnaround: Leading stressed colleges and universities to excellence*. Baltimore: The Johns Hopkins University Press.

Jongbloed, B. (2008). *Funding higher education: A view from Europe*. Paper presented at the seminar Funding Higher Education: A Comparative Overview. Retrieved from http://www.utwente.nl/mb/cheps/summer_school/Literature/Brazil%20funding%20vs2.pdf

Kaiser, F., Vossensteyn, H., & Koelman, J. (2001). *Public funding of higher education: A comparative study of funding mechanisms in ten countries*. Enschede, The Netherlands: Center for Higher Education Policy Studies.

Kwiek, M. (2006a). *Academic entrepreneurship and private education in Europe.* Retrieved from www.cpp.amu.edu.pl/pdf/Kwiek_Entrepreneurialism_PHE.pdf

Kwiek, M. (2006b). The European integration of higher education and the role of private higher education. In S. Slantcheva, & D. C. Levy (Eds.), *Private higher education in post-communist Europe: In search of legitimacy.* New York: Palgrave.

Levy, D. (2006). Private-public interfaces in higher education development: Two sectors in sync? In *Proceedings of the 2007 World Bank Regional Seminar on Development Economics.* Retrieved from siteresources.worldbank.org/INTABCDE2007BEI/Resources/Daniel-Levy.PDF

Maringe, F., Foskett, N., & Roberts, D. (2009). I can survive on jam sandwiches for the next three year: The impact of the new fees regime on students' attitudes to HE and debt. *International Journal of Educational Management, 23*(2), 145–160. doi:10.1108/09513540910933503

Miroiu, A., & Aligica, P. D. (2002). *Public higher education financing: A comparison of the historical and formula-based mechanism.* Academic Press.

Reichert, S. (2009). *Institutional diversity in European higher education: Tensions and challenges for policy-makers and institutional leaders.* Brussels: EUA.

Stiglitz, J. E. (1988). *Economics of the public sector.* New York: Norton.

Tomusk, V. (2004). *The open world and closed societies: Essays in higher education policies in transition.* New York: Palgrave. doi:10.1057/9781403979476

Vandenberghe, V., & Debande, D. (2008). Refinancing Europe's higher education through deferred and income-contingent fees: An empirical assessment using Belgian, German & UK data. *European Journal of Political Economy, 24,* 364–386. doi:10.1016/j.ejpoleco.2007.09.005

ENDNOTES

[1] In cases where there are several education systems inside one country (as is the case with Belgium and the UK) we have included all into one column, considering the mechanism applied if one of the systems applies it.

Section 2
Cross-Cultural Teamwork

Chapter 4
Teamwork in Medical Organizational Cultures

Simona Vasilache
Bucharest University of Economic Studies, Romania

ABSTRACT

The chapter discusses the specificities of organizational culture in healthcare environments, taking into account general managerial theories and their suitability to particular professional settings. The challenges of teamwork and the things to be particularly considered by decision-makers in the healthcare system are discussed and critically analyzed.

DISCUSSION ON ORGANIZATIONAL CULTURES

The acceptance or rejection of an organizational culture, the decision to consolidate it or, on the contrary, to change it, is based both on humoral reactions, and also on certain compatibility matrices between types of employees, types of objectives, and types of cultures. Thus, the study of these matrices emerged.

A pioneer in this direction is Harrison, who speaks, in 1972, of *organizational ideologies*. Ideologies are defined by Beyer (1981) as relatively coherent systems of opinions and values that keep people together and explain the actions to which they resort in order to achieve specific purposes. This approach does not differ much from the definition, perhaps the best known, which Schein (1992) gives to the organizational culture: "set of unanimously shared basic concepts that the group has learned during the adaptation to the external environment and integration in the internal environment" (p. 12, t.m.). Meyer (1982) speaks of organizational ideologies in the hospital environment, in the context of the learning experience caused by a strike of the doctors. Depending on their ideologies, some

DOI: 10.4018/978-1-4666-4325-3.ch004

hospitals learn from this experience, adapt, while others reject it without processing it.

As stated by Ashkanasy, Wilderom and Peterson (2000), managerial ideologies can be related to the so-called competing values theory (competing values framework - CVF). Quinn and McGrath have developed this theory in the early 80s, by organizing polarized values on two axes: interior-exterior and flexibility-control.

According to their study, the orientation towards control is correlated with the focus on external coercion elements (rules, taboos, etc.), and the inclination towards flexibility has its origin inside the organization, in creating a sense of belonging, through training and socialization. By transferring to the organizational context the distinction made by Dodds (1951) at socio-cultural level, between shame cultures and guilt cultures, the shame cultures are those in which the external control is very emphasized – you do what you are required because you are ashamed to be marginalized, and the guilt cultures are those primarily based on being conscious of one's own role and responsibilities, which are accomplished through belief rather than through a conditioned reflex of control.

In other words, there are cultures, and implicitly organizational cultures, able to choose, take decisions based on considering each alternative and reach, with certain costs, a consensus, and organizational cultures in which the decision is institutionally imposed by the existence of a more or less inflexible set of rules, which provide the control component.

The human relationship model, as a closed but flexible system, brings a sense of family within the organization. The organization that adopts this model values relationships of trust between its members, and transforms its leaders into mentors, mediators, by no means autocrats. Decision-making within the organization is decentralized, which lowers the degree of control. Leaders are trusted with the same trust encountered in interpersonal relationships within the organization, which generates a relatively low resistance to change, given the authority earned, not imposed, by the one that proposes the change, and the consensus within the organization.

The open systems model gives great importance to the external environment from which the organization obtains its resources. The acquisition of resources needed by the organization, considering the uncertainty of the external environment and the limited adaptability of the internal environment, requires the presence of a leader who is oriented towards innovation and change. The learning organization theory best fits this quadrant of the "map" of organizational cultures, flexible and oriented towards the external environment (to a certain extent a paradoxical hybrid, since flexible cultures are more likely to "grow" from inside) from where the directions of change that the organization must face come.

The internal process model is based on stability and control, on maintenance, rather than on innovation. Being, strictly chronologically, the oldest of the models, it is related to the scientific management theory and with Weber's bureaucracy, his ideal type of organization. It is a reductive, closed model, operating *caeteris paribus*, thus assuming the absence of any external environmental factors that might influence processes that take place within the organization. The typical leader in this model is a coordinator, a monitor-evaluator, according to the roles in a team proposed by Belbin (1985). Foss (1997) speaks of an administrative optimum, in which we can see the ideal of this kind of model. Once this optimum, which is basically a sum of routines, is reached, and assuming that there are no disturbing external influences, the organization could ideally function, without any type of management. It would therefore be an administrative utopia. Given that external influences are often intentionally reduced to zero, by oversimplifying the model, we can say that there are not few the organizations in which this utopia is functional. Their resistance to change comes exactly from the perception of optimum - why replace something that works? - from better accepting a static model, with a single point of optimum, instead of a dynamic model with certain degrees of optimum, not at all with plane, long periods of uncommitted practice of some verified routines.

Finally, the model of rational objectives is an open system, but based on rationality. Its main challenge is to keep a "rationality" of actions within the organization, other than the individual one, of its members, taking into account the permanent aggression of the external environment, which imposes rapid and unpredictable changes. The two systems, the external environment and the organization, simultaneously evolve, but at different speeds.

If the open systems model is the closest one to organizational learning, the rational objectives model best questions the organizational intelligence, as an adaptation to the external environment, on the premises of certain patterns of thinking which can be viewed as long-term plans, independent to a point from fluctuations in the external environment. The existence of certain patterns of thinking in organizations (Arango, 1998) and their effectiveness in given situations which are related to a certain configuration of the external environment, are topics not quite explored in the speciality literature. We can, however, advance the hypothesis, starting from Schein's definition, which includes the idea

of aggregate, of conglomerate, that organizational culture does not rely on values as such, but on the conjunction or disjunction of these values, on certain areas of constructive interference, respectively destructive interference. These areas are the organizational, functional, respectively the dysfunctional mental models.

From this perspective, myths and metaphors accumulated in organizations are an inferior stage of thinking patterns, a primitive way of explaining the unexplainable, resembling in this respect, with the primitive thinking of civilizations that mythological explained phenomenon that were beyond their control and incomprehensible to them. Not accidentally these less developed forms of organizational mental models have high remanence, and are difficult to change. They are the first to fill an absolute void, and giving them up creates the feeling of insecurity, of loss of group identity, in relation to the external environment. As organizational mental models are refined, and gain a greater explanatory power, in other words, they rationalize, by replacing resistance to the external environment with applied attempts of getting closer, of understanding the external environment and the exact mechanisms by which it exercises its influence, then the strategy replaces the myth.

We notice, in organizations, the evolution from one type of highly structured culture, the so-called Greek temple, to a highly individualized culture, based on concentrations of people who, at a certain moment in time, share some common values. According to Handy's metaphorical approach, every culture is governed by a god, the extremes being those which we have already been mentioned - the Apollo (the temple) and the Dionysian (the cluster). Apollo's cult urges on moderation, balance, on *institutional*, at the expense of individualism. In other words, the system is stronger than the individual, and it is considered normal to be this way. Temple cultures are stable and less prone to change.

The Dionysian embodies precisely the exit, punishable in terms of measure, of excess avoidance, from the system's frames. It is an existentialist trend emphasizing the individual freedoms, more important than the system. The organization exists to support the individual to achieve his goals. It is the philosophy on which, at least theoretically, all professional organizations are based.

The club culture, governed by Zeus, exhibiting the so-called *country club management*, in which relationships are placed before the structure. Basically, the organization is composed of some permanently forced learning patterns. What does Zeus, other than to identify some opportunities, even by arousing indignation, which otherwise accompanies any denial of the template? Empathy plays an essential role in this culture, as essential as the speed of reaction, or attention.

The network culture, governed by Athens, is the closest one to the issue of organizational intelligence. Power within the organization is everywhere and nowhere, its source is ubiquitous and is related to the flexibility of the network. Power in the culture governed by Athens is given by expertise, it is the expert's power. It is a creative culture in which the team and the enthusiasm have the central role.

Certainly, from the point of view of the stringency, of the metaphorical emancipation, Handy's approach could seem too impressionistic. It is, nevertheless, an useful and picturesque systematization of the trends capable of modeling an organization, although it subliminally induces the idea that any organizational culture starts from an idol, that a certain type of relationship, on the ver-

tical, is privileged with regard to the rest of the relationships which are on the horizontal.

Bringing together the two main approaches, and also the idea of material culture, complementary to the immaterial culture, I propose a synthetic classification of the organizational cultures:

1. **Static Organizational Cultures:** Are cultures dependent on structures, on the honeycomb. These are classified, pushing somehow the terminology, in purely *material* cultures, and *material-immaterial* cultures. Matter-or-fact, the purely material cultures for which the communication and the interaction are solely sets of written rules, represent an abstraction. The excessive formalization, static by definition, is a cultural tendency relatively widely spread. Its relationship with the avoidance of responsibility, of the relational stress, is another matter of discussion. The *material-immaterial* cultures, that are closer to reality, are the ones in which although the relational element is present, the structural, institutional element, is overwhelming. These are cultures in which the "whisper down the lane", the informal communication, harmful, as long as is has no chance to initiative, to speech.

2. **Dynamic Organizational Cultures:** Are cultures characterized by evolution, based rather on relationship that can be done and un-done, which can reshape, redefine, than on rigid structures. These can be classified in *immaterial-material cultures*, and *immaterial cultures*. Again, likewise the material cultures, the purely immaterial cultures do not exist, because any relationship needs a minimal structures, so as the remark of

Alan Bennet (We started off trying to a set a small anarchist community, but people wouldn't obey the rules) is not just a simple paradox. The immaterial-material cultures, on the other hand, are orientated towards relationships, towards the exploration and exploitation of individual capacities, rather than on the system stability. Highly communicative cultures, and contextualized, which having a predisposition to adaptation, in a dynamic environment, can nevertheless create adaption problems for their members.

Therefore, culture can be a prevailing structural capital or a prevailing relational capital. It can be oriented, autocratically speaking, by the leader's attitude, or it can be created at the intersection of the various changes among the people constituting the organization.

The organizational culture, as a result of certain practices accepted by all the members of a group, depends on the mission of the organization, but it also influences it, being capable of easily transforming it into a shape without a background, if nothing or almost nothing in the behavior of the organization supports the declared purpose of its existence. In the case of hospitals, the organization culture influences the quality of the medical services offered (Cooke and Rousseau, 1988; Klingle et al., 2008). One of the heavers of this influence is, as it will be shown, the organizational learning, which is dependent on the organizational culture.

As sinergies, as well as bottlenecks may occur between the organizational learning and the individual learning, studies concerning the organizational culture discuss about the *person-culture fit* (Vanderberghe, 1999), about the congruence of the personal values with the organizational ones, which determines the fidelity of an employee for a certain working place (O'Reilly, Clatman and Caldwell, 1991).

The clinic (from the Greek *klinein*, to lay in bed) is a department in which learning (where students and residents learn) and scientific activities take place. This meaning comes up more often than the similar English meaning, for instance, where clinic generally means an ambulatory, a place where patients receive health care services without being hospitalized (*dentistry clinics*). The clinic, being managed by a docent or by an academic, is a constitutive part of a hospital, clinic or university, to which it is subordinated, from an administrative point of view. Thus, the clinic can be seen as a learning core, and less as a managerial core, which induces a schism in the way in which its culture has the configuration: in collaboration with the rest of the hospital clinics, in order to stimulate an integrated learning, or in a strict hospital administration dependency, with all the animosities that flow from here. Giving credit to the first model of course, I will show, using the case studies, how the administrative component can be limited in favor of the learning one.

There are two great schools that approach the organizational culture, the structuralistic and the functionalistic, not necessarily taking the same difference from anthropology and opposing in this way Durkheim to Lévi-Strauss. The first attempts to determine how the culture is composed, out of the tangible and intangible elements of the organization, and the second one is rather interested in the functioning of the culture, in its influence upon the forms of organizational capital.

The first approach is metaphorical, according to Schein and Pettigrew, in the attempt to associate the independent phenomena that contribute to the creation of the organizational culture. In the mid '30, Lewing was talking about the "virtue space", a symbolic reunion of all the experiences of an individual. Then he extended this concept by studying the way in which the individuals can similarly perceive common experiences. The individual psychology, based on certain symbols, beliefs, value, attitudes, has socialized.

Frost et al. (1981) talks about the generalization of symbols, like the configuration of Kunda (1992), or Alvesson (2002), of the external perspective upon culture, seen like a cohesion factor, which is shaped outside individuals, practically representing an autonomous grid of interpreting reality, to which they sometimes adhere. That is why I named this perspective *structuralist.*

In the structuralisic perspective there is the idea of *integrator, as it has been defined by* Brătianu, Jianu, Vasilache (2006): "An integrator is a strong force field, capable of combining two or more elements in a new entity, based on interdependency and synergy. These elements can be physical or virtual, and must have the capacity of interacting in a controlled manner". Based on this concept, I approach the organizational culture in the university clinic as an integration level, intermediating between the individual and organizational intelligence.

One of the particularities of the organizational culture in an university clinic derives from the degree of exploitation of the three components of the intellectual capital. The three forms of capital integrated in the intellectual capital, human, structural and relational capital, that generate on the organizational level knowledge, intelligence and values, dependent on the individual knowledge, intelligence and values (Brătianu, 2008) do not have in the university clinic the same share.

Traditionally, the hospitals were based almost entirely on the human capital, on very well trained and devoted doctors and nurses, ignoring the importance of procedures and relationships in ensuring quality services (Tucker and Edmonson, 2002). The passion of some patients who have been more involved in the care process and who are more qualified than in the past (Baggs and Schmitt, 1998) obliges to a reexamination of the organizational processed, in order to identify errors and try to eliminate their causes, achieving a first step towards the organizational learning. Put another way, the structural capital, which stores the hospital routines, on one hand, and the university ones, on the other hand, and the relational capital that generates the capacity of the clinic to learn from its patients, to integrate their feedback in the care process and to flatten the hierarchies, which were traditionally very rigid, in the favor of some collaborative structures, has begun to gain importance.

A second particular element of the organizational culture of a university clinic is the social pressure. At least from a theoretical point of view, the medical organization is unlimitedly responsible for the results it obtains, even if, obviously, like in the case of any other organization, there are numerous factors which are beyond its power of control, factors concerning the general external environment (for example, the patients' living conditions), as well as the pseudo-competitive environment (the performance of other system elements, with which the patient comes across). Most often, the hospitals are on one hand the victims of an austerity budget, insufficient as the cases become more complicated, university hospitals being clearly disadvantaged from this point of view, and on the other hand, they are under the expectations of the society, which are very high, obligating them to get closer to excellence. Concerning the medical services, because of obvious causes which relate to the consequences of errors, the tolerance for mistake is minimal. From this stems the existing pressure upon the university clinics.

From the social pressures derives a third characteristic, solidarity. A certain esprit de corps is perceived as being specific to the medical profession. The existence of a residual hazard, which even in ideal conditions the clinic cannot eliminate, is partly because of the above mentioned factors, but also because of some other intrinsic factors, which are related to the on-going processes in the clinic, determining this solidarity. From the point of view of the beneficiary however, the procedural solidarity does not determine a procedural uniformity of performance, in the physician-clinic relationship. Put another way, there is always the distinction between the performance of a certain physician within the clinic and the global performance of the clinic. This thing, correlated with the much greater importance of the human capital in comparison to the other forms of capital, sends to the conclusion that, although characterized by solidarity, the organizational culture of the university clinic is lax, keeping the focus on the individual and on his or her performances, in the disadvantage of the organization. The idea of "medical school", the perfect synthesis of the procedural solidarity and of the quasi-homogenous performance levels, tends therefore to remaining a historical reference.

A study from 2003, of Mohr et al., that included over 8000 employees of American hospitals, proposed four types of organizational cultures, respectively entrepreneurial, collegial, bureaucratic and rational, testing the patient's level of satisfaction in each of the cases, has obtained the following results: the majority of the hospitals have a bureaucratic, rigid culture, which is correlated with low patients' satisfaction scores. The collegial culture, the second as frequency, positively influences the level of the patients' satisfaction.

The other two types of culture are not significantly correlated to the level of the patients' satisfaction, which could be explained by the fact that in a large hospital the attention and customized services are lowered, and on the other hand the time pressure and competition increase.

According to Durkheim (in Turner, 1990), the level of consensus with respect to cognitive orientation and the cultural codes adopted by the members of a population is indirectly related to their structural difference, and directly related to the number of the interpersonal interactions, with the degree of emotions awareness, and with the frequency of the rituals.

The university clinic culture is from the point of view of the structural difference, composed of all the subcultures of the groups involved in the clinic processes, physicians, nurses, orderly, laboratory technicians, patients. Obviously, there are between these groups barriers of education, differentiated by responsibilities, of the perspective each one of them has on the common scope, which is to ensure, on the short run good quality for each patient, and to contribute on the long run to the medical progress. From here stems the difficulty of integrating the subcultures and of adopting common mission and vision.

LITERATURE REVIEW

Medical practice constitutes a very complex process based predominantly on knowledge dynamics and continuous learning. A discussion by Van Beveren (2003) draws attention to the particular issues raised by knowledge management in healthcare. He speaks of hospitals as "collections", rather than teams of professionals, who are working separately, in fragmented departments, which prejudices knowledge transfer, while still delivering care. Quoting Schneider (1993), he concludes that a model based on teamwork is also problematic, in healthcare, as it confuses tasks and diminishes authority. While the teamwork approach is more of an intuition-based, know-how sharing, personalized knowledge management (Sheffield, 2008), healthcare organizations tend to prefer the codified approach, based on precise and sometimes rigid routines and procedures. Teamwork is widely recognized as being Achilles' heel in medical practice and education (Burford, 2012; Curran et al., 2007; Wilkinson, 2002). It is a sensitive issue impacting largely on the quality of care, because the two processes of the medical profession, *learning* and *doing*, can hardly be set apart, in the 'learning together to work together' paradigm (Thistlethwaite, 2012). This paradigm also considers the prepositions of learning, *with*, *from*, and *about*, which include the classical triad of *knowing what*, *knowing how*, and *knowing whom*, but go beyond it, in stressing the blending of collaborative, peer-to-peer learning with learning from models (Bratianu and Vasilache, 2012). Although this standardization is widely popular in healthcare nowadays, in the form of evidence-based medicine (Bossuyt & Kortenray, 2001), we claim that standardization may benefit from teamwork learning, as knowledge, in medical practice, is not always explicit. Initiatives like "clinical excellence" (Wailoo et al., 2004) should take into account the role of tacit knowledge diffusion in medical practice. Our discussion on learning and knowledge dynamics will, then, be an integrative approach to the

types of knowledge and conversion from tacit to explicit, and to intergenerational transfer.

According to Ryu (2003), knowledge transfer within professional groups, especially physicians, is a highly researched topic, recently. Ryu motivates his choice for physicians based on the fact that they are the main professional group in hospitals, and they get involved in knowledge-intensive processes. In a behavioral framework, he investigates intention of the physicians to share knowledge. The focus is, thus, intrinsic. In our research, the focus is rather on the organizational culture components influencing the working of teams and the inter- and intra-team knowledge sharing processes. We base our perspective on a study by De Long and Fahey (2000), also quoted in Wang and Noe's (2010) review, showing that organizational values and organizational climate are key contextual factors in enabling or disabling knowledge sharing processes. Studies by Wang (2004), Holste and Fields (2010), or Willem and Scarbrough (2006) have distinguished trust as a major ingredient of teams promoting knowledge sharing. This *willingness to be vulnerable* (Lencioni, 2002) makes people cooperate, in order to balance their strengths and weaknesses, rather than compete. In highly competitive environments, as it is the case with medical teams (Porter and Teisberg, 2007), cooperation is a lesson to be learnt.

Husted and Michailova (2002) and Lam and Lambermont-Ford (2010) investigate the reasons why individuals avoid involving in knowledge sharing. Among the prejudices mentioned, the authors include *potential loss of value and bargaining power*, *unwillingness to spend time on knowledge sharing*, *fear of hosting "knowledge parasites"*, *avoidance of exposure*, *high respect for hierarchy*. As far as the first prejudice is concerned, they refer to the link between the years spent educating oneself and the sense of knowledge ownership developed, a knowledge which is usually hardly acquired. In the medical profession, experiencing a lengthy apprenticeship, this kind of perception is a threat to knowledge sharing. As far as time spent with knowledge sharing is concerned, we presume that, in the medical practice, knowledge sharing opportunities abound, as individuals already spend much of their working time together, in teams. The fear of exposing one's possible errors and uncertainties while sharing knowledge is, in our opinion, another valid threat to knowledge sharing in hospitals, especially in the case of older, well established professionals, placing great emphasis on prestige and being challenged by newer techniques they haven't assimilated. Also, as a Romanian surgeon, when asked why he doesn't overtly share his experience with his apprentices replied – "a surgeon's knowledge is hardly won; I will not offer for free something which had cost me years of work" – the fear of nurturing knowledge parasites is present, as well. From the side of the apprentices, the tendency to reject already tested knowledge and to reinvent their own can be noticed. The link between learning cultures and knowledge sharing has been often confirmed (Lee, Kim, and Kim, 2006; Reychav and Weisberg, 2010), and it is known that learning organizations are usually mistake-tolerant, seeing errors as opportunities to evolve. Still, in medical practice, due, mainly, to the high costs of errors and to the social pressure, the *who is to blame culture* (Husted and Michailova, 2002) seems to be prevalent. Thus, in order not to endanger one's professional status and career, knowledge is to be exercised individually, enhancing this way the stickiness tendency (Szulansky, 2000).

The medical system, especially in teaching and research hospitals, which are the focus of our research, is mainly vertically structured, with a significant emphasis placed on hierarchy, on formal relations, while knowledge sharing is largely horizontal: "Knowledge sharing is a more subtle concept, and is seen as a dual process of enquiring and contributing to knowledge through activities such as learning-by-observation, listening and asking, sharing ideas, giving advice, recognizing cues, and adopting patterns of behaviour (Bosua and Scheepers, 2007, p. 95)." Thus, knowledge sharing becomes possible in environments where individuals are categorized based on their respective knowledge levels, not on any other types of hierarchies. A knowledge level is given by the integrative result of tacit and explicit knowledge

RESEARCH CONTEXT

Medical migration used to be an issue of the post-colonial world, involving physicians migrating from the African countries, or India, to Europe or US (Hagopian et al, 2005; Astor et al., 2005). Recently, physicians from less prosperous European countries, with low budgets allocated to healthcare, migrate to the West, creating nearly insurmountable problems to the system. In 2008, WHO has warned Romania that its medical migration, of over 2% (4% in 2007), endangers severely the system, bringing it near to collapse. Presently, Romania only has 1.9 physicians per 1000 inhabitants, as compared to 3.3 physicians per 1000 inhabitants, the European average. Migration is more intense at the entry-level, of recent graduates starting their medical training in teaching and research hospitals. Their presence in these large hospitals, confronted with very diverse and complex medical cases, removed some of the burden of ordinary, routine work, allowing professionals to focus on performance in research and healthcare. Thus, their migration not only diminishes the replacement rate, in professional teams, but also forces older and more skilled doctors to take over routine tasks, and reduce the time allocated to learning and sharing knowledge. The quality of the knowledge intensive processes is consequently lower, and so is the quality of the medical act.

As far as teams are concerned, in the context of medical migration they tend to be more unstable, exhibiting lower levels of enthusiasm and a general climate of transition. Knowledge transfer, as a basic mechanism for learning, under these circumstances, is expected to be less systematic, depending more on nuclei of good practice and less on procedures that can be traced at the scale of an entire medical section, or hospital. Given that national professional record and recommendations are little or not taken into account in international recruitment procedures, physicians aiming to leave are not interested in building a strong reputation inside their present teams.

Considering the context sketched above, and the findings in literature, we advance the following working hypotheses:

- The learning process is based mostly on the knowledge conversion from tacit to explicit knowledge;
- Knowledge sharing is practiced mostly by younger physicians;
- Intergenerational and inter-teams knowledge transfer are relatively less important in the medical learning process.

Based on these hypotheses, we have investigated the learning processes, intra- and inter-teams, in Romanian teaching and research hospitals. The methodology of the research, as well as the results and discussions, are expanded in the next sections.

METHODOLOGY

We have selected students and interns from Romanian teaching and research hospitals, using a snow-ball sampling technique, which lead to a sample of 500 students and interns actively involved in conferences and congresses participation, on-line debates, on dedicated forums, and medical publishing. Out of this sample, we obtained 282 valid sets of answers to our questionnaires. The aim of the questionnaire was to distinguish between passive knowledge transfer, and student-specific knowledge transfer in medical practice, linking them to the perceived outcomes of learning. We have also assessed the organizational climate parameters, and their relationship with learning. The selection variable, in the first case, was *trust in one's medical skills* (trmsk), while in the second case the selection variable was *fit with the clinic culture* (fitcc).

The independent variables were assessed on a 1 to 5 Likert scale, 1 being least true, while 5 being most true.

We performed factorial analysis, in order to identify the factors of trust in the outcomes of learning, depending on knowledge transfer strategies used, and also to identify the factors of cultural fit, depending on clinic's characteristics. We then performed cluster analysis, to match types of knowledge transfer strategies with types of clinical contexts.

The descriptive statistics for the *trust* variables is presented in Table 1.

Table 1. Descriptive statistics for trust variables

	N	Minimum	Maximum	Mean	Std. Deviation
Own errors were discussed	282	1	5	2.24	.915
General errors were discussed	282	1	5	3.11	.793
Practical demonstrations made to you	282	1	5	1.22	.327
General demonstrations	282	1	5	2.19	.923
Supervised practice	282	1	5	2.66	.811
Unsupervised practice	282	1	5	3.04	.724
Valid N (listwise)	282				

It may be seen that the mean scores are generally higher for non-personalized practices than for personalized knowledge sharing. It may be also seen that, for instance, in the case of individually-targeted practical demonstrations, the sample's answers are more consensual.

The descriptive statistics for the *fit* variables is presented in Table 2.

As it may be seen, the respondents in the sample are, on average, at the age of becoming independent, from the point of view of formal supervision, but needing, however, collegial training. They do not characterize themselves, often, as team players, but indicators of individualism are also low, as criticism and initiative are usually not habitual. The clinical climate is perceived as not being very permissive to learning.

The results of the analysis are presented in the next section.

RESULTS

We have performed factorial analysis on the *trust* and *fit* variables, with Varimax rotation and Kaiser normalization. We took into consideration only items with factor loadings greater than 0.5. The results of the analysis are presented in Table 3.

The first factor, accounting for 77% of the variance, groups variables related to student-oriented learning. The only exception is the variable *practical demonstrations made to*

Table 2. Descriptive statistics for fit variables

	N	Minimum	Maximum	Mean	Std. Deviation
Age	282	20	35	31.82	11.23
Team player	282	1	5	2.15	.971
Free to ask	282	1	5	3.22	.729
Free to criticize	282	1	5	2.09	.954
Good learning opportunities	282	1	5	1.86	.827
Mentor supervision	282	1	5	1.52	.416
Clinical leadership	282	1	5	2.21	.832
Valid N (listwise)	282				

Table 3. Factorial analysis for trust variables

	1	2
oerrd	.714	-.271
gerrd	.638	-.213
gdem	.644	-.330
spract	.552	-.540
pdemy	-.087	.748
unspract	.059	.598
a. Extraction method: Principal component analysis b. 2 components extracted.		

Table 4. Factorial analysis for fit variables

	1	2
age	.629	-.413
teampl	.512	-.292
frcrit	.534	-.021
mentor	.587	.113
frask	-.019	.528
cllead	-.215	.592
glopp	.319	-.120
a. Extraction method: Principal component analysis b. 2 components extracted.		

you, as they are not very common, not even in the most student-centred learning climates in university hospitals in Romania. The second factor groups variables related to passive learning. The factorial analysis for *fit* variables is presented in Table 4.

The items related to age, team spirit and freedom to criticize, as well as to the existence of a mentor, are seen as related, grouped into a factor we have named *school*. The other factor identified, grouping clinical leadership and freedom to ask, was labelled as *frame*. In other words, knowledge transfer can be more structured, in a school-like manner, or less structured, diffused in the organizational context. It may be seen that learning opportunities do not seem to belong to neither of the two factors, as respondents may feel that

they are included in the aggregation of the other items mentioned.

By clustering the responses, we obtained four possible situations, illustrated in Figure 1.

The last scenario, which is also the most unfavourable to effective knowledge transfer in medical practice, is the most frequent (61% of the cases), while the first scenario is the least frequent (8% of the cases). The second scenario takes place in 16% of cases, while the third scenario happens in 15% of the cases. While the first scenario, of the student-centred learning in a context which is more structured, would be the ideal case, the last scenario reflects a *sauve qui peut* situation, quite common in the sampled clinics. The intermediate scenarios can be transformed towards either of the two extremes. The stu-

Figure 1. Knowledge transfer scenarios

Student-centred learning in a *school* environment	Student-centred learning in a *frame* environment
Passive learning in a *school* environment	Passive learning in a *frame* environment

dent-centred learning in a *frame* environment may give the student broad guidance and the opportunity to ask. If trust in one's own abilities is enabled by a focus on student, during practical interventions, this moderately guiding learning environment may prove very beneficial, especially for students in their last years of study and interns. Passive learning in a *school* environment implies that the beneficiary of the learning process lags behind the group, being frustrated and lacking trust in one's own skills. In this situation, *fit* is gradually lost. Thus, *fit* without *trust* seems to be, considering the particularities of the medical profession, very independent, despite the amount of teamwork it involves, more dangerous that *trust* without *fit*. If, at the team level, *trust* is properly stimulated, through particularized knowledge transfer strategies, the clinical context seems to influence less the final outcome. Otherwise said, a highly supportive clinical context is not necessarily needed.

CONCLUSION

Our analysis was based on two parameters, *trust* in one's own medical skills and *fit* with the clinic culture. We assessed, based on the scenarios combining the factors of trust with the factors of fit, the influence of each in effective knowledge transfer. Trust seems to be more relevant than fit, when analysing the efficiency of knowledge transfer in Romanian hospital clinics.

Although contexts enabling knowledge transfer are less frequent, at the moment of the survey, there are premises that, for young doctors trusting their skills and well defining their learning objectives, moderately structured organizational cultures are also

creators of learning opportunities. However, a state of passivity, in both learning strategies and organizational contexts, seems to prevail, leading to a poor identification of the young doctor with the clinic, contributing to high turnover (influenced by extrinsic motivators), and to a poor level of self-awareness, as a professional, and low trust in one's medical skills. These are the aspects, revealed by the research, which have to be corrected, by both pro-active, student-focused learning practices, and by a more enabling and better structured organizational context.

REFERENCES

Alvesson, M. (2002). *Postmodernism and social research*. Buckingham: Open University Press.

Arango, J. B. (1998). *Helping non-profits become more effective*. Retrieved from http://www.algodonesassociates.com

Ashkanasy, N. M., Wilderom, C. P., & Peterson, M. F. (Eds.). (2000). *Handbook of organizational culture and climate*. Thousand Oaks, CA: Sage Publications.

Astor, A., Akhtar, T., Matallana, M. A., Muthuswamy, V., Olowu, F. A., Tallo, V., & Lie, R. K. (2005). Physician migration: Views from professionals in Colombia, Nigeria, India, Pakistan and the Philippines. *Social Science & Medicine*, *61*(12), 2492–2500. doi:10.1016/j.socscimed.2005.05.003 PMID:15953667

Baggs, J. G., & Schmitt, M. H. (1997). Nurses' and resident physicians' perceptions of the process of collaboration in an MICU. *Research in Nursing & Health*, *20*, 71–80. doi:10.1002/(SICI)1098-240X(199702)20:1<71::AID-NUR8>3.0.CO;2-R PMID:9024479

Belbin, M. (1985). *Management teams: Why they succeed or fail*. London: Heinemann.

Bishop, P. B., & Wing, P. C. (2006). Knowledge transfer in family physicians managing patients with acute low back pain: A prospective randomized control trial. *The Spine Journal, 6*(3), 282–288. doi:10.1016/j.spinee.2005.10.008 PMID:16651222

Bontin-Foster, C., Foster, J. C., & Konopasek, L. (2008). Physician, know thyself: The professional culture of medicine as a framework for teaching cultural competence. *Academic Medicine, 83*(1), 106–111. doi:10.1097/ACM.0b013e31815c6753 PMID:18162762

Bossuyt, P., & Kortenray, J. (Eds.). (2001). *Evidence-based medicine in practice*. Amsterdam: Uitgeverij Boom.

Bosua, R., & Scheepers, R. (2007). Towards a model to explain knowledge sharing in complex organizational environments. *Knowledge Management Research and Practice, 5*(2), 93–109. doi:10.1057/palgrave.kmrp.8500131

Bratianu, C. (2009). The frontier of linearity in the intellectual capital metaphor. *Electronic Journal of Knowledge Management, 7*(4), 415–424.

Bratianu, C. (2010). A critical analysis of the Nonaka's model of knowledge dynamics. In *Proceedings of the 2nd European Conference on Intellectual Capital*. Lisbon, Portugal: ISCTE Lisbon University Institute.

Bratianu, C., & Andriessen, D. (2008). Knowledge as energy: A metaphorical analysis. In *Proceedings of the 9th European Conference on Knowledge Management*, (pp.75-82). Reading, MA: Academic Publishing.

Brătianu, C., Jianu, I., & Vasilache, S. (2007a). Integratori pentru capitalul intelectual al unei organizaţii (I). *Revista de Management şi Inginerie Economică, 6* (2), 11-23.

Brătianu, C., Jianu, I., & Vasilache, S. (2007b). Integratori pentru capitalul intelectual al unei organizaţii (II). *Revista de Management şi Inginerie Economică, 6* (2), 39-49.

Bratianu, C., Jianu, I., & Vasilache, S. (2011). Integrators for organizational intellectual capital. *International Journal of Learning and Intellectual Capital, 8*(1), 5–17. doi:10.1504/IJLIC.2011.037355

Bratianu, C., & Orzea, I. (2010). Tacit knowledge sharing in organizational knowledge dynamics. In *Proceedings of the 2nd European Conference on Intellectual Capital*, (pp. 107-114). Reading, MA: Academic Publishing.

Bratianu, C., & Vasilache, S. (2012). Knowledge transfer in medical education from a teamwork perspective. *Management & Marketing, 7*(3), 381–392.

Burford, B. (2012). Group processes in medical education: Learning from social identity theory. *Medical Education, 46*, 143–152. doi:10.1111/j.1365-2923.2011.04099.x PMID:22239328

Cooke, R. A., & Rousseau, D. M. (1988). Behavioral norms and expectations: A quantitative approach to the assessment of organizational culture. *Group & Organization Studies, 13*(3), 245–273. doi:10.1177/105960118801300302

Cooke, R. A., & Rousseau, D. M. (1988). Behavioral norms and expectations: A quantitative approach to the assessment of organizational culture. *Group & Organization Studies, 13*(3), 245–273. doi:10.1177/105960118801300302

Curran, V. R., Sharpe, D., & Forristall, J. (2007). Attitudes of health sciences faculty members towards interprofessional teamwork and education. *Medical Education, 41*, 892–896. doi:10.1111/j.1365-2923.2007.02823.x PMID:17696982

Dodds, E. R. (1951). *The Greeks and the irrational.* Berkeley, CA: University of California Press.

Foss, N. J. (1997). *Resources, firms and strategy: A reader in the resource-based perspective.* Oxford, UK: Oxford University Press.

Frost, P. J., Moore, L. F., & Louis, M. R. (1991). *Reframing organizational culture.* Thousand Oaks, CA: Sage.

Gauthier, N., Ellis, K., Bol, N., & Stolee, P. (2005). Beyond knowledge transfer: A model of knowledge integration in a clinical setting. *Healthcare Management Forum, 18*(4), 33. doi:10.1016/S0840-4704(10)60067-1 PMID:16509279

Geisler, E., & Wickramasinghe, N. (2009). *Principles of knowledge management: Theory, practice, and cases.* New York: M.E.Sharpe.

Gillespie, B. M., Chabover, W., Longbottom, P., & Wallis, M. (2010). The impact of organizational and individual factors on team communication in surgery: A qualitative study. [PubMed doi:10.1016/j.ijnurstu.2009.11.001]. *International Journal of Nursing Studies, 47*(6), 732–741.

Gupta, K. S. (2008). A comparative analysis of knowledge sharing climate. *Knowledge and Process Management, 15*(3), 186–195. doi:10.1002/kpm.309

Hagopian, A., Thompson, M. J., Fordyce, M., Johnson, K. E., & Hart, L. G. (2004). The migration of physicians from sub-Saharan Africa to the United States of America: Measures of the African brain drain. *Human Resources for Health, 2*, 2–17. doi:10.1186/1478-4491-2-17 PMID:15078577

Handy, C. (1995). *Gods of management: The changing work of organizations.* Academic Press.

Harrison, R. (1972). Understanding your organization's character. *Harvard Business Review, 5*(3), 119–128.

Huggins, R., & Izushi, H. (2008). *UK competitiveness index 2008.* Centre for International.

Ichijo, K., & Nonaka, I. (2007). *Knowledge creation and management: New challenges for managers.* Oxford, UK: Oxford University Press.

Jansen, L. (2008). Collaborative and interdisciplinary health care teams: Ready or not? *Journal of Professional Nursing, 24*(4), 218–227. doi:10.1016/j.profnurs.2007.06.013 PMID:18662657

Kalisch, B. J., & Begeny, S. (2005). *Improving patient care in hospitals, creating team behavior.* Organizational Engineering Institute. Retrieved from http://www.oeinstitute.org/articles/improving-patient-care.html

Kerner, J. F. (2006). Knowledge translation versus knowledge integration: A funder's perspective. *The Journal of Continuing Education in the Health Professions, 26*, 72–80. doi:10.1002/chp.53 PMID:16557513

Klingle, R. S., Burgoon, M., Afifi, W., & Callister, M. (1995). Rethinking how to measure organizational culture in the hospital setting. *Evaluation & the Health Professions, 18*(2), 166–186. doi:10.1177/016327879501800205 PMID:10143010

Klingle, R. S., Burgoon, M., Afifi, W., & Callister, M. (2008). Rethinking how to measure organizational culture in the hospital setting. *Evaluation & the Health Professions, 18*(2), 166–186. doi:10.1177/016327879501800205 PMID:10143010

Kunda, G. (1992). *Engineering culture: Control and commitment in a high-tech corporation.* Philadelphia: Temple University Press.

Kyndt, E., Dochy, F., & Nijs, H. (2009). Learning conditions for non-formal and informal workplace learning. *Journal of Workplace Learning, 21*(5), 369–383. doi:10.1108/13665620910966785

Landry, R., Saihi, M., Amara, N., & Ouimet, M. (2010). Evidence on how academics manage their portfolio of knowledge transfer activities. *Research Policy, 39*(10), 1387–1403. doi:10.1016/j.respol.2010.08.003

Legare, F., Ratte, S., Gravel, K., & Graham, I. D. (2008). Barriers and facilitators to implementing shared decision-making in clinical practice: Update of a systematic review of health professionals' perceptions. *Patient Education and Counseling, 73*(3), 526–535. doi:10.1016/j.pec.2008.07.018 PMID:18752915

Lencioni, P. (2002). *The five dysfunctions of a team.* San Francisco: Jossey-Bass.

Lin, C., Tan, B., & Chang, S. (2008). An exploratory model of knowledge flow barriers within healthcare organizations. *Information & Management, 45*(5), 331–339. doi:10.1016/j.im.2008.03.003

Liveng, A. (2010). Learning and recognition in health and care work: An inter-subjective perspective. *Journal of Workplace Learning, 22*(1/2), 41–52. doi:10.1108/13665621011012843

Macdonald, M. (2003). Knowledge management in healthcare: What does it involve? How is it measured? *Healthcare Management Forum, 16*(3), 7–11. doi:10.1016/S0840-4704(10)60225-6 PMID:14618826

Mandruleanu, A., & Ivanovici, M. (2008). Knowledge management implications. *Management & Marketing, 3*(2), 105–116.

Martin, G. P., & Learmonth, M. (2012). A critical account of the rise and spread of 'leadership': The case of UK healthcare. *Social Science & Medicine, 74*(3), 281–288. doi:10.1016/j.socscimed.2010.12.002 PMID:21247682

Mayer, R. E. (2010). Applying the science of learning to medical education. *Medical Education, 44*, 543–549. doi:10.1111/j.1365-2923.2010.03624.x PMID:20604850

Mennin, S. (2010). Self-organisation, integration and curriculum in the complex world of medical education. *Medical Education, 44*, 20–30. doi:10.1111/j.1365-2923.2009.03548.x PMID:20078753

Meyer, A. D. (1982). Adapting to environmental jolts. *Administrative Science Quarterly, 27*(4), 515–537. doi:10.2307/2392528 PMID:10257768

Mohr, J., Batalden, P., & Barach, P. (2004). The clinical microsystem and patient safety. *Quality & Safety in Health Care, 13*, 34–38. doi:10.1136/qshc.2003.009571 PMID:15576690

Morgan, L., Doyle, M.E., & Albers, J.A. (2005). Knowledge continuity management in healthcare. *Journal of Knowledge Management Practice, 6*.

Nissen, M. E. (2006). *Harnessing knowledge dynamics: Principled organizational knowing & learning*. Hershey, PA: IGI Global.

Nixon, I., Smith, K., Stafford, R., & Camm, S. (2006). *Work-based learning: Illuminating the higher education landscape*. York, UK: Higher Education Academy.

Nonaka, I. (1994). A dynamic theory of organizational knowledge creation. *Organization Science, 5*(1), 14–37. doi:10.1287/orsc.5.1.14

Nonaka, I., & Takeuchi, H. (1995). *The knowledge creating company: How Japanese companies create the dynamics of innovation*. Oxford, UK: Oxford University Press.

O'Reilly, C., Clatman, J., & Caldwell, D. (1991). People and organizational culture: A Q-sort approach to assessing fit. *Academy of Management Journal, 34*, 487–516. doi:10.2307/256404

Pawlowsky, P. (2001). The treatment of organizational learning in management science. In *Handbook of organizational learning & knowledge*. Oxford, UK: Oxford University Press.

Porter, M. E., & Teisberg, E. (2007). *Redefining health care: Creating value-based competition on results*. Cambridge, MA: Harvard Business School Publishing.

Prugsamatz, R. (2010). Factors that influence organization learning sustainability in non-profit organizations. *The Learning Organization, 17*(3), 243–267. doi:10.1108/09696471011034937

Prusak, L., & Weiss, L. (2007). Knowledge in organizational settings: how organizations generate, disseminate, and use knowledge for their competitive advantage. In *Knowledge creation and management: New challenges for managers*. Oxford, UK: Oxford University Press.

Ratto, M., Propper, C., & Burgess, S. (2002). Using financial incentives to promote teamwork in health care. *Journal of Health Services Research & Policy, 7*(2), 69–70. doi:10.1258/1355819021927683 PMID:11934370

Reddy, M. C., & Jansen, B. J. (2008). A model for understanding collaborative information behavior in context: A study of two healthcare teams. *Information Processing & Management, 44*(1), 256–273. doi:10.1016/j.ipm.2006.12.010

Roos, G., Pike, S., & Fernström, L. (2005). *Managing intellectual capital in practice.* Amsterdam: Elsevier.

Ryu, H. (2003). *Modeling cyclic interaction: An account of goal-elimination process.* Paper presented at the CHI 2003. Ft. Lauderdale, FL.

Schein, E. S. (1985). *Organizational culture and leadership.* San Francisco: Jossey-Bass.

Sheffield, J. (2008). Inquiry in health knowledge management. *Journal of Knowledge Management, 12*(4), 160–172. doi:10.1108/13673270810884327

Teece, D. J. (2009). *Dynamic capabilities & strategic management: Organizing for innovation and growth.* Oxford, UK: Oxford University Press.

Thistlethwaite, J. (2012). Interprofessional education: A review of context, learning and the research agenda. *Medical Education, 46,* 58–70. doi:10.1111/j.1365-2923.2011.04143.x PMID:22150197

Tucker, A. L., & Edmondson, A. C. (2002). Managing routine exceptions: A model of nurse problem solving behavior. *Advances in Health Care Management, 3,* 87–113. doi:10.1016/S1474-8231(02)03007-0

Turner, J. (1990). Emile Durkheim's theory of social organization. *Social Forces, 68,* 1089–1103.

Vandenberghe, C. (1999). Organizational culture, person-culture fit, and turnover. *Journal of Organizational Behavior, 20,* 175–184. doi:10.1002/(SICI)1099-1379(199903)20:2<175::AID-JOB882>3.0.CO;2-E

Vikis, E. A., Mihalynuk, T. V., Pratt, D. D., & Sidhu, R. S. (2008). Teaching and learning in the operating room is a two-way street: Resident perceptions. *American Journal of Surgery, 195*(5), 594–598. doi:10.1016/j.amjsurg.2008.01.004 PMID:18367140

Wailoo, A., Roberts, J., Brazier, J., & McCabe, C. (2004). Efficiency, equity, and NICE clinical guidelines. *British Medical Journal, 328,* 536–537. doi:10.1136/bmj.328.7439.536 PMID:15001481

Wang, S., & Noe, R. A. (2010). Knowledge sharing: A review and directions for future research. *Human Resource Management Review, 20*(2), 115–131. doi:10.1016/j.hrmr.2009.10.001

Wang, Z. T. (2004). *Knowledge system engineering.* Beijing, China: Science Press.

Warren, K. (2008). *Strategic management dynamics.* Chichester, UK: John Wiley & Sons.

Wilkinson, T. J. (2002). Teaching teamwork to medical students: Goals, roles and power. *Medical Education*, *36*, 1089–1090. doi:10.1046/j.1365-2923.2002.13385.x PMID:12406275

Willem, A., & Scarbrough, H. (2006). Social capital and political bias in knowledge sharing: An exploratory study. *Human Relations*, *59*(10), 1343–1371. doi:10.1177/0018726706071527

Chapter 5
Dimensions of Culture in Hospital Teamwork

Anna Rosiek
Ross Medica, Poland

Krzysztof Leksowski
Military Clinical Hospital, Poland & Collegium Medicum Nicolas Copernicus University Chair of Public Health, Poland

ABSTRACT

The chapter discusses, on research-based findings, the particularities of culture in hospitals, in a cross-cultural perspective with a particular focus on the Polish case. The findings of the study point to the fact that exterior factors and perceptions have a decisive impact on the patient evaluation of the hospital experience, so hospitals should dedicate some of their efforts to improving organizational culture and its perceived effects on patients.

1. INTRODUCTION

The issues, raised first by the European Union, largely contributed to actions which were undertaken later and which would result in improving the quality of health care service in medical units in Poland. Beside that, the significant structural changes in the social and economic systems in Poland have led to transformation and commercialization of many aspects of life, including the medi-cal service sector. The changes affected not only structures, but also the patients' thinking mode, their way of seeing a health care unit and the services it offers. Patients have become more demanding, they have started to behave like customers (clients) and expect the same quality of service as in the case of consumer goods.

Such a situation is caused by the entry of medical services into the market of consumer goods, into the area of competitive medical

DOI: 10.4018/978-1-4666-4325-3.ch005

units. This new situation requires a medical organization to take into consideration patients' needs, to listen to them and to improve the quality of its services.

Specifics of medical service – its professional and interpersonal aspects – are extremely important in health care. Those specifics concern the highest values, that is: health and human life. However, concentrating on providing high quality medical service in its technical aspect is not sufficient in contemporary market environment. Therefore, in order to obtain patient's positive opinion on medical services provided by health care units, such a unit has to take care of those factors which pertain directly to its image as seen by the customer. Those factors are highly subjective; they include patient's feelings and experience in previous contacts with a health care organization, his/her trust and satisfaction and also the commitment of the whole organization to the treatment process and improvement of patient's physical and psychological state. Those factors, as peculiar determinants of medical service, have direct influence on shaping the image of a health care unit on the service market. Emphasizing this issue is extremely important now because in everyday medical practice in hospitals, we encounter depreciation of work and stance of medical personnel, specifically doctors and nurses. In the long run, such a situation leads to the decrease of trust, decrease in satisfaction, contributes to negative viewing of a medical unit and leads to deterioration of quality of medical service and that in turn gives a health care unit bad image. Furthermore, the managers of health care units, focused on solving system problems, often forget that an organization's success lies in

its image and how it is perceived, and also in the quality of services it provides, in the way it communicates with its patients and its identity. There is, therefore, a need for specific indication and appreciation of medical personnel as an important part of the organization, influencing its image through the quality of services offered to a patient. Creating and ensuring the quality of the relations between a service provider (in this case a hospital) and a patient; relations based on connections, both rational and emotional, and also determining critical areas in an organization, which affect the way this organization and the quality of medical services are perceived by a patient, will allow to create a medical service which will fulfill patient's expectations. By the same token, it will also help to build a solid image of a health care unit, which will be based on trust, satisfaction and partnership, with special emphasis on many levels and areas of quality in medical service, in relation to the ongoing process of evaluation and increasing expectations of customers (patients). The aforementioned premises became the starting point for a discussion about quality improvement in medical services in the aspect of hospital's image-creation on the service market. They also inspired work on creating an eventual model of medical service that would be aimed at the service's quality, for the goal is to effectively build a hospital's image that would be based on satisfaction, trust and good relations with others.

The aim is, therefore, to create a medical service model and a management model that would help to create a good image through improvements in quality of offered medical services. The general aim can be further described in the following specific aims:

- The analysis of the process of shaping and evaluation of the definitions of medical service quality as perceived by a patient.
- Determination of rational and emotional factors which influence the quality of medical service and hospital's image in the light of offered medical service.
- Creating a model of medical service in a health care unit, which would allow the effective building of hospital's image.
- Determination of differences between a medical service provider and a patient's expectation as far as quality in medical service is concerned.

2. WELL-BEING ACROSS CULTURES

2.1. The Quality of Medical Service

The quality of medical service is the basis of a health care organization aiming at perfection. Orienting a hospital's goals at quality improvement is the basis of its functioning and requires the involvement of all hospital's employees. At the foundation of this philosophy lie everyday contacts between medical personnel and patients. To this way of thinking the work of managers of public hospitals ought to aspire; the aim being the ensurance of the quality of all the processes in an organization. How perfect a health care unit is depends on how a patient sees it, and even more, on the quality assessment, that is the quality of medical service and the level of attention patient experienced during his/her stay at a hospital. This way of viewing the problem of quality in patient's mind, causes the medical organization to stay in the patient's

mind for a longer time, and also allows the long-term and effective creation of medical unit's image. There appears, therefore, a new definition of medical service quality which is based on feelings and experiences of a patient, which in turn are connected to subjective feelings on offered medical service, and not on the medical service provided in reality. The new definition of quality is close in its meaning to patient's satisfaction. Effectiveness of health care service, the timing, information, the way of communicating, patient's opinions and observations are the key elements influencing patient's experience and satisfaction with medical service quality and they also define said quality. Such a way of perceiving the quality of medical service is connected to accreditation, certification and research into patient's satisfaction with the service the health care organization provides. European Commission's and National Committee for Quality Assurance's introduction of such a requirement as obligatory additionally emphasizes the importance of the problem and indicates that patient's satisfaction is crucial from the point of view of an organization that provides medical services.

As we can see, the clinical quality is not seen by a patient as an indicator of the quality of health care offered by a hospital. Patients more often remember the general impression of staying at a hospital and the care being bestowed on them, instead of clinical quality of their stay. Patient's perception of medical service quality boils down to judging everything he/she is able to observe at a hospital or a clinic during his/her stay there, and that includes the relations between a patient and service provider (hospital, staff). Therefore, we can say that everything that is in some relation to a hospital (its surroundings, internal culture and employees) influences patient's perception of medical service quality. Additional benefit resulting from the patient's stay at a hospital and one that testifies to the quality of medical service is the improvement of patient's clinical parameters and in consequence, the patient's state of health. Cunningham says that the quality of medical service from patient's point of view includes nine elements: good care of the patient, timely personnel reaction to patient's signal, good doctor, good reputation of the health care unit among the patient's friends and family, adequate equipment supply, cleanness, adequate meals, lack of disturbances, precise discharge papers.

As we can see, most of the factors that influence patient's satisfaction with the quality of medical service are not strictly clinical elements. They pertain instead to kindness and empathy of the medical personnel, and specifically to sympathy, care, readiness to help and the feeling of comfort.

The quality of medical services, as seen form patient's point of view, is always connected to all the elements which influence the perspective of the person being hospitalized. These elements include: timeliness of medical procedure (the procedure being performed on time), personnel's attitude towards the patients, easy to understand and precise information for patients. Using thusly defined term "quality", the managers of medical units, aiming for improvement of managing processes and also improvement of the quality of medical service – having in mind creating a positive image for a hospital – should create and support all quality processes which would help the employees form right conclusions, create an organizational culture that would be based on competence, unite hospital's mission with hospital's goals, measure and analyze processes present in an organization

in specially dedicated for this purpose teams. Success in correct carrying out of processes contributing to improvement of medical services and hospital's image, translates not only into patient's satisfaction, but also into the hospital's employees' satisfaction, and it also brings substantial profits to the organization. It translates into financial profits for the organization, which come from investing in high standard treatment, because the cost generated as a result of low quality relationship between a patient and the hospital's personnel, directly influences the efficiency indicators of stationary health care, such as: making the most use of hospital's beds and the length of patient's stay at a hospital, and more expensive of treatment.

This area of interest is important from the hospital's manager point of view - in his/her hands lies caring for creating high quality medical service through personnel engagement and he/she should include in the managing process those elements that in the long term will positively influence the image of a hospital.

Hospitals are the most complex of purposeful organizations and they exist in the most turbulent specific industry environment. Hospitals constantly deal with life and death matters and must address their service to patients who are not directly paying for the service they receive. In many cases, patient is completely unaware of the costs of hospital treatment and procedures. Hospital managers often have very little say in the major decisions made and medical service providers rarely are employees of the organization. This is one reason why hospital management must reform and continuously improve the level of quality in hospital department especially level of teamwork, the quality of relationships within teams, communications with patient and his/

her family and also amongst organizational teams and build a positive hospital image. Many organizations, particularly hospitals because of their complexity, are seeking new paradigms that will improve their efficiency and effectiveness regardless of the outcome of the current reform debate. Implementing an organizational change model, specifically team driven improvement, can lead to more teamwork, better communication and as a consequence improved patient service delivery in all areas of hospital operations which influence patient's satisfaction and create a positive image for a hospital.

Health care quality and patient satisfaction, and also patient safety, are common mantra of all health care providers in many countries including Poland. Over the years, a variety of models and schemes for hospital intervention and development have been deployed (Friesner, Neufelder, Raisor, & Bozman, 2009). A typical approach is to hire external consultants to plan and implement organizational change efforts with the use the Malcolm Baldridge Award model for quality improvement in hospital wards. With implementation of this quality control model, however, the observed progress is rather small. Changing basic practices in complex massive healthcare organizations will be especially challenging in hospital's day-to-day practices (Isern & Pung, 2007). Mohr Burgess and Young suggest that teamwork culture in a hospital can reduce turnover thus providing cost saving and higher quality service for patients. Poland's experience and research in this area show that teamwork culture and good communication in a hospital ward positively influences patients satisfaction, his/her recovery speed and ability to recommend the hospital to the patient's friends or family.

3. INTEGRATORS OF MEDICAL TEAMS

3.1. Teamwork: Implementation of the Quality System

All of the staff members at hospital wards tend to perceive the quality process positively and judge it to be useful for them and their department. From staff member's point of view, improvement process in a hospital is a way to improve the quality of the health care provided to the patient, and also to improve the medical staff's working conditions. All medical staff in a hospital understand that quality process would increase their ability to take on responsibility in particular due to writing-up and communications protocols in many aspects in health care organizations. As we can see each clinic is a specific microsystem with its own characteristics, which are very specific in health care sector (Table 1) and focus on patient, community and improvement of treatment process.

This specific healthcare clinical microsystem can be defined as the combination of a small group (team) of people who work together in a defining setting on a regular basis or if needed provide care, and the individuals who receive that care are patients. As a functioning unit, a team has clinical and also business aims, it links processes within organization, shares information and technology environment and produces service and care which can be measured as performance outcomes. These systems evolve over time and are embedded in larger systems which are all about organization (hospital environment). As any living adaptive system each microsystem must do the work, meet the members' needs and maintain itself as a functioning medical unit. Teamwork systems in hospital

Table 1. Characteristics of medical (clinical) microsystem in a team work concept (based on "Teamwork as an Essential Component of High-Reliability Organizations, page 1583" with author's own modifications)

		Characteristic of Clinical Microsystem	Definitions
Hospital Image	teamwork (relationship)	Leadership	The role of the leaders in hospital is to balance setting and reaching collective goals, and to empower individual autonomy and accountability through building knowledge, skills, attitude, respectful action, reviewing and reflecting.
		Staff fokus	There is selective hiring of right people. The orientation process is designed to fully integrate all staff into culture and roles. Taking care of patient with full responsibility during treatment process.
		Interdependance	The interaction of staff is characterized by trust, collaborative willingness to help each other and also by contact with patients, respect and recognition that all contribute individually to a shared purpose
	patient satisfaction (trust)	Patient fokus	This is characterized by meeting all patient needs, listening, informing (educating about treatment process), responding to patient's special requests and also respect for all human rights and patient safety. All of this contributed to smooth service flow.
		Community and Information	The medical community is a resource to the microsystem and establishes good relationship with patients and their family by the process of good communication. Information is the connector - staff to patient, staff to staff. Effective communication on each level in a hospital is paramount and multiple formal and informal channels are used to keep everyone informed all the time.
	outcomes (value)	Process improvement	The atmosphere for learning and redesign is supported by the continuous monitoring of care, use of benchmarking, frequent testing of the change progress.
		Performance results	Performance focuses on patient outcomes, avoidable costs, streamlined service delivery, using data feedback, promoting positive competition

as a specific organization were successful. Although the most common was staff focus, their competences and technical (medical) experience, the presence of interdependence, process improvement, leadership and patient focus suggest that all these aspects of the microsystem must be considered when designing the work. The design of work systems and deep understanding of the process are major contributors to success for medical organization such as hospital. Indeed the higher degree of process awareness often drives the design of the work. This is an important reason why organizations such as hospitals and other medical institutions should be implemented with efficient and effective teamwork system in each department or ward. Understanding how success's characteristics relate to each other can help in self-assessment in organiza-

tion and understanding the challenges of high performance and what it means exactly in everyday practice will be much easier if the teamwork systems are implemented.

Teams and Teamwork

There is a general consensus in the research literature that a team consists of two or more individuals, who have specific roles, perform interdependent tasks, are adaptable, and share a common goal (Salas, Dickinson, & Converse,1992). To work effectively together, team members in hospital must possess specific medical knowledge, skills – sometimes manual, for example surgeons – and attitudes. In practice it could be knowledge of their own and teammate's task and responsibilities, the skill in monitoring each other's performance and a positive disposition toward working in a team. Based on its definition alone, it is easy to see how teamwork is critical for the delivery of health care. Physicians, nurses, pharmacists, technicians, and other health professionals must coordinate their activities to deliver safe and efficient patient care. Their right coordination of all activities during patient's stay in a hospital ward influences patient's satisfaction, mental condition before and after medical procedure and in consequence makes for a faster improvement of the patient's health.

As we can see, health care staff perform interdependent tasks (e.g., a surgeon cannot operate until a patient is anesthetized,) while functioning in specific roles (e.g., surgeon, surgical assistant, anesthesiologist, nurses) and sharing the common goal to provide a patient of safe care. However, despite the importance of teamwork in health care, most clinical units (hospital wards) continue to function as discrete and separate collections of professionals (Knox & Simpson, 2004). This is partially due to the fact that members of these teams are rarely trained together; furthermore, they often come from separate disciplines and diverse educational programs.

Given the interdisciplinary nature of the work in medicine and the necessity of cooperation among the workers (staff members) who perform it, teamwork is critical for ensuring patient safety and satisfaction with his/her stay at a hospital. Teams make fewer mistakes than do individuals, especially when each team member knows his or her responsibilities, as well as those of other team members (Smith-Jentsch, Salas & Baker,1996; Volpe, Cannon-Bowers, Salas, & Spector,1996). However, simply installing a team structure does not automatically ensure it will operate effectively.

To create a good and effective team in a medical unit, we must remember that teamwork is not an automatic consequence of co-locating people together and depends on a willingness to cooperate for a shared goal. Teamwork does not require that team members work together on a permanent basis. Teamwork is sustained by a commitment to a shared set of team knowledge, skills and attitudes rather than permanent assignments that carry over from day to day (Morey et al., 2002). This reason is very important in patient's treatment process, because co-operation within a team influences service, the treatment process itself and patient's satisfaction with his/her hospital stay.

Lack of teamwork always plays significant role. Specifically, poor communication in a hospital ward contributes to patient's dissatisfaction, and less comfortable stay in a surgery ward. Also with the absence of teamwork there is a lack of mutual performance cross-monitoring, inadequate conflict resolution, poor situational awareness, and work overload. These are the main reasons of patient's dissatisfaction. Patient as a good observer who assesses each staff member in hospital, can feel uncomfortable if the communication is poor among the team members. A patient is the first person who asks a doctor or a nurse about the possible outcomes of the treatment process and said patient does it as a person vitally interested in his/her own health. This is why the patient is the first person to assess and evaluate the lack of team work in front of service, lack of proper communication and work overload. Good teamwork is much more important in aspect of improvement of both quality of management and quality of care at a hospital ward and in consequence influences the hospital image.

3.2. Critical Components of Teamwork

Extensive research on teamwork during last year suggests that teamwork is defined by a set of interrelated: knowledge, skills and attitudes that facilitate coordinated, adaptive performance (Baker, Beaubien, Holtzman, 2003; Baker, Gustafson, Beaubien, Salas, Barach, 2003). Teamwork is distinct from taskwork (e.g., surgical skill) but both are required for teams to be effective in complex environments (Morgan & Schwab, 1986). Furthermore, in health care, knowledge and skill at the task are not enough. Teamwork depends on each team member being able to anticipate the needs of others. Adjust to each other's actions, and have a shared understanding of how a procedure should happen (e.g., knowing the steps in an appendectomy or cholecystectomy procedure).

Recently, researchers have begun to identify skills in hospital practices that define team performance in health care. This line of research began with the work of Gaba, Howard, Fish, Smith, & Sowb in 2001, who developed Anesthesia Crisis Resource Management (ACRM). It was designed to help anesthesiologists effectively manage crises by working in multidisciplinary teams that included physicians, nurses, technicians, and other medical professionals (Howard, Gaba, Fish, Yang, & Sarnquist, 1992; Gaba et al., 2001). Anesthesia Crisis Resource Management uses patient simulators to provide training in specific technical and generic teamwork skills. The simulated anesthesia environment consists of a real operating room with standard equipment and situations requiring actual performance of clinical interventions. A life-like mannequin with appropriate breath and heart sounds permits team members to per-

form clinical procedures such as endotracheal intubation and infusion of intravenous drugs. Scenarios presented include overdose of inhalation anesthetic, cardiac arrest, and complete power failure (Holzman et al., 1995). The team skills trained in this simulated environment include making inquiries and assertions, communicating, giving and receiving feedback, exerting leadership, maintaining a positive group climate, and reevaluating actions.

In addition to anesthesia, a number of researchers have recently begun to identify the knowledge, skills and attitudes requirements of teamwork in other health disciplines. For example, Healey, Undre, and Vincent (2004) have developed the Observational Assessment for Teamwork in Surgery (OTAS) to assess cooperation, leadership, coordination, awareness, and communication in surgical teams (Healey et al., 2004). Thomas, Sexton and Helmerich in 2004 developed ten behavioral markers for teamwork in neonatal resuscitation teams; also Filn and Maron in the same year have identified nontechnical skill requirements for teams in acute medicine.

These studies encapsulate the core three elements such as knowledge, skills, and attitude requirements for physicians, nurses, and other health care professionals to function effectively in a wide variety of health care teams. Different researchers use different terminology to define these specific medical knowledge, manual skills, and attitudes requirements (Thomas et al., 2004); some additionally identify the behavioral markers such as "information sharing," while others identify a requirement for "communication" (Leonard, Graham, & Bonacum, 2001; Flin & Maron, 2004). To Salas, Sims and Klein these generic elements of: knowledge, skills and attitudes can be clustered into eight broad competencies of teamwork. These competencies must be possessed by health care professionals so they can perform in the variety of teams of which they are part and a variety of tasks requiring coordination in day-to-day medical practice (McAlearney,2008; Shortell, Casalino, & Fisher, 2010).

Everyday experience shows that it is rather a kind of mixture of those elements: specific knowledge, skills and attitudes of people working together which creates an effective team work in a hospital environment. This mix of elements and behavior specific to hospital environment is presented in Table 2. The table presents a mix of elements such as behavior and skills, their definition, and behavioral examples which should be observed in medical practices to create effective teamwork.

These are the key reasons why hospitals should implement effective teamwork. Focus is on three basic themes:

- **First:** The delivery of health care. An organization such as hospital is a high reliability organization and as such provides the service. Patients expect error-free care, good communication and re-

specting of the human rights (Knox & Simpson, 2004).

- **Second:** Improving of teamwork is an essential component of complex and perfect organization which is a hospital. Although not the sole determinant of high reliability, HROs (high reliability organizations) are typically comprised of teams embedded in multiteam systems and effective teamwork is critical for success in environments that demand high reliability (Wilson, Burke, Priest, & Salas, 2005).

- **Third:** The easiest way of improving quality of service and hospital image is by teamwork and the continuous personal training both in communication and medical practice skills. Team training has been effectively implemented in the commercial airlines and the military with positive results (Thomas et al., 2004). Their positive experience shows that training program in teamwork minimalizes the risk of unwanted incidents, improves communication among team members and builds strong inter-

Table 2. Mix of elements and behavior that creates effective teamwork in hospital environment

Complex teamwork in perfect hospital organization	Training (improving of teamwork medical skills)	Delivery of healthcare	Team leader	Establish and revise team goals and plan, take care of team members, have a clear common purpose, conduct effective period meeting. Usually this is a role of the chief medical doctor.
			Personnel behavior	Support each other, regularly provide feedback about patient treatment to each other, learn about new, innovative treatments and attend special training courses provided for medical staff
			Monitoring performance	Periodically diagnose team effectiveness, including the results of the teamwork and monitor medical errors in working teams to ensure patient's safety. Monitoring of performance in professional health care
	Training (improving of teamwork effective communication)		Communication	Frequent communication and information exchange, both formal and informal, on each level in hospital environment to provide better health care service

Source: Author's own study

personal relationships. Such training programs are now emerging in health care with potentially similar benefits (Baker, Beaubien & Holtzman,2003). Finally, health care must work to integrate teamwork throughout every level of training and education of health care professionals. Using this approach, team concepts become a part of everyday practice.

Teamwork is an essential component of achieving high reliability for health care organizations. High Reliability Organization environments demand teamwork and, as a result, the science of team training can provide great insights and proven techniques for improving performance within such health care organizations.

Team Work in Surgery

Performing safe surgery relies on the ability of surgical team members to combine professional knowledge and technical expertise with non-technical skills e.g. communication, teamwork, situation awareness, leadership, decision-making (Yule et al., 2006). Mastery of both types of skills is essential (Mazzocco et al., 2009). The surgical team is a dynamic, multi-disciplinary team and consists of surgeons, anaesthetists, operating theatre (OT) nurses and nurse anaesthetists. Many errors that occur in the OT are attributed to the non-technical skills of the surgical team (Yule et al., 2006; Makary et al., 2006). In order to work safely and effectively in a surgical environment, with a minimum of technical errors, the non-technical skills of communication, teamwork and situation awareness are the most important (Flin et al., 2003). In the context of the Operating Theatre com-

munication is defined as 'skills for working in a team context to ensure that the team has an acceptable shared picture of the situation and can complete the tasks effectively', and teamwork is defined as 'skills for working in a group context, in any role, to ensure effective joint tasks completion and team member satisfaction'' (Flin & Maran, 2004). Furthermore, situation awareness is defined as 'developing and maintaining a dynamic awareness of the situation in theatre based on assembling data from the environment, understanding what they mean and thinking ahead what might happen next'

Procedures in the OT are complex and demand intense interaction between team members. Surgical teams should be cohesive and have similar perceptions of communication and teamwork to collaborate effectively, establish common goals for improving team performance, and ensure patient safety (Leonard, Graham, & Bonacum, 2004; Mills, Neily, & Dunn,2008). Therefore, work processes should emphasize the interdependency of team members and support a good understanding of each team member's tasks, roles and responsibilities within the surgical process. This facilitates effective teamwork, ensures that action is linked to reflection, and creates a culture that is open to change (Lingard at al., 2008; Undre et al., 2006).

The main conclusion is that developing a culture of collaboration and coordination in health care requires a commitment to engage in shared learning and dialogue. Dialogue with staff focus, interdependence, information and communication and also process improvement with patient focus has the potential to encourage collegial learning, change thinking, support new working relationships and improve patient care. Assessment of an organization by cultural criteria especially their inside characteristics offers a powerful new way to think about performance at the frontlines of healthcare and in the future it could be gold standard for assessing the success of an organization.

4. HEALTHCARE ENVIRONMENT COMMUNICATION

4.1. Communication as an Aspect of Safety and Satisfaction for Patients in Surgical Ward

Safety is a fundamental patient right, though not a certainty (Knox & Simpson, 2004). When patients arrive at a health care organization, they expect to leave that institution in equal or better health. Patients and their families do not expect physicians, nurses, and other hospital staff to make mistakes, or worse yet cover up as opposed to communicate errors. Historically, physicians, nurses, and other health care professionals have functioned as discrete parts. The new character of medical services, and higher expectation of patients are the main reasons of higher standard for professionals. As a result of this new quality the Institute of Medicine recommended that interdisciplinary team training programs be established, based on sound principles of team management, to improve coordination and communication among health care staff (Kohen, Corrigan, & Donaldson, 1999).

It is easy to see how teamwork is critical for the delivery of health care. Physicians, nurses, pharmacists, technicians, and other health professionals must coordinate their activities and communication to deliver safe and efficient patient care.

Given the interdisciplinary nature of the work and the necessity of cooperation among the workers who perform it, teamwork is critical for ensuring patient safety. Teamwork depends on each team member being able to anticipate the needs of others; adjust to each other's actions, and have a shared understanding of how a procedure should happen. Therefore communication in team is the basis. Complex hospital procedure require not only technical skills but also communication skills and respecting the patient's needs especially in aspects of communication, (doctor-nurse, patient-doctor, and nurse -patient).

Communication studies suggest that patient socio-demographic factors are embedded within medical encounters and impact patient expectations, judgments, and outcomes, such as satisfaction. Physician chatting has been suggested as one way to enhance patient satisfaction. However, little is known about chatting within the context of the clinical encounter or of the interaction of chatting with patient socio-demographic factors and patient satisfaction. Chatting behavior can be viewed as the verbal communication of topics unrelated to the diagnosis, treatment, or management of a medical or healthcare condition. Physician chatting has been suggested as one way to enhance patient satisfaction (Daaleman and Mueller, 2004).

In addition, the potential contribution of physician chatting as a patient-centered communication behavior, such as data gathering, relationship building, partnering, and counseling, remains unclear. We can see however that chatting has been strongly recommended as a way to enhance patient satisfaction.

Physicians should initially recognize that all patients bring a set of silent and spoken expectations and assumptions to the medical encounter. Patient characteristics such as age, race/ethnicity, and health status, impact these expectations and are also strongly predictive of satisfaction. Although many of these characteristics are not amenable to physician intervention, clinicians may potentially impact two modifiable factors – chatting behavior and visit length – in a more global or relationship-centered fashion. Perhaps doctor's communication with patient and visit duration may be viewed as key facilitators to the physician's understanding of the patient's experience of health and illness. If this assumption is correct, chatting and communication process with patient during hospital stay, should be considered a more-inclusive part of history-taking and family information gathering rather than a task that is independent of these processes (Young, Materko, & Desai, 2000).

Measuring the patient safety and satisfaction, communication is a very important issue that will help very much in improving the service provided to patients and improve the level of satisfaction with treatment. To evaluate patients' satisfaction and identify any areas for improvement, there is a need of taking into account the out-patient consultation, pre-assessment clinic, surgery and post-operative care, and also patients' comments relating to service provision.

Patient satisfaction is important health outcome. Full understanding both the domains of satisfaction as well as their relative importance to patients is necessary to improve the overall quality of patient care. Meeting the doctor, presenting all relevant information and giving printed information are very important factors in improving the patient satisfaction with surgery and staying at the surgical ward and the feeling of safety.

The patient satisfaction significantly increases with meeting the doctor and knowing more about the surgery itself. Similar information was found by Elder and Suter (2004) who found that it is important to meet the surgeon,

know the advantages and disadvantages of possible treatments, the common risks and complications, the operative technique, and discussion of the rare risks of the operation. Comprehensive preoperative information causes little or no increase in overall patient anxiety (Dawes & Davison, 1994; Newton-Howes, Bedford, Dobbs, & Frizelle,1998). Poor patient recall of verbal pre-operative information is well documented (Nisselle,1993; Morgan and Schwab,1986; Garden, Merry, Holland, & Petrie, 1996) and most patients wanted written preoperative information. A standard written information sheet may also be the best medium in which to mention rare complications, leaving time for the surgeon to verbally discuss the particular risks and postoperative expectations pertaining to a particular patient.

Many of the studies and documentations show, that the patient satisfaction was significantly increased by giving them printed information. The overall patient satisfaction from being listed for surgery to discharge was as high as 85%, while Chet and McCluskey (2004) who compared public and private patients priorities and satisfaction found that 90% of private patients were satisfied with the information they received regarding surgery, while in public sector 45% of patients wanted more information. This tendency prevails in the European health care sector as well.

4.2. Verbal Communication and Human Right's in Hospital

Inform the Patient about Treatment

Informing the patient about treatment during the hospital stay is a guaranty for patient's mental and physical health, patient safety climate and increase in their satisfaction. In the Polish health care system's reform programmes, the 'quality communication' concept involves two dimensions: technical and interpersonal. The former looks for achieving better results through the conduct and application of health care and scientific research. The latter comes from concerted efforts to increase respect for patients as human beings and improve their satisfaction with the health care services they receive. Health care leaders and managers have developed a heightened awareness of the importance of the moral dimension of health care service provision. This has resulted in a rapid proliferation of professional codes of ethics, codes of conduct for health professionals and patients' rights documents, and assessment of the quality of care as a obligatory to each hospital. Many researchers show that showing on patient honest and sensitivity and so called "human approach" are main determinants of performance quality in hospital environment. So as we can see verbal communication, especially in the aspect of informing the patient about the treatment and drug therapy provided during hospitalization is important both from patient's and quality point of view in hospital practice. Patient like to be educated by nurses and doctors about they situation, and also pay special attention to additional information material available on a hospital ward.

Interactions between practitioners and patients occur in an organizational and social context and within a system of infrastructure. These contextual differences exist in a unique space and time within and across nations. The provision of care for any specific diagnostic group of patients is influenced by where, when and with whom it is happening. It will also depend on the availability of technical and financial resource in hospital and also on the health care system in a particular country. Regardless of advances in information technology, medical care will continue to involve direct communication between individuals (Miller et al., 2001) and patient education is one way to prevent medical errors (Sulzer-Azaroff & Austin, 2000) in hospital practices. When patients know the questions to ask and feel they can effectively communicate with caregivers, they are providing prompts to activate safe health care behaviors. Effective communication between the empowered patient and receptive caregiver not only helps alleviate patient concern about experiencing a negative outcome (Sulzer-Azaroff and Austin, 2000), it also adds a patient-centered, customized set of cues to prompt the occurrence of critical safety-related behaviors.

Human Rights

Medical practitioners have a key role to play in protecting, promoting and fulfilling human rights. An organization called Physicians for Human Rights works closely with many human rights organizations in the world and The American College of Physicians has an active human rights committee. Also, other medical organizations in Poland are becoming more active in this area. Amnesty International defines human rights defenders as 'individuals or groups of people who promote and protect human rights through peaceful and non-violent means. Examples include judges, lawyers, religious leaders, educators, etc. In the Declaration on Human Rights Defenders, the United Nations calls upon professionals to uphold human rights and freedoms. The promotion of human rights is in keeping with the medical professional code. Peel states in *Human Rights and Ethics* that 'Human rights and medical ethics are complementary (Peel, 2005).

Approaching human rights has to start by asking how the practicing physician confronts human rights issue in daily clinical situations. Our research, conducted in surgery clinics in Poland on patients after laparoscopic cholecystectomy, shows everyday problems related to human rights in public hospital. The learning objectives for the issue of medical and human rights in clinical situations are:

1. Understanding the physician's role as an advocate for human rights in surgery clinics.
2. Identifying ways in which physicians can participate in providing health care for patient after laparoscopic cholecystectomy.
3. Recognizing that surgeons have been used as agents of the state in abusing human rights.
4. Recognizing how health professionals may be involved in the documentation and adjudication of cases of human rights abuses.

Abuse of human rights is a worldwide problem, and it demands the attention of physicians everywhere. As a member of the World Medical Association (WMA), the Polish Medical Association is committed to realizing the mission of the WMA—to uphold the highest possible standards of ethical behavior and care by all physicians, at all times. Although, they have a long way to go before the aspirations of "human rights" declarations (Universal Declaration of Human Rights, 2004), conventions (European Convention for the Prevention of Torture and Inhuman or Degrading Treatment or Punishment, 2004) and treaties (International Covenant on Economic, Social and Cultural Rights, 2004) are fully realized. As physicians, they have a special responsibility to be defenders of human rights, responsibility that is grounded in their heritage of caring for the sick and suffering.

Surgical interventions are increasingly important to public health and must be included in contemporary discussions on health and human rights. The large amount of diseases with surgical interventions known to avert disability and death, along with cost effectiveness of the intervention, are evidence that some surgical procedures should be prioritized for delivery in all countries, and that the status of these specific procedures must be elevated from important to an essential element of the right to health. The current disparities in global surgical care are unacceptable. Because of that short- and long-term plans to improve access to surgical care in these environments are important. As a starting point, this includes critical appraisal and action in areas of the world's surgical workforce, integration of surgical services in ongoing health policy initiatives, and agreement on indicators that can be used to measure progress. Health care personnel, as a working team involved in delivery of surgical services, have much to learn from the practical applications of human rights principles and the essential role they must fulfill in research and advocacy to improve availability for surgical care globally.

Investing in surgical services would be beneficial for all sectors in medicine and help to provide upholding of human rights on a better level in hospital practices even despite the fact that the researched parameters related to human rights are not statistically significant when it comes to patients' opinions but are important when we assess team–work in surgery wards, especially in aspect of communictation with patient and the aspect of quality care in hospital surgery ward.

We can show specific positive obligations for the medical profession. Positive obligations in surgeons' profession are: protecting individuals' rights, fulfilling human rights and promoting rights of patients. These functions of Human Rights in Medicine are realized in hospital clinics as a concept of high quality standards by informing patients about their rights, teaching new doctors how to speak to patients and how to provide the service in surgery clinic. Each doctor must provide proper documentation on injury, they must respect the patients' privacy and protect detainees form abuse by third parties. In hospital practice, communication with patients is one of the aspects that should be improved.

It would be beneficial to establish broader definitions of medical ethics or create new international communication codes in human rights aspect of physician – patient communication. What is needed are procedures for implementing, monitoring, and enforcing existing standards and codes, as well as an increased awareness by the medical community of its human rights obligations. Additionally paying attention to patient's rights influences patient safety culture and factors in overall perception of safety in surgery ward. The best way to achieve this would be to make "medicine and human rights" a significant part of the ethics curriculum in medical health schools. Also perception human rights influent on patient safety culture factor of overall perception of safety in surgery ward.

4.3. Non–Verbal Communication in Hospital Ward

Non–verbal communication is a subtle form of communication that takes place in the initial three seconds after meeting someone for the first time and can continue throughout the entire interaction. Thus it is important for health care provider to be aware of the non-verbal messages they convey to their patients. Non – verbal communication significantly influenced patient satisfaction. Apart from technical skills and competences, information sharing about patient's illness, also non verbal expression and perceived empathy were the main predictor variables of patient satisfaction with health care provider interaction. In other words, better demonstration of empathy, situation awareness and greater efforts to improve patient enablement could positively affect the patients perception of the provider's competency and consequently their satisfaction.

Empathy

Empathy is crucial to effective achievement of patient centeredness in that it encapsulates sensitivity to both informational and emotional aspect of communication. Patient providers usually feel pressured to see more patients in the short time, leading to concerns that patient provider (doctor) is less engaged in the healing process of a particular patient.

In the field of patient safety in hospital environment apart from epidemiology and treatment, patient attention has been paid to the importance of shared attitudes, beliefs, and value that underline how people perceive and act on safety issue in organization. These shared characteristics are often referred as a safety culture. Developments and changes in practices and procedures within the hospital practices are thought both to share and reflect the safety culture of that organization in a dynamic and evolving way. Positive safety culture in healthcare we can describe as a dependent on the quality of staff and managers communication which is based on mutual trust and openness, and also sharing the emotional connections with patient (empathy). Shared perception is an important aspect of safety and influences patient satisfaction.

Patient's trust, satisfaction and the relationship between hospital personnel and a patient are the factors which can be identified as important elements that testify to high quality of offered service and key elements in creating the image of a hospital. It should be noted that such factors as: brand loyalty, brand value, and brand recognition have indirect influence on a hospital's image. These elements are, however, dependant on trust, satisfaction and relationship with a client, although they influence the opinion on how good the medical service is, equally strongly.

Trust

In the context of health care, trust is worked on in a changing environment, where a hospital fulfills its mission, trying simultaneously to provide a higher standard of health care and gain financial profits. Trust building became a certain standard for a hospital and its employees, which the hospital is able to offer its patients in order to improve the quality of medical service. In the context of medical market, trust should be viewed and considered in four categories. First, the intentions of all interested parties should be known, in this case, the relation between a doctor and a patient (Moorman, Zeltman, & Deshpande, 1992; Montaglione, 1999). Moreover, factors such as: belief in doctor's good will and right diagnosis and following the doctor's orders should be involved, because they are the basis for building relationships in this business (Suchurr & Ozanne,1985).

Patient's Satisfaction

Patient's satisfaction with his/her stay at a hospital is the result of his/her positive experience during hospitalization. Satisfaction is defined as recognizable state, that allows the expression of positive emotions or identifying bad experiences (Westbrook, 1981). It is also the emotional response of a patient to a particular situation, that is related not to the whole medical market, but to a product (hospital), medical service, a person characteristics and behavior repeated and observed during patient's stay at a hospital.

Francken and Van Raaij (1981) say that satisfaction is determined by difference between real and expected situation and also by appearance of internal and external barriers, which make it impossible for the expected (wanted) situation to occur (Francken and Van Raaij 1981). Patient whose expectations are not fulfilled, will be unsatisfied and the consequences of that will be negative for his/her perception of medical service and for the health care unit.

Relationship with Patients

Research in the field of medicine emphasizes that relationships with patients in a medical unit are very generalized. They narrow down to defining the roles between a patient and a doctor, define their style of communication. They do not show, however, the factors that would motivate a patient to continue communicating with the doctor after the end of hospitalization (Barksdale, Johnson, & Suh, 1997). Wanting to gain patient's trust and ensure his/her satisfaction, and in consequence create a positive image of a hospital, a doctor should strive for creating such a relationship with a patient that would fulfill his/her expectations. The doctor should support a patient and actively take part in the process of determining the correct course of treatment (Ouschan, Sweeney, & Lester, 2006) during hospitalization. The accessibility of medical personnel on a hospital ward and their accessibility for a patient is a factor that influences substantially the improvement of medical service quality and hospital's image.

Creation of the hospital's image and desire to maintain the positive image through high quality of medical service (in patient's opinion) is a process that requires constant improvement. The improvement in this area should be conducted on the basis of creating such a model that would lead to improvement of patient's comfort of living and, similarly, would lead to patient's positive opinion regarding functioning of a hospital. As a consequence, we will be able to observe the development of the positive image of a medical unit that would result from increased patient satisfaction with his/her stay at a hospital.

In the current model of how public health care units function in Poland, processes related to improvement of a health care unit through high quality medical service are under appreciated and sometimes disregarded altogether by hospital's managers. Seeing how market works, it seems unwise. After all, hospitals – similarly to companies – started to function on the market and are surrounded by increasing competition. As a consequence, they started to try to attract patients, their loyalty, satisfaction and trust. Wanting to maintain its position on the market, a hospital should take care of improving managing processes on all the levels of organization's functioning. Reasons for today's state, i.e. the lack of those improvements, are rooted in the fact that regulations pertaining to how a hospital

functions are not adjusted to realities of Polish medical market. The new law for health care units does not "force" the effective proprietory supervision and does not indicate precisely the mechanisms which should be introduced in order to improve managing processes. In the light of such a gap, it is difficult for anybody to make decisions about introducing improvements in health care. The fact that health care units managers try to operate according to a mass of unclear laws and regulations, under the threat of public finance discipline, is an additional factor that is conducive to the gaps widening and imperfections in medical units management growing. This, in consequence, does not contribute at all to improvement in how hospitals function, and that does not lead to creation of a positive image for a hospital as far as quality is concerned. If we want to improve the medical service quality model and create a stable and positive image for a hospital, we should ensure that patients trust a hospital, are satisfied with the service and relationship with hospital's staff, because these things are the basis for improving the quality of medical service. It's these non-material factors, which are additionally highly subjective, that indirectly contribute to creating a brand for a medical unit. They show hospital's strength, value and patient's loyalty to the brand and, in consequence, high quality of offered medical service (Figure 1).

Patient's satisfaction is a key element in measuring quality in medical units. The measuring of satisfaction is important in every branch of business because customer's satisfaction translates into his/her loyalty. Scientific studies show that a patient who is satisfied, is more likely to recommend the hospital he/she was at, and return there if such a need occurs or when their life and health are in danger (Bruke-Miller et al, 2006). In

Figure 1. Strategy for improving the medical service and hospital's image through trust, satisfaction and interpersonal relations
Source: Author's own study based on: "Brand Equity in hospital marketing" Kyung Hoon Kim, Kang Sik Kim, Dong Yul Kim, Jong Ho Kim, Suk Hou Kang, Journal of Business Research 61 (2008) 75-82.

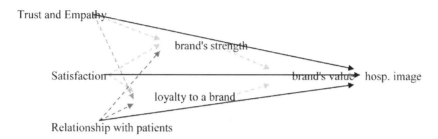

health care, patient's satisfaction is very important because satisfied patients are the group in whose case the treatment administered by a medical unit ended successfully (Lee, 2005). Therefore, patient's satisfaction with the effects of the treatment translates to both, patient's health and smaller cost of health care. That's why it is so vital for a health care unit to strive for improving patient's satisfaction with the treatment. It should be noted that in a situation where patients have the option of multiple choice, sometimes they will not recommend the medical unit they stayed at, even though they were satisfied with their stay. Sometimes it is due to the fact that patient's general satisfaction was caused by the general health improvement (Sitza and Wood, 1997). On the other hand, patient's willingness to recommend a health care unit and his/her desire to return to the same unit are caused by objective assesment of said health care unit. It needs pointing out that the quality of care, willingness to recommend a medical unit or desire to return to it are three unique variables, which carry with them certain priorities for the patients and which influence patients' satisfaction (Burroughs, Waterman, Cira, & Dunagan, 1999).

Patient's positive impressions, his/her satisfaction, are an important source of information for the hospital. They help to identify problems, solve them and allow to use such solutions that would aim for quality improvement in the organization's functioning (Levine, Plume and Nelson, 1997).

In some countries, the measuring of patient's satisfaction became obligatory. For example in France, such studies are conducted in medical units since 1996. The examination of patient's satisfaction is a tool used by hospital's managers to improve the quality of work in the hospital environment, to improve the quality of medical service, to attract patient's attention and it also helps to introduce convenient solutions for a consumer (Labrere et al., 2001; Labrere and Francois, 1999). The results of satisfaction surveys are given to the personnel working at a hospital (Boyer, Francois, Doutre, Weil, & Labarere,2006). Patient's satisfaction became an essential term for a medical organisation and the results obtained in periodical surveys show the ways in which a patient appreciates hospital's achievements in such areas as quality improvement in the hospital's functioning and image building. Conducting such surveys periodically allows the managers to draw conclusions on whether a hospital meets patient's expectations, and they also show what changes should be introduced in the future for the hospital to succeed on the medical market.

5. PERFORMANCE AND PRACTICES OF LEADING HOSPITALS (LEADERSHIP)

Leadership is especially important at a time of dramatic changes in healthcare systems in the world. As the United States makes significant investments in health care reform initiatives, quality and patient safety improvements, and information technology, the capability to assimilate these massive changes must also be built. Fortune 500 businesses have understood that these huge investments have the best chance of delivering their expected return when they attend to the human side of the equation: ensuring that the skills, rewards, talent management, and overall organizational culture are aligned with the intended change. This is achieved when leadership best practices are adopted, cultivating the necessary competencies to inspire and manage in a challenging and changing environment. Without adequately and pervasively preparing health care leadership to effectively implement new capabilities, many transformational components of health reform may have a lower probability of succeeding or meeting the public's expectations.

Leadership development and succession planning are also crucial for the strategic development of health care organizations. According to leadership best practices, "an effective leadership development program has broad organizational reach, touching both employees and affiliated professionals and spanning the organization. With this reach, leadership development programs can be used to help new and established leaders, as well as those in administrative and clinical roles, to improve their leadership skills and abilities to perform their job functions"(McAlearney, 2008).

Health care must address critical issues regarding leadership and organizational performance such as:

- How to assure the availability of leadership prepared to address future challenges and lead transformation.
- How to transform health professionals working as individuals into high-performing teams.
- How to align management systems to support culture change and continuous professional development.
- How to create an organizational culture dedicated to crossing the quality chasm (Roberts, 1990).

The complexity of health care today and the changes needed to reform and improve our health care system require that providers have the skills and tools to address the questions raised. These include, in particular, the use of evidence-based care management processes, the adoption of continuous quality improvement techniques, the ability to develop effective teams, also the implementation of electronic health records and registries. Much has been written about each of these skills and tools, but they need to be considered as an integrated set of competencies required to effectively respond to the new payment incentives for providing better-coordinated, cost-effective care. Over the last decade, the National Center for Healthcare Leadership (NCHL an organization in U.S which names and assesses leaders on the medical market) has served as catalyst in bringing the leadership agenda to the forefront in health care and advocating for the adoption of evidence based best practices. Although much of what needs to be done is already known to the field, a greater challenge is putting this knowledge into action and broadly implementing best practices that have been developed in other industries or among thought-leader health care providers into day-to-day operations. The intent of the leadership survey is to raise awareness of leadership best practices and to provide hospitals and health systems with the capability to benchmark and examine their own progress with regard to these practices.

Despite the apparent lag in adoption of leadership development best practices by health care organizations, certain hospitals are engaging in leadership development and succession planning in response to changing policy and economic conditions. The leadership survey enabled organization to identify the level to which hospitals and health care systems have adopted these leadership development best practices and to identify if specific organizational characteristics were associated with their adoption.

The assessments measure alignment of core processes and strategies that define a systematic and sustainable approach to leadership development in health care organizations. The survey enabled NCHL to assess the degree to which evidence-based leadership development best practices are used and to study the relationship between the talent management core processes and certain organizational performance measures, such as mortality, readmissions, patient satisfaction, and quality process measures. The survey also enabled hospitals and health care systems to compare their leadership development efforts with evidence-based best practices and benchmarks. Thanks to that, benchmark organizations experiences are used as a comparison point for the survey results and indicate that these benchmark organizations have been more widely adopted human resource best practices than is demonstrated by hospitals

Table 3. Hospital analysis in aspect of cross-cultural leadership experiences

Type of existing hospitals in countries dependend on:	USA	France	Poland	Patient Preferences
Number of Beds				
Small (6–99)	x	X	x	x **
Medium (100–299)	x	X		
Large (300 and more)	x	X	x	
Ownership				
Public		X	x	
not-for-profit	x		x	x
for profit	x	X		
Federal	x			
Teaching Hospitals				
Non - Teaching	x	X	x	x
Teaching	x	X	x	
Services				
Med./Surg/Gen	x	X	x	x **
** most impotant elements from patient point of view in hospitals which are leaders				

Source: Author's own study

and health systems in various countries. To better evaluate and understand this problem Table 3 compares hospitals of USA, France and Poland, in the aspects of the number of beds, ownership types, service type.

In order to understand the effect of foreign cultural experience on hospital personal values, leadership behavior and the correlation between them, USA and France leaders with foreign cultural experience and Poland leaders without cultural experience were studied. The findings showed that no significant difference was observed when leadership behavior and personal values of the two groups were compared separately. However, considerable differences were found in the correlation of leadership behavior and personal values between the two groups. Leadership behavior was more predictable and highly influential values-in-use were identified in the case of Taiwanese leaders without foreign cultural experience. In contrast, leadership behavior of foreign leaders with cultural experience was more complex than could be accounted for by those personal values evaluated in Poland. Moreover, no common values-in-use which motivated more than three leadership behaviors were found in this group. These findings indicate that individuals' foreign cultural experiences do impact on their motivation of leadership behavior, and, possibly, transform their personal values. An important contribution of the present study is that it provides a starting point for future study of correlations of leadership behavior and personal values for leaders with different cultural experience. Only with more empirical research from different countries of origin, or of Polish leaders possessing different cultural experience, can we enrich knowledge of

correlations of leadership behavior and personal values.

Cross-cultural studies into the correlation between personal values and behavior present great empirical evidences that personal values and leadership behavior differ from one culture to another. The majority of studies, however, focus on identifying universality and uniqueness of values and leadership behavior across cultures (Schwartz, 1994; House et al., 2004). In contrast, less attention has been paid to understand the effect that experience of a foreign culture has on personal values and leadership behavior. Moreover, there has been a lack of integration concerning the relationship between specific medical and personal values and leadership behavior.

5.1. Leadership Behavior in Hospital Study

Leaders are respected by followers not because of their skills, but because of their behavior. Leadership is 'the behavior of an individual when he is directing the activities of a group towards a shared goal' (Hemphill & Coons, 1957, p.7). Yukl (2006) suggested that one of the useful ways to study leadership is to examine leadership behavior or what leaders do. The two most frequently used leadership behavior dimensions in research are initiation of structure and consideration. These were identified in a study which spanned the years 1953-1962 conducted by The Ohio State University. Leaders who are friendly, supportive, welfare caring and consultative are thought to be considerate. Leaders who define roles, create standards, set up deadlines and follow procedures are thought to be initiating structure (Burns, 2005). The conclusion of the study was that leadership is not inherited traits of great-man, but rather that effective leadership can be developed through training. In other words, hospital leaders can be made, and created continously (Horner, 1997).

A major problem encountered by researchers in leadership behavior is how to define and classify behavior of medical staff in hospitals, when they are studied cross-culturally (Smith, Peterson, & Schwartz, 2002). A behavior that is clearly defined in one culture may be defined totally differently in another. For example, criticizing a subordinate directly and privately is considered appropriate behavior in the United States. However, in Chinese society, the same leadership behavior would be seen as inconsiderate. Many studies support the idea that concepts of leadership differ as a function of cultural differences (House et al., 2002). Therefore, understanding the meaning of leadership behavior in different cultures is not only a challenge but is also essential for global leaders on hospital market. Recent research in this domain mainly focus on investigating commonness and divergence of leadership behavior from culture to culture (House et al., 2004; Connerley & Pedersen, 2005). Such studies are certainly helpful on understanding the effect of contextual factors on leadership effectiveness for organizations operating globally, but they leave a gap that needs to be filled in relation to understanding how leadership behavior is transformed when leaders possess experience of a foreign culture. Knowing the effects of foreign cultural experience on the transformation of leadership behavior can provide the knowledge that is required for selecting, fostering and developing potential global leaders.

Leadership capability in the form of transformational style (meaning: transformational leadership has four dimensions: (1) idealized influence or charisma, (2) inspirational motivation, (3) individualized consideration, and (4) intellectual stimulation. Implementing these dimensions, a set of practices shown by the transformational leaders to their followers are: set vision, aligned followers to the vision through effective communication, and motivated followers to achieve that vision (Bass & Avolio, 1994) combined with the best practice capability is the key determinants to organizational success.

Effective management approach is the one that nurtures organizational change which emphasizes key aspects of future-oriented elements; transformational leadership and internalizing best practice. The ability to weld these capabilities into the hospital organization's change effort proves highly effective means to progress to world-class standard. Leadership and its relations to success of TQM programs has been discussed in many studies before (Waldman,1994; Ahire and Shaughnessy, 1998; Choi&Behling,1997).

TQM gurus such as Deming, Crosby and Juran clearly recognized the role of top managers as key factor to effective quality management in each company and also in health care systems in many countries. Consistent with the calls by all the quality gurus, and for this reason, almost all excellence models include leadership as enabling driving contributory element (EQA, 1994; MBNQA, 1997; Kanji, 1998; NPC, 2000). Waldman (1994) in discussing the theoretical consideration of leadership and its relation to TQM emphasizes the importance of management long-term commitment to innovation and creativity. In their study, Ahire and O'Shaughnessy (1996) split the sample between high and low top management commitment and they found that firms with high top management commitment produce high quality products, the same is in hospitals. Good and high quality management provide health care services in the best way, because they understand that patient expectations and their assessment of hospital ward may be important for future leadership building on hospital market both in global and in local aspects. Choi and Behling (1997) attempted to clarify why certain TQM programs ended up with failures. By studying the managers' attitudes towards time, market and patients, they discovered that those leaders who have positive inclinations toward these factors seem to have more proactive type of quality programs, which consequently affect their company performance. Miller and Cangemi (1993) consistent with Zairi (1994) concluded that one of the most important reason for TQM failure was lack of total ownership among the leaders.

Experience of French Hospitals

The leading hospital on a medical market conducts regular quality assessment of its structures. It regularly assesses not only patient's expectations but also staff work and teamwork. Patient's words are an important source of information in screening for problems and developing an effective plan of action for quality improvement and building strong leadership position on market. This assessing of patient satisfaction as a mandatory is used by hospital managers to improve the hospital environment, patient amenities and facilities in a consumerism context of health care service. Leadership experience from France has shown that satisfaction surveys are generally considered useful in improving health care delivery process and service. This type of feedback triggers a real interest that can lead to a change in hospitals' culture and

in their perception of patients. Effects of this positive feedback seem to announce profound modifications in the hospital setting such as: integration of patient satisfaction into the continuous quality improvement and changes in the relationship across the various types of care providers with the development of multidisciplinary group discussions.

Experience of American Hospitals

Hospital leadership is a critical part of the quality in healthcare on the medical market in the States. Quality and outcome are often measured with structure and process. Outcomes include such traditional measures as morality and functional environments. Patient satisfaction is also part of this dimension. Hospitals that are leaders are interested in patient satisfaction for many reasons. The same as in other industries, customer satisfaction (patient satisfaction) is important because satisfied patients are loyal and the patients who are satisfied tend to comply with the treatment prescribed by a healthcare provider and they are also more likely not to go doctor shopping when they get better (Zendbelt, Smets, Oort, Godfried,& de Haes,, 2007). They will rather stay with the same doctor. Hospital leadership experience showed that satisfied patients are more likely to recommended their providers to their friends and to return when they need care again. It also showed how care attributes influence overall patient satisfaction. US Leadership experience indicated three variables that are important for organization that wants to create the best service. Those variables are: evaluation of overall quality of care, willingness to recommended and willingness to return and they may be affected differently by the patient care experience.

Experience of Polish Hospitals

Hospital leadership on the medical market in Poland could be assessed similarly to the US and France. Experience of these countries showed that leadership on competitive medical market, also in Poland is build through effective improvement of the quality in many aspects of the organization. An important aspect of leadership for a medical organization is also patients' point of view, their perception of services services, and overall hospital quality. Surveys researching patient satisfaction show that hospital patients put a various priorities on the staff's reactions and care attributes. The nursing and doctor's care attributes such as empathy, trust, are clearly more influential than other staff care attributes in the evaluation of overall quality of care construct. Also staff care attributes such as willingness to help if a patient has a question, helpfulness, staff explanations about medications, are clearly more influential than the nursing and doctor care attributes when it comes down to patient's willingness to recommend a particular hospital and return. Also room conditions attributes are clearly more influential than other elements of hospital care in patient's willingness to recommend particular hospital and overall quality of care in Polish hospitals. Professional working in high performing teams and creation of organizational culture dedicated to improving quality help a medical organization build a leadership position on medical service market.

To become a world-class organization on medical market, hospitals must not only know what others are doing in the market but should constantly evaluate and compare its own achievement and processes with the more superior standard that may exist in other countries. Therefore, it is critical for the hospitals to search for best practices and methods and subsequently internalize them into their own core processes. There are many ways, relative to the selected benchmark on the medical market, that can define business practices. In the search for a performance-driven definition, "best practices" are considered as a business method that provides competitive advantage through improved customer/patient service, better asset utilization, or reduced costs of patient hospitalization and whole treatment (Webb, 2000). In reality, it is hard to find best practices in everything a hospital does, thus there are no best practice medical healthcare organizations that achieved success in everything.

Leadership style on a hospital market has a positive structural relationship with financial performance and patient satisfaction, his/her willingness to recommend and return. This implies that transformational leadership is deemed suitable for managing Polish and American medical organizations. Hospitals that have leadership capability to change its management approach using best practice will further improve their performance. Best practice is considered a capability that, given proper resources, can be used to enhance profitability and financial soundness of the hospital procedures. Therefore, a hospital which wants to adopt best practice approach must resource their initiatives and increase the transformational style of managing to better understand the competition on the market, patients' expectations and must also train the staff to express empathy. Because both, transformational leadership and best practice management, work to nurture improved performance, they are complementary capabilities that should be given serious attention by medical and hospital organizations aiming to be world class.

6. TEAM EFFICIENCY INDICATORS ACROSS CULTURES

Many organizations, particularly hospitals, because of their complexity are seeking new methods that will improve their efficiency and effectiveness regardless of the outcome of the current restructuring taking place in Poland. Implementing an organizational-specific socio-technical system can lead to teamwork better, communication and improving patient service delivery in all areas of hospital process. Team efficiency indicators can help develop quality process a toward patient expectations by doing a number of things, which also help to create a positive hospital image such as:

- Clearly identify outcomes and empower employees to achieve those goals.
- Build cultural competence into quality process.
- Integrate quality development team to establish quality metrics in hospital environment.
- Align the organization's mission to the overall quality of care.

Team efficiency indicators across cultures help managers in hospital quality process. Also managers can expect a considerable return on investment, satisfied patients and staff and improved clinical outcomes. Managers have a great influence on control of efficiency in a team and can fulfill patient's expectation of quality and service by focusing first on their employees. Managers should remember that front line staff including nurses, laboratory technicians and receptionists are extremely important contributors to quality and team efficiency indicators. Receptionists have the first and last role in each healthcare organiza-

tion, and as such they give the first and last impression of the hospital or clinic which is critical for any hospital ward. Healthcare customers are the same as any business customers, so they should be greeted with the same all quality customer service attitude. In other words, healthcare customers desire to be treated with dignity, respect and care. We can see that without satisfied and confident employees quality practices have no hope of being successful. It means that satisfied employees are excellent representation of good healthcare organization and provide stellar service to all patients which adds to the total experience and is in turn perceived as high quality by patients. If we talk about team efficiency indicators we must always remember that in each organization culture staff and their behavior significantly influence teamwork efficiency indicators, so it is important for managers to continuously control employees behavior.

6.1. Responsibility of a Hospital Efficiency Indicator for Medical Service the Hospital Provides

Hospital, as an organization dealing with health care, in the service of improving the quality and comfort of patient's life, takes responsibility for the medical services being offered on the hospital grounds. By the same token, the organization is responsible for all the processes taking place there. Realization of a medical service is the outcome of many processes within the organization efficiency, and they are often very complicated and related to one another. The organization of processes connected to medical service on the hospital grounds is focused on: therapeutic processes, administrative processes, communication

Figure 2. Connections of processes influencing the offered medical service and teamwork
Source: Author's own study

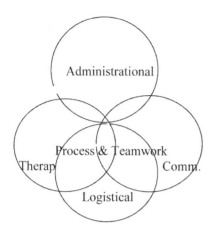

processes and logistical processes. Internal connections and influence of those processes on offered medical service can be presented on a simple scheme (Figure 2).

The common area where all the processes within the organization converge defines the area characteristic for medical service offered by a health care unit. Therefore, for the processes to work efficiently and without problems, it is important for the organization to clearly state organization's mission and constantly strive for perfection via eliminating existing imperfections, striving for optimalizing reserves and solving problems that arise in hospitals. As we can see, each process in healthcare needs an efficiency indicator. The relationship between that and good teamwork of the hospital team is a guaranty for not only perfect service, patient satisfaction and high quality of health care provided by hospital, but also a healthy proportion between personnel team management and all processes in an organization. Taking responsibility for the correct realization of medical procedure and all the processes involved in it, boils down

– in the simplest terms – to detailed analysis of Walter Shewart cycle which involves Planning, Doing, Checking and Action.

7. FEEDBACK ACROSS CULTURES IN SURGERY WARD

Successful surgery and health care processes in hospital practice in general depend on effective teamwork and communication on each level in a medical organization. Changes in surgical environment, technology and procedures further exacerbate this problem. In healthcare organization it is important to understand what makes an effective team in terms of structure and process. Teamwork is integral to professional skills set for work both in the operating theater as in the field of patient communication and communication with other members in a hospital ward. Communication failures are frequent. Communication is often too late, incomplete or not received by those concerned and left unresolved. In one third of all ineffective communications recorded there were visible effects on team process, including team tension, resource waste, delay and sometimes procedure deviation. Teamwork model in each healthcare organizations must drive from an analysis of tasks in their natural context. Teamwork behaviors are contingent upon the tasks and process that serve a particular function in surgery ward in hospital. In other words they are task dependent. Traditional model of teamwork in surgery ward in hospital practices showed that the main tasks depend on a bidirectional exchange of objects and information. Both the nurses and doctors (surgeons) need skills in timing their exchange, and ensuring that what is communicated is clear and comprehensible.

The people present in surgery unit (operating theatre) need to monitor one another's states and doings. Because the nurses must anticipate the surgeons' requests and the surgeons must appreciate that the nurses depend on others to work effectively. As we can see professional skills are highly integrated and interdependent and must be continuously trained both in technical aspect and in communication aspect because it is the only way to perfecting a complex delivery of healthcare services. Simplifying the complexity of a unit of team work in description of surgery ward is necessary. In every day practices between surgeons and nurses, and also other staff members, we observe teamwork as a following construct:

- **Cooperation:** Response of team members to one another's request.
- **Communication:** Clarity of information exchange between staff members and patients.
- **Coordination:** Objects and information exchange on each level of operating area.
- **Leadership:** Effectiveness of team control.
- **Control:** Assessing and monitoring one another's work and situation in a surgery ward.

This suggests, and means, that teamwork is not only a task but also generic behavior. Communication can amount to tasks in a work protocol. Dialogue has a potential to encourage collegial learning, change thinking between team members, support new working relationships and also improve patient care and their image about the hospital ward, and professionals working there.

Health care system in which patient complexity outcome indicators and informed families are representative of current reality and interdisciplinary approach to care, is crucial to successful navigation of patient's positive experience in the surgery ward in hospital. Lack of communication and interdisciplinary collaboration among team members may be responsible for delays, errors and in consequence patient dissatisfaction.

Organization factors indicated that in hospital practices there are many challenges for established standardized, efficient and effective teamwork and training, because working in this special environment is a cross cultural process when the treatment is a key element from quality, organizational, staff and patients' point of view. Because of this the conditions for such collaboration on many levels in organization and between each participant in medical environment we defined as a learning culture that has yet established. Structures for promoting this safety culture in the workplace do exist and a considerable body of knowledge and guidance is available on teamwork and team performance in other domains. This should help the development of teamwork in health care. To develop this model of performance and quality control and implement it in hospital practice, there needs to be a joint investment of resources at all levels within a generative healthcare organization.

CONCLUSION

Analyzing the problem of patient's satisfaction through the prism of external environment, (such as patient's family assessment of hospital image, communication culture, teamwork in medical environment, quality of care in hospital ward, and elements which are important from patient's point of view) we can say that a well-managed hospital that wants to constantly improve its image, should pay close attention to quality of the offered service, to efficient functioning within the limits of pre-established low cost, and to striving for patient's satisfaction. Such actions are the way to creating a strategy for improving the medical service quality and building a positive image for a hospital through quality and patient's satisfaction. At the same time, they guarantee patient's loyalty. Medical personnel treats patients as partners whose support in the world of increasing competition should

be ensured and whose perception of medical service and hospital itself should be positive. The results indicate that the factors pertaining to the material area – especially those related to living conditions – and also those related to empathy, personnel's competences and their communication with patients (sharing with a patient the information about his/her state of health and engaging a patient in the healing process) have very significant influence on patient's satisfaction with his/her stay at a hospital ward. Fulfilling patient's needs in functional quality area increases patient's comfort and, as a consequence, translates into satisfaction with the hospitalization.

REFERENCES

Ahire, S. L., Golhar, D. Y., & Waller, M. A. (1996). Development and validation of TQM implementation constructs. *Decision Sciences, 27,* 23–56. doi:10.1111/j.1540-5915.1996.tb00842.x

Ahire, S. L., & O'Shaughnessy, K. C. (1998). The role of top management commitment in quality management: An empirical analysis of the auto parts industry. *International Journal of Quality Science, 31,* 5–37. doi:10.1108/13598539810196868

Baker, D. P., Beaubien, J. M., & Holtzman, A. K. (2003). *Medical team training programs: An independent case study analysis.* Washington, DC: American Institutes for Research.

Baker, D. P., Gustafson, S., Beaubien, J., et al. (2005). Medical teamwork and patient safety: The evidence-based relation: Literature review (AHRQ Publication No. 05-0053). Rockville, MD: Agency for Healthcare Research and Quality (AHRQ).

Baker, D. P., Gustafson, S., Beaubien, J. M., Salas, E., & Barach, P. (2003). *Medical teamwork and patient safety: The evidence-based relation.* Washington, DC: American Institutes for Research.

Barksdale, H. C., Johnson, J. T., & Suh, M. (1997). A relationship maintenance model: A comparison between managed health care and traditional-free for service. *Serv. Journal of Business Research, 40,* 237–247. doi:10.1016/S0148-2963(96)00240-8

Bass, B. M. (1985). *Leadership and performance beyond expectations.* New York: Free Press.

Bass, B. M., & Avolio, B. J. (1994). *Improving organizational effectiveness through transformational leadership.* Newbury Park, CA: Sage.

Boyer, L., Francois, P., Doutre, E., Weil, G., & Labarere, J. (2006). Perception and use of the result of patient satisfaction surveys by care providers in a French teaching hospital. *International Journal for Quality in Health Care, 18*(5), 356–364. doi:10.1093/intqhc/mzl029

Bruke-Miller, J. K., Cook, I. A., Cohen, M. H., Hessol, N. A., Wilson, T. E., & Richardson, L. et al. (2006). Longitudinal relationship between use of highly active antiretroviral therapy and satisfaction with care among women living with HIV/AIDS. *American Journal of Public Health, 96*(6), 1044–1051. doi:10.2105/AJPH.2005.061929 PMID:16670232

Burns, C. (2005). *Leadership.* University of Strathclyde.

Burroughs, T. E., Waterman, A. R., Cira, J., & Dunagan, W. C. (1999). Understanding patient willingness to recommend and return: A strategy for prioritizing improvement opportunities. *Joint Commission of Quality Improvement, 25*(6), 271–287. PMID:10367265

Chet, K., & McCluskey, P. (2004). Public versus private patient priorities and satisfaction in cataract surgery. *Clinical & Experimental Ophthalmology, 32,* 482. doi:10.1111/j.1442-9071.2004.00868.x PMID:15498059

Choi, T. Y., & Behling, O. C. (1997). Top managers and TQM success: One more look after all these years. *The Academy of Management Executive, 11*(1), 37–47.

Code de la Sante Publique. (1996). Ordonance no 96 – 346 du 24 avril 1996 portant reforme de l'hospitalization publique et privee. *Journal Officiele de la Republique Francaise*, 6324-6336.

Connerley, M. L., & Pedersen, P. (2005). *Leadership in a diverse and multicultural environment: Developing awareness, knowledge, and skills*. Thousand Oaks, CA: Sage Publications.

Council of Europe. (n.d.). *European convention for the prevention of torture and inhuman or degrading treatment or punishment*. Brussels: Council of Europe.

Cunningham, L. (1991). *The quality connection in health care: Integrating patient satisfaction and risk management*. San Francisco, CA: Jossey-Bass.

Daaleman, T. P., & Mueller, J. (2004). Chatting behavior and patient satisfaction in the outpatient encounter. *Journal of the National Medical Association*, 96(5), 666–670. PMID:15160982

Dawes, P., & Davison, P. (1994). Informed consent: What do patients want to know? *Journal of the Royal Society of Medicine*, 87, 149–152. PMID:8158593

Elder, M. J., & Suter, A. (2004). What patients want to know before they have cataract surgery. *The British Journal of Ophthalmology*, 88, 331–332. doi:10.1136/bjo/2003.020453 PMID:14977762

European Quality Award (EQA). (1994). *TI Europe excellence*. Retrieved from http://www.ti.com/europe/docs/busex/winner.html

Flin, R., Fletcher, G., & McGeorge, P. et al. (2003). Anaesthetists' attitudes to teamwork and safety. *Anaesthesia*, 58, 233–242. doi:10.1046/j.1365-2044.2003.03039.x PMID:12603453

Flin, R., & Maran, N. (2004). Identifying and training non-technical skills for teams in acute medicine. *Quality & Safety in Health Care*, 13(Suppl. 1), i80–i84. doi:10.1136/qshc.2004.009993 PMID:15465960

Francken, D. A., & Van Raaij, W. F. (1981). Satisfaction with leisure time activities. *Journal of Leisure Research*, 13, 337–352.

Friesner, D., Neufelder, D., Raisor, J., & Bozman, S. C. (2009). How to improve patient satisfaction when patients are already satisfied: A continuous process-improvement approach. *Hospital Topics*, 87(1), 24–40. doi:10.3200/HTPS.87.1.24-40 PMID:19103585

Gaba, D. M., Howard, S. K., Fish, K. J., Smith, B. E., & Sowb, Y. A. (2001). Simulation-based training in anesthesia crisis resource management (ACRM): A decade of experience. *Simulation & Gaming*, 32, 175–193. doi:10.1177/104687810103200206

Gaba, D. M., Howard, S. K., Flanagan, B., Smith, B. E., Fish, K. J., & Botney, R. (1998). Assessment of clinical performance during simulated crises using both technical and behavioral ratings. *Anesthesiology*, 89, 8–18. doi:10.1097/00000542-199807000-00005 PMID:9667288

Garden, A. L., Merry, A. F., Holland, R. L., & Petrie, K. J. (1996). Anaesthesia information – What patients want to know about anaesthesia. *Anaesthesia and Intensive Care*, 24, 594–598. PMID:8909673

Geneva Convention. (1949, August 12). *Convention (III) relative to the treatment of prisoners of war*. Geneva, Switzerland: Geneva Convention.

Healey, A. N., Undre, S., & Vincent, C. A. (2004). Developing observational measures of performance in surgical teams. *Quality & Safety in Health Care*, *13*, i33–i40. doi:10.1136/qshc.2004.009936 PMID:15465953

Hemphill, J. K., & Coons, A. E. (1957). Development of the leader behavior description questionnaire. In *Leader behavior: Its description and measurement*. Columbus, OH: Bureau of Business Research of The Ohio State University.

Holzman, R. S., Cooper, J. B., Gaba, D. M., Philip, J. H., Small, S. D., & Feinstein, D. (1995). Anesthesia crisis resource management: Real-life simulation training in operating room crises. *Journal of Clinical Anesthesia*, *7*, 675–687. doi:10.1016/0952-8180(95)00146-8 PMID:8747567

Horner, M. (1997). Leadership theory: Past, present and future. *Team Performance Management*, *3*(4), 270–287. doi:10.1108/13527599710195402

House, R. J., Hanges, P. J., & Javidan, M. et al. (2004). *Culture, leadership, and organizations: The GLOBE study of 62 societies*. Thousand Oaks, CA: Sage.

House, R. J., Javidan, M., & Hanges, P. et al. (2002). Understanding cultures and implicit leadership theories across the globe: An introduction to project GLOBE. *Journal of World Business*, *37*(1), 3. doi:10.1016/S1090-9516(01)00069-4

Howard, S. K., Gaba, D. M., Fish, K. J., Yang, G., & Sarnquist, F. H. (1992). Anesthesia crisis resource management training: Teaching anesthesiologists to handle critical incidents. *Aviation, Space, and Environmental Medicine*, *63*, 763–770. PMID:1524531

Isern, J., & Pung, C. (2007). Driving radical change. *The McKinsey Quarterly*, *4*(24).

Kain, Z. N., Wang, S. M., Caramico, L. A., Hofstadter, M., & Mayes, L. C. (1997). Parental desire for perioperative information and informed consent: A two-phase study. *Anesthesia and Analgesia*, *84*, 299–306. PMID:9024018

Kanji, G. K. (1998). Measurement of business excellence. *Total Quality Management*, *9*, 633–643. doi:10.1080/0954412988325

Kaplan, R. S., & Norton, D. P. (1996, January-February). Using the balance scorecard as a strategic management system. *Harvard Business Review*, 11.

Knox, G. E., & Simpson, K. R. (2004). Teamwork: The fundamental building block of high-reliability organizations and patient safety. In *Patient safety handbook*. Boston: Jones and Bartlett.

Kohn, L. T., Corrigan, J. M., & Donaldson, M. S. (1999). *To err is human*. Washington, DC: National Academy Press.

Labarere, J., & Francois, P. (1999). Evaluation de la satisfaction des patients par les etablissements de soins: Revue de la literature. *Revue d'Epidemiologie et de Sante Publique*, *47*, 175–184. PMID:10367304

Labrere, J., Francois, P., & Auquier, P. et al. (2001). Development of a French impatient satisfaction questionnaire. *International Journal for Quality in Health Care, 13*, 99–108. doi:10.1093/intqhc/13.2.99 PMID:11430670

Lee, K. J. (2005). A practical method of predicting client revisit intention in a hospital setting. *Health Care Management Review, 31*(3), 157–167. doi:10.1097/00004010-200504000-00009 PMID:15923917

Leonard, M., Graham, S., & Bonacum, D. (2004). The human factor: The critical importance of effective teamwork and communication in providing safe care. *Quality & Safety in Health Care, 13*(Suppl. 1), i85–i90. doi:10.1136/qshc.2004.010033 PMID:15465961

Levine, A. S., Plume, S. K., & Nelson, E. C. (1997). Transforming patient feedback into strategic actions plan. *Quality Management Care, 5*, 28–40.

Lingard, L., Regehr, G., & Orser, B. et al. (2008). Evaluation of a preoperative checklist and team briefing among surgeons, nurses, and anesthesiologists to reduce failures in communication. *Archives of Surgery (Chicago, Ill.), 143*, 12–17. doi:10.1001/archsurg.2007.21 PMID:18209148

Lonsdale, N., & Hutchison, G. L. (1991). Patients' desire for information about anaesthesia. *Anaesthesia, 46*, 410–412. doi:10.1111/j.1365-2044.1991.tb09560.x PMID:2035796

Makary, M. A., Sexton, J. B., & Freischlag, J. A. et al. (2006). Operating room teamwork among physicians and nurses: Teamwork in the eye of the beholder. *Journal of the American College of Surgeons, 202*, 746–752. doi:10.1016/j.jamcollsurg.2006.01.017 PMID:16648014

Malcolm Baldrige National Quality Award (MBNQA). (1997). *The Malcolm Baldrige criteria for performance excellence*. Author.

Mazzocco, K., Petitti, D. B., & Fong, K. T. et al. (2009). Surgical team behaviors and patient outcomes. *American Journal of Surgery, 197*, 678–685. doi:10.1016/j.amjsurg.2008.03.002 PMID:18789425

McAlearney, A. S. (2008, September/October). Using leadership development programs to improve quality and efficiency in healthcare. *Journal of Healthcare Management*. PMID:18856137

Miller, M. R., Elixhauser, A., & Zhan, C. et al. (2001). Patient safety indicators: Using administrative data to identify potential patient-safety concerns. *Health Services Research, 36*, 110–132. PMID:16148964

Miller, R. L., & Cangemi, J. P. (1993). Why total quality management fails: Perspective from top management. *Journal of Management Development, 12*(7), 40–50. doi:10.1108/02621719310044956

Mills, P., Neily, J., & Dunn, E. (2008). Teamwork and communication in surgical teams: Implications for patient safety. *Journal of the American College of Surgeons, 206*, 107–112. doi:10.1016/j.jamcollsurg.2007.06.281 PMID:18155575

Montaglione, C. J. (1999). The physician-patient relationship: Cornerstone of patient trust, satisfaction, and loyalty. *Managed Care Quarterly, 7*(3), 5–21. PMID:10620959

Moorman, C., Zeltman, G., & Deshpande, R. (1992). Relationship between providers and users of marketing research: The dynamic of trust within and between organization. *JMR, Journal of Marketing Research, 29*, 314–329. doi:10.2307/3172742

Morey, J. C., Simon, R., Jay, G. D., Wears, R., Salisbury, M., Dukes, K. A., & Berns, S. D. (2002). Error reduction and performance improvement in the emergency department through formal teamwork training: Evaluation results of the MedTeams project. *Health Services Research, 37,* 1553–1581. doi:10.1111/1475-6773.01104 PMID:12546286

Morgan, L. W., & Schwab, I. R. (1986). Informed consent in senile cataract extraction. *Archives of Ophthalmology, 104,* 42–45. doi:10.1001/archopht.1986.01050130052018 PMID:3942543

Newton-Howes, P. A., Bedford, N. D., Dobbs, B. R., & Frizelle, F. A. (1998). Informed consent: What do patients want to know? *The New Zealand Medical Journal, 111,* 340–342. PMID:9785548

Nisselle, P. (1993). Informed consent. *The New Zealand Medical Journal, 106,* 331–332. PMID:8341472

NPC. (2000). *Prime minister's quality award: Regulation and application procedure.* Kuala Lumpur: Jabatan Percetakan Negara.

Ouschan, R., Sweeney, J., & Lester, J. (2006). Customer empowerment and relationship outcomes in healthcare consultations. *European Journal of Marketing, 40*(9/10), 1068–1086. doi:10.1108/03090560610681014

Pattison, S., & Pill, R. (2004). *Values in professional practice: Lessons for health, social care and other professionals.* Oxford, UK: Radcliffe Medical Press.

Peel, M. (2005). Human rights and medical ethics. *Journal of the Royal Society of Medicine, 98,* 171–173. doi:10.1258/jrsm.98.4.171 PMID:15805563

Roberts, K. H. (1990a). Managing high reliability organizations. *California Management Review,* 101–113.

Salas, E., Dickinson, T. L., & Converse, S. A. (1992). Toward an understanding of team performance and training. In *Teams: Their training and performance.* Norwood, NJ: Ablex.

Schurr, P. H., & Ozanne, J. L. (1985). Influences on exchange processes: Buyer's preconception of a seller's trustworthiness and bargaining toughness. *The Journal of Consumer Research, 11,* 939–953. doi:10.1086/209028

Schwartz, S. H. (1994). Are there universal aspects in the structure and contents of human values? *The Journal of Social Issues, 50,* 19–45. doi:10.1111/j.1540-4560.1994.tb01196.x

Schwartz, S. H. (1996). Value priorities and behavior: Applying a theory of integrated value systems. In *The psychology of values: The Ontario symposium.* Mahwah, NJ: Lawrence Erlbaum Associates.

Schwartz, S. H. (2005). *Human values.* Brussels: European Social Survey Education Net.

Schwartz, S. H. (2005b). Robustness and fruitfulness of a theory of universals in individual human values. In *Valores e trabalho.* Brasilia: Editora Universidade de Brasilia.

Shortell, S. M., Casalino, L. P., & Fisher, E. S. (2010, July). How the center for medicare and medicaid innovation should test accountable care organizations. *Health Affairs*. doi:10.1377/hlthaff.2010.0453 PMID:20606176

Sitzia, J., & Wood, N. (1997). Patient satisfaction: A review of issues and concepts. *Social Science & Medicine*, *45*(12), 1828–1843. doi:10.1016/S0277-9536(97)00128-7 PMID:9447632

Smith, P. B., Peterson, M. F., & Schwartz, S. H. (2002). Cultural values, sources of guidance, and their relevance to managerial behavior: A 47-nation study. *Journal of Cross-Cultural Psychology*, *33*(2), 188–208. doi:10.1177/0022022102033002005

Smith-Jentsch, K. A., Salas, E., & Baker, D. P. (1996). Training team performance-related assertiveness. *Personnel Psychology*, *49*, 909–936. doi:10.1111/j.1744-6570.1996. tb02454.x

Sulzer-Azaroff, B., & Austin, J. (2000). Does BBS work? Behavior-based safety and injury reduction: A survey of evidence. *Professional Safety*, *45*, 19–24.

Surgical Checklist, W. H. O. (2010). UK pilot experience. *BMJ (Clinical Research Ed.)*, *340*, 133–135.

Thomas, E. J., Sexton, J. B., & Helmreich, R. L. (2004). Translating teamwork behaviors from aviation to healthcare: Development of behavioral markers for neonatal resuscitation. *Quality & Safety in Health Care*, *13*, i57–i64. doi:10.1136/qshc.2004.009811 PMID:15465957

Undre, S., Sevdalis, N., & Healey, A. N. et al. (2006). Teamwork in the operating theatre: Cohesion or confusion? *Journal of Evaluation in Clinical Practice*, *12*, 182–189. doi:10.1111/j.1365-2753.2006.00614.x PMID:16579827

United Nations. (n.d.a). *International covenant on civil and political rights*. New York: UN.

United Nations. (n.d.b). *International covenant on economic, social and cultural rights*. New York: UN.

United Nations. (n.d.c). *Universal declaration of human rights*. New York: UN.

Volpe, C. E., Cannon-Bowers, J. A., Salas, E., & Spector, P. E. (1996). The impact of cross training on team functioning: An empirical investigation. *Human Factors*, *38*, 87–100. doi:10.1518/001872096778940741 PMID:8682521

Waldman, D. A. (1994). Designing performance measurement systems for total quality implementation. *Journal of Organizational Change Management*, *7*(2), 31–44. doi:10.1108/09534819410056113

Webb, D. A. (2000). E-marketplace best practices. *Industrial Distribution*, *89*(9), 122.

Westbrook, R. A. (1981). Sources of satisfaction with retail outlets. *J Retail*, 68-85.

Wilson, K. A., Burke, C. S., Priest, H., & Salas, E. (2005). Promoting health care safety through training high reliability teams. *Quality & Safety in Health Care*, *14*, 303–309. doi:10.1136/qshc.2004.010090 PMID:16076797

World Medical Association. (n.d.). *Declaration of Tokyo. Author.*

Young, G., Materko, M., & Desai, K. (2000). Patient satisfaction with hospital care: Effects of demographic and institutional characteristics. *Medical Care, 38,* 325–334. doi:10.1097/00005650-200003000-00009 PMID:10718357

Yukl, G. (2006). *Leadership in organizations* (6th ed.). Upper Saddle River, NJ: Prentice Hall.

Yule, S., Flin, R., & Paterson-Brown, S. et al. (2006). Non-technical skills for surgeons in the operating room: A review of the literature. *Surgery, 139,* 140–149. doi:10.1016/j.surg.2005.06.017 PMID:16455321

Zairi, M. (1994). *Measuring performance for business result.* London: Chapman & Hall. doi:10.1007/978-94-011-1302-1

Zandbelt, L. C., Smets, E., Oort, J., Godfried, H., & de Haes, H. (2007). Medical specialists' patient-centered communication and patient reported outcomes. *Medical Care, 45*(4), 330–339. doi:10.1097/01.mlr.0000250482.07970.5f PMID:17496717

Chapter 6
Concept and Types of Organizational Cultures of Hospitals

Łukasz Sulkowski
Jagiellonian University, Poland

Joanna Sulkowska
University of Social Sciences, Poland

ABSTRACT

This chapter sets out to analyze the problem of defining the concept of organizational culture as well as models and typologies used in reference materials. It presents various issues of organizational culture: paradigms of organizational culture, definitions of organizational culture, and two-dimensional typologies of organizational culture. The single-dimensional classifications present the following dichotomies: 1) weak culture – strong culture, 2) positive culture – negative culture, 3) pragmatic culture – bureaucratic culture, 4) introvert culture – extrovert culture, 5) conservative culture – innovative culture, 6) hierarchic culture – egalitarian culture, 7) individualist culture – collectivist culture. Furthermore, this chapter includes: multidimensional typologies of organizational culture, corporate identity – alternative approach to organizational culture and relations between culture, and structure, strategy, and organization setting. Moreover, based on the quality pilot study, it strives to explain peculiarity of this concept in relation to Polish hospitals. Results of pilot studies of organizational cultures of hospitals in Poland relate to four hospitals in Lodz Province.

INTRODUCTION

Organizational culture proved to be a difficult research issue, firstly due to ambiguity of the very term, but also because of the lack of effective tools which would allow to look into given organizational cultures. The problem seems to intensify in the case of such organizations as hospitals, where organizational culture is also influenced by values and professional standards of doctors and medical staff. Nonetheless, organizational

DOI: 10.4018/978-1-4666-4325-3.ch006

culture in hospitals constitutes a significant theoretical issue, mainly due to the fact that the problem has not been conceptualized yet, and, at the same time, is of pragmatic importance, as organizational culture often establishes social norms which may hamper organizational changes.

PARADIGMS OF ORGANIZATIONAL CULTURE

The cultural movement in management is struggling with the basic epistemological problems relating to the ways of defining culture. There is no consensus among scholars as to the ways of understanding or paradigms of organizational culture. Indeed, this is an issue related to the ambiguity of cultural studies in general (Kroeber & Kluckhon, 1952). We can distinguish a number of paradigms of understanding culture, and, which follows, organizational culture. Looking for paradigms of thinking about culture in general, we must identify at least three orientations: functional-structuralist trend (closely related to NFS), interpretative-symbolic approach (identical with IS paradigm) and postmodernism (also called radical humanism) and poststructuralism (associated with the critical trend – CMS) (Sułkowski, 2005). In cultural studies the classical approach was functionalism, whose foundations were created in the first half of the twentieth century and led to structuralism. The development of hermeneutics, and humanistic sociology and cultural anthropology became the basis for the emergence of the symbolic-interpretative paradigm. In the eighties and nineties of the twentieth century due to critical philosophy and cultural anthropology, the role of poststructuralist and postmodernist orientation increased.

A similar distinction paradigms can be applied to organizational culture. M.J. Hatch proposes to distinguish four paradigms in the sciences of management: classical, modernist, interpretative-symbolic and postmodernist (Hatch, 2002). Current organizational culture did not function in classical approaches to management. Modernism puts an organizational culture in terms of functionalist and structuralist as one of the subsystems of organization and refers to the methodology of representative comparative studies. The need to control the organizational culture is suggested, leading to its instrumentation. Interpretative-symbolic approach describes it as a process of constructing and reading of social reality and symbolic organization of language in human activities in the group. Qualitative methodology is preferred, such as organizational ethnography. It is sceptical to assess the possibilities of instrumental development of organizational culture. Postmodernism emphasizes the defragmentation, cultural and epistemological relativism, textual and narrative approach. The sense of creating a methodology is neglected, and the flagship 'anti-method' 'becomes a deconstruction (Hatch, 2002).

L. Smircich reviews the paradigms underlying the concept of binding the culture of the organization (Smircich, 1983b). He finds five common areas: (1) cross-cultural comparative studies, (2) internal corporate culture, (3) cognitive theory of organization, (4) organizational symbolism (5) unconscious and subconscious processes in the organization (Table 1).

Organizational culture can be interpreted as an independent variable (external) - due to the impact of the environment on the organization, the internal variable of the organization or a root metaphor (Thompson & Luthans,

Table 1. Typology of cultural research in the theory of organization from the point of view of the assumptions related to culture and its role in organizational reality

Culture as Independent Variable	Culture as Internal Variable	Culture as Root Metaphor
Cross-cultural management National styles of management. Similarities and differences in management practices in different countries. Relation between effectiveness and national culture. Globalization of corporate culture.	**Culture of a company** Management of company culture. Relation between effectiveness and corporate culture. Changes and classifications of corporate cultures.	**Cognitive approach** Organization as a cognitive venture. **Symbolist approach** Organization – symbolic discourse. **Drama approach** People as actors of an organization. Organization as a theatre. **Interpretative approach** Organizational reality as an intentional construct of consciousness. **Psycho-dynamic approach** Study of organization as a form of human expression.
FUNCTIONALISM		**NON FUNCTIONALIST PARADIGMS**

Source: On the basis of M. Kostera, 1996.

1990). Culture seen in the perspective of cross-cultural comparative research in management is an independent variable affecting the organization (Kostera, 1996). In this regard, it is understood in functionalist terms, and a specific context exerts influence on the management process. This approach included the study of social and national leadership and management styles, and the comparative study of the impact of cultural context on organizations. Culture - the internal variable is formed as a result of the organization, is peculiar for it. Organizations in this perspective can shape organizational culture. Studies relate primarily to its creation and development, typology and the relationship with the efficiency of the entire organization. Culture can also be understood as an root metaphor, in terms of different paradigms of functionalism. Organizational culture is identified within them with the organization itself. Organizations are understood primarily as symbolic activities, a form of human expression and creativity, cognitive ventures or symptoms of deep structures of human mind or the com-

munity. A change of perspective is based on these paradigms. Economic organizations cease to be primarily economic projects, but the accents are different - psychological, social and symbolic aspects of their existence.

J. Martin performs the classification of the concept of organizational culture approach by analyzing more than 70 researchers and classifying them into one of three theoretical perspectives. The prospect of integration focuses on the pursuit of homogeneity and stability of organizational culture, in which it resembles the functionalist-structuralist paradigm. The prospect of differentiation allows for the possibility of divisions, tensions, conflicts, creation of subcultures and separation, in which it is closer to interpretative-symbolic paradigm. The prospect of flow-oriented fragmentation, division and constant change of ungraspable culture lies closest to the postmodernist and poststructuralist paradigm (Martin, 2002).

Apart from these three similar paradigm concepts of organizational culture, many researchers present their own proposals of paradigms, schools or approaches to organizational culture usually neglecting the fact that the genesis of culture lies in the research culture in general (O'Donovan, 2006).

DEFINITIONS OF ORGANIZATIONAL CULTURE

The consequence of the absence of a single paradigm, and even the consent of the researchers regarding one way to organize approaches to organizational culture, is the multitude of definitions of organizational culture and of the descriptions of its components, typologies and relationships with other areas of the organizations with the environment. In the literature dozens of different definitions that can be classified as belonging to different paradigms can be encountered (Table 2).

Definitions of organizational culture are so dispersed due to difficulties in creating coherent research programs and case studies. Organizational culture becomes too capacious and too difficult to be operationalized. Researchers dealing with cultural studies rarely take advantage of their colleagues' contributions while the research output is not compiled as it should be.

Despite the different descriptions of organizational culture, there are certain characteristics that are commonly associated with this concept. These include: 1) a system of values (ideology of the organization shared by its members), 2) organizational climate (shared perceptions of organizational situations), 3) system of beliefs (culture of a group with respect to patterns of effective action).

In summary, it can be said that organizational culture is a social product, created and maintained by a group of people who form an organization. To a large extent, it exists in the minds of employees, their feelings, reactions to and perceptions of different situations. It is also a way of understanding and identifying one's own organization. Organizational culture is related to the rituals and symbols specific to the organization, it is a kind of collective thinking. It should be emphasized that it is subject to change, although the changes are usually introduced gradually and slowly.

Table 2. Definitions of organizational culture

Author	Definitions of Organizational Culture
E. Jacques	Habitual or traditional manner of thinking and acting, to some extent shared by members of an organization and at least partially accepted by employees.
E. Schein	The paradigm of shared and fundamental assumptions created by a given group when solving the issues of environmental adaptation and internal integration. The paradigm may be deemed conventional. New members of organization must accept it as a proper method of solving organizational problems.
H. Schenplein	Values, norms and beliefs that are commonly accepted in organization as a part of the entire system.
G. Hofstede	"Mind programming" directed at organization members, constitutes a set of values, norms and organizational rules effectively inculcated into the group (Hofstede, 2000).
P.M. Blau	Specific, unwritten "game rules" in social organization allowing participants of the social life to properly understand organization and identify with it (Blau, 1974).
L. Smircich	Networks of meanings created by people in the course of organizational process (Smircich, 1983a).
R. Deshapande, R. Parasurman	Unwritten, usually subconsciously perceived rules filling the gap between unwritten area and situation actually taking place in the organization (Deshapande & Parasurman, 1987).
J.M. Kobi, H. Wüthrich	Organizations not only have culture, but also constitute culture themselves (Kobi & Wüthrich, 1991).

Source: Own study.

MODELS OF ORGANIZATIONAL CULTURE

E. Schein dealt with systematization of the components of organizational culture. The author emphasizes that organizational culture exists partly to respond to two types of problems that affect every organization: (1) problems in adapting to the environment of the organization and (2) problems of internal integration (Schein, 1983; Schein, 1984; Schein, 1985). His model consists of the elements called the levels of culture that have been isolated because of their durability and visibility. The author sees the culture of the organization as a set of dominant values and norms of behaviour characteristic of a given organization, encouraged by the assumptions about the nature of reality and manifesting itself through artefacts - external and artificial creations of a culture (Schein, 2010). According to this author, culture exists on three levels: on the surface there are artefacts, below there are values and norms of behaviour, and on the lowest level there are the main, the basic assumptions.

The artefacts can include: logo, look and design of buildings, dress code, signs of status, common expressions and mental shortcuts, jargon, slogans, myths, legends, ceremonies and rituals. Regarding the norms and values, it can be divided into those that are declared (declaring that the organization is good, what is laudable and what is wrong and reprehensible) and observed (that can be learned from a variety of informal talks and behaviours). The foundation and core of the organizational culture are the assumptions, i.e. sets the basic patterns of orientation and ideas and the philosophical and ideological assumptions guiding perception and action.

Since there are numerous concepts to describe organizational cultures, there are also a variety of typologies. The dimensions used in different models of types of organizational cultures emerge partly during the exploration of researchers to address the specific characteristics of national cultures differentiating in cross-cultural research.

TWO-DIMENSIONAL TYPOLOGIES OF ORGANIZATIONAL CULTURE

Among scholars there is disagreement as to the dimensions of organizational culture, but regardless of their opinions, most of them see the relationship between dimensions of culture proposed by Geert Hofstede, such as individualism versus collectivism and power distance and corporate culture (Kanungo & Jaeger, 1990; Mendonca & Kanungo, 1990).

Reviewing the literature, number of typologies and classifications of organizational culture can be found. Some of them are based on simple dichotomies investing culture of the organization on the continuum of intensity of a particular trait. Others are more complex two-fold, and sometimes multi-dimensional models.

The analysis can be started from single-dimensional classifications. Among the most common in the literature, the following dichotomies can be indicated:

1. Weak culture – strong culture,
2. Positive culture – negative culture,
3. Pragmatic culture – bureaucratic culture,
4. Introvert culture – extrovert culture,
5. Conservative culture – innovative culture,
6. Hierarchic culture – egalitarian culture,
7. Individualist culture – collectivist culture.

1. Weak Culture – Strong Culture

Please see Table 3.

2. Positive Culture – Negative Culture

The criterion to distinguish positive culture from negative culture (Table 4) is above all its impact on the long-term effectiveness of the organization. Positive culture should favour reaching the objectives set by the management, while a negative culture may hinder the achievement of these objectives. P. Bate, on the basis of studies, described the syndrome of negative organizational culture, which may be contrasted with a positive culture (Bate, 1984).

Manifestations of 'negative cultures' are associated with the threat of passivity (subordination), and conservatism. Passivity may

Table 3. Weak culture versus strong culture

Features	Strong culture	Weak culture
Degree of acceptance of organizational values and norms.	Consensus regarding organizational norms and values.	Conflict regarding organizational norms and values.
Feeling of community among the employees.	Strong feeling of community among the employees.	Feeling of conflict of interests and aiming at confrontation.
Degree of formalization of norms.	Unwritten, generally accepted norms.	Formalized rules, often neglected.
Commitment of employees in company matters.	High degree of company's commitment.	Low degree of company's commitment.
Degree of employees' loyalty to the company.	High degree of employees' loyalty to the company.	Low degree of employees' loyalty to the company.
Emotions related with being a member of the organization – pride or shame.	Pride related with belonging to the company.	Shame related with belonging to the company.
Employee emotions – feeling of appreciation or humiliation.	Feeling of employee's appreciation in the company.	Feeling of employee's humiliation. in the company..

Source: Own study.

Table 4. Negative culture versus positive culture

Features	Negative Culture	Positive Culture
Emotions	Emotional coldness – avoiding expressing emotions and feelings.	Moderate or strong emotional character – sharing emotions with others.
Personalization of corporate ties.	Depersonalization of interpersonal relations – high degree of formalization.	Personalization of relations in a company – personal, direct messages, lower degree of formalization.
Activity of employees.	Subordination – waiting for superiors' cues in order to solve the problem.	Active character – aiming to independent decision-making and solving problems by the employees themselves.
Attitude to changes.	Conservatism – lack of flexibility in new situations.	Flexibility – openness to changes and readiness to implement them.
Isolation.	Concentration on one's own responsibilities, specialization.	Wider look on the functioning of the company, generalization attempts.
Attitude to other organizations.	Antipathy – people are opponents rather than supporters (individualism).	Sympathy – people are supporters rather than opponents (collectivism).

Source: Own study on the basis of P. Bate, 1984.

result from the dominance of paternalistic management style. A sense of safety resulting from the submission of the organizational power frees employees from having to decide. Conservatism on the other hand is combined with the desire to maintain the known, secure *status quo*. However, in situations of turbulence in the environment of the organization both passivity and conservatism contribute to decreasing the competitiveness of the company

3. Pragmatic Culture – Bureaucratic Culture

Bureaucratic culture is fettered by a number of formalized rules, orders and prohibitions governing life in detail the organization. It is the culture of the written word, with limited and routinized interpersonal contacts. Pragmatic culture is characterized by the lack of specific organizational regulations. There is a clear orientation towards verbal contacts of interpersonal nature.

4. Introvert Culture – Extrovert Culture

Analogy of introvert culture versus extrovert culture was moved from the level of personality to the organizational one (Sikorski, 1990) shown in Table 5. Simply phrased, it can be said that the introverted personality is focused on oneself and closed to other people, while the extrovert personality is focused on other people, and therefore open. By moving to the classification to the level of organizational culture, introverted culture can be described as closed, and extroverted – as open ones.

Family businesses are threatened with introvercy, which is manifests itself by closing organization from external influences. Employees representing the family dominate in the organization are characterized by a distrust of strangers, which creates a kind of hermetic culture. Managers must pay attention to the need to open the organization to external influences.

5. Conservative Culture – Innovative Culture

Conservative culture is combined with the desire to reduce uncertainty, to operate in a low risk environment, to maintain the *status quo* and emphasize the stabilizing role of the organization. The role of tradition is emphasized in the company. Options have been created and the scenarios are deterministic, it is assumed to avoid risk, minimize the information deficit

Table 5. Introvert cultures versus extrovert cultures and organizational culture

Features	Introvert Cultures	Extrovert Cultures
Tolerance against others.	Low tolerance against different views and values.	High tolerance against different views and values.
Knowledge of other employees' problems.	Large degree of knowledge of other employees' problems.	Low degree of knowledge other employees' problems .
Sensitiveness towards other employees' feelings.	High sensitiveness towards other employees' problems.	Low sensitiveness towards other employees' problems.
Suspicion towards new employees in the organization.	High degree of distrust towards new employees.	Conventional trust towards new employees.
Attitude towards changing a job.	They do not plan, neither imagine, changing a job.	They may plan changing a job depending on offers on the market.

Source: Own study, on the basis of: Cz. Sikorski, 1990.

and to adopt one-option planning. Changes are primarily regarded as a threat.

Innovative culture is oriented to changes and is associated with a willingness to deal with the deficit of information and the propensity to take risks. Organizations characterized by a high tolerance for uncertainty do not seek to maintain the status quo, but are willing to accept external changes and to implement transformations. Adaptation to changes in the environment is usually easier for them, they are more flexible. They give more importance to being open organizations rather than to their stability (Sułkowski, 2002) (Table 6).

The danger of conservatism is one of the key cultural threats to contemporary organizations operating in a high volatility environment. The key is to strive to maintain and transmit the same values, traditions are cultivated, the aim is to operate in the conditions of *status quo*. Although the conservative orientation is conducive to the stability of the company, too strong conservatism may be dangerous for each economic entity. Conservative enterprises isolate themselves from information and resist to changes. They can be effective only under conditions of considerable stability of the sector, which happens more and more rarely.

6. Hierarchic Culture – Egalitarian Culture

Preferring hierarchy is associated with the belief that people are different and the organization reflects this diversity. Thus, in the organization there should occur multiple levels of management and there should be a significant variation in the rights, privileges and benefits of different groups of workers. Particular attention is paid to maintaining discipline and strengthening the authority of management. The hierarchical organization involves domination of the strong acceptance of the diversity of employees. There is a clear preference for elitist thinking. Accented is the importance of discipline and order, created by a power structure.

The desire for equality stems from the conviction that people are entitled to similar rights and the organization is a reflection of this basic equality. Thus, the organization should have a flat structure and limit the maximum number of levels of management. Significant variations of powers, privileges and benefits among employees are not encouraged. Equality raises the following attitudes in organizations: accentuation of similarities between the workers, the preference for

Table 6. Conservative culture and innovative cultures

Features	Conservative Culture	Innovative Culture
Change-orientation	Orientation to maintain the *status quo* in the organization.	Orientation to change in the organization.
Entrepreneurship	Low level of entrepreneurship and innovation.	High level of entrepreneurship.
Attitude to tradition	Respect and tradition are treated as model.	Distance, tradition is treated as a burden.
Respect to authorities	High respect towards experienced persons in the organization.	Undermining the authority, promoting 'fresh blood'.
Attitude towards information	Striving to work in the conditions of full information. .	Acceptance of taking actions in the information deficit conditions.

Source: Own study.

egalitarian thinking, focus on spontaneity and flexibility of the structures and power relations (Sułkowski, 2002) (Table 7).

Hierarchy-equality dimension is primary in relation to another one defined as authoritarianism - the democracy (participation). Authoritarianism is the tendency to single, undisputed method of decision making in the organization, while the democratic means striving toward the group (fully participatory) decision-making. Hierarchy-equality dimension is also primary in relation to the dimension of the centralization of power (Harrison, 1972). In G. Hofstede's concept the hierarchy-equality dimension corresponds to the distance in relations of power. A large distance is a hierarchical orientation, and small – that of equality (Hofstede, 2000).

7. Individualist Culture – Collectivist Culture

Individualism is putting the individual above the welfare of a social group (Table 8). It is associated with a desire for individual freedom and the conviction that the welfare of the individual is essential. According to this, the organization should focus on the motivations and competencies of individuals, not teams. Implementation of individual good can consequently lead to the success of the organization, since it prefers competitive attitudes and non-conformist behaviour. The organization is perceived here as a collection of individuals with conflicting interests. S. Lukes emphasizes: human dignity, self-determination and autonomy of individuals, respect for privacy and the possibility of self-realization as the basic components of individualism (Lukes,

Table 7. Hierarchic and egalitarian cultures

Feature	Hierarchic Culture	Egalitarian Culture
Inequalities between positions	Striving to strengthen inequalities between working positions.	Striving to eliminate differences between working positions.
Pay discrepancies	Acceptance of high pay discrepancies between working positions.	Striving to eliminate pay discrepancies.
Management style	Autocratic	Participational
Decision centralization degree	Centralization of decision-making	Decentralization of decision-making
Origin of organizational hierarchy	Natural, objective, belief that lower level employees have usually lower abilities and skills than higher level staff.	Social, conventional, hierarchy is related with playing different roles defined due to pragmatic reasons.
Stability of the hierarchy of power	Hierarchy should be stable.	Hierarchy should be flexible and undergo changes.
Dependency relations between employees	Subordinates depend on their superiors.	Superiors and subordinates depend on each other.
Privileges of higher level staff	Higher level staff should be privileged.	Everybody should have equal rights in the organization.
Concept of executing power	Concepts underlying the importance of superiors and of the process of managing employees are dominant.	Concepts underlying the importance of employees and their commitment and participation in the management process are dominant.

Source: Own study.

1973). Individualism in organizations is expressed in: (1) placing individual liberty as the supreme value in organizations, (2) acceptance of the independence aspirations of individuals, (3) a preference for the good of individuals, (4) in competitive orientation in organizations, (5) the creation of the cult of individuals.

Collectivism - the idea that good of a social group is more important than the good of the individual, in organizations it is reflected as orientation towards the objectives of the group, even against the interests of individuals, and attitudes of conformity and cooperation are preferred. Stressing the value of group solidarity, the organization is often perceived as a social group or team. Success is achieved through its cooperation and consensus, therefore individuals should identify themselves with the group. Teams are motivated in the first place, and only then – the individuals. Collectivism manifests itself in: (1) recognition of the common good as superior, (2) highlighting the importance of cooperation in a social group, (3) emphasizing the importance of community, (4) the orientation towards cooperation and unity in the organization, (5) the creation of the cult of team work.

MULTIDIMENSIONAL TYPOLOGIES OF ORGANIZATIONAL CULTURE

Distinguishing organizational culture models and typologies from general models of organizations or its selected areas seems to be the basic cognitive problem. Since we have both theoretical and operational problems

Table 8. Individualist cultures and collectivist cultures

Features	Individualist Cultures	Collectivist Cultures
Priority of interests in the organization.	Individual interest is more important than that of the organization.	Interest of the organization is more important than that of the individual.
Core of the organization.	Organization is a group of individuals with differing interests.	Organization is the group of cooperating people.
Work relations	Competition between employees is necessary.	Cooperation between people is necessary in the organization.
Perspective of the importance of individuals.	Organization is based on eminent individuals..	Organization is based on teams.
Convergence of the interests of the organization and individuals.	Interests of the organization and individuals are divergent.	Interests of the organization and employees are convergent.
Attitude to individual liberty.	Organization functions thanks to freedom of individuals.	Organization functions thanks to group solidarity.
Degree of conformism.	In the organization, people should have their own opinion and be able to express it (nonconformism).	In the organization, one should adjust to the opinion of the group (conformism).
Attitude to conflict.	Conflicts can contribute to the development of the organization.	In the organization, one should strive towards harmony and avoid conflicts.
Attitude to familism.	Ideal interpersonal relations in the organization are different from the ones in the family because they are based on a contract guaranteeing mutual benefits.	Ideal interpersonal relations in the organization should resemble family relations.
Importance of private life in the organization.	It is necessary to have a clear division between professional and private lives in the organization.	In the organization private and professional lives of employees are intertwined.

Source: Own study.

connected with separating the organizational culture from the entire organizational system, we find it difficult to describe and classify it. By distinguishing five basic organizational configurations, such as: simple structure, machine bureaucracy, professional bureaucracy, divisionalized form and adhocracy, H. Mintzberg, in fact, relates to the organizational culture, even if he focuses on the structure (Mintzberg, 1983). Ch. Perrow described types of organizational cultures by creating the matrix of technologies based on the changeability parameters and the degree of analyzability (routine, engineering, craft and non-routine) (Perrow, 1967). A sieve and human capital models are two opposite ideal types of organizational culture. A similar situation exists in the case of models of leadership, power, organizational learning or managing human resources. They depict the entire organization or its selected area and, at the same time, may be perceived as a model or typology of organizational culture. Too excessive capacity and ambiguity of organizational culture makes it impossible to analytically separate organizational culture from other areas of organization.

Reference materials provide a great number of models and typologies for organizational culture. Most often quoted concepts were created by the following researchers: E. Schein, W. Ouchi, T. Deal and A. Kennedy, T. Peters and R. Waterman, G. Hofstede and Ch. Handy. (Peters & Waterman, 1980) All of them have been implicitly constructed upon the functional structuralism. While analyzing those concepts in terms of convergence, it can be observed that they are in accord as far as organizational elements of culture are concerned. Majority of authors, following the example of E. Schein, agree that organizational culture includes several of these elements:

values, norms, basic assumptions, cultural patterns, language, symbols, artefacts, rituals and taboos (Schein, 1992). Models of organizational culture are, on the other hand, very diverse in terms of the proposed dimensions of values and typologies. After all, some of them were created as a result of speculations and consulting practice rather than in the course of scientific research. T. Deal and A. Kennedy differentiate organizational culture according to the degree of risk and feedback speed. Blend of these dimensions allows to create the typology of cultures: tough guy/macho, work hard/play hard, "be your company" and process oriented (Deal & Kennedy, 1988). Concepts of Ch. Handy, W. Ouchi as well as T. Peters and R. Waterman are similarly simplistic and have not been rooted in a wider frame of scientific research. The last three concepts bear the hallmarks of good "marketing products", since they were based on a spectacular idea and were intensively promoted as popular handbooks. Unfortunately, to achieve higher sales, it was necessary to simplify the reality. Even if they may seem witty and inspiring for managers, it would be difficult to claim that they were shaped by solid empirical foundations. The situation is different in the case of G. Hofstede's concept which evolved from the studies of enterprises, carried out on a small scale but with the use of the sophisticated research program focused on quality and quantity. Based on the analysis of the above mentioned elements of organizational culture, six dimensions for analysis were distinguished: willingness to retain the procedures – willingness to achieve the best results; care for employees – care for production; membership – professionalism; open system – closed system; slight control – strict control and normativity – pragmatism (Hofstede & Hofstede, 2007). Organizational culture dimensions proposed by G. Hofstede differ significantly from dimensions proposed by other authors creating models based on empirical studies. Therefore, what we experience here, is the "jungle" of models, dimensions and typologies of organizational cultures (Goffee & Jones, 1998).

As has already been pointed out, culture is based on the beliefs, norms and values shared by the employees of the organization. Many scientists have conducted research into the relationships which exist between culture and organizational effectiveness (Quinn & Rohrbbaug, 1983). These studies made it possible to differentiate the following types of organizational cultures (Quinn, 1988). (1) The culture of the clan, which is characterized by a friendly working relationship. Members of organizations believe they are a part of one big family. Leaders here are seen as mentors. A high degree of commitment to their tasks can be noticed, and the loyalty and tradition bind the organization together. Emphasis is put on long-term benefits. The organization is characterized by a striving for consensus and is focused on interpersonal relationships. Leadership skills in managing teams and employee development are critical; (2) culture of adhocracy. It encourages creativity and dynamic development. Employees of the organization are not afraid to take risks and to experiment. A typical leader of the organization is an innovator, a visionary. Managerial skills in innovation management, attitudes to the future, management of continuous improvement are critical; (3) culture of hierarchy, which is typical of a formalized organization. A typical type of leader is here a coordinator, organizer and observer. Work must be carried out without interference, it must also be made on time. There is a rule pursuant to which control fosters efficiency. Managerial

skills in the management of assimilation (clear formulation of expectations and standards), system control and coordination are critical; (4) culture of the market, for which a typical leader will be the supervisor, competitor, producer. A characteristic feature of this type of organizational culture is to achieve goals and overcome competition. It is important to carry out the tasks, results and achieve success. Managerial skills to mobilize workers and promote the adoption of customer-oriented attitude are critical.

While clan culture and adhocracy are characterized by flexibility and freedom of action, culture of hierarchy and the market values the stability and control. The first two are cultures are also oriented on internal issues and integration, while in two latter cases we are dealing with an orientation to the position in the environment and diversity.

The literature proposes the types of cultures described by one, two or more variants. One-dimensional models are presented by: E.T. Hall, who because of the situational determinants of communication (context) distinguishes high and low context cultures (Hall, 1984); L. Zbiegień-Maciag, who reviews the one-dimensional models detailing the cultures: positive and negative, introvert and extrovert, conservative and innovative, male and female, bureaucratic and pragmatic, elitist and egalitarian, strong and weak (Zbiegień-Maciąg, 1999); RR Gesteland, who applied the criterion of division due to the concentration of the transaction (pro partner and pro trading cultures), due to the form of desired and inappropriate behaviour (ceremonial and non ceremonial cultures), due to the common forms of behaviour (verbal, nonverbal and verbal para-verbal expressive and restrained cultures), due to the approach to time (monochronic and polychronic cultures);

R. Rutka and M. Czerska who differentiate cultures from the perspective of praxeological evaluation criteria (pro-efficiency and anti-efficiency cultures) (Rutka & Czerska, 2002); Cz. Sikorski, who presents cultures derived due to the degree of uncertainty avoidance (cultures of high and low of tolerance of uncertainty) (Sikorski, 1999).

It should be emphasized that the use of one-dimensional models, simplifies, reduces and often brings the typology to only two types of cultures. The multivariate models, which describe many types of cultures, cause blurring of the boundaries and overlaps in the characteristics of individual cultures. The most popular are two-dimensional models, distinguishing four types of cultures. In addition to the one already described above, R.E. Quinn's model, other noteworthy characteristics of the cultures include the ones by R. Harrison and Ch.B. Handy, T.E. Deal A.A. Kennedy, N.H. Snyder, T.J. Peters, Cz. Sikorski and R. Goffee and G. Jones.

Division of R. Harrison and Ch. Handy is one of the earliest and also the most popular typology of cultures. The concepts of both authors were developed independently, but include the same values. R. Harrison lists four types of organizations that make up a specific culture. These organizations are oriented to power, role, tasks and people. Each of them prefers a defined system of values. Value system shared by the employees of the organization determines the alignment of interests with the interests of its staff, and shapes the ability to cope with the environment by the company. Typically, in the organizations rarely can we meet all four types of culture in its pure form, but most companies tend to focus on a particular system of values (Bratnicki, Kryś & Stachowicz, 1988). Characteristics of types of cultures proposed by R. Harrison and CH. B. Handy is presented in Table 9.

In turn, T.E. Deal and A.A. Kennedy applied two criteria relating to the organization to describe the cultures. They are, in this case, the risk level of activity and rate of getting to know the results of operations. Intersection of the two criteria allows distinguish four cultures (Deal & Kennedy, 1982). At the intersection of high-risk activities and the immediate feedback we have:

1. **Hard Macho Culture:** Young, educated, brilliant characters dominate here. They are dynamic and have a lot of ideas.

Table 9. Types of culture by R. Harrison and Ch. B. Handy

Types of Culture→	Culture of Power	Culture of Role	Culture of Tasks	Culture of People
Aspirations	rivalry, will to dominate the environment	order, stability	orientation to tasks, achieving the goal, development	meeting employees' needs, orientation to own success
Power and system of work	centralization of power, a high degree of internal control, autocratic style, paternalism	strong hierarchy, high formalization, procedures	cooperation, teamwork, the power of distributed and based on experience, knowledge and competencies of employees. flexible organization	lack of hierarchy and control, experts work independently
Shared values	rivalry, competition	sense of security, competence	setting and achieving objectives, cooperation, self-control	self-reliance, individual skills, freedom of action

Source: Own study on the basis of: R. Harrison, 1972; Ch. B. Handy, 1976.

The work atmosphere is dominated by young people, the climate of rapid action, taking high risks. Organizational culture is characterized by struggle and individualism. What matters is success.

2. **Company-Oriented Culture:** The heroes of the organization are people who insist on implementing their plans. They are mature, act peacefully. They are a kind of mentors. They assume that the environment is a source of danger to the organization so it is better to make thoughtful, appropriate decisions. Orientation to the group and partnership. Importance of hierarchy, much attention is paid to meeting agendas and speeches at meetings. Scientific and technical work atmosphere is dominant.

And at the crossroads of low risk activities and delayed feedback there emerge:

3. **Culture of 'Work Hard and Have Fun':** The protagonists are active people, committed to work. They believe that they must work hard and have fun with it. Personal contacts are also important here. Many meetings, celebrations are organized together. Many people believe that the environment of the organization is full of possibilities that need to be skilfully exploited.

4. **Culture of the Process:** In an organization subordination to the rules, impersonality, and minimalism dominate. At work stability is important as well as performance of tasks based on rules and procedures. The heroes are hard working people who value stability, who commit no errors, even in difficult situations. The role of hierarchical order and formal positions held by individual members of the organization is also emphasized. Interpersonal relationships are artificial.

Due to the need to develop pro-efficiency culture one should also look at the concepts that distinguish types of cultures that favour change. One of the models that allows for analysis of the convergence of culture with the possibility of changing is the model by NH Snyder. In this model two dimensions have been highlighted: (1) orientation to the organization and (2) focus on achievement. There arise then four types of organizational cultures: the culture focused on quality (that values effective planning, accepts change, focused on problem solving), creative culture (which is dominated by innovation, entrepreneurship, risk taking and initiating change), productive culture (characterized by efficiency, coherence, strict procedures and rituals in the proceedings, and resistance to change) and supporting culture (referring to the teamwork, cooperation, growth and response to change) (Rowe, 1990). Peters's model (Table 10) follows a similar convention. He distinguishes four types of cultures, depending on how they influence innovation, action, control and harmony of culture in the organization.

Presenting the typologies of organizational cultures, one should also be aware of the concepts of Polish authors. The most frequently cited include typologies by M. Dobrzynski, and Cz. Sikorski. In M. Dobrzynski's concept there appears the definition of the organizational climate (Dobrzyński, 1977). It is the climate what employees of the organization believe exists, and not necessarily what actually takes place there. The author lists four types of organizational climates:

Table 10. Types of culture by T.J. Peters

	Employee-Orientation	**Work-Orientation**
External Orientation	**Culture of Innovation** Organizational culture focused on innovative change, willingness to take risks. Dominated by informal contacts, direct. The possibility of chaos.	**Culture of Action** The organizational culture focused on performance, achievements, results. Initiative counts. Rewarded with flawless, professional operation. The organization is characterized by the acceptance of change. There may be problems with the delegation of powers.
Internal Orientation	**Culture of Harmony** Organizational culture, where deliberation dominates. People and team activities matter. External values are accepted only if they correspond to the values shared in the organization. The priority of the cultural values influencing strategic decisions. Insusceptibility to change.	**Culture of Control** Organizational culture oriented to strong control. Dominated by conservatism and bureaucratism. A hierarchical structure. Formal relations prevail. Written communication. Risk aversion. Changes encounter considerable resistance on the part of subordinates. Closed organization.

Source: Own study on the basis of: L. Zbiegień-Maciąg L., 1993.

autocratic, bureaucratic, innovative and sociable. Climate that is typical of the organization is the result of the dominance of a particular type of managerial motivation - motivation of achievement, power, security and belonging. Consequently, the power motivation as a result of the need to influence and dominate others causes the authoritarian climate. Power and strength of influence dominate, as in the culture of power by R. Harrison. In the relationships rule can be seen on the one hand, on the other one – submission. Promotion is associated with the faultless performance of top-down commands. The power of organization focuses its efforts on controlling the flow of information and increasing subordination of others. Achievement motivation contributes to the climate of innovation. In this culture creativity, knowledge, skills and qualifications that are most useful in the implementation of current tasks dominate. The management is focused on getting the best possible result, encouraging employees to be active and creative. The organization of this type adapts to the type of tasks and requirements of the environment flexibly. With regard to the motivation security it should be noted that efforts to minimize the risks of physical and social develops the bureaucratic climate. It specifically aims to stabilize based on the norms, rules and procedures. Executives are protected by preventing unexpected phenomena and avoiding risky ventures. Hierarchy plays an important role in the organization. The organization is formalized. Employees are passively subjected to rigid rules of action, on which they have no influence. The development of employees is mainly based on the careful assimilation of rules, regulations, and formally certified skills. As for the motivation of belonging to a group, it is a social climate condition. In this climate networking skills and team work, are valued employees are equal partners jointly shaping their own activity. The dominant value in the organization is the acceptance by the environment. The management focuses on the alignment of the influence of individual employees, to develop social awareness, habits of help and support.

Cz. Sikorski, in turn, divides organizational cultures due to the attitude of members of the organization to cultural dissonance (Table 11). Cultural dissonance is related to differences in the ways of thinking and behaviour of employees in different organizations. It is the most common cause of conflicts and misunderstandings. Cultural dissonance is an impediment to the functioning of the organization, especially in the case of multi-cultural organizations, multinational corporations or organizations in which there are many different subcultures. The attitude to this phenomenon is such an important feature of organizational culture that should be considered as a separate criterion for the typology of organizational cultures (Sikorski, 2002).

R. Goffee and G. Jones, on the other hand, assume that the cultural patterns prevailing in the organization can be effectively explained by sociological methods (Goffee & Jones, 1996). It is therefore necessary to evaluate cultures in relation to sociability and solidar-

ity. By sociability is understood here sincere sympathy prevailing among the members of the community. Solidarity is understood as the capacity of workers to achieve common goals. R. Goffee and G. Jones' model allows to extract four typologies of cultures. The combination of a high level of solidarity with an equally high level of sociability leads to the isolation of communal culture. Its characteristic feature is the development of friendships at work and beyond. Justice and reduction of anxiety in situations of uncertainty. Sharing clear, deeply-rooted values. Equal sharing the risks and rewards. Clearly defined competencies and assessment system. Social events are important, which means a strong emphasis on ritual of this culture. The high level at the interface between solidarity and low sociability emerging mercantile culture, characterized by quick and efficient and effective use of opportunities repulsing threats. To make mistakes and shortcomings in the work is perceived as something wrong. An

Table 11. Division of cultures by Cz. Sikorski

	Acceptance of Cultural Dissonance	**Lack of Acceptance of Cultural Dissonance**
Antagonist Relations	**Culture of Competition** Organizational culture is characterized by strong competition and the belief of its members about the need to prove their own superiority. The need for participation and team achievements. Collectivist culture. Focus on the roles performed by the people. Heterogeneous culture. Clashing of different cultural patterns is noticeable. Orientation to the present.	**Culture of Domination** A characteristic feature of this culture is the belief of its members of their natural advantage. Homogeneous culture due to the occurring patterns of behaviour consistent with the traditional ones. The tendency to subordinate the organization patterns to that of the national culture. Strong need for security, and hence strong uncertainty avoidance. Collectivist culture. Paternalistic management style. Orientation to the past.
Non-Antagonist Relations	**Culture of Cooperation** The culture is characterized by a routine operations in a competitive environment. The focus on quality relationships and dialogue between people is noticeable. Heterogeneous culture. The principle of autonomy, equality, respect for diversity. The principle of harmony with the environment, enhanced concentration and focus on customer needs than on the competition. Identification with the culture. Women's culture - to avoid conflicts and rivalries. Democratic style of management.	**Culture of Adaptation** Culture oriented on non-routine activities in a competitive environment. Focus on the quality of relationships and dialogue between people. Homogeneous culture in the sphere of values. Subordination to the formal goals of the organization. Focus on customer needs and one's own professional development. Strong need for achievement and internal motivation. High tolerance of uncertainty. Small power distance (partner nature of the relationship). Individualistic orientation to achieve in conjunction with an objective assessment of one's own and others' needs and goals. Orientation to the future.

Source: Own study on the basis of: Cz. Sikorski, 2002.

important role is played by reports containing specific data. All tasks are centrally coordinated, and their implementation is not negotiable. Subordinate personal interest often coincides with the objectives of the organization. It often happens, however, that employees are not characterized by too much loyalty. Frequently they remain in the organization as long as it serves their interests. The separation between personal and professional life is noticeable. Only successful major strategic events are celebrated together. Another type of culture highlighted by the authors mentioned above is the culture of the network. It arises at the interface between the low level of solidarity and a high level of sociability. This culture is oriented to strong personal relationships, deepening personal relationships and skipping formal procedures. It is typical to meet in the offices, to gossip and casual chats. Acquaintances and family affinities matter. Unlike the mercantile culture, numerous meetings are often organized at work for social purposes, birthdays, holidays, etc. are celebrated together. Large role of rituals. The last type of culture emerging at the intersection of low level of solidarity and low sociability culture is not uniform. Its characteristic feature is the pursuit of individual goals. Failure to identify with the objectives of the organization. Non-compliance of managers at various levels regarding strategic objectives and development standards. In the organization of this type it is undesirable to manifest emotions and attempts to behave sociably. Professional life is separated from personal matters. Members of the organization assume that all sorts of rituals are a waste of time. Reluctance to change and development is stressed. There is distrust and reluctance to provide information (Goffee & Jones, 1996; Goffee & Jones, 1998).

RELATIONS BETWEEN CULTURE AND: STRUCTURE, STRATEGY AND ORGANIZATION SETTING

The relations between organizational culture and other areas of organization, including strategy, structure and organization setting are also unclear. Several approaches and differentiation criteria may also be indicated here.

Separation of the organizational culture from other elements of organization is the first problem. Functionalists usually opt for the possibility of theoretical and practical separation of cultural, structural and strategic areas, while interpretivists and postmodernists tend to tacitly assume, or even explicitly indicate, inseparable connection between these semantic areas (Smircich, 1983a).

Establishing a priority is the second issue. One has to answer the question whether organizational culture is more important, equally important or perhaps less important than other management areas. Obviously, majority of researchers dealing with cultural phenomena pronounce for superiority or at least equivalency of culture in organization management (Kobi & Wüthrich, 1991). Outside the cultural mainstream, however, it would be easy to find supporters of the theory that strategy predominates over organizational culture (Wit & Meyer, 2007).

Establishing the relation between organizational culture and the organization setting, constitutes, in my opinion, the third and the key issue. Reference materials provide a vast number of studies and analyzes devoted to the relationship between culture *per se* and other elements of social and economic setting (Bogalska-Martin, 2007). This abundant scientific material includes classical studies carried out by M. Weber (Weber, 2002), analyses of the relationship between the culture and the wealth of nations: F. Fukuyama (Fukuyama, 2001), DS. Landes (Landes, 2000), as well as multicultural comparative studies: G. Hofstede, A. Trompenaars and Ch. Hampden-Turner, R. Hous and R. Inglehart (Hofstede, 1984; Hampden-Turner & Trompenaars, 1998; House, Hanges & Ruiz-Quintanilla, 1997; Inglehart, 1997). All of these works, however, do not relate to the relationship between organizational culture and social, economic or even cultural setting. If we assume that organizational cultures are "immersed" in the cultures of given societies and constitute a different set of values, what kind of transmission is there between these areas then? Vast majority of researchers assume that the values and norms of the society diffuse into the organizational culture. Obviously, any opposite influence is also possible, even if the range is usually smaller due to the size of the community and strength with which these values and norms may become entrenched. Still, a homogenous model defining the relationship between the culture of society and organizational culture has not been created. There are no decisive solutions which would allow to determine the cohesion level between culture of a society and organizational culture. Some authors depict organizational cultures and cultures of the societies employing completely different models and dimensions of values (Hofstede & Hofstede, 2007). Others assume larger coherence and use the same or similar models and dimensions of values (Sułkowski, 2002).

Lack of conclusions in terms of the relationship between the organizational culture and other elements of the organizational system results in making very diverse empiric and research assumptions in this area. Theorists and managers include both enthusiasts and sceptics of using organizational culture for the purpose of organization management.

CORPORATE IDENTITY – ALTERNATIVE APPROACH TO ORGANIZATIONAL CULTURE

Development of the trend of social research in the sciences of management has led to the rise of the idea of organizational identity. Decades of research on the phenomenon of organizational culture, which is still unclear, do not inspire optimism for the new concept of the area. Is the transfer of another uncrystallised concept of the humanities to the sciences of management going to offer any cognitive benefits? To answer this question one need to consider the following:

1. The definition of organizational identity,
2. The purposefulness of introducing the concept of organizational identity,
3. The links between organizational identity and culture.

'Identity' is a key concept in the interpretative trend in social sciences (Sułkowski, 2009). It is located primarily at the level of compression of individual consciousness with the collective one. Ii is defined as 'the concept of self' (Brittan, 1977), 'symbolic interpretation of the individual, referring to what one is in their opinion, and what they would like to be'

(Rodriguez-Tomé & Bariaud, 1980), 'whole body of constructs of the subject referred to each other, which is not a simple sum of its parts, but their synthesis' (Bausinger, 1983). 'Identity' is a concept important in the social sciences, but rather ambiguous, and forming a 'problem area' rather than a conceptual core (François, 1980). Among the vast literature and numerous studies on the identity the classic authors should be mentioned: G. H. Mead (Mead, 1975), H. Tajfel and J. Turner (Tajfel & Turner, 1979) and E.

Goffman (Goffman, 1981). Studies of identity conducted on the basis of social psychology and sociology were related to the formation and development of 'social self' by individuals. Should they, therefore, be referred to the level of collective actor, which undoubtedly is the organization?

Many researchers have opted for the transfer of the concept of identity on the collective ground, including organizations. R. Jenkins uses the term 'collectively shared identity' (Jenkins, 1996). M.J. Hatch and M. Schultz, referring to the concept of G.H. Mead suggest that the organization has an identity ('object-self' and 'subject-self') (Hatch & Schultz, 2004). J. Dutton and J. Dukerich describe the process of reflecting the identity of the organization in its image (Dutton & Dukerich, 1991). Therefore one can see the process of rooting the concept of identity in the theory of management sciences.

Organizational identity is a response to organization members of the following questions: 'Who are we as an organization?' And 'Who would we like to be?'. If we assume that the organization is more than just a set of actions of individuals, it seems sensible to be searching for social forms of organization such as culture, management, strategy and structure. Defining identity as a 'symbolic, collective interpretation of people forming the organization, referring to what is and what the organization wants to be' is clear. However, for that concept to be fruitful, it is necessary have the identification diversity of culture, image and organizational mission and vision.

The identity remains in stable conditions in the organizations the subject of collective organization, often default, consensus. *Explicite*, the problem occurs only in times of tension and changes, while the key questions of values consistently return and contradictory values of organization development clash. S. Albert and D.A. Whetten proposed that the effect of this search which is the fruit of a collective consensus on: the values, organizational culture, philosophy of action, orientation, market position, domains of activity, mission and vision and membership of an organization, should be regarded as manifestations of organizational identity (Albert & Whetten, 2004). Thus, the organizational identity should meet the following key criteria.

1. The criterion for determination of the key features of the organization. The identity of the organization should reflect its essence, the basic 'existential' questions, around which a consensus of members of the organization arose.

2. The criterion for determination of differentiation. Organizational identity is created by members of the organization as a sense of separateness. They identify with the organization by defining its boundaries, belonging and exclusion criteria.

3. The criterion of continuity over time. Identity is the result of a sense of temporal continuation. The organization is integrated by legal and managerial conventions. These in turn are supported by convincing its members and others in the environment of the continued existence of the organization itself despite the ongoing changes (Albert & Whetten, 2004).

4. To the above three criteria proposed by S. Albert and D.A. Whetten I propose to add a fourth one. The 'identity of the organization' is a more than unitary and social phenomenon. The sense of existence (esprit du corp), differentiating and supported by its members over time

is a manifestation of the functioning of a social group, not just selected individuals (such as owners, managers or other stakeholders).

Is it possible to do without the concept of 'identity' when analyzing social aspects of the organization? B.E. Ashforth and F. Mael suggest that the process of obtaining social identity is a prerequisite for taking any group action. 'Psychological group' is defined in terms of membership. Identification with the group is also the most important mechanism for participation. Among the signs of the emergence of social identity a sense of group separateness, striving to maintain its position and prestige of the group can be identified (Ashforth & Mael, 2004). The concept of identity is closely related to the establishment of identification or identification with a group. Theories of social identification is enriched by an understanding of organizational identity. However, most research on organizational culture and leadership identification with the organization was mixed with the internalization of its values and commitment. Identification with the group means to identify with it, and the internalization of the adoption and assimilation of the values espoused by the group. Identification with an organization does not have to result in internalization of organizational values and identification with the whole organization is conditioned by identifying with its members. Commitment, in turn, refers to the emotional connection and taking relatively little effort in working for the organization and its source may, but does not need to identify with the group. The distinction between these three concepts can point to identification, as a the source of organizational identity, and the internalization as a mechanism for its consolidation and dissemination

to others. Organizational identity formation takes place in the processes of communication and negotiation of meaning, which suggests that it is strongly rooted at the group and team level, while its occurrence on the level of all large organizations leads, according to many authors, to theoretical problems (Ashforth & Mael, 2004). Therefore it seems that the discussion about the identity should not be neglected while analyzing the functioning of the organization. The issue remains whether it is appropriate to create the theory of 'the identity of the organization' understood as a whole and examine the processes of creating, maintaining, and changes in group identity.

Reflections on a relatively permanent and distinctive organization's core values refer not only to the concept of organizational identity, but also to its mission, vision, organizational culture and image. It is necessary to distinguish between these concepts and identify points in common.

Mission and vision of the organization are taken from the formulation of strategic management. They are defined in different ways. L.W. Rue and P.G. Holland noted that the mission defines the essence and meaning of the organization by defining its most general purpose and domain of activity (Rue & Holland, 1989). J. Brilman defines vision as a short formula specifying the main vocation and goals (Brilman, 2002). The mission of the organization should be based on culture and identity of the organization, but it must include only those values that were considered worth promoting, creating a positive image of the organization. Vision is usually created by the managers, it does not have to be disseminated and serves as a projection of the development of the organization based on its objectives and values. Both these terms are then close in meaning and refer to the conscious, prospective and explicit aims and core values. Mission and vision are deliberately created, conscious and usually disseminated in order to be achieved in the future. The mission, therefore, differs from the identity of the organization, though it often plays an important role in its formation (Leuthesser & Kohli, 1997). Interrelation can be seen between the organization's mission and its identity and culture.

Organizational culture and identity are based on core values and arise due to the interdependence of spontaneous and intentional collective action (Table 12). Thus, the question of the distinction between identity and organizational culture poses some problems. The definitions of organizational culture are so broad that they typically include at least a part of the organizational identity. For example, it happens both in the case of the historical definition by E. Jacques (Jacques, 1952) as well as in the ones by E. Schein (Schein, 1982) and H. Schenplein (Schenplein, 1988). Aforementioned definitions of culture also meet selected criteria for distinguishing organizational identity proposed by S. Albert, D.A. Whetten (Table 12).

Comparing the organizational culture definitions to the criteria for defining organizational identity certain similarities can be seen and as well as some differences. All three cited formulations include the continuity of time and social constitution of organizational culture, which is also characteristic of organizational identity. Two newer definitions also meet the first criterion for defining a culture similar to the identity as key values (the 'essence'). The difference is the lack of criterion for distinguishing the organization's unique configuration value that is characteristic of identity.

Despite the proximity of the terms of the organizational culture and identity, it seems that it is appropriate to introduce a clear separation of these concepts. Strategor differentiates culture from identity placing culture on the level of symbolic space (ideas, values, norms, beliefs, myths), but the identity of the organization on the level of individual interpretation of this space – the internal image (fantasy, passion and complexes) (Strategor, 1997). It is a term referring to the psychosocial understanding of identity.

M.J. Hatch and M. Schultz clearly differentiate between culture, identity and image of the organization while pointing to their mutual dependence. 'Organizational identity is not entirely culturally conditioned nor fully the resulting image of the organization, it is

Table 12. Definitions of organizational culture and criteria for defining organizational identity

Author	Definition of Organizational Culture	Comparison to Organizational Identity
E. Jacques	Conventional or traditional way of thinking and acting, which is to some extent shared by members of the organization, and that new employees must at least partially accept.	Criteria meet: continuity over time (3) and social constitution (4).
E. Schein	A model of shared, fundamental assumptions that the group created by solving the problems of adaptation to the environment and internal integration. The model can be considered as obligatory. It is instilled to new members of the organization as a proper way of solving problems.	Criteria meet: 'the essence' of the organization (1), continuity over time (3) and social constitution (4).
H. Schenplein	Values, norms and beliefs generally accepted in the organization and forming the system.	Criteria meet: 'the essence' of the organization (1), continuity over time (3) and social constitution (4).

Source: Own study.

rather formed by the interaction of these two spheres' (Figure 1) (Hatch & Schultz, 2000).

The interaction between organizational culture, identity and image is reflected in the four interpretative processes taking place between these spheres. The first is the mirroring of the images of the organization itself created by others in its identity. Mirroring links the image of the organization related (her image in the eyes of others - the environment) with its identity. Secondly, we deal with the process of rooting (reflecting) the identity in the organizational culture. Identity has an impact on the shape of values, norms and patterns of cultural organization, it must be embedded in the culture. This leads to expressing organizational culture by the identity. Organizational culture is known and disseminated by the expressed formulation of identity based on culture. The identity gives the impression (impressing) on others through the image. The whole model is based on the inter-relation scheme (Hatch & Schultz, 2004).

It seems that it would be advisable to add the mission and vision, which also constitute a kind of idealized picture of the organization and its future, often developed for internal use. Thus, next to the image of the organization, there are a mission or vision to manage impressions and they should be placed beside the image in the proposed scheme.

The adoption of such way of understanding and differentiation of organizational identity allows to transfer the concept of 'identity' to the management sciences. To what extent is this transplantation fruitful? It is worth to consider the applications of the concept of organizational identity.

Organizational identity is an expression of organizational community's efforts to broaden its influence, and simultaneously it is the reflection of the play of internal interests. Therefore it remains unstable, variable and is expressed in different ways depending on context. This is reflected in the form of the concept of multiplicity and flexibility of organizational

Figure 1. Dynamics of organizational identity
Source: M.J. Hatch & M. Schultz, 2004.

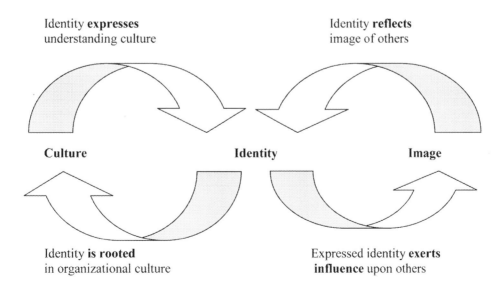

Identity **expresses** understanding culture

Identity **reflects** image of others

Culture   **Identity**   **Image**

Identity **is rooted** in organizational culture

Expressed identity **exerts influence** upon others

identities (Hatch & Schultz, 2004). M.G. Pratt and A. Rafaeli propose a multi-layered concept of organizational identity, manifested by the study of organizational symbols and artefacts such as e.g. clothing and costumes (Pratt & Rafaeli, 2004). D.A. Gioia, M. Schultz and K. Corley describe the 'adaptive instability' of ways of defining organizational identity allowing on the one hand to maintain the continuity of a sense of belonging to the same organization, and on the other hand to adapt to change in the environment (Gioia, Schultz & Corley, 2004). 'Identity work' is present in each organizational interaction, both having the nature of the routine maintenance of existing patterns of action and interpretation as well as their radical changes (McDermott & Church, 1976). Studies of N. Monin and B. Czarniawska-Joerges examine the concept of narrative creation of an organizational identity (Monin, 2004; Czarniawska-Joerges, 2004). The sphere of analysis of the relationship between creating power and organizational and identity (Alvesson & Willmott, 2004), as well as communication and identity (Cheney & Christensen, 2004) seems very promising. A very interesting area of research is the search for dysfunction in the processes of development of organizational identity. M.J. Hatch and M. Schultz write about two main possibilities: organizational narcissism and organizational hyperadaptation. The authors define, following A.D. Brown, organizational narcissism as a lack of will or the ability of organizations to respond to its own image circulating in the environment (Brown, 1997). This is due to loss of interest in the opinions of external stakeholders, focus on maintaining one's own self-esteem, fantasizing about ones greatness and disorder of perception and interpretation of information from the environment. M.J.

Hatch and M. Schulz diagnose narcissism as a manifestation of disorders of organizational identity, distinguished by its domination through reference to the organizational culture. In the relationship culture-identity-image, the latter element loses its importance. Focus on developing a strong culture, placing the identity in culture (reflecting), and expression of culture through the identity (expressing) without concern for the image are the mechanisms of organizational narcissism (Hatch & Schultz, 2004). Narcissism threatens the organization. The authors cite the example of Royal Dutch Shell, which ignored the protests of environmentalists who opposed the flooding an used oil platform in the North Sea. Schell's engineering culture and identity led to the narcissistic interrelation completely rejecting the rapidly deteriorating image of the company. Only a series of successive crises in the company led to a profound reflection, opening to contacts with stakeholders and the rejection of narcissism. The opposite of narcissism is the organizational hyperadaptation, which means a close interrelation between the image and the identity of the organization. The organization focused on the external image, opinions of stakeholders and market studies may lose the sense of its own existence. The need to continuously adapt to external changes contributes to the detachment from cultural heritage. M.J. Hatch and M. Schultz show the risk of hyperadaptation involving the loss of continuity, external steering and weakening of the organizational culture. Hyperadaptation actions such as: attempts to introduce New Coke in place of the classic Coca-Cola and transitional break with the cultural heritage of companies Gucci and Yves Saint Laurant are cited as examples (Hatch & Schultz, 2004). Opinions on the subject of 'losing culture' are, however, varied. M. Alvesson suggests that the replacement of the organizational culture by rapidly changing perception of the customer-dependent image, is a normal condition of contemporary flexible organization and has no significant dysfunctional characteristics (Alvesson, 1990). Regardless of opinions on this issue, studying the interaction between culture, identity and image of the organization seems to be interesting and unexplored area. In Poland, the concepts of organizational identity is not yet widespread, and the first research have been conducted by: K. Konecki, A. Zarębska and L. Sulkowski (Konecki, 1999; Zarębska, 2009; Sulkowski, 2006)

RESULTS OF PILOT STUDIES OF ORGANIZATIONAL CULTURES OF HOSPITALS IN POLAND

Initial results included in this study cover a series of free-form interviews with managers and employees from four hospitals located in the Lodz Province in Poland. In total, 15 interviews were conducted which aimed at gathering different opinions concerning the description of: culture, norms, key social values and tensions typical of hospitals. Provided interpretations should be perceived merely as initial and quality conclusions, any generalization would require wider and more representative studies.

Interviewed managers and employees were employed in 4 hospitals in Lodz Province. Brief description is provided next:

Hospital No. 1: a public unit with over 2500 employees. This is a specialist hospital, with gynaecologic, obstetric and paediatric wards, in a difficult financial condition undergoing a restructuring process. The hospital was founded by the Ministry of Health.

Hospital No 2: a university hospital employing over 1000 people. The hospital was founded by the Medical University. This is a multi-specialist hospital with, among others, such wards as: cardiology, pneumology, diabetology, dialysis, allergology, neurology, neurosurgery, general and transplantation surgery or laryngology. The hospital remains in a good financial condition and has been developing its infrastructure and improving specialist medical equipment for many years now.

Hospital No. 3: a multi-specialist hospital employing over 500 people. The hospital was founded by the Ministry of Interior and Administration. This is a multi-specialist hospital. For the last three years, the unit has undergone a deep restructuring change which allowed to improve its financial condition. In spite of onetime debts, the hospital currently does not generate any liabilities.

Hospital No. 4: a district hospital, in 2009 was transformed into a company with 100% shares owned by the local government. Currently, the hospital employs 750 people and specializes, among others, in: surgery, internal diseases and infectious diseases. A number of medical services which are rendered is outsourced to small entities affiliated with the hospital. The hospital has undergone a deep restructuring change, which allowed to settle former debts and regain a financial balance.

Tension between the subcultures is the main conclusion in the cultural area. The strongest subcultures relying on their own values and norms and displaying the high level of self-identity, include the following professional groups: doctors, managers, nurses, other medical employees (e.g. paramedics). The dynamic social balance based on power play and clashes of cultural patterns and norms can easily be observed between those groups.

The second conclusion shows the correlation between the organizational culture of hospitals and professional cultures. Organizational culture in hospitals is created by tension between the values of professional cultures, especially cultures of doctors and nurses, and organizational culture of the hospital, that is a business entity operating on the commercial market. This clash between the two systems of values reduces effectiveness of managerial activities. Medical ethos based on the Hippocratic Oath urges medical professionals to care about health and life of the patient. This is an auto telic, basic and core value deeply rooted in the medical culture (Nawrocka, 2008). On the other hand, organizational culture of hospital managers who have to work during transformation period and strive to lower operational costs, is increasingly similar to the values and norms typical of a competitive enterprise. What predominates then, is an ongoing pursuit for costs optimization and financial surplus which would allow to expand the hospital activity. These two approaches

tend to be contradictory, which is evidently reflected in the hospital organizational structure (Table 13).

The described dualism of organizational cultures in hospitals leads to a series of organizational consequences. Firstly, three distinct subcultures may be easily distinguished: doctors, nurses and managerial-administrative staff, which clash with one another more and more often. Hospital managers, most often doctors (as in the four analyzed hospitals), intuitively or with perfect awareness understand this tension within organizational culture perceiving it as a peculiar "split personality of managers". Being doctors, they wish to conform with the medical ethos, but, at the same time, they are also obliged to take into account economic and managerial logic.

According to the third aspect, as it was proved by the conducted interviews, organizational culture is, above all, interconnected with organizational structure of hospitals. The strategy is perceived by managers as a formalized document which does not provide any innovative solutions since the dynamic setting demands the implementation of incremental strategies while organizational structure was often believed to be coupled with culture.

Table 13. Cultural dualism of hospitals in Poland

Criterion	Professional Medical Culture	Hospital Organizational Culture
Key values	1. Providing the highest quality medical services 2. Taking care for a patient 3. Using the latest methods of medical treatment 4. Striving to cure a patient regardless the costs	1. Lowering operational costs 2. Taking care for the hospital development 3. Generating balance surplus amounts 4. Abandoning unprofitable medical services
Sense of community	Bonds and values of the given professional group, built upon the community	Communication and loyalty of the organization members, built upon collaboration
Sense of autonomy	1. Strong sense of community and professional autonomy 2. Hermetical groups of doctors and nurses	1. Separation from the surrounding and competitiveness 2. Responsibility of managers
Sense of continuity	Professional associations, maintaining contact with professional environment	Continuity of employment and hospital activity Continuity of management

Source: Own study.

For instance, culture of hospitals No. 1 and 2 was built upon bureaucratic patterns, culture of hospital No. 3 goes in line with pragmatic patterns, while culture in hospital No. 4 is an equivalent of entrepreneurial patterns.

To sum up, based on initial quality studies of organizational cultures, it can be observed that there are significant differences between culture of enterprises and culture of hospitals. Specificity of hospital cultures lies in significance of professional cultures and the peculiar tension between organizational and professional cultures. The phenomenon of hospital culture in Poland seems to be of great importance and has not been properly explored yet.

REFERENCES

Albert, S., & Whetten, D. A. (2004). Organizational identity. In M. J. Hatch, & M. Schultz (Eds.), *Organisational identity: A reader*. Oxford, UK: Oxford University Press.

Alvesson, M. (1990). Organisation: From substance to image. *Organization Studies, 11*, 373–394. doi:10.1177/017084069001100303

Alvesson, M., & Willmott, H. (2004). Identity regulations as organisational control producing the appropriate individual. In M. J. Hatch, & M. Schultz (Eds.), *Organisational identity: A reader*. Oxford, UK: Oxford University Press.

Ashforth, B. E., & Mael, F. (2004). Social identification theory and the organisation. In M. J. Hatch, & M. Schultz (Eds.), *Organisational identity: A reader*. Oxford, UK: Oxford University Press.

Bate, P. (1984). The impact of organisational culture on approaches to organisational problem solving. *Organization Studies, 5*.

Bausinger, H. (1983). Sensless identity. In *Identity: Personal and socio-cultural: A symposium*. Łódź: Wydawnictwo Uniwersytetu Łódzkiego.

Blau, P. M. (1974). *On the nature of organizations*. New York: John Wiley & Sons.

Bogalska-Martin, E. (2007). Wprowadzenie do teorii kulturowych uwarunkowań rozwoju gospodarczego. In R. Piasecki (Ed.), *Ekonomia rozwoju*. Warszawa: PWE.

Bratnicki, M., Kryś, R., & Stachowicz, J. (1988). *Kultura organizacyjna przedsiębiorstw: Studium kształtowania procesu zmian zarządzania*. Wrocław: Ossolineum, PAN.

Brilman, J. (2002). *Nowoczesne koncepcje i metody zarządzania*. Warszawa: PWE.

Brittan, A. (1977). *The privatized world*. London: Routledge and Kegan Paul.

Brown, A. D. (1997). Narcissism, identity and legitymacy. *Academy of Management Review, 22*.

Cheney, G., & Christensen, L. T. (2004). Organisational identity: Linkages between internal and external communication. In M. J. Hatch, & M. Schultz (Eds.), *Organisational identity: A reader*. Oxford, UK: Oxford University Press.

Czarniawska-Joerges, B. (2004). Narratives of individual and organisational identities. In M. J. Hatch, & M. Schultz (Eds.), *Organisational identity: A reader*. Oxford, UK: Oxford University Press.

de Wit, B., & Meyer, R. (2007). *Synteza strategii*. Warszawa: PWE.

Deal, T. E., & Kennedy, A. A. (1982). *Corporate cultures: The rites and rituals of corporate life. Boston*. Cambridge: Perseus Publishing.

Deal, T. E., & Kennedy, A. A. (1988). *Corporate cultures: The rites and rituals of corporate life*. London: Penguin Books.

Deshapande, R., & Parasurman, R. (1987). Linking corporate culture to strategie planning. *Organizacja i Kierownictwo, 6*.

Dobrzyński, M. (1977). Klimat organizacyjny jako wyznacznik stylu zarządzania. *Przegląd Organizacji, 1*, 54–64.

Dutton, J., & Dukerich, J. (1991). Keeping eye on the mirror: Image and identity in organisational adaptation. *Academy of Management Journal, 34*, 517–554. doi:10.2307/256405

François, F. (1980). Identité et hétérogénite de l'espase discursif. In P. Tap (Ed.), *Identités collectives et changements sociaux*. Toulouse: Privat.

Fukuyama, F. (2001). Culture and economic development. In N. J. Smesler, & P. B. Baltes (Eds.), *International encyclopedia of the social and behavioral sciences*. Oxford: Pergamon. doi:10.1016/B0-08-043076-7/04584-8

Geertz, C. (1973). *The interpretation of cultures*. New York: Basic Books.

Gioia, D. A., Schultz, M., & Corley, K. (2004). Organisational Identity, image and adaptive instability. In M. J. Hatch, & M. Schultz (Eds.), *Organisational identity: A reader*. Oxford, UK: Oxford University Press.

Goffee, R., & Jones, G. (1996, November-December). What holds the modern company together? *Harvard Business Review*.

Goffee, R., & Jones, G. (1998). *The character of a corporation*. New York: Harper Collins Publishers.

Goffman, E. (1981). *Człowiek w teatrze życia codziennego*. Warszawa: PIW.

Hall, E. T. (1984). *Poza kulturą*. Warszawa: PWN.

Hampden-Turner, C., & Trompenaars, A. (1998). *Siedem kultur kapitalizmu: USA, Japonia, Niemcy, Wielka Brytania, Szwecja, Holandia*. Warsaw: Dom Wydawniczy ABC.

Harrison, R. (1972). Understanding your organisation character. *Harvard Business Review, 4*, 119–128.

Hatch, M. J. (2002). *Teoria organizacji*. Warszawa: PWN.

Hatch, M. J., & Schultz, M. S. (2000). Scaling the tower of Babel: Relational differences between identity, image and culture in organizations. In M. S. Schultz, M. J. Hatch, & M. H. Larsen (Eds.), *The expressive organisation: Linking identity, reputation and the corporate brand*. Oxford, UK: Oxford University Press.

Hatch, M. J., & Schultz, M. S. (2004). The dynamics of organisational identity. In M. J. Hatch, & M. Schultz (Eds.), *Organisational identity: A reader*. Oxford, UK: Oxford University Press.

Hofstede, G. (1984). *Culture's consequences*. Beverly Hills, CA: Sage Publications.

Hofstede, G. (2000). *Kultury i organizacje: Zaprogramowanie umysłu*. Warszawa: PWE.

Hofstede, G., & Hofstede, G. J. (2007). *Kultury i organizacje*. Warszawa: PWE.

House, R. J., Hanges, P., & Ruiz-Quintanilla, A. (1997). GLOBE: The global leadership and organizational behavior: Effectiveness: Research program. *Polish Psychological Bulletin, 28*(3), 215–254.

Inglehart, R. (1997). *Modernization and postmodernization: Cultutal, economic and political change in 43 societies*. Princeton, NJ: Princeton University Press.

Jacques, E. (1952). *The changing culture of a factory*. New York: Fryden Press.

Jenkins, R. (1996). *Social identity*. London: Routledge.

Kobi, J.-M., & Wüthrich, H. (1991). *Culture d'entreprise: Modes d'action: Diagnostic et intervention*. Paris: Nathan.

Konecki, K. (1999). Transformacja tożsamości organizacyjnej. *Master of Business Administration, 4*.

Kostera, M. (1996). *Postmodernizm w zarządzaniu*. Warszawa: PWE.

Kroeber, A. L., & Kluckhon, C. (1952). Culture: A critical review of concepts and definitions. *Peabode Museum of American Antropology and Ethnology Papers, 47*(1).

Landes, D. S. (2000). *Bogactwo i nędza narodów: Dlaczego jedni są tak bogaci, a inni tak ubodzy*. Warsaw: Muza.

Leuthesser, L., & Kohli, C. (1997). Corporate identity: The role of mission statements. *Business Horizons*. doi:10.1016/S0007-6813(97)90053-7

Lukes, S. (1973). *Individualism*. Oxford, UK: Oxford University Press.

Martin, J. (2002). *Organizational culture: Mapping the terrain*. London: Sage.

McDermott, R. P., & Church, J. (1976). Making sense and feeling good: The etnography of communication and identity work. In L. Thyayer (Ed.), *Communication and identity*. Author.

Mead, G. H. (1975). *Umysł, osobowość, społeczeństwo*. Warszawa: PWN.

Mintzberg, H. (1983). *Structures in five: Designing effective organizations*. Englewood Cliffs, NJ: Prentice-Hall.

Monin, N. (2004). *Management theory: A critical and reflective reading*. London: Routledge. doi:10.4324/9780203356814

Nawrocka, A. (2008). *Etos w zawodach medycznych*. WAM.

O'Donovan, G. (2006). *The corporate culture handbook: How to plan, implement and measure a successful culture change programme*. Dublin, Ireland: The liffey Press.

Ouchi, W. (1980). Markets, beaucracies and clans. *Administrative Science Quarterly, 25*.

Perrow, C. (1967). A framework for comparative organizational analisis. *American Sociological Review, 32*(2). doi:10.2307/2091811

Peters, T. J., & Waterman, R. H. (2000). *Poszukiwanie doskonałości w biznesie*. Warsaw: Medium.

Pratt, M. G., & Rafaeli, A. (2004). Organizational dress as a symbol of multilayered social identities. In M. J. Hatch, & M. Schultz (Eds.), *Organisational identity: A reader*. Oxford, UK: Oxford University Press.

Quinn, R. E. (1988). *Beyond rational management: Mastering the paradoxes and competing demands of high performance*. San Francisco: Jossey-Bass.

Quinn, R. E., & Rohrbbaug, J. (1983). A spatial model of effectiveness criteria: Towards a competing values approach to organizational analysis. *Management Science, 29*(3). doi:10.1287/mnsc.29.3.363

Rodriguez-Tomé, H., & Bariaud, F. (1980). La structure de l'identité à l'adolescence. In P. Tap (Ed.), *Identités collectives et changements sociaux*. Toulouse: Privat.

Rowe, A. J. (Ed.). (1990). *Strategic management: A methodological approach*. Reading, MA: Addison-Wesley Pub. Co.

Rue, L. W., & Holland, P. G. (1989). *Strategic management. Concepts and experiences*. New York: McGraw-Hill.

Rutka, R., & Czerska, M. (2002). Wpływ kultury organizacyjnej na metody i narzędzia pełnienia ról kierowniczych. In J. Stankiewicz (Ed.), *Nowoczesne zarządzanie przedsiębiorstwem*. Zielona Góra: Redakcja Wydawnictw Matematyczno-Ekonomicznych.

Schein, E. H. (1983). The role of the founder in creating organizational culture. *Organizational Dynamics*, 13–28. doi:10.1016/0090-2616(83)90023-2

Schein, E. H. (1984). Coming to a new awareness of organizational culture. *Sloan Management Review*, 3–16.

Schein, E. H. (1985). How culture forms, develops and changes. In R. H. Kilmann (Ed.), *Gaining control of the corporate culture* (pp. 17–43). Academic Press.

Schein, E. H. (1992). *Organizational culture and leadership*. San Francisco: Jossey-Bass.

Schein, E. H. (2010). *Organizational culture and leadership: A dynamic view*. San Francisco: Jossey-Bass.

Schenplein, H. (1988). Kultura przedsiębiorstwa i jej rozwój. *Organizacja i Kierowanie, 7/8*.

Sikorski, C. (1990). *Kultura organizacyjna w instytucji*. Łódź: Wyd. UŁ.

Sikorski, C. (1999). *Zachowania ludzi w organizacji: Społeczno-kulturowe skutki zachowań*. Warszawa: PWN.

Sikorski, C. (2002). *Kultura organizacyjna*. Warszawa: C.H. Beck.

Smircich, L. (1983a). Organizations as shared meaning. In *Organization symbolism*. Greenwich, CT: JAI Press.

Smircich, L. (1983b). Studing organisations as cultures. In G. Morgan (Ed.), *Beyond method: Strategies for social research*. Thousand Oaks, CA: Sage.

Strategor. (1997). *Zarządzanie firm: Strategie, struktury, decyzje, tożsamość*. Warszawa: PWE.

Sułkowski, Ł. (2002). *Kulturowa zmienność organizacji*. Warszawa: PWE.

Sułkowski, L. (2005). *Epistemologia w naukach o zarządzaniu*. Warszawa: PWE.

Sułkowski, Ł. (2006). Tożsamość organizacyjna a kultura organizacyjna – Problemy metodologiczne. In T. Listwan (Eds.), Sukces w zarządzaniu kadrami: Kapitał ludzki w organizacjach międzynarodowych. Wrocław: Wydawnictwo Akademii Ekonomicznej im. Oskara Langego.

Sułkowski, Ł. (2009). Interpretative approach in management sciences. *Argumenta Oeconomica, 2*.

Tajfel, H., & Turner, J. (1979). An integrative theory of intergroup conflict. In W. G. Austin, & S. Worchel (Eds.), *The social psychology of intergroup relations*. Oxford, UK: Oxford University Press.

Thompson, K. R., & Luthans, F. (1990). Organisational culture: A behavioural perspective. In B. Schneider (Ed.), *Organisational climate and culture*. Oxford, UK: Jossey-Bass.

Weber, M. (2002). *Gospodarka i społeczeństwo: Zarys socjologii rozumiejącej*. Warszawa: PWN.

Zarębska, A. (2009). *Identyfikacja tożsamości organizacyjnej w zarządzaniu przedsiębiorstwem*. Warszawa: Difin.

Zbiegień-Maciąg, L. (1999). *Kultura w organizacji: Identyfikacja kultur znanych firm*. Warszawa: PWN.

Chapter 7
The Role of the Personal Culture in the Management of a Multicultural Team

Tatiana Segal
Bucharest University of Economic Studies, Romania

ABSTRACT

The chapter reviews the clash between personal and organizational culture in multicultural settings, advancing ways to mediate between the two and to apply proper strategies in order to establish sound interpersonal relations while not losing sight of the general objectives of the business organization.

INTRODUCTION

In a multicultural organization, the role of the "head" (from foreman to general manager through all hierarchical levels), is characteristic both for the smooth running of the business and, especially, for establishing interpersonal relationships based on universals of diversity that each team member represents. Geert Hofstede and Fons Trompenaars (Netherlands), Edward Thomas and Mildred Reed Hall (USA), Michael Bond (Canada) and many other researchers, as a result of studies carried out have established the basic criteria based on which the cultural traits that distinguish human communities (people) can be determined (Hunter, 2005). But, in fact, given the unprecedented development of information systems, mergers and relocations, mobility studies and work, these differences are preserved, they tend to increase, or decrease? What role does the"head"has under "democratization" employment relationships, according to the American model?

DOI: 10.4018/978-1-4666-4325-3.ch007

In order to answer these questions, and to find out the characteristics of the personal culture, that play a decisive role in biunivocal adaptation of the manager to the differences in a multicultural group and of each of the members to the manager, we turned to a company with international experience of about 30 years, Ubisoft.

BRIEF OVERVIEW OF UBISOFT

Originally called UbiSoft Entertainment (Ubi the acronym for Union des Bretons Indépendants) and having as object of activity development and distribution of video games, the French company known today as Ubisoft, one of the world's leading developers and publishers of video games was founded in 1986 by the five Guillemot brothers in Rennes where it continues to have its registered office, even though, nowadays the Administrative and international headquarter is in Montreuil.

The first video game, Zomby, due to the innovative features in brought, enjoys a great commercial success. Ubisoft is experiencing a rapid development and, until 1989 when the turnover reaches $ 10 million, it annually releases on the market a few games.

The first distribution subsidiaries of the group are open in 1991 in the UK, Germany and the U.S., countries that currently account for 40% of turnover. Next, from 1992-1996, it opens production studios in Romania and France, and the distribution extends to Japan, Italy and Australia.

During the next years many other branches were opened, so that the company currently has 24 studios in 18 countries, employing over 6,700 employees, out of which 80% in development.

Ubisoft creations present five online games, including one called Might and Magic: Heroes Kingdom is the best known. The administration of such games is very complicated, because it requires continuous communication with both players to manage any conflict arose within the community and to fix the programming errors that participants confront. It is in fact the role employees called "masters of the game". They work in teams of 10-12 people and are responsible for the operation of a server. Each team is coordinated by a team leader, manager, the only one connected to the core company. His role is to manage the group of "game masters", to assure performance and to send to the superiors all the "discoveries" of the team.

PRELIMINARY CONSIDERATIONS AND METHODOLOGY

We chose such a team in order to highlight the personal culture and validate/invalidate the cultural traits partially attributed to different populations in literature. There are many reasons for this choice. Firstly, the extremely high diversity of team composition: basically, every person is from another country (other cultures) of Europe. Secondly, the manager comes from Romania, one of the first countries that Ubisoft has opened branches, characterized by high power distance, but also by a high collectivist spirit. Becomes interesting to see to what extent such a leader can adapt to the individualistic nature of Western colleagues, or can transform them into a stronger team spirit and also what are the personal culture that helps to fulfill the mission (Johnson, 2011). Another reason is represented by the specific way of working: each team member is working at home and communicating with each other only via videoconference. As a result, the cohesion factor represented by the entrepreneurial culture, which is usually formed by direct and daily interaction, where the non-verbal communication plays a more prominent role than verbal sometimes, is practically excluded (Ferraro, 2010). The manager has the task and duty to mitigate "roughness" and achieve team cohesion. He is the only one having direct contact with the company – transmitting the business values and norms of Ubisoft, not only to the employees, but to all the stakeholders (Zeigler, 2008).

The method used was a questionnaire survey, sent by mail to the respondents.

Target Group: the Ubisoft team that includes a Greek, a Dutchman, English, a Romanian, a Frenchman, a German, and manager (also Romanian).

Period: One week in May 2012

Study Objectives:

1. The identification of the cultural features of the team members and managers;
2. The identification of the cultural differences in the Working Group (Head and subordinates);
3. The identification of the effects of the cultural differences on group performance;
4. The identification of the elements of the personal culture that helps the manager to manage the team.

Apparently having a range of a few people, sampling was not necessary. However, in a micro group (10-12 people) the presence of 3-4 respondents from the same country may tilt the balance in favor of the features of such persons. An average of their responses, just fade personal cultural elements. That is why, we didn't conduct a full survey, but we chose randomly one representative from each country. Under these circumstances, we believe that the sample is representative and the margin of error limited to 0.05.

For the investigation we used the Likert Reusis scale, with which it is estimated the extent to which respondents agree with a set of statements.

The questionnaire is divided into three parts, each aimed at highlighting key information on respondents' personal culture.

In the present survey we asked respondents to give honest answers regarding their wishes and thoughts on a particular topic and avoid answers considered as being „correct" in theoretical ideal conditions.

Due to the fact that they are working in an area, subject to permanent technological changes, the respondents are younger than 35 years.

Assumptions

1. Assuming that each worker's education received and personality are mostly responsible for the personal cultural differences, the first part aims to identify the preferences and opinions of the manager and team members on general aspects of everyday life (family life, social relationships, education, and employment). We expect this section to record high diversity of opinions (Lewiss, 2006).
2. As is well known, national culture has a remarkable influence on each person, and for the manager it will be very difficult to avoid conflicts of this nature in the multicultural team. Therefore, the second section is structured as role-plays and approaches sensitive and controversial issues, such as religion, ethics, solidarity and attitude towards power.

3. The third working hypothesis was that the Ubisoft team does not want to cooperate with strangers, but the nature of the service requires them to have such relationships. Therefore, the last section is to providing details on respondents' attitudes towards multicultural cooperation.

Personal Culture

The first part of the questionnaire is divided into three sections, which seek to identify basic information about the team members and the manager. The aim is to determine the components of their personal culture and how they are affecting working relations and multicultural collaboration.

Initial section includes 11 general statements on various personal relationships, ways of spending the free time and spirituality. Respondents were asked to assess, on a scale from 1 = not at all, 5 = very much, the degree of these assertions.

The first issue analyzed relates to family relationships, in order to identify the extent to which each team member is attached to the family. As it is known, the family is, by definition, the core for formation and development of the personal culture. The family role and commitment of people towards it, varies from one culture to another, but in general, having good family relationships is beneficial. For example, people who have brothers are negotiating better, collaborate more easily with colleagues and can quickly find solutions to conflicts. Reporting to power, dichotomy individualism/collectivism and all other dimensions of personal culture are first expressed in the family. At the same time, sometimes family can be a learning environment of negative characteristics such as stereotypes or discrimination.

Questioned about the extent to which they agree with the statement "My family is the most important thing for me" (Q/R 1.) Team gave the answers in Figure 1.

It is noted that for the majority of the respondents family is indeed an essential part, three of them giving it the maximum score. The team, including the manager, received an overall score of "4", which demonstrates a strong attachment to the family and its values, and a good relationship with it. Lowest score was, surprisingly, the Romanian one. A score of "2" indicates a cold relationship with the family.

Another factor to consider is that of social relations (Q/R 2 "I like to make new friends"). It almost goes without saying that a person who likes to make new friends is sociable, works better in teams and easily adapts to cultural differences. Therefore, based on the extent to

Figure 1. Family relations

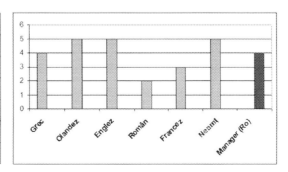

Greek	4	
Dutch	5	
English	5	
Romanian	2	
French	3	
German	5	
Manager (Ro)		4

which they make new friends, we aimed to reveal the introvert/extravert character of the team members. The respondents' role was to mark the extent to which assertion represents them (Figure 2).

The results are slightly surprising because they show a slight reluctance of the respondents regarding the establishment of new relations of friendship. The team received a score of 3.5 which places it in a medium, neutral zone. This attitude can be explained by the fact that most people think that they can only make new friends by participating in various festivals or tours, activities related to leisure, not work. Very few people regard their colleagues as friends or potential friends, not just associates.

Unlike most of the team, the manager seems to be an open person, always ready to meet other people, an attitude that should inspire the entire team. It is his duty to convince subordinates that at work there may be other relationships outside (in addition to) the strictly professional. The easiest and best solution to this would be organizing interactive activities to stimulate team members to get to know each other better. Having friendly relations with colleagues, especially those from different cultures may act to reduce tension and eliminate conflicts within the group.

Another factor considered in achieving the cultural profile of the manager and the team was the attitude. A modest and moderate attitude is often characteristic of a balanced person, who does not like conflict and can collaborate with others without major difficulties. That is a person aware of her skills, but down to earth. On the contrary, the fact of displaying an attitude of superiority is not tolerated in some cultures and often proves to be a source of conflict. Therefore, the statement "Being modest and thrifty are two of the principles that govern my life" (Q/R 3), we sought to highlight these qualities. The results are found in Figure 3.

The team achieved an overall score of 3.5, three people standing at extreme right: the French and the English are the people that are extremely modest and sensible, while Romania held that modesty doesn't characterize him at all. The manager, although Romanian, described himself as modest, the essential characteristic of someone who wants to be respected and appreciated by his colleagues.

Once again it has been proven productively that, in our analysis, we used individual personal culture, even though the number of respondents is very small, and we did not make an average of personal culture of the teams' countrymen.

Figure 2. Social relations

Greek	4	
Dutch	3	
English	3	
Romanian	3	
French	5	
German	3	
Manager (Ro)		4

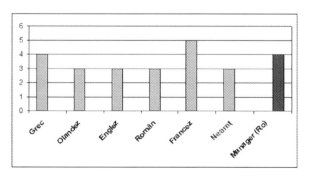

Figure 3. Attitude towards others

Greek	3	
Dutch	4	
English	5	
Romanian	1	
French	5	
German	3	
Manager (Ro)		5

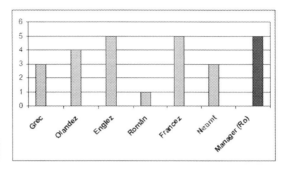

The fourth question touches a sensitive topic: spirituality. Nowadays religion plays, at least apparently, in some cultures, a role increasingly insignificant. The significant moments are respected, but their appearance is more mundane than pious. This means, in special cases, that at the request of the boss, people put aside holidays and fulfill their service obligations. However, there are cultures where faith still plays a role so important that all activities are conducted in accordance with religious precepts. In this case, you may not ask the practitioner to put job duties before the religious ones. An effective manager must know the religious belonging of his collaborators and what they imply, for any mistake in this area, made by him or any member of the team is not only inexcusable, but also can lead to conflicts, sometimes irreconcilable.

Therefore, it is good to know, from the outset the team's attitude towards this subject. Respondents' position Q/R 4 "I believe that God helps me to manage my work" is illustrated in Figure 4.

The results are, at first sight unexpected, because the team is proving not be religious. Of all respondents, only the Frenchman corresponds to the known portrait type: a strictly secular education system for more than 200 years makes leaves its mark. The responses of the Greek and the Romanian are a bit curious, because both belong to cultures in which faith plays a very important role in people's lives. In what concerns the manager's reluctant attitude to the role that divinity plays in everyday life can be explained by the fact that he's a young person coming from an urban area.

Figure 4. Role of religion

Greek	1	
Dutch	1	
Greek	1	
Dutch	1	
English	1	
Romanian	1	
French	1	
German	2	
Manager (Ro)		2

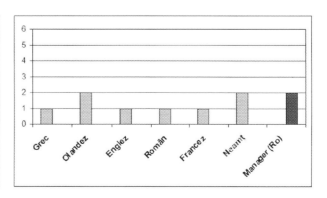

The only conclusion that is necessary for such a result is that, at least in European countries, faith plays an increasingly reduced role in social life and is limited to only a part of the intimate personal culture, and has nothing to do with the achievements of each of us.

The next point of analysis refers to the confidence that each one gives his colleague, and mutually enjoys. Without trust in the others, members of a team cannot collaborate together. By definition, man is a social animal who can only be by interacting with his peers. Cooperation based on mutual support was a key factor in the survival and development of mankind (from the tribal family to the forming of mankind). Throughout life we are often put in a position to collaborate with others (colleagues, friends, business partners, etc..) in order to carry out a job, to achieve a common goal or even learn something. The poet also tells us that "Where there's just one there's no power" and when many people work for the same cause, the chances of success increases exponentially.

However, nowadays, the process of computerization, the fact that a number of works can be performed at home, alone, has developed individualistic traits, such as "every man for himself" working, extremely complex, with plenty of cargo psychological becoming almost an accident. Even at work where service tasks require the formation of groups that must work within them and cooperate with each other welding process of a team is difficult. Occurrence suspicion, distrust between teammates lead to the outbreak of conflict both objective and subjective reasons, such as that rarely anyone is free to choose which team to join one or more colleagues do not job and then others have to work for them or as bad, make mistakes so large that the whole team put in a bad light. Therefore,

instead of leading to the fulfilment faster and better cooperation can be a nuisance for each participant.

From the point of view of the manager responsible for the results obtained, a crisis team should be avoided at all costs. However it cannot ensure quality results only work by the entire team. Therefore, a good manager must learn to trust his colleagues and to stimulate that, in turn, their trust in colleagues and ask them not to impede to finally get the best results. System is applied, at least in theory, very simple: those who do not work are punished and those who have exceptional activity (including those that are lazy job) are rewarded.

By saying "If you want something to be well done, you must do it myself" (Q / A 5) we sought to verify the extent to which each of the respondents are convinced that everyone else will like them all their best to get the best results.

The results are illustrated in Figure 5.

Overall score obtained is 3.6 and shows a medium level of confidence among team members that can be correlated with pronounced individualism of some respondents. As expected, representatives of Western (English, the German, Dutch and French) believes that, to ensure that work is good, you have to do it themselves. At the opposite end, Greece and Romania.

Manager, and he came from a collectivist culture type has a similar attitude Orientals (Greek and Roman). In fact, the very position they occupy within the team, the boss forces him to trust his teammates. Unit difference might explain the problems which had to face: definitely not had time to finish, to complete, to develop work performed by subordinates.

A healthy life requires the existence of free time. This course can be devoted to family and relaxation, but can be used by working more.

Figure 5. Trust in the others

Greek	2	
Dutch	4	
English	5	
Romania	2	
French	4	
German	5	
Manager (Ro)		3

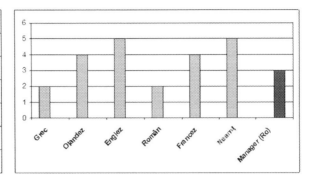

Including the statement "I prefer to do overtime than to spend time with family", we wanted to highlight the position of respondents to report work/rest.

The results are found in Figure 6.

According to the results, the only Englishman who prefers to devote his spare time business activities, not family or leisure. All others choose to spend their leisure time more enjoyable with family. Even the manager, by marking the option "such and such" confirms the idea that whenever one can enjoy while enjoying to spend it with family.

Only answer Englishman stands out. Do not be misunderstood statement? Was not honest answer? Correlating this option with the first statement on relations with family (where all the box "a lot" was marked) we see that, in fact, family is everything to him.

And then? The answer comes indirectly: it is the oldest hovering between 31-35 when the family (wife, children, elderly parents) were most in need of support material. So, from his point of view, it is normal to express feelings to loved ones doing overtime to earn more.

A matter of personal cultural interaction multiculturalism is shown in the following assertion: "I love to travel and live as foreigners" (Q / R 7). Left the country, not necessarily to work abroad, but to travel, is for many an obstacle difficult to overcome, for where they go home they will not find habits. Other rules and other rules of conduct, other food ... And simply travelling can be hard, but to work among strangers. Naturally, it is easier to collaborate with people from the same cultural background, and if you have worked with people from other cultures is preferable

Figure 6. Work vs. others' rest

Greek	2
Dutch	2
English	5
Romanian	1
Franch	2
German	3
Manager (Ro)	3

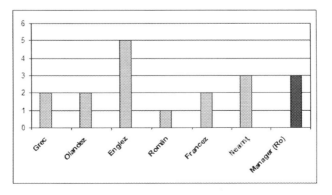

that the general environment is usually home. In practice, it often happened that people sent to work abroad, even well trained and with a wealth of multicultural experience, cannot adapt to new conditions. Therefore we asked Ubisoft team members to think about this situation and assess the possibility of overcoming cultural barriers to work/travel abroad.

Responses are summarized in Figure 7.

In this case the diversity of responses is much higher for the response to appeal not only to personal culture, but a lot of other factors together including temperament, family situation, health etc momentary. One can see that those Anglo-Saxon origins are tied to the land than others. However, the average score of 3.5 team stands in a centre which could be interpreted as an acceptance of work/travel abroad, although if you can choose, each would prefer to stay in his system of values.

Manager, as teammate Romanian, speaks loudly for working/travelling abroad. It is difficult to assess, but compared to this response, the extent to which lies manager position is due to their experience, expertise loved ones (family, friends) or unique motto neighbours' goat "who still fat and milk".

Continuing our analysis we put it another complex factor strongly dependent on the respondent's personality, attitude or in case of conflict.

Workplace, disputes, conflicting discussions more or less are inherently bright. The more they are inevitable in the team. What is, however, different is the attitude of each team member to such a situation. In a group, more or less united, there are people who detest conflict situations and prefer to remain neutral, to be silent, even though I know well that such behaviour will not solve the tension, as there are people who like to strongly support option, even though I know that by their attitude merely create a conflict or put fuel on the fire, if it broke.

For the manager how subordinates are positioned against a statement like "I do not like conflicts and I try to avoid them" (Q / R 8) is a useful information for the management team. He will pay more attention to those impulsive, prone to argue, to prevent them or at least to intervene before disaster occurs.

The answers of the persons who answered this question can be find in Figure 8.

As shown, the majority of the team is working to avoid conflict. The French and the German, whose history is dotted with numerous armed conflicts, is categorically against any conflict. In the background, but having a similar opinion is the Greek and the English.

Figure 7. Grade of adjustment abroad

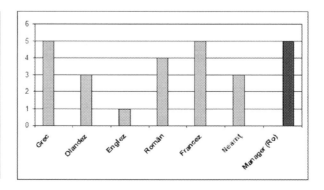

Greek	5
Dutch	3
English	1
Romanian	4
French	5
German	3
Manager (Ro)	5

Figure 8. Attitude towards conflict

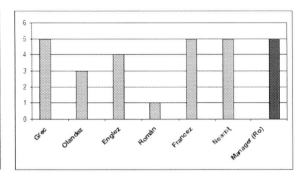

Greek	4	
Dutch	3	
English	4	
Romanian	1	
French	5	
German	5	
Manager (Ro)		

The Dutchman is located in a median plane, meaning that he does not like conflictual situations, but were there no choice, he will not remain neutral. Conversely, the first one to argue whenever possbile, is Romanian. Given the general characteristics of the Romanians, namely friendly, conciliatory, open, we believe that this attitude is either circumstantial or temperamental.

The manager's response is typical of a leader whose role, regardless of temperament, ethnic, religious, political creeds and so on, is to settle and resolve incidents occurred within the team.

The following statement, "If I need to make a decision, I spend more time analyzing alternatives" (Q / R 9), concerns the decision making process in different situations, not only in a strictly professional sense. We wanted to see how each team member behaves when they are forced to make a decision whether it is a trivial or a crucial event for him. In fact, respondents were asked to evaluate themselves and position themselves in the category of the thoughtful, rational or, conversely, of those impulsive, instinctive.

Results are found in Figure 9.

All team members, including the manager, were characterized as highly rational people who do not ever take any decision without assessing all possibilities. In an work relationship, such an attitude is desired and is well received because a careful analysis of all alternatives always leads to the best solution for everyone.

Another topic discussed was that of culture, specifically the preferences of the respondents' cultural activities. Certainly, the statement.

Figure 9. Making decisions

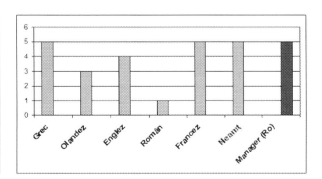

Greek	5	
Dutch	4	
English	5	
Romanian	5	
French	4	
German	4	
Manager (Ro)		5

"I like to go to the theater, opera ..." (Q / A 10) refers strictly to the performing arts, in this answer, to the theater and opera. Our limitation is exclusively due to the desire for brevity, not to the fact that we would despise other artistic fields. In fact we believe that the usual cultural events participants, if not opera amateurs, for example, but who appreciate fine arts, will not feel excluded from the discussion and will show great interest in cultural life.

Participation from early childhood to cultural events play a key role in shaping personal culture. In fact, those "exposed" to cultural life are more open when it comes to establish new human relationships or to deal with unforeseen circumstances.

The results are illustrated in Figure 10.

The German and the Romanian declared themselves the biggest amateur of performances (theater, opera), followed closely by the Greek. The French and the Dutch situate themselves in the middle ranks in the sense that they do not dislike to go to shows, but do not do go too often or if something more enticing comes up, the renounce the cultural challenge. English is the only one who states that he does not like to participate in such activities. May be, of course, a personal opinion pertaining to education, but also to the more subjective and less controllable passions,

preferences, phobias etc. We can, however, explain this refuse to go to the theater because of financial reasons: it is well known that, in England, performances (especially theater) are of high quality, and ticket prices keep up with the quality. In these circumstances, not everyone can afford a ticket. And thus, going to the show with the family one night could cost as much as a holiday.

The manager is characterized as an avid viewer of shows whenever he can.

Finally, the last assertion of this first section of the survey relates to people's ability to work under pressure. A team whose members can cope with stress is less exposed to conflict situations (this can reconfirm the previous stance on Q / R 8).

The statement we submitted to a review was "I hate working under presure " assuming that people prefer to work in a relaxed, calm atmosphere. The answers can be found in Figure 11.

Contrary to our expectations, but according to the logic of the attitudes towards conflict response, all team members said they are able to work under pressure empire without any problems.

Such an attitude, which corresponds to the manager, too, gives assurance that the team can function as a well-tuned mechanism under all

Figure 10. Cultural activities

Greek	4	
Dutch	3	
English	1	
Romanian	5	
French	3	
German	5	
Manager (Ro)		4

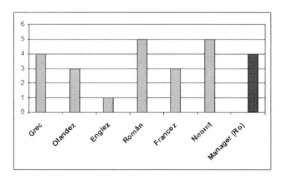

Figure 11. Working under pressure

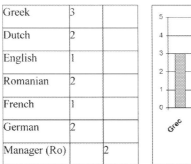
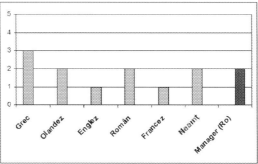

Greek	3	
Dutch	2	
English	1	
Romanian	2	
French	1	
German	2	
Manager (Ro)		2

conditions. Also, the task of the manager to manage the team in difficult times is relieved even by his colleagues, they showing willing to face stress without generating conflicts between them.

Once this section of the questionnaire is completed we can fulfil a comparative analysis of the responses (Figure 12).

It is noted that although there is some variation in responses between the manager and the team, both follow the same general trend.

Significant differences appear, in our opinion, just in the case of key issues on the management team, such as adaptation to work abroad (and with foreigners), attitudes towards conflict, decision making.

In fact, it is normal to have a manager to differentiate from the team, with a stronger behavior when it comes to conflict management, adapting to working with foreigners or decisions, because they are, in fact, traits which are indispensible to this position.

Figure 12. Comparative analysis

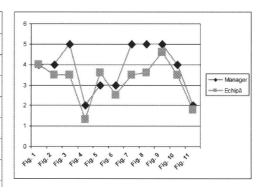

	Manager	Team
Fig. 1	4	4
Fig. 2	4	3,5
Fig. 3	5	3,5
Fig. 4	2	1,3
Fig. 5	3	3,6
Fig. 6	3	2,5
Fig. 7	5	3,5
Fig. 8	5	3,6
Fig. 9	5	4,6
Fig. 10	4	3,5
Fig. 11	2	1,8

REFERENCES

Ferraro, G. (2010). *The cultural dimension of international business*. Upper Saddle River, NJ: Prentice Hall.

Harvard Business Essentials. (2005). *Time management*. Cambridge, MA: Harvard Business School Publishing Corporations.

Hunter, M. (2005). *Guide to managerial communication*. Upper Saddle River, NJ: Prentice Hall.

Johnson, M. (2011). *The diversity code*. AMA Printer House.

Lewis, D. R. (2006). *When cultures collide. WS*. Bookwell Printing House.

Whalen, D. J. (2007). *The professional communication toolkit*. Thousand Oaks, CA: Sage Publications.

Zeigler, K. (2008). *Getting organized at work*. New York: McGraw-Hill Printing House.

Chapter 8
Communication in a Healthcare Company

Dina Rusnac
Bucharest University of Economic Studies, Romania

ABSTRACT

The chapter discusses the marketing strategies of private Romanian healthcare clinics from a communication perspective, advancing methods to improve customer outreach. The study puts together data from the private medical services market and comparatively analyzes the marketing strategies, making recommendations towards the optimal cost-benefit mix.

1. THE MARKETING AND COMMUNICATION STRATEGIES OF THE PRIVATE CLINICS FROM ROMANIA

The Concept of Strategy in a Firm

The strategy in a firm is the pattern of the major objectives, purposes or goals and essential policies and plans for achieving those goals, stated in such a way as to define what business the company is in or is to be in and the kind of company it is o it is to be.

It is considered that a company needs a strategy when the resources are finite, when there is uncertainty about competitive strengths and behavior, when commitment of resources is irreversible, when decisions must be coordinated between far-flung and over time and when there is uncertainty about control of the initiative. Strategy provides a unified sense of direction to which all members of the organization can relate (Payne, 1993).

Strategy is concerned with the deployment of potential for results and the development of a reaction capability to adapt to environmental

DOI: 10.4018/978-1-4666-4325-3.ch008

changes. Generally, organizations have identifiable existing strategic perspectives, however not many organizations have an explicit strategy for the intended future. The absence of an explicit strategy is frequently the result of a lack of top management involvement and commitment required for the development of proper perspectives of the future within the scope of current corporate activities.

- Strategy specifies the direction. Its intent is to influence the behavior of competitors and the evolution of the market to the advantage of the company making the strategy. A strategy statement includes a description of the new competitive equilibrium to be created, the cause-and-effect relationships that will bring it about, and the logic to support the course of action.

Defining the Marketing and the Communication Strategies

The *marketing strategy* can be defined as an endeavor by a corporation to differentiate itself positively from its competitors, using its relative corporate strengths to better satisfy customer needs in a given environmental settings. It is the marketing concept of building an organization around the profitable satisfaction of customer needs and it has helped firms to achieve success in high-growth, moderately competitive markets (Porter, 1981).

The formation of marketing strategy requires the following three decisions:

1. **Where to Compete:** That is, it requires a definition of an market (for example, competing across an entire market or in one or more segments).

2. **How to Compete:** That is, it requires a means for competing (for example, introducing a new product to meet a customer need or establishing a new image for an existing product).

3. **When to Compete:** That is it requires timing of market entry (for example, being first in the market or waiting until primary demand is established).

Many companies are trying to develop unique strategic marketing procedures, processes, systems and models. Experience shows, however, that most companies' marketing strategies are burdened with undue complexity. They are bogged down in principles that produce similar responses to competition. In order to be successful and competitive, companies should take into consideration several facts about the marketing strategy implementation that is as important as the strategy creation. So, the following are the common problems associated with marketing strategy formulation and implementation:

1. Too Much Emphasis on "Where" to Compete and not Enough on "How" to Compete

Experience shows that companies have devoted a lot more attention to identifying markets in which to compete than to the means to compete in these markets. Information on where to compete is usually easy to copy. "How" information, on the other hand, is tough to get and tough to copy. It concerns the fundamental workings of the business and the company.

In the next era of marketing, companies will need to focus more on how to compete in entirely new ways. In this endeavor, creativity will play a crucial role.

2. Too Little Focus on Uniqueness and Adaptability in Strategy

Most marketing strategies lack uniqueness. For example, specialty stores increasingly look alike because they use the same layout and stock the same merchandise. In the 1970's, when market information was scarce, companies pursued new and different approaches. But today's easiest access to information often leads companies to follow identical strategies to the detriment of all (Schultz et al., 1993).

Ideas for uniqueness and adaptability may flow from unknown sources. Companies should, therefore, be sensitive and explore all possibilities.

3. Inadequate Emphasis on "When" to Compete

Because of the heavy emphasis on where and how to compete, many marketing strategies give inadequate attention to "when" to compete. Any move in the marketplace should be adequately timed. The optimum time is one that minimizes or eliminates competition and creates the desired impact on the market; in other words, the optimum time makes it easier for the firm to achieve its objectives. Timing also has strategy implementation significance. It serves as a guide for different managers in the firm to schedule their activities to meet the timing requirement (Subhash, 1993).

Decisions on timing should be guided by the following:

1. **Market Knowledge:** If you have adequate information, it is desired to market readily; otherwise you must wait until additional information has been gathered.
2. **Competition:** A firm may decide on an early entry to beat minor competition, you may delay entry if necessary; for example, to seek additional information.
3. **Company Readiness:** For a variety of reasons, the company may not be ready to compete. These reasons could be lack of financial resources, labor problems, inability to meet existing commitments, and others.

The *marketing communication process* is the process of informing, reminding, and persuading the consumers about a particular product or service. The various promotional tools involved in product promotion comprise the communications mix of an organization. Marketing communication is instrumental in influencing the purchase decision of the consumer. Integrated Marketing Communication (IMC) is the judicious and efficient use of the product promotional tools so that a universal, clear and effective promotional message is communicated amongst the target audience. The paper examines IMC strategy and management.

IMC is a term used to describe a holistic approach to marketing communication. It aims to ensure consistency of message and the complementary use of media. It is the integration of all marketing tools, approaches, and resources within a company which maximizes impact on consumer mind and which results into maximum profit at minimum cost. Using outside-in thinking, IMC is a data-driven approach that focuses on identifying consumer insights and developing a strategy with the right (online and offline combination) channels to forge a stronger brand-consumer relationship. This involves knowing the right touch-points to use to reach consumers and understanding how and where they consume different types of media. Regression analysis and customer lifetime value are key data elements in this approach.

Integrated marketing communication is a new way of looking at the whole, where once we only saw parts such as advertising, public relations, sales promotion, purchasing, employee communications and so forth. It's realigning communication to look at it the way the customer sees it – as a flow of information from indistinguishable sources. IMC means talking to people who buy or don't buy based on what they see, hear, feel, etc.- and not just about the company's product or service. It means eliciting a response, not just conducting a monologue. And it means being accountable for results, not just readership scores or day-after recall – delivering a return on investment, not just spending a budget.

IMC is more than the coordination of a company's outgoing message between different media and the consistency of the message throughout. It is an aggressive marketing plan that captures and uses an extensive amount of customer information in setting and tracking marketing strategy. Steps in an Integrated Marketing System are:

1. **Customer Database:** An essential element to implementing Integrated Marketing that helps to segment and analyze customer buying habits.
2. **Strategies:** Insight from analysis of customer data is used to shape marketing, sales, and communications strategies.
3. **Tactics:** Once the basic strategy is determined the appropriate marketing tactics can be specified which best targets the specific markets.
4. **Evaluate Results:** Customer responses and new information about buying habits are collected and analyzed to determine the effectiveness of the strategy and tactics.
5. **Complete the Loop:** Start again at #1.

The Healthcare System in Romania

The Romanian health system has remained unchanged in many aspects for the last 30 years. It is a system based on social insurance and has as a goal the insurance of an equitable access to a basic package of services for all of the insured persons.

In 1997, Romania has introduced a new system for the health insurance through the Law nr. 145/1997, based on a modified version of the Bismarck's model. Nowadays, the Romanian sanitary system is based on several structures of the following models (taking into consideration the main way the system is financed):

1. **Semashko Model:** The sanitary system is financed through the state social insurance budget (state treasury account).
2. **Beveridge Model:** The principle of the "filter" role, patients are freely selecting the family doctors they prefer and they are financed through taxes.
3. **Bismark Model:** Based on social health insurance system (based on compulsory insurance bonuses, based on income).

The share of public expenses on health from GDP has varied between 3.6% and 3.7% during the last years, and since 2007 it started to be around 4%. For the last years, the budget for the healthcare system has increased in values, from 90 € / per citizen to 200 € / per citizen, as well as a share from the total GDP, from approximately 3% to over 4% during the same period.

Though there was an increase in the share of spending on the healthcare system from the GDP, still the financing level remains very low, compared to other EU member states. The financing of the healthcare system continues to be inefficient and inadequate. The Romanian healthcare system is considered to be chronically subsidized and lacking foreign investments. The allocation of resources is not made in a transparent manner, but rather on a very vague criterion. So, there are very big differences in the allocations of these subsidiaries between different regions of the country, types of healthcare services provided and different healthcare institutions.

The compulsory health insurances, as well as the optional ones administrated by the insurance houses, collect the taxes according to the income of each person and distribute them as benefits in the moment of usage of the medical services.

Funding resources of the health system:

1. The state budget
2. The budget of the National Common Fund for Health Social Insurance
3. The local budgets, private income, external credits
4. The non-refundable external funds, donations and sponsorships.

The majority of funds are directly or indirectly controlled by the state. The system is build around the central administration, while the medical personnel, patients and their representatives have very little power to influence the system that they are financing.

The single big modification that was made during the last years was the introduction of the health insurance system that has as an objective the consolidation of the responsibilities of the major buyer of medical services that is the Insurance House.

At the beginning, it was intended that the National Health Insurance House (Casa Naţională pentru Asigurări de Sănătate) had direct responsibility for the population's health and benefited of large autonomy for the collection and management of the health insurance funds. But as a matter of fact, the Parliament voted for a big modification in the legislation and made the National Health Insurance House a centralized institution that is controlled by the Ministry of Public Health and the Ministry of Public Finances. Now, the institution has a low level of autonomy and is managed simultaneously by several other institutions.

The Ministry of Public Health is the central authority in the healthcare system. It is an organizational structure that, unfortunately, doesn't really understand what are the real health needs and necessities of the population.

The World Health Organization considers that Romania needs to concentrate mostly on the following three areas:

1. The improvement of the population's health.
2. The increase of the response rate compared to population's expectations.
3. Insurance of equity in terms of financial contribution.

Taking into consideration these areas, nowadays, Romania is situated on the 99-th place in the world, after such countries as Albania, Slovakia, Hungary, Turkey, etc.

The comparison with other EU member states, as well as the comparison made between the different regions from Romania, states that the Romanian healthcare system is situated in an alarming situation. It is so, because of the existing big differences between the offered medical services across the country, the access to them and the sanitary indicators. There are regions in Romania, where the number of medical personnel is far below the medium level across the country. The access to medical services is highly restricted in most of the regions, especially in the rural areas. The rural areas have the lowest indicators regarding the number of doctors, pharmacists and assistants reported to population.

Drugs represent the biggest expense of the insurance system in Romania after the expenses with the personnel. Drugs represent almost a quarter of the Romania's total budget for sanitary system, which means that it is much bigger than the average of the European countries.

Though more than 50% from the total population from Romania lives in the rural area, only 30% of the total number of pharmacists and only 20% of doctors work in these areas.

The Decentralization and the Reform of the Health System

The decentralization of the health system plays an important role in the process of reforming the healthcare system in Romania. The reorganization and the decentralization of the funds and supply of medical services have started with the introduction of the health insurance system. This time, the patient/the citizen is situated in the center of the healthcare system and has the possibility to freely choose the supplier of medical services that he desires.

The EU laws will have a great impact on the supply of medical services in Romania, though the national government tried in many ways to maintain the control over the health system. Nether-the-less, it would take some time before the EU laws and regulations could be implemented in Romania, because the system is very rigid and difficult to change in a short period of time.

The Analysis of the Private Healthcare Market in Romania

The medical services market from Romania is formed of suppliers both from the private and from the public sector (Table 1).

The public sector that supplies medical services is trying to make some reforms and changes in its activity in order to increase the quality of the supplied services. One decision it made was to externalize some of its processes. This decision has as an aim the implementation of an efficient management system that would increase the quality and the diversity of the supplied services.

The private sector is continuously developing. On the one hand they are externalizing some of the activities of the public health institutions. On the other hand they are constantly growing by extending their network and supplying their services in more and more cities from Romania.

In a word, the private market of medical services from Romania had an ascending development during the last period and in 2008 it has reached the highest results for the last 10 years.

In 2010, the Romanian private healthcare market is expected to develop by around 13% to €373 million, according to estimates included in the report "Private healthcare market in Romania 2010, development forecasts for 2010-2012" written by PMR, a research and consulting company.

Growth is expected to continue on the private medical services market in Romania in 2010 despite the unfavorable economic conditions. All leading medical chains in the country expect their sales to increase in 2010 by 10-50%. "According to PMR forecasts, in 2010 the market, which consists of out-of-

Table 1. SWOT Analysis of the Romanian healthcare system

Strengths	Weaknesses
- contribution to the health insurance houses and participation to costs; - the development of the private healthcare system; - almost complete coverage of the population with medical services; - free access of the population to medical services;	- low access to medication; - the consumer's rights and information are very poor; - lack of specialists; - imbalance of the geographical distribution of the medical assistance; - the system is build around the central administration; - duplication of the medical acts; - bad evidence of the patients; - situated on almost the last place in the European healthcare system ranking;
Opportunities	**Threats**
- the formation, training and managing of the human resources; - improvement of the professional abilities of the medical personnel through trainings; - increasing the percentage of the primary medical assistance; - the computerization of the medical services system and the client's course follow up; - fostering the continuity of the medical services through hospital planning programs; - the adoption of some standards for medical products, medical technologies, medical trainings and information networks; - the improvement of the population's health condition and the equitable access to medical services for everybody; - the financial reorganization and decentralization;	- the financial resources for the medical services are not concentrated to stimulate the continuity of the medical services; - the absence of an institution that would evaluate and promote the continuous supply of medical services and the quality of the supplied medical services; - the unequal distribution of funds, the inefficient coordination of funds between the different sources of financing; - bad coordination of costs and the inefficient use of money are the major problems of the Romanian health system.

pocket payments for medical services, medical subscriptions (along with occupational healthcare services) and health insurance, will grow by 13% and develop even more rapidly in 2011 and 2012" says Monika Stefanczyk, PMR's Head Pharmaceutical Market Analyst and the report's coordinator.

Against a background of difficulties in public healthcare, private spending on healthcare has grown constantly in recent years, and this is expected to continue. Compulsory health insurance almost covers payment for treatment at public clinics in full, but Romanians, in general, complain about the quality of service in the public system and also the lack of special sophisticated treatments which are available at private hospitals. Another important matter pertaining to customer choice is the fact that private healthcare chains attract the best doctors, by offering them higher salaries. At

public hospitals doctors can earn around €200-350, whereas salaries at private facilities are several times this amount.

In 2010 difficulties with public healthcare funding are expected, and this will affect quality of service at public hospitals and encourage more customers to migrate to private clinics. With improvements in quality of life and increasing affluence, Romanians are no longer willing to tolerate bad management, an unprofessional appearance and a lack of individual care and courtesy at public clinics. Another important reason for the progress of private healthcare is the prevalence of bribery in the public healthcare system. People give bribes to doctors for quality of treatment and attention, and the total costs of treatment at public and private clinics are often comparable.

In anticipation of this trend, leading private suppliers of medical services are planning to invest more than €200 million within two or three years in hospitals alone to meet growing demand, according to our estimates. Although the private healthcare services market in Romania is not highly saturated, key players are expecting tough price competition in 2010, particularly with regard to corporate users.

Because there were, for many years, no legal provisions aimed at helping the private health insurance market to take off in Romania, the country has, over the past five years, seen a booming subscription market which has been acting as a substitute for insurance plans. The medical subscription market in Romania has been driven by mandatory occupational medical services, introduced in 2002, when the Health Ministry adopted a directive which forced both public and private employers to offer their staff medical examinations on a regular basis. Subscriptions to private medical services became a standard offer in the employee packages of large companies in Romania. Here, we are talking about the occupational medicine, which means that employees, according to their profession, have to do on a yearly basis a list of analysis and consultations.

In total, according to data gathered by PMR, in 2009 there were approximately 380,000 subscribers to private medical services in Romania. Subscriptions usually guarantee a minimum set of services, and it is necessary to pay additional fees for more expensive treatment.

In 2010 providers of medical chains expect stagnation on the corporate market and a boom in retail. Private medical companies have reported that the fees-for-services arena was already booming in 2009.

Most medical subscriptions developed in the fields of dental services, laboratory diagnostics, maternity and gynecology. Providers usually operate as a clinic. There are only two companies which have hospitals in their organizations: CMU and MedLife.

In 2010 most of the operators expect consolidation of the supply of medical services. Large chains of clinics already have a network of smaller partners which are expected to be acquired. In 2009 investment funds paid more attention to private healthcare and acquired, for example, MedLife (taken over in late 2009 by Societe Generale Asset Management).

The health insurance market has developed relatively slowly in the absence of legal provisions which would redefine the basic package of services and fiscal incentives. At present, the package covers a wide range of services, which prevents private insurers from creating comprehensive and more sophisticated offers for their clients. At the same time, the poor condition of medical facilities in Romania has discouraged patients from purchasing such products.

Development of health insurance is expected to take place in the next few years and to begin to take clients from private healthcare providers in the short term. The corporate subscription market is believed to have reached saturation and some customers might switch in future years to private health insurance, which is believed to be more comprehensive than the services offered by a network of medical facilities. However, this will depend largely on the expansion of private healthcare facilities in the country. Most operators expect the private healthcare services market to consolidate this year, and large chains already have smaller partners in their networks, which they intend to buy.

Also, private healthcare services providers plan to invest over €200 million in private hospitals in Romania over the following two or three years.

According to private medical companies operating in Romania, the market has a total potential of €400 million, but only about 12% of this can be achieved by 2012, according to the most optimistic scenarios.

Describing the Main Players on the Healthcare Market in Romania

The main players on the private market of medical services are as follows: Medicover, Centrul Medical Unirea, Medcenter, Medsana, Sanador, Hipocrat and Romar.

One of the most important players on this market is *Medicover*. First of all, I would like to mention that is a multinational company. Medicover is the largest health services company in Central and Eastern Europe providing compassionate, world-class medical care that meets the highest international standards. The company serves more than 6000 companies and more that 400,000 employees in Poland, Romania, Hungary, Czech Republic, Slovakia, Germany, Ukraine and Estonia. Being one of the largest private sector employer of medical professionals, Medicover serves both prepaid members and fee-for-service patients in its health centers, as well as through an extensive network of medical professionals. The company provides all primary and specialty care, diagnostic tests and follow-up care. In Romania the company does not have a hospital yet.

The company is mostly focused on occupational health. It works with large and small companies to develop programs custom-designed to meet their needs. These range from annual health exams to Medicover-staffed, on-site company clinics.

The company's clinical diagnostic laboratory services are supplied through its laboratories Synevo and IMD that provide efficient, timely services to all clients and the resulting measurable cost savings is passed along to companies and members.

In 1997 the company has launched its operations in Romania. Medicover's operations in Romania began with the purchase and merger of Rombel Medical Laboratories and Brimax International Medical Centre. Over the next dozen years, four additional health centers were added in Bucharest and in 4 other cities. During this time Rombel maintained its laboratory business, which merged in 2004 with Nova Medical Polska to form Synevo. *(Source:* www.medicover.ro*)*

Another important player on the market is *Centrul Medical Unirea (CMU)*. The company was created in 1995. It started its activity as a cardiology cabinet in a small apartment on the Unirea Boulevard. In 1996 they have introduced the concept of medical subscriptions. In 1999 they have launched officially their first medical center with multiple specialties.

Nowadays, the company has a large network of clinics in Bucharest and in the country. It has the CMU Kids clinic that offers medical services only for children; the Diagnostic and Treatment Center that offers medical services for people with rare and complicated illnesses; the Gynecologic and Obstetric Hospital that offers specialized medical services for women and finally the Stem-Health Unirea, that offer their patients to collect and keep the stem cells in a special bank. *(Source:* www.cmu.ro*)*

In 2010 the company was acquired by an investment fund named Advent International and it was considered to be one of the most important transactions that took place on the healthcare market. CMU offers to its clients diagnostic tests and analysis, imagistic services, hospital services, occupational medicine services, consultations and many other.

According to the results of IMAS"s recent poll, regarding Romanian private medical service providers, MedLife grabbed the top spot when it comes to notoriety among Romanian consumers.

When asked "Which private medical services providers did you hear about?", MedLife was the first name mentioned by the people participating in the poll. On a national scale, MedLife"s aggregated notoriety (spontaneous and assisted) was 14.6%, followed by Medcenter (12.9%), Medsana (12.1%), and almost tied for the 4th and 5th spot, were Unirea Medical Center (CMU) and Sanador with 11.6%, and 11.3%, respectively.

MedLife has been operating on the Romanian market since 1996, and currently is the largest private medical services provider on the domestic market. The company holds 4 hyper clinics in Bucharest and in the country, 5 analysis laboratories, and one medical center in each of the following cities: Cluj-Napoca, Arad, Braşov, Ploieşti and Năvodari. It has a network of over 120 partner clinics all across Romania.

MedLife owns the largest Romanian private clinic - Life Memorial Hospital - which is the result of an investment worth more than €10 million. The company was the first to attract the first major private investment in the sector, IFC - the consulting division of the World Bank, which became a majority shareholder holding a 20% stake. MedLife currently has approximately 1000 employees. (*Source:* www.medlife.ro)

Sanador Medical Center, that is the next competitor on the health care market in Romania, offers a broad range of medical services for individuals and their families, for national and multi-national companies. Founded in 2001, Sanador Medical Center has been continuously evolved, now operating two clinics, a fully-equipped medical labora-tory and private medical reserves located in "Floreasca" Emergency Hospital. Sanador is a top Medical Center in Bucharest and the only private clinic which has the ability to cover a full range of medical services due to its highly specialized medical staff and state of the art equipment. Sanador's medical data processing system offers a safe, confidential and convenient way to schedule for appointments and to archive the patient's private files for future reference.

Personalized medical packages are available depending of each client's personal needs in order to benefit of prompt high quality medical services in all Sanador centers delivered to you by a dedicated medical team and state of the art medical equipment.

Due to its highly specialized physicians and medical staff Sanador Medical Center has the ability to cover a broad range of full medical services such as specialty investigations, lab tests and diagnosis, imagistic explorations (3D/4D Ultrasound, Gastroscopy, Colposcopy, Magnetic Resonance Investigations, Computed Tomography, Mammography, Radiology, Osteodensitometry, a.s.o.), Stomatology and dental radiology, Emergency services, employment screening and periodic medical check-up, prophylactic programs for employees, work-place assessments and counseling, first aid at work training, vaccination. Sanador Medical Center is authorized to serve as International Vaccination Centre.

2. THE MEDCENTER'S MARKETING AND COMMUNICATION STRATEGY

About the Company - Business Description

MEDCENTER is a Medicarom Group company and it represents one of the most important suppliers of clinical and laboratory medical services from Romania. Having over 12 years experience in this field, Medcenter has developed itself as a reliable partner for state and private companies from different fields of activity at national level. Currently, the company benefits of national coverage, operating through a network of 42 centers, with a different range of medical services. Medical centers are located in the following cities: Bucuresti, Iasi, Baia Mare, Cluj-Napoca, Brasov, Focsani, Buzau, Braila, Tecuci, Adjud, Rm Sarat, Codlea, Panciu, Turda and Constanta.

Medcenter's history started in 1998, when its thirst medical center opened in Iasi. That time, the market of private medical services was juts beginning to develop. The need for private medical services aroused as the state health system was not satisfying and fulfilling the needs of people. As people saw that they couldn't find the services they needed at the quality level they wanted, more and more people started to address to private medical services, where their needs were satisfied.

Medcenter has an ascending evolution during these 12 years, but the most spectacular years were 2003 and 2004, the years when Medcenter changed its status from a local supplier of medical services into a national supplier by opening two more centers and winning the tender for externalization of 2 state hospitals. From that moment, Medcenter started to strengthen its network by opening new medical centers all over the country.

Most Important Achievements of Medcenter during its Evolution

See Tables 2 through 4 and Figures 1 and 2.

1. **Decentralization of Decision-Making Power:** A new approach of decision-making power and responsibilities in hierarchies;
2. Implementing a system of centralized tracking and reporting sales;
3. Implementing target for the sales force, for each center;
4. **Building a Seals Team in each Center:** Trained and dedicated to increase seals in the private sector;
5. **Re-Branding Medcenter:** Implementation of a new identity (brand's logo, image, marketing strategy and advertising themes) which lead to the repositioning of the company and moving it up-market;
6. Creating a unitary identity for Medcenter, a "label" applied in all Medcenter clinics;
7. Obtaining certifications and quality credentials for Medcenter clinics (RENAR Quality Certificate, IQNet Certification, SRAC Certification) – this had 2 major advantages: obtaining a major score for CASMB/J and creating the image of a top quality supplier;
8. Implementing a new system of professional training and yearly evaluation for our staff.

Medcenter Evolution in Figures

1. Making outsourced hospitals efficient has turned them into profitable unit and generated an upward trend;
2. Both Private Contracts and Cash have an upward trend; since 2006, Private Contracts have registered a growth of approximately 50% from year to year;

Starting with 2007-2009, changes has been made in the sales structure of laboratory tests - focus on selling the more expensive tests

Medcenter has built a team of 480 employees, made of highly trained personnel, dedicated to manage a portfolio of over 500

Table 2. Percentage growth of turnover and yearly number of laboratory tests 2005-2009

growth %	2005	2006	2007	2008	2009
turnover	99.20%	15.14%	59.57%	32.84%	-16.67%
no of analysis	101.13%	20.77%	42.02%	16.55%	1.45%

Source: Internal data from Medcenter

Table 3. Lines of income of Medcenter (RON)

	2001	2002	2003	2004	2005	2006	2007	2008	2009
CASH	394,023	559,797	654,726	943,062	2,644,242	3,395,968	4,436,304	5,878,744	8,604,558
CAS	227,666	2,606,962	2,579,800	5,258,602	5,793,766	4,775,524	11,741,551	15,289,396	4,976,773
PRIVATE CON-TRACTS	97,587	78,674	85,634	131,268	1,303,818	3,188,420	5,050,965	7,415,427	7,479,783
HOSPITAL				1,219,940	5,303,756	5,963,990	6,415,431	8,137,806	9,537,409
total	719,276	3,245,433	3,320,160	7,552,873	15,045,581	17,323,903	34,516,107	46,137,105	30,774,202

Source: Internal data from Medcenter

Table 4. Yearly number of analysis made in Medcenter

	2001	2002	2003	2004	2005	2006	2007	2008	2009
no of analysis	200,670	411,558	452,592	1,185,178	2,383,786	2,878,849	4,088,670	4,765,522	4,834,471
growth %		105.09%	9.97%	161.86%	101.13%	20.77%	42.02%	16.55%	1.45%

Source: Internal data from Medcenter

Figure 1. Income evolution of Medcenter between 2001 and 2009
Source: Internal data from Medcenter

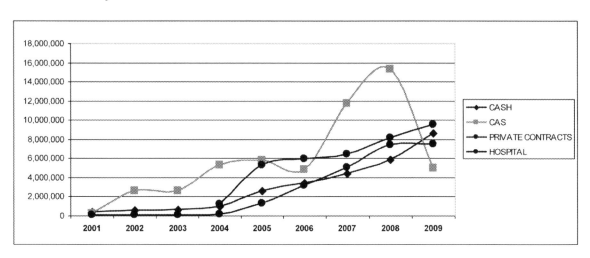

Figure 2. Yearly number of analysis made in Medcenter laboratories between 2001 and 2009

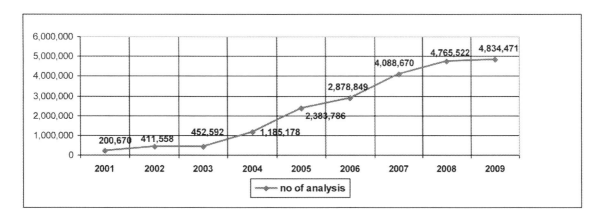

companies and over 50.000 private health subscriptions, 70 000 patients each month and over 4 500 000 analysis per year.

The company's mission is to ensure a correct health evaluation of its pacients, through an accurate and fast diagnosis, all its centers providing medical services based on modern equipment, coordinated by specially trained and highly-qualified personnel.

The company's future plans are aimed for acquiring the status of a national and international supplier of clinical and laboratory medical services by developing current centers of Medcenter, by opening new medical and laboratory centers and also by externalizing other laboratories and other partnerships.

Medcenter activity is primarily focused on clients form the private sector, which can be classified as it follows:

- Companies from all field of activities
- Medical companies
- Insurance companies
- Private persons (majority)

Medcenter activity also includes services for clients from public sector:

- Public hospitals
- Health Insurance House

Medcenter's Products and Services

The Medcenter clinics offer a wide range of clinical and laboratory medical services, as follows:

- Medical specialties
- Diagnostic tests
- Laboratory analysis
- Family medicine
- Occupational medicine

The Medcenter services are mostly oriented to clients form the private sector and are aiming to satisfy as best as possible their needs, whether they are private companies or physical persons.

The Medcenter's activity is strictly regulated by the implementation of the quality standard SR EN ISO 9001:2001 and the activity of the Medcenter's laboratory of medical analyses is accredited by RENAR according to SR EN ISO/CEI 17025:2000. Medcenter has outstanding equipment in its medical centers and laboratories and this is one of the most improtant reasons for the company's constant development and a basis for its customers' satisfaction.

The Relationship between Marketing and Selling in a Company

Marketing is a systematic design of business activities for planning pricing, distributing and promoting a good or service to the target market. American Marketing Association defines it as "Marketing is the performance of business activities that direct the flow of goods and services from producer to consumer or user".

Business organizations conduct their marketing activities under five marketing concepts. These concepts are based on the philosophy of the company to decide whether the interest is society or customers. Marketing has evolved out of these concepts. During the late 80s in the initial stages of Industrial revolution, there was no competition and producers believed in production concept which means consumer prefer inexpensive and widely available products, so major emphasis was on high production efficiency. But as more companies came in, product concept emerged where companies started to improve their product features.

Later, in 1920s selling concept came into being, where producers believe in aggressive selling and promotion of a product or service to sell their products. And as the competition increased producers started realizing the value of customer and customer satisfaction. Companies started analyzing what customers need or want and the main idea was to satisfy customers and maximize profits. Customer is considered as a king.

Many people think selling and marketing as the same thing. Bus a successful manager should know the difference between them. Selling is to sell what producer produces, rather than selling what a customer wants, whereas marketing is satisfying customers by the means of product. Selling aims at sales maximization. Marketing aims at profit maximization. Marketing is a vital activity of a business process. It holds an important place in the enterprise as it helps to increase sale and earn revenue. It helps to create utilities of time, place and possession. It increases per capita income and raise the standard of living. It ensures the better services to the consumer and creates employment in the field of marketing.

Marketing in a developed economy gets the advantage of the matured marketing system. Due to lack of effective competition, seller's domination in the market, low income groups, lack of knowledge and less supporting services. Marketing involves four basic activities: product, pricing, physical distribution and promotion. Combining these four activities in the right proportion to achieve the target goal is known as a marketing mix. These basic elements, according to Kotler, are the four P's of the marketing mix. If the company is unable to design an effective marketing mix, it will not be able to succeed and achieve its marketing goals and selling the company's products.

The terms "marketing" and "selling" are often used interchangeably and can be confusing to new business owners. In addition, since home business owners typically perform most tasks associated with their business, the lines between marketing and selling can become even more blurred.

Why is it important to make the difference between these 2 important concepts for an organization? Knowing the difference between marketing and selling can help identify and clarify where your efforts, as a manager, are successful and where they need improvement. To succeed you have to identify and build on your strengths and correct your weaknesses. The company's marketing efforts may be producing hundreds of leads, but if you, as a manager, don't know when and how to switch gears to make the sale, you won't produce the income results you want. Marketing can be thought of as all the activities that go into making people aware that your company and products exist. Selling involves the steps taken to convince the potential customer to make the actual product purchase. Marketing makes the company and product known to potential customers. It creates a demand for the company's products or services. Marketing involves a good deal of research to identify groups of potential buyers. That research determines what customers want and what they're willing to pay for it. The company's marketing message conveys why someone should choose that company or product over all the others. It describes how the company can meet your customers' wants and needs; how it can solve their problems. In a word, *marketing produces leads*.

Selling is what turns those leads into paying customers. It is more closely associated with a process called overcoming objections. Part of the marketing process is to actually uncover potential objections which might prevent a prospect from being converted to a customer. Selling is where all that marketing research is applied at the point of sale. It is a much more intimate, one-to-one technique where a buyer "assists" a prospective customer in making a "buying decision" (Porter, 1981).

If a sales person market primarily online, his research can be done using search engines or keyword searches, and using specialized programs as well as various other methods. In mere minutes the online marketer can accumulate highly accurate real-time data on what people are looking at, or looking for online, and fairly easily conduct other research such pricing, packaging, and availability. The value of this powerful research capability cannot be understated.

Once the company's research has identified its potential customers, the marketing plan will include all the activities that reach them and encourage them to visit its sales pages. Online marketing may include your website, search engine optimization, advertising, social media marketing, article marketing, blogging, press releases, podcasting, email marketing, networking, video marketing, and link building.

All of the company's marketing activities will funnel prospects to your sales page(s) where customers will ultimately click the "buy now" button and complete the purchase. By the time prospects hit the company's sales page its marketing message will have convinced them that the company is trustworthy and they'll be open to the idea of buying from it. Selling answers their questions about how they will personally benefit from that product. It's a call to action.

If we think about traditional brick-and-mortar stores, marketing involves all of the activities that get a potential customer to walk in the door. Selling occurs inside the store and involves interaction with a sales clerk. For direct sales party plan consultants, much of the marketing is done by the company you are associated with. It's the company that has done the market research, established pricing, developed advertising materials, catalogs, brochures, sales party procedures, and more. Independent consultants can focus more on selling, but should also engage in marketing themselves. A consultant's marketing plan should focus on why customers should choose her over the thousands of other consultants offering similar products from other companies and over others in the same company.

Marketing can also be best described as getting the product to market, whereas selling involves actually closing the sale with a potential customer. Some people also refer to closing the sale as the "conversion," referring to the fact that the potential customer is converted into an actual customer.

There are some areas where marketing and sales intersect or overlap. One area is when you create the "pitch." Most people are familiar with the term "sales pitch," but the sales pitch is not about selling alone. It is also about the development and delivery of that marketing message so that consumers will receive it.

Effective marketing then also includes clear effective delivery of the "pitch" to consumers. This should be done through whatever means you use to communicate with your potential customers-including in print or media advertising or through point-of-purchase displays and other means. Your "pitch" or your message should be clear and professional and build trust.

Many sales people consider selling as a way of overcoming objections. If a consumer is considering the purchase of a product, they already desire the product, but chances are they have objections that stand between that desire and making the actual purchase. The research conducted during the marketing process should identify all the potential objections that might arise prior to a sale. It can also help address some of these concerns

and objections up front. Then, you increase your odds of closing the actual sale.

Marketing then is a lot about numbers, research, and statistics. But that's not enough by itself. Marketing is also an art. It involves understanding human motivations, as well. Those motivations determine how, when, what, and why they buy.

Internet marketing-and in fact, all marketing-seems to be focused on numbers. You will often hear the media focusing on how many potential customers you can reach via a particular means of advertising or by sending emails, etc. But just because you expose your message to thousands or millions of people does not guarantee success.

You won't automatically get a particular percentage of people to purchase from you just because they hear about you. It's not that simple. Certain groups of people are going to be more inclined to purchase your product or service based on their specific motivations. So rather than just putting your message out there for everyone (and paying to do that), good marketing focuses on speaking to and being heard by the right demographic group that is more likely to purchase what you are selling.

Marketing - when done well - is pretty seamless. Compelling ad copy and attractive graphics make it seem easy. Effective marketing uses these tools to convey the appropriate message to the target market. When marketing is well done, products or services seem to almost sell themselves.

Understanding the difference between marketing and selling will help focus your efforts and improve your profits. A successful marketing plan will get the marketing message in front of the right people at the right time, and these targeted customers will become excited to buy the product. Selling is what closes the deal.

CREATING A NEW MARKETING AND COMMUNICATION STRATEGY FOR MEDCENTER AND EVALUATING ITS EFFECTS ON THE COMPANY'S SALES

Describing the Current Marketing and Sales Strategy of Medcenter

At the present moment, Medcenter has a quite big a sales department and very small marketing department that is made out only of 2 persons. It is important to mention that the company is not investing so much financial resources in marketing, as it is considered to be a waste of money by the management of the company. As I have already mentioned, in my final paper I will not try to understand why is this happening in Medcenter, rather I will try to create a new strategy for the company, create some ways of implementation and try to show methods of evaluating the results of the strategy.

Now, I will try to make a short description of the sales and marketing department in Medcenter the relationship between them.

The sales department in Medcenter is composed of 15 sales agents and 5 support employees. Medcenter's selling activity is primarily focused on clients form the private sector, which can be classified as follows:

1. Companies from all Fields of Activity
2. Medical Companies
3. Insurance Companies
4. **Private Persons:** This category is most targeted category for the sales department.

Medcenter's selling activity also includes services for clients from the public sector, like:

- Public Hospitals
- National Health Insurance House

Medcenter sells several categories of services, as follows:

Occupational Medicine and Medical Subscriptions for Companies

Occupational medicine is the branch of medicine that deals with the prevention and treatment of diseases and injuries occurring at work or in specific occupations. In accordance with the Health Ministry Directive no.933 /Nov. 2002, Medcenter provides the following services:

- Medical check-up at hiring (employment screening);
- Adaptation medical check-up;
- Periodic medical check-up;
- Medical check-up after medical breaks.

The company will also provide:

- Work-place assessments;
- Employers counseling regarding special work conditions for employees;
- Rehabilitation, reorientation and professional reintegration.

Laboratory Analysis

Medcenter's laboratory activity is working in accordance to the quality standard SR EN ISO/CEI 17025:2000, accredited by RENAR. Medcenter has outstanding equipment in its medical centers and laboratories and this is one of the most important reasons for the company's constant development and a basis for its customers' satisfaction. The company's laboratory offers a range of more than 400 different tests, from the following categories: Hematology, Coagulation, Immunohematology, Chemistry, Viral markers, Endocrinology markers, Tumor markers, Cardiac markers, Immunology and Serology, Microbiology, Molecular biology, Allergies, Toxicology, Drugs in urine, Pathological anatomy.

Family Medicine

Medcenter offers also family medicine services, there are more 30 family doctors all over the company's network. Any person can have a personal family doctor, all you have to do is just to choose one of the doctors and make an appointment.

Medical Specialties

The medical specialties that are available in Medcenter's clinics are as follows: Allergology, Infectious diseases, Balneophysiotherapy, Cardiology, Dermatology, Diabetes and Nutritious diseases, Echography, Endocrinology, Physiotherapy, Gastroenterology, Gynecology, Hematology, Hepatovirusology, Chirotherapy, Family medicine, General medicine, Internal medicine, Occupational medicine, Neurology, Ophthalmology, Otolaryngology, Orthopedics, Pediatrics, Pneumology, Psychiatry, Psychology, Rheumatology and Urology.

Diagnostic Tests

In Medcenter patients can benefit from the following diagnostic tests that are available in all centers all over the country, as follows: Audiogram, Colposcopy, Echography, Effort electrocardiogram, Electrocardiogram, Osteodensitometry and Test respiratory.

Medcenter is also a reliable partner in many fields, like:

Partner of Insurance Companies

The company provides the best national coverage to its partners in insurance field, delivering top quality services and a problem – solving oriented attitude towards their customers. Thus, the company's network of medical centers and laboratories is continuously growing, having as target the coverage of minimum 50% of the entire country until 2012. Medcenter collaborates with most of the insurance companies, such as Allianz Tiriac, Interamerican, Omniasig, Signal Iduna, etc.

Partner in Clinical Studies

Medcenter has 10 years of experience in providing clinical laboratory services and over 5 years in participation in national clinical studies, implemented by pharmaceutical companies and other partners in the field.

The company provides excellent territorial coverage, both through its own clinics as well as through the medical teams. The company has developed its own infrastructure of blood samples collection and transportation that ensures the delivery of services to any of the locations included in the study. Also, Medcenter uses its own integrated software system which offers the beneficiary real time access to the requested reports. Medcenter has implemented its own Standard Operating Procedures – SOP – which ensures the accuracy and speed of execution in all medical processes.

Naturally, the quality control is extremely important for the company and in this regard it has implemented both internal and external control procedures, provided by prestigious laboratories from Germany, UK, Finland, etc.

Partner with other Medical Companies

Medcenter collaborates with other 200 medical companies which have chosen to request medical services from Medcenter. Among them there are Centrul Medical Unirea, Medsana, Euroclinic, International Healthcare System, etc. The company's 10 years experience in providing medical services, as well as the excellent coverage of regional clinics and the quality standards implemented in each medical center have made the company a reliable partner in this field.

Outsourcing Laboratories

Medcenter is one of the most important players in the field of outsourcing laboratories, winning the public tenders for outsourcing the laboratories of three County Hospitals: Focsani, Braila and Buzau. The company entirely took-over the County Hospitals Laboratories and made great investments in both the building itself, as well as in the laboratory equipments and personnel.

This offers great advantages to the company's medical partners, as it is able to:

- Deliver laboratory tests in a 24/7 regime
- Perform specific medical tests that are only allowed in a hospital laboratory
- Provide professional services and equipment for blood collection and analysis, as well as the highest hygienic conditions for performing the medical activity in the hospital laboratories.

These are the main services available at Medcenter. Nether-the-less, most of the income in the company comes from selling occupational medicine services and private subscriptions. That is why the company has invested a lot of money in its sales team that sells these kinds of services. As an evidence of this, is the process of selling occupational medicine and private subscriptions to companies that was implanted in the company.

The following persons are involved in the process of selling and execution of a contract of Occupational Medicine: Account manager, Sales coordinator, Director of the sales department, Coordinator of contract operations, Project Manager and the doctors. I will present below the steps that are followed in this process.

One of the first steps in the selling process in any company, not only at Medcenter, is the finding of new customers. In this company there are several methods that are used at this stage.

The Account Manager can prospect himself the market in order to find the clients, usually by searching on websites for this information. He is searching mostly for companies that are more exposed to accidents at work or those companies that have to correspond to some special sanitarian conditions, like public alimentation companies or construction companies. Also, the Account Managers get some prospect clients from the Sales coordinator. They may ask the current clients for recommendations.

After the clients are contacted, the Account Manager is setting a meeting with the potential client in order to present the offer and discuss about it. Afterwards the client signs the contract; its employees are programmed by the Project Manager for medical examinations. After the examinations are made, the employees get an aptitude file from Medcenter that proves that they are suitable for the job they execute. On the other hand, with this aptitude file, the employer has a document that proves that he is in accordance with the current legislation.

The costs that are involved for executing the process of selling Occupational medicine services to clients include the current expenses like: salaries for employees, depreciation of the equipment that is used for executing the medical examinations, maintenance of the sales agent's cars, fuel and other current expenses.

Creating a New Marketing and Communication Strategy for Medcenter

It was observed that during the last 9 months, there was a constant decrease in sales in Medcenter. The company tries to figure out why this thing happens. Is it only the cause of the economic crises from the country or is it also something else? From my point of view, one of the major problems of Medcenter is the fact that the company's name is not so well-known. Very few people and companies know about Medcenter and this is of course because the company did not invest important sums of money in marketing and in creating an image for Medcenter. The management of the company think that the company should be promoted through its sales force and it would be sufficient for having good sales and a good image. But, as time showed, Medcenter had excellent results only before the crises came. Nowadays, other medical companies invest money in marketing and sales and they try to attract new clients by all means.

At the present time, Medcenter's marketing activity consists of creating marketing materials, like brochures, flyers with medical centres, visit cards, etc. The company has also some accounts on specialized medical sites, where it gets some messages from the sites visitors. Also the company has a quite complex and interesting site, that is also administered by the marketing team. That is in major the main activities that are done by the marketing department.

Elaborating the Marketing Goals and Objectives for Medcenter

Now, I would like to think about and try to create a new marketing strategy for the Medcenter and show its way of implementation. I will not be able to know what would be the real results of this strategy, as it is only a supposition and a vision of mine, but I will present methods to evaluate if my strategy will work or not. So, if my strategy would be implemented, the management of the company knew how to evaluate the return on the investments they did.

In order to create a good marketing strategy for this company we should try to find out what are the objectives of this firm from the marketing and communication point of view.

Marketing objectives are the key term in a marketing strategy plan. The objectives consist from marketing direction – it highlights the purpose of the market and its desired outcome. It is normally written in a statement which forms the highest level of purpose for a business. Some of the most common marketing objectives are the market share and the revenues. It is considered, that in order to fulfill the market share objective it is necessary to acquire 50% of the total marketing volume for a market segment. As for the revenue objective, it is considered to be an increase in sales.

Marketing goals and objectives are derived to assist in directing the strategic marketing plan toward its outcomes. Goals and objectives are the results we hope to achieve with the marketing program. As a differentiation, goals are the broad or macro level outcomes we desire to achieve from the marketing plan. Marketing objectives are the specific o micro-level outcomes we hope to achieve and are associated with further defining a specific goal. Each goal lays the framework for developing objectives. A marketing goal is typically more generic and vague. Therefore a *marketing goal* answers the question: "What broad desired results do we want to achieve with our strategic marketing plan?" While the *marketing objectives* answer the question: "For each goal, what are the specific outcomes we hope to achieve with the marketing plan?"

For Medcenter, the marketing objectives would be:

- Increasing the company's notoriety among customers
- Creating a brand image for Medcenter
- Attracting new customers
- Promoting the existing services and creating new ones
- Increasing the Medcenter's site visitors and page rank
- Increasing the number o signed contracts with 30%
- Increasing the number of laboratory tests with 15%
- Increasing the number of patients with 20% in the clinics
- Fidelization the visitors of the website
- Market positioning of the new opened centers

All these marketing objectives should help the company to fulfill its general goal that is increasing the sales and the revenues of the company.

Actually, raising awareness of your product in your target market is where sales begin, and this is where marketing communications activities begin the selling process. With today's multiple channels for content to reach potential customers, the art and science of marketing communications has become increasingly important.

The marketing communications function (commonly called "marcom") has many communication tools available. Some companies in an industry might rely on paid advertising in print and online media. While other companies in the same industry might rely on a very different media mix, such as public relations and events. However, no company can be sure they are using the most efficient media mix without creating a marcom strategy that is aligned with their overall strategic marketing direction. For Medcenter we will use both of the communication tools available, as the company didn't do anything of this kind before and it is really necessary to raise the company's image among customers.

The marketing communications strategy process usually begins with creating a "messaging strategy", that is determining the consistent theme or fundamental selling message that will be used in all marketing materials. Medcenter has such a message that is used in all its materials, like brochures, flyers, the site, etc. This message is "It's about your health!". This message wants to relate the fact that any person should be conscious about the importance of their health and the importance of choosing a good supplier of medical services that will give you a correct diagnosis.

Another key part of the messaging process is creating the positioning statement. This two sentence statement tells what you sell, to whom, and why customers should buy it. The positioning statement for Medcenter would be: "Medcenter focuses on selling highly qualitative services, by this fulfilling the needs of customers, whether they are companies or persons." The company's mission is to become the preferred top supplier of medical and laboratory services, proved by the proficiency the company offers and by respecting the standard of quality implemented in all of the medical centers.

As you move through the process of creating a positioning statement, you'll want to capture your brainstorming results, such as in your marketing strategy mind map. Then, refine and test those creative approaches until you settle on your company's positioning statement. Your positioning statement is critical to making all of the other parts of the marketing communications strategy work well. This is because every awareness-building and product information program needs to paint a clear, concise picture of what you sell and how customers will benefit from using your products.

Once you have settled on a strong positioning statement, you can develop sound strategies for your marketing programs. For most companies this means considering programs such as:

1. Public relations
2. Advertising
3. Web site
4. Seminars
5. Conferences and trade shows
6. Downloadable materials
7. Direct marketing (offline & online)
8. Packaging
9. Event sponsorships
10. Merchandising promotions

A mind map is a good way to capture ideas about which programs look like they will be most effective. Add these programs to the Marketing Communications section of your strategic marketing mind map. Later, evaluate each program to see if it should be in your final strategic marketing plan.

In large companies where each marketing program has its own manager, you can link your main strategic marketing mind map to each program's own planning mind map. In companies where the whole marcom strategy is implemented by one team, you can add details about marcom programs in the team's main marketing mind map.

New Vision on Medical Marketing

There are always medical breakthroughs on the horizon that will change the way diseases are treated. And while there always will be dramatic changes in medical treatments and technologies, there also will be a dramatic evolution in how the healthcare industry relates to its customers. One area in healthcare that is changing, but will be even more striking in the near future, is relationship marketing. As technologies related to the medicines and procedures themselves change, so must the marketing that supports them.

Trends are emerging and show us the future of relationship marketing in healthcare. While some of these trends might not come to pass, it is known for sure that one trend will continue: *Healthcare marketing must improve patient health.* Consumers, physicians, payers, legislators and the general public will reject anything else. The healthcare industry will continue to receive unfair criticism, but it can begin to win over opponents by clearly showing the reason why it exists in the first place: to improve the lives of patients. Every marketing effort should help deliver this goal.

There must be considered the following trends in consumer's behavior, while creating a marketing strategy for your clinic:

Healthcare Information 24/7

This means that consumers will demand immediate access healthcare information. The information that consumers will have access to and will use to make decisions will continue to increase in volume and availability. A simple search on Google can yield reliable disease-state information and treatment options. Consumers now can get reports about the effectiveness of a particular hospital or clinic to check not only mortality rates of a particular procedure, but also cost. This type of information will only increase in use and no longer do consumers need to be at home to find it. Growing use of mobile Internet applications will make it easy for consumers to find out anything they want – anytime they want it. Healthcare companies must embrace this fundamental change by allowing easy access to information for consumers wherever they are.

Consumers as "Physicians"

As in many other industries, consumers will generate more and more of the available content. With the staggering increase in bloggers, user-generated media (such as YouTube), and social networking, end users are creating and controlling more and more of the content available online. This will begin to extend to healthcare to a greater degree during the next five years. For healthcare companies, this represents both an opportunity and a threat. The opportunity is that with wide networks and vocal brand advocates, your massage can be spread quickly for little expense. However, the negative side is particularly dangerous in healthcare. Like other industries, for every positive mention of a brand, there is likely also a negative one. In the case of healthcare, incorrect negative information puts patient's health in risk – something every company must be vigilant about monitoring to protect their brand and the lives of their customers.

Internet: A Trusted Source

It is considered that the internet will become the primary site and, potentially most trusted source for healthcare information for the vast majority of consumers. All other forms of media already fall behind the Internet. This is true across all age ranges and demographics. Savvy baby boomers will only accelerate this change. Friends and family are trusted sources, but they never will be as comprehensive as the Internet for sheer volume of information. With more social networking and peer sharing opportunities on the Internet, many consumers will turn to their "online" family for information. Likely, physicians will remain the most trusted source of information, but it is likely that most patients will go online before or after talking with a physician to "double-check" the information they received. Healthcare companies must be aware of this change and quickly move to become trusted, objective, and valuable source of information online (Kotler et al., 2002).

It's their Data, Not Yours

Advances in technology and consumer adoption will allow consumers to track and control all of their healthcare data in one place, making it available anywhere at any time. Throughout the country, hospitals and individuals are slowly adopting technologies such as electronic medical records that have existed for a number of years. However, in these cases physicians, hospitals, and managed care companies continue to "own" the data. This includes data regarding past test results, physician notes, medical history, and allergies, for example. In future, consumers will have more control on this data. Services such as

Microsoft HealthValut and Google Health are one of the ways that allow consumers to maintain all of their healthcare information. This allows them to track their health over time when they want it, not just during a doctor's visit. In addition, in emergencies all of their data is immediately available. This is something that's been promised by the healthcare system for many years, but consumers have grown tired of waiting and are simply doing this on their own. Healthcare companies must embrace this change and make it simple for consumers to track the usage of their products or services. It will be critical to provide integration instead of yet another system for them to use.

Healthy Social Networking

Finding a world of people they can relate to online, patients will begin to form more formal and informal networks seeking advice of their peers instead of their physicians. Because of the sheer number of people utilizing the Internet, it is possible to find people who share the same experiences as you. This even becomes true for those with the rarest conditions. Patients will use these networks to share treatment ideas, provide moral support, recommend physicians, advocate for causes and demand action from the medical community. Using the power of numbers, patients now will be able to pressure healthcare companies on a much larger scale. Healthcare companies must respond to these networks appropriately and see them as partners or they will face negative repercussions, ranging from bad press to boycotts.

Constant Contact, Constant Care

Health-monitoring technologies will put doctors and patients in constant contact. Some technologies to monitor patients' health, now in early development and still largely cumbersome and not embraced by the public, will become more widespread. These include vital-sign monitoring to check on patients after surgical procedures, drug compliance programs and constant health status updates via the Internet. All of these data, once captured and interpreted, will allow doctors and patients to become more closely connected. An office visit will no longer be necessary to see if a new blood pressure medication, for example, is working. The doctor simply can access the patient's information online and adjust the medication instantly via a message to the pharmacy. Patients will become more accepting of these technologies will form lasting bonds with consumers and early adopters, gaining a big competitive advantage and increasing barriers to entry for others later on.

Evaluating the Results of the New Marketing Strategy for MedCenter

In order to evaluate the results of a marketing strategy there can be used several tools, like: Consumers surveys, focus groups, interviews, patient surveys, discharge surveys, etc. This process also helps to identify what they consider to be the key benefits from a particular service.

Telemarketing is another tool which is beginning to finally be used by health marketers. Telemarketing is a form of using the telephone or computer to make contact with the health consumer. Traditionally, the access to people came from patient records or telephone directories. Now the computerized random digit dialing makes any connected telephone a potential part of the survey. Telephone interviews are excellent for gathering a small amount of information from a large number of people. Since contact is by voice, questions must not require visual aids or thorough understanding of complex topics by the interviewees. A telephone interview may last 10-15 minutes with many close-end questions, that is, question for which a list of answers is provided. Surprisingly, telephone respondents may actually provide more information or be more honest than in-person interviews. Consumers tend to be more open since the telephone becomes the defense mechanism for anonymity. Telephone interviews do have some disadvantages. For example, answers must be shorter and not as in-depth as those obtained in other methods. There is no opportunity to use any visual aids or props. However, these disadvantages are minimal in comparison to the strong cost-benefit aspects of comparing personal versus telephone interviews. Because of its low-cost, high response rate, and small time requirements, the telephone survey is often the best method to use in surveying the general community.

Videotex is an interactive electronic system in which data and graphics are transmitted from a computer network over telephone or cable lines and displayed on a subscriber's TV or computer terminal screen. Marketing research firms see videotex systems as a major consumer auditing tool for the future. On the research side, surveys can be done directly to consumers through the personal computer. As households continue to add computers to their possessions, the health industry will be later able to survey consumers directly and instantaneously through a videotex system. The industry can also use the system as a key educational tool for self-diagnosis, preventive health, and for marketing their specific services. Videotex systems are currently used sporadically in health organizations, but the potential and outlook is for much greater utilization of this effective marketing tool. The future of improving marketing techniques in health care will be related to making better use of the telecommunication technology that is already available.

Other forms of typically used marketing research techniques include direct observations, personal interviews, mail surveys, and consumer panels. Since the costs of marketing research continue to spiral, mechanisms which provide a leveraged or multiplier impact are being utilized more frequently. This means that more people need to be contacted in the shortest amount of time and at the least cost. This again puts the emphasis on telemarketing, mail-surveying and group sessions. Large amounts of information can be gathered through a mail survey. Respondents tend to give more thorough answers since the interview is anonymous. Since no one is there to provide guidance to the questions, the questionnaire form must be made as easy as possible to follow with primarily close-ended questions. Data gathering by mail is relatively inexpensive. The main costs are for the mailing list, the questionnaire forms and postage. Mail questionnaires ordinarily have a fairly low return rate. At 30 to 40 percent response to a mail questionnaire is considered normal. Obtaining a return of 60 to 70 percent is exceptional. All results depend, of course, on the service interest, quality of the questions, and the accuracy of the mailing list. Mailing lists can be purchased directly from research and consumer behavior firms in local cities.

For Medcenter there will be created a survey that will help the company to find out whether its objectives are fulfilled or not, whether its customers are receiving the services they have been expected to receive, whether it should change something in its strategy or not.

REFERENCES

CMU. (n.d.). Retrieved from www.cmu.ro

Kotler, P., Roberto, N., & Lee, N. (2002). *Social marketing: Improving the quality of life.* Thousand Oaks, CA: Sage.

Medcenter. (n.d.). Retrieved from www. medcenter.ro

Mediafax. (n.d.). *Romania private healthcare market seen up 13 this year.* Retrieved from http://www.mediafax.ro/english/romania-private-healthcare-market-seen-up-13-this-year-to-eur420m-report-5767473/

Medicover. (n.d.). Retrieved from www. medicover.ro

Medlife. (n.d.). Retrieved from www.medlife. ro

Payne, A. (1993). *The essence of services marketing.* Hemel Hempstead, UK: Prentice Hall.

Porter, M. E. (1981). *Competitive strategy: Techniques for analysing industries and competition.* New York: Free Press.

Sanador. (n.d.). Retrieved from www.sanador.ro

Schultz, D. I., Stanley, I., Tannenbaum, I., & Lauterborn, R. (1993). *Integrated marketing communication: Putting it together & making it work.* NTC Publishing Group.

Subhash, C. J. (1999). *Marketing planning and strategy* (6th ed.). South-Western Publishing Co.

Winston, W. J. (1985). *How to write a marketing plan for health care organizations* (Vol. 2). Haworth Press, Inc.

Chapter 9
A Multi-Level Analysis of the Change in Teaching Methods in Post-Communist Romania

Oana Gauca
Bucharest University of Economic Studies, Romania

ABSTRACT

The chapter provides an overview of the changes suffered by the secondary and higher education systems in the communism to post-communism transition and discusses the transformation of the teaching methods and the impact of these transformations. Most teachers aspire to make critical thinking the main objective of their instruction; most of them do not realize that to develop as thinkers students must pass through stages of development in critical thinking. The conclusions point to the fact that most teachers are unaware of the levels of intellectual development that students go through as they improve as thinkers. The research shows that significant gains in the intellectual quality of student work will not be achieved if teachers do not recognize that skilled critical thinking develops only if properly cultivated and only through predictable stages.

1. LITERATURE REVIEW

In the 1960s and early 1970s, analytic philosophers of education were engaged in trying to find a definition for teaching. Much of the debate centered on the question of whether teaching implies learning or merely resumes to the act of sharing knowledge. John Dewey had set the stage by writing:

Teaching may be compared to selling commodities. No one can sell unless someone buys. We should ridicule a merchant who said that he had sold a great many goods although no one had bought any. But perhaps there are teachers who think that they have done a good day's, teaching irrespective of what pupils have learned. There is the same exact equation between teaching and learning that there is between selling and buying (1933, pp. 35–36).

DOI: 10.4018/978-1-4666-4325-3.ch009

This may appear as teachers are to be blamed for student failure and lack of learning. Aristotle pointed out that teaching is an activity finding its results in the learner, not in the teacher. Were there no need for learning, there would be no need for teaching. This does not mean, however, that teaching must always produce learning but it must be constructed around the perceived need for learning.

More important, however, is what we mean by learning. Discussion of the meanings and types of learning would be somehow superfluous as they would go on forever, but we should note that some spend perhaps too much time defending one form of learning (e.g., constructivist learning) over all others.

A potentially more fruitful approach would study what the best teachers do to answer the question: what form or level of learning is called for by *this* topic, for *this* student, in *this* situation? Furthermore, learning may occur without (or even contrary to) the teacher's intention (Jackson, 1992), and this possibility suggests that teachers must be aware of and reflective about what they are conveying to students through their manner. Scheffler's criterion of manner has come to be known as the 'rationality' criterion. He wanted to preserve a significant place for human teachers in an electronic age, and he hoped also to exclude indoctrination and other scripted forms of producing learning from the category of 'teaching.'

Teaching, for Scheffler, must display respect for the student's rationality. This take on teaching seems to capture teaching at its deepest and best. The rationality criterion should be met when we look at a teacher's overall performance. But surely, even teachers who are dedicated to 'rationality' in Scheffler's sense sometimes use methods that are not clearly marked by the criterion. Should we say that, at these times, they are not teaching?

And suppose that a given teacher rarely meets the rationality criterion but, through methods such as direct instruction (telling), conditioning or even indoctrination, secures a considerable amount of learning. Is he / she not teaching? It might be better to include all of these activities on a 'teaching continuum' (Green, 1968) and give our attention, as suggested above, to matching each to appropriate learning goals.

As Martin Buber said, students learn from teachers with whom they work closely something about 'the ourstery of personal life' (1965, p. 90). This sort of learning is not usually recognized as the learning for which formal schooling was established. Yet it has always been involved in teaching— both formal and informal, and it may be inherent in the teacher–learner relation. It does not have to be intended.

However, the teacher-student relationship has evolved over time and has been affected by various conceptions, by the society as whole, by the political systems and by individuals. Therefore, we shall capture the main factors that lead to change of teaching methods in Romania, whether they existed in the past or not and what type of impact they have, as well as at what level.

Assessment of this relationship can be done on more than one side, taking into consideration every link of the relationship. A different approach to it could be the evaluation of students' attitudes, perspectives and personality traits and objectives. Furthermore, the political systems and reforms can be evaluated so as to indicate the path and objectives they set.

Kugel's (1993) speculative account of how teachers develop focuses on separate stages, where a focus on the content precedes a focus on students as individuals and then on students as learners of the content. Alexandersson (1994) dealt with this by claiming that for some teachers the focus was on the students, for others on activity in itself, and for others the focus was on the content.

In the case of university teaching, the direct object of teaching can be seen as very similar to the constituted object of study (Martin et al, 2000). The two are not theoretically identical. The focus in researching the object of study (Martin et al, 2000) is on the something being taught. The starting points in Martin et al's study were on the structure of the subject matter and how it was conceived in relation to it being taught and learned. In more complete ways of experiencing, the constituted object of study is a relation between the something and the students, while in the less complete, it focuses only on the something which is taught.

The act and indirect object of teaching are the intertwined parts of how the teacher teaches. The relationship between them is one of intentionality. The teacher uses particular acts that are directed towards bringing about certain things beyond the actual teaching event. The act and indirect object are very similar to the teacher's approach to teaching (Trigwell et al, 1994; Trigwell & Prosser, 1996; Martin et al, 20001), where the act could be seen as the strategy aspect of an approach and the indirect object as the intention aspect.

Conceptions of teaching and approaches can be seen as closely related when described in relation to the same teaching situation. According to Trigwell and Prosser (1996), student-focused conceptions of teaching are related to approaches to teaching in which student- focused strategies are aimed at helping students to develop or change their conceptions. Teacher-focused conceptions are related to approaches to teaching in which teacher-focused strategies have the intentions of transmitting infom1ation to students or having them acquire concepts. The intentions of

the approaches are related directly to the how aspect of conceptions of teaching.

The how aspect of conceptions of teaching and the intentions of approaches to teaching can also be seen as logically related to the *what* aspects of teachers' conceptions of student learning (Trigwell & Prosser, 1996). Student-focused conceptions and intentions are related to conceptions of student learning as conceptual development or conceptual change (what) to satisfy students' internal demands (how).

Teacher-focused conceptions are related to conceptions of student learning as accumulating information or acquiring concepts to satisfy external demands.

In technical education, the teacher is seen as the provider of knowledge. The student receives the "truth" from the experts - in this case, the teacher and the text. The teacher decides what information and facts are important for the students to know. Plans are then made to give that information to the student and provide ways for the students to use and remember it.

The focus is on knowledge and skill, the "how to" actions (Wilkosz, 1983). Problem-solving when based on technical action, can be successful within the classroom. However, the assumption cannot be made that the students' lives are changed because of their gained knowledge. The meaning of concepts is comprised of knowledge, its relevance, the emotional response of the learner, and the context for use of that knowledge (Caine & Caine, 1991).

Meaning is constructed by the students. Jensen (1998) cautions teachers to "never assume that because something is relevant to you, it's relevant to your students" (p. 92-93). Motivation and readiness are important factors to consider when looking at the long-term impact of technical education (Morgaine, 1992).

Another important factor for conveying meaning is communication and the means of communication. That brings us to the term communicative education, which is based on interpretive knowledge and is "concerned with meanings and interpersonal communication of meanings" (Thomas, 1998). It recognizes the role of the student in the learning process. The teacher and student share the responsibility of learning. Everyone in the classroom exchanges understandings and experiences. "Truth" comes out of this interaction (Redick, 1995). Everyone's experiences are valid and students are encouraged to listen to and respect the ideas of each person in the classroom. However, not all "opinions" are given equal credence. The students examine and question the ideas. As a result, students learn to give reasoned, logical arguments in order to gain respect for their ideas.

Communication, empathy, and reasoning are emphasized in communicative teaching. Dialogue and mutual support are used as primary methods for communicative teaching (Morgaine, 1992).

Planning lessons with an emphasis on communicative education requires a teacher to create an atmosphere of trust so all students feel comfortable in sharing their ideas and experiences. The teacher must model the behavior that is required by encouraging students to express their ideas and responding to the ideas in a positive manner. Concerns about respect and confidentiality may also need to be addressed (Thompson, 2000).

In communicative education, the students are "active participants in considering the context of a specific problem affecting a family, the desired results, the alternatives available for problem resolution, and the potential con-sequences of various alternatives" (Copa & Mileham, 1998, p.40). The students may not be accustomed to taking this responsibility for their education or having the right to choose the direction in which it goes. The teacher will need to guide the students in this process by selecting relevant resources and carefully planning activities and discussion questions.

Communicative action in the classroom is cognitive reasoning. However, it is not critical thinking. "In order to be critical thinking in the strong sense, students must seek solutions to problems that require them to make value, moral, and ethical judgments" (Kowalczyk, Neels, & Sholl, 1990).

As any other social segment, teaching is affected by change, in turbulent times. Both internal and external forces (Yee, 1998) drive the need for change. Referring to "change drivers", large scale forces that produce complex change, Swenson (1997) notes that "globalisation" of society has produced an imperative for continual reappraisal of practices in order to maintain a competitive edge.

Teaching and therefore teaching methods are faced, just as I mentioned beforehand, with multiple external pressures from governments, employers, the forever changing social, economic and technological contexts, as well as the needs and desires of students. There are demands to improve teaching quality, to present information in different ways, to develop critical thinking, to make schools and universities more accountable and to make education, especially higher education, more relevant to a rapidly changing econouur. Globalization and technological advances are bringing increased competition, but also create opportunities for very different learning experiences for students and teachers. In the face of these environmental changes, teachers are expected to improve the quality of their teaching and their students' learning outcomes at the same time as being more efficient and taking on new and expanded roles (Taylor, 1999).

Moreover, other forces that have governed change in education and teaching, for the last 20 years are:

- **Educational Reforms:** With the 1989 democratic revolution that brought down communism, the Romanian education system began the process of reform. Education reform was adopted, but implementation of that reform was a slow process and continues to be one, especially in the rural area of the country. With every change of government, the system suffered modifications, which were hard to be absorbed by the immediate affected mass: teachers and students.

A great number of the qualified teachers in Romania during the immediate post revolution were members of the communist intelligentsia and/or the communist party. Therefore, the implementation problem that existed in the post revolution continued in a number of schools because new curricula had not been swiftly adopted and communist ideas remained among the teachers.

However, the last few years have changed the system, as well as the resources the schools and universities have to work with. Romania adopted the Bologna system and separated the cycles of study on 3 years for bachelor degree, 2 years for master degree and 3 years for PhD. Moreover, for the secondary school and high school, there were implemented alternative manuals of study (selected by the teacher in each school) and the final papers which have unique test subjects all over the country.

This change factor is actually closely connected to decrease in funding from government sources – this is associated with two discernible shifts in the perception of the government: (1) education is not really a public good but a private benefit and (2) funds are not really an investment but a cost;

- **Growing Expectations:** As fees rise continually, even in public schools, students expect more and are more willing to complain about the quality of what is delivered; Tutoring is therefore a major problem in Romania, because of the fear of the parents that their children might fall behind their classes, because of inadequate and poor quality of teaching.
- **Low Financial Benefits:** The salaries of teachers have been a subject of argue and protests in the last 5-7 years. These have either decreased or remained steady, while the economy went from a boom period to an economic crisis. Moreover, the promises of the government have not been accomplished for three years. All of these lead to a shortage in teachers "supply" and a diminished quality of teaching.
- **The Rapid Spread of Communication and Information Technologies:** Whereas schools and universities once held monopoly over the high – quality information, now it is available at lower costs and multiple resources, on the Internet.

Further external pressures are coming from the overall pace of change in the world in which university students and teachers live and work, a world characterized by uncertainty a super - complexity (Barnett, 2000). As

Bowden and Marton (1998) argue, universities are preparing students for a largely unknown future in a rapidly changing world. Students are expected to graduate with degrees relevant to the demands of current workplaces as well as a capacity for lifelong learning, to enable them to adapt to the unknown situations they will face in their future lives. This means a different curriculum which goes beyond that of the traditional discipline-based university course. It is no longer enough for teachers to be experts in the knowledge of their discipline or profession, and to teach this knowledge in traditional ways.

Teachers need to learn how to design and teach in graduate attributes-based courses, how to work in multi-disciplinary teams and how to foster student inquiry and research. This is a dramatic change for many teachers, both in the content that they teach and in how they go about teaching. If teachers are to help students to develop the capacity to learn for an unknown future, they also need to possess this capacity in relation to their own teaching and academic work.

The challenges facing education systems and teachers continue to intensify. In modern knowledge-based economies, where the demand for high-level skills will continue to grow substantially, the task in many countries is to transform traditional models of schooling, which have been effective at distinguishing those who are more academically talented from those who are less so, into customized learning systems that identify and develop the talents of all students. This will require the creation of "knowledge-rich", evidence-based education systems, in which school leaders and teachers act as a professional community with the authority to act, the necessary information to do so wisely, and the access

to effective support systems to assist them in implementing change.

Romania, even though struggling to make its way and align to international educational systems, it loses more and more ground to better ranked universities, where a growing number of students choose to learn. Recent studies have shown that this shift starts to affect even high school students, who choose to study outside our borders. If this may not be regarded as an important driving factor for a teaching and educational change, the rankings of Romania in international knowledge tests, should.

One of the most comprehensive surveys currently applied also in Romania is PIRLS. This report compares the performance of U.S. students with their peers around the world and also examines how the reading literacy of fourth-grade students has changed since the first administration of PIRLS in 2001.

Results are presented by student background characteristics (sex and race/ethnicity) and by contextual factors that may be associated with reading proficiency (school characteristics, instructional practices and teacher preparation, and the home environment for reading).

The results of 2006 show a decrease of performance for Romanian students, from a score of 512 in all levels to the results in Table 1.

The results of the PIRLS test as well as of TALIS (conducted by OECD) suggest that, in many countries, education is still far from being a knowledge industry in the sense that its own practices are not yet being transformed by knowledge about the efficacy of those practices.

Naturally, policy solutions should not simply be copies of other educational systems

Table 1. PIRLS results

Average combined reading literacy score	Average literary subscale score	Average informational subscale score
1 Russian Federation 565	Canada, Alberta 561	Hong Kong, SAR1 568
2 Hong Kong, SAR1 564	Russian Federation 561	Russian Federation 564
3 Canada, Alberta 560	Canada, British Columbia 559	Singapore 563
4 Canada, British Columbia 558	Hong Kong, SAR1 557	Luxembourg 557
5 Singapore 558	Hungary 557	Canada, Alberta 556
6 Luxembourg 557	Canada, Ontario 555	Canada, British Columbia 554
7 Canada, Ontario 555	Luxembourg 555	Canada, Ontario 552
8 Hungary 551	Singapore 552	Bulgaria 550
9 Italy 551	Italy 551	Italy 549
10 Sweden 549	Germany 549	Sweden 549
...	...	...
35 Norway3 498	Romania 493	Norway3 494
36 Romania 489	Moldova 492	Romania 487
37 Georgia 471	Georgia 476	Georgia 465
38 Macedonia 442	Macedonia 439	Macedonia 450
39 Trinidad and Tobago 436	Trinidad and Tobago 434	Trinidad and Tobago 440
40 Iran 421	Iran 426	Iran 420
41 Indonesia 405	Indonesia 397	Indonesia 418
42 Qatar 353	Qatar 358	Qatar 356
43 Kuwait 330	Kuwait 340	Morocco 335
44 Morocco 323	Morocco 317	Kuwait 327
45 South Africa 302	South Africa 299	South Africa 316
PIRLS scale average 500	PIRLS scale average 500	PIRLS scale average 500

or experiences, but comparative analysis can provide an understanding of the policy drivers that contribute to successful teacher policies and help to situate and configure these policy drivers in the respective national contexts.

2. METHODOLOGY

2.1. Previous Studies

From our literature research, it resulted that five empirical, interview-based studies have focused on teachers' conceptions or orientations towards teaching and have outcomes in the form of an internally related set of ordered or hierarchical categories.

All five studies identified similar ranges of conceptions or orientations, but there were differences in their methodologies, in the aspects of teaching which delimit some of the categories and in the way that relations between categories are constituted or constructed.

Three of the studies were phenomenographic, focusing on conceptions of teaching. These studies constituted hierarchical (or semi-hierarchical) sets of categories of description which related to different conceptions (Dall'Alba 1991; Martin and Balla, 1991; Prosser, Trigwell & Taylor, 1994). Dall'Alba (1991) interviewed 20 teachers from four disciplines, and described an ordered set of seven qualitatively different categories. Ordering was based on "less to more complete understandings of teaching" (p. 296) so can be seen in terms of hierarchically expanding levels of completeness.

Martin and Balla (1991) interviewed 13 teachers taking a course in higher education. They described seven hierarchically related categories clustered into three major levels: presenting information, encouraging active learning and relating teaching to learning. There are shifts in the teachers' focuses within these levels.

Prosser et al (1994) interviewed 24 teachers of first year physical sciences, and their analysis focused on the structural and referential (meaning) components of the conceptions and the relations between them. They described six hierarchically related categories, with the least complex four forming two pairs depending whether knowledge is seen as coming from the teacher or the syllabus.

The two other studies in the group focused on teachers' characteristic orientations towards teaching, describing the relations between these in terms of their constituent belief dimensions (Samuelowicz and Bain, 1992'; 2001).

The earlier study, from interviews with 13 teachers of science and social science, identified five "conceptions" representing different profiles on five bipolar belief dimensions: the learning outcome as knowing more or differently; the nature of knowledge as curriculum bound or interpreting reality; students conceptions taken into account or not; teaching as one way transmission or two way co-operation; content as teacher or student controlled.

The later study, from interviews with 39 teachers across a wider range of disciplines, identified seven conceptions and nine belief dimensions. Dimensions not included in the previous study included the purpose of teacher-student interaction as well as its direction, the responsibility for organizing and transforming knowledge, whether students' professional development is stressed or not and whether interest and motivation are provided by the teacher or arise through student engagement.

Ordering the results, they can be grouped in two categories: teacher focused and student focused.

Teacher-Focused/Teacher-Centered Categories

In all categories in each study, teaching was described as imparting, presenting or transmitting information. Teachers focus on their delivery skills and/or on the pieces of information to be delivered. Communication is one-way from teachers to students and information has a taken-for-granted quality, existing in the syllabus, textbooks, the teachers' knowledge and/or the lecture notes. Desired learning outcomes were not considered.

Student-Focused Categories

The student-focused groups of categories are distinguished from the teacher-focused categories by a number of features that are consistent across studies. Teachers perceive a need to identify and relate to students' existing understandings in order to help students to develop or change their understandings. Teaching is an interactive process where meaning is negotiated.

Knowledge is seen as being developed, transformed or personalized by students, rather than acquired from external sources. Students are therefore expected to actively engage in learning in order to develop or change their knowledge of the subject matter and/or the world.

The second group of categories is distinguished from the previous one by two features common to all studies. Teachers focus on organizing the content and on their students acquiring it. Content still comes from the teacher or syllabus, but the focus is on concepts and their inter-relations rather than fragments. Teachers perceive that they can assist acquisition through. structuring the content to make it easier for students to "understand" Kernber (1997, p. 264) labels this group as "transmitting structured knowledge".

Several studies have two categories that fit into this second group, and they delimit these in different ways. It is still primarily one-way from teacher to student, but may include two-way interaction to maintain attention or to check and clarify students' understanding.

According to Kernber (1997) the two broad groups of categories described above relate to an overall teacher-centered, content oriented orientation, consistent with the knowledge transmission orientation from his studies of teachers' and departments' orientations towards teaching

A third category is represented by those situated in the middle.

Categories in the Middle: Transitional, Provisional or Unclear

Conceptions in the middle of the sets described in some studies can also be seen to include focuses on student activity or practice, and/or on forms of "understanding" or capability that students will acquire or develop. Not all studies include categories of this kind, and there are different ways of delimiting them.

2.2. Research Design

The research is based on a triangulation of the methods and of theoretical perspectives (Campbell & Fiske, 1959; Web, 1966; Denzin, 1978; Sandelowski, 2000; Johnson, 2007), on a mix of approaches and measurements.

The qualitative approach is corroborated with the quantitative approach and also completed by it. In the study, there were also used the triangulation of data (collecting data about different persons within the same field of activity, at different moments in time and in different organizational contexts) and the theoretical triangulation, combining two perspectives from which the relations between and among variables can be interpreted: one perspective, the institutional one, takes as a premise the idea that the educational system is the one that allows / doesn't allow change in teaching methods or practices, and the second one, individual, takes as a premise the idea adaptability and dealing with change in teaching method genuinely resides with the teacher / professor.

This research was conducted in order to determine whether methods of teaching have changed within the last 20 years and if there is any sign of change in the future. Data gathered from this research instrument were then computed for interpretation. Along with primary data, it was also made use of secondary resources in the form of published articles and literatures to support the survey results.

The descriptive method of research was used for this study. To define the descriptive type of research, Creswell (1994) stated that the descriptive method of research is to gather information about the present existing condition. The researcher used this kind of research to obtain first hand data from the respondents so as to formulate rational and sound conclusions and recommendations for the study.

The descriptive method is advantageous for the researcher due to its flexibility; this method can use either qualitative or quantitative data or both, giving the researcher greater options in selecting the instrument for data-gathering. The primary data were derived form the answers the participants gave during the survey process. The secondary data on the other hand, were obtained from published documents and literatures that were relevant to change management and teaching methods. With the use of the survey questionnaire and published literatures, this study took on the combined quantitative and qualitative approach of research. By means of employing this combined approach, we were able to obtain the advantages of both quantitative and qualitative approaches and overcome their limitations.

The quantitative approach chosen for this study is more related the detailed description of a phenomenon, in this case the pattern of implemented teaching methods and their adaptability in time; it basically gives a generalization of the gathered data with tentative synthesized interpretations.

The purpose of the quantitative research is:

- Identification of independent and dependent variables, in the analysis of the pattern of implemented teaching methods and their adaptability in time;
- Determining the nature of the relationship among variables, on the basis of which decisions and predictions can be made.

The quantitative research, as it has been designed, satisfies the three particular conditions, meaning:

- The condition of simultaneous variation, which states that the dependent and independent variables have to vary simultaneously (to rise or to fall at the same time);

- The occurrence condition, which assumes that the variation of the independent variable to take place before or at the same time with that of the dependent variable;
- The condition of the absence of their factors that can explain the variation of the dependent variables. In reality, it is very difficult to exclude all the factors that can influence a variable, factors which are not identified or controlled by the research.

Hypothesis testing was also used for this sample. The formal steps in testing hypotheses about the population mean (or proportion) are as follows:

1. Assume that μ equals some hypothetical value $\mu0$. This is represented by H0: $\mu=\mu0$ and is called the null hypothesis. The alternative hypotheses are then H1: $\mu\neq\mu0$ (read " μ is not equal to $\mu0$), H1: $\mu > \mu0$, or H1: $\mu < \mu0$[1], depending on the problem.
2. Decide on the level of significance of the test (usually 5%, in this case) and define the acceptance region and rejection region for the test using the appropriate distribution.
3. According to the obtained value, decide if the null hypothesis can be rejected and if, implicitly, the mean is statistically different to the tested value $\mu0$.

The research is based on non-comparative techniques with Likert scales. The common scale has been used, in five stages, which stands for linearity. The scale used is correlated with other measurement of similar construction which is as well valid, the rankings covering the entire frame of the respondents' attitudes towards a certain item.

The questionnaire includes 44 structured questions, having the possibilities of answer ranked on the classic Likert scale, questions that are graded from "never" to "very often", in what concerns the change in time of the frequency of use of the teaching methods, as well as three other identification questions.

The objectives of the questionnaire design were:

- Formulating the information that is to be collected in a precise way;
- Encouraging the respondents to answer in a complete manner (minimizing the non-responsiveness rate);
- Encouraging the respondents to answer correctly (minimizing the responsiveness errors).

The sentences have been formulated in such a way as to minimize the effort of the respondents, stimulating the respondents to speak freely, with no incurred idea. Unsatisfying answers (like incomplete answers) have been treated as missing values and introduced in SPSS as missing values.

The participants for the case study were professors of Academy of Economic Studies in Bucharest, teachers from high schools in Petrosani, Brasov and Oradea, as well as teachers from elementary and secondary school, from Petrosani and Brasov.

The sample consisted of 100 professors and teachers, chosen randomly, taking into account all the years of study.

The distribution of the teachers based on their experience can be seen in Figure 1.

The majority of the questionnaires were distributed to be completed and collected immediately, which lowered the rate of non-responsiveness and it was also a convenient methods regarding the time and the administrative costs. The other part was surveyed by email, in an interactive PDF form.

The questions were codified and the data were transferred to a SPSS file.

The sources of error are the questionnaires that were wrongly filled in, the non responses, the misjudgment of some questions and other variables that can influence the ability of the respondents to state their opinions truthfully (uncertainty, fear, not trusting the anonymity of questionnaires). We can also mention lack of attention, of interest, lying etc.

Figure 1. Sample distribution based on their teaching experience

As this study required the participation of human respondents, specifically human resource professionals, certain ethical issues were addressed. The consideration of these ethical issues was necessary for the purpose of ensuring the privacy as well as the safety of the participants. Among the significant ethical issues that were considered in the research process include consent and confidentiality. In order to secure the consent of the selected participants, the researcher relayed all important details of the study, including its aim and purpose. By explaining these important details, the respondents were able to understand the importance of their role in the completion of the research. The participants were not forced to participate in the research. The confidentiality of the participants was also ensured by not disclosing their names or personal information in the research. Only relevant details that helped in answering the research questions were included.

The results obtained through the analysis are relevant for our purpose, as they reveal the methods of teaching used nowadays, as well as their frequency. Moreover, it reveals the factors that may affect the way teaching is implemented in schools and how they affect the outcomes of teaching.

2.3. Descriptive Statistics

It can be observed that in terms of relationship, most of the respondents indicated values very close to the mean, and in some cases even close to complete acceptance of the affirmation (Table 2). Therefore, on average the respondents agree to the affirmation that teaching methods and strategies are discussed with other professors/teachers, all the other situations being +/_ 0.96 diverged from this value of 4. This shows a unitary view of the participants, in terms of collaboration and discussion with peers.

However, in terms of resources, on average respondents did not agree nor disagree with the affirmation "Video equipment, tapes and films are readily available and accessible in all the classrooms of your school/university", by obtaining a mean of 3.09. This rather reveals the fact that resources are still a problem for our schools, as not all are fully equipped and can use projectors or video equipment at their disposal. However, a bias of this answer could be the fact that part of the respondents were from Petrosani, a less developed and poorer area of our country.

Analysis shows that the highest mean of 4.11, was obtained for the encouragement of

Table 2. Descriptive statistics (internal environment)

Variable	N	Min.	Max.	Mean	Std. deviation
In your school/university, teachers/professors usually discuss teaching methods and strategies with each other.	100.00	1.00	5	4.02	0.964
Teachers/professors are encouraged to be innovative in the school/university you are currently employed in.	100.00	1.00	5	4.11	0.952
Video equipment, tapes and films are readily available and accessible in all the classrooms of you school/university.	100.00	1.00	5	3.09	1.286
New and different ideas are implemented in your school/university.	100.00	1.00	5	3.77	1.072
Strict discipline is needed to control many of the students you teach to.	100.00	1.00	5	2.61	1.190
Valid N (listwise)	100.00				

innovation in schools, which means that the majority of the participants involved, feel that they are not only allowed to be innovative, but also pushed towards innovation in their schools. This is a very important result, because lack of innovation acceptance is among the factors that could have been considered resistant to change and can now be taken out of that list.

This result is also sustained by the question "new and different ideas are implemented in your school/university", by obtaining an average of 3.77. This shows that on average, people agree almost completely with this affirmation, which was in fact a test of consistency in answers. Therefore, it can be concluded that teachers do not only feel that they are allowed to be innovative, but that this actually happens and it is put into practice, even though in a smaller percent.

The lowest score was obtained for the affirmation "Strict discipline is needed to control many of the students you teach to", with the mean of 2.61. This question tried to reveal how teachers see their relationships with their students, whether in terms of authority or of collaboration.

Results indicate that on average, teachers disagree with this affirmation, which I might say is a very good result and also a primary indicator of change. If in the past, the strict authority of the professor was a must in the classroom, it seems that now, on average, teachers don't consider this to be an imperative.

Data analysis reveals that the perception of change (Table 3) for the professors is somewhere in the middle, which to me indicates the fact that they are not decided about where things are heading.

The highest value was obtained for the question "There is a great deal of resistance to proposals for curriculum change in the board of your school/university.", with a mean of 3.91. This shows that on average, teachers inclined to agree with this affirmation, the standard deviation being of only 0.879.

This result is a resistant to change factor, the acceptance of the school management for curriculum change, and it is exactly one of the sociological items mentioned in the PEST analysis. The motivation of this resistance may lie in many different answers: either it is the bureaucracy, the fact that people in the management don't actually understand the reasons something needs to be changed or it can be part of the cultural dimension that plays its role.

It is sure however, that in a change process, management shall be affected, but not only at school level, but also at a class level (lower level action) and at an educational level (upper level action).

Table 3. Descriptive statistics (perception of change)

Variable	N	Min.	Max.	Mean	Std. deviation
Within the last 10 years, you feel that the changes concerning teaching methods are more frequent.	100.00	1.00	5	3.84	0.877
You feel that you have the possibility to implement a new method of teaching, without being limited by the educational plan.	100.00	1.00	5	2.50	0.966
There is a great deal of resistance to proposals for curriculum change in the board of your school/university.	100.00	1.00	5	3.91	0.879
Valid N (listwise)	100.00				

Close to the value of this variable, was that obtained for "Within the last 10 years, you feel that the changes concerning teaching methods are more frequent", revealing a mean of 3.84. This indicates a positive fact, that of perception of the people within the system, who feel, on average, that the frequency of change in teaching methods has increased within the last 10 years.

The lowest value was 2.50, which means that on average, teachers don't agree with the affirmation "You feel that you have the possibility to implement a new method of teaching, without being limited by the educational plan". This value is also close to the neither agreement nor disagreement vale, which may indicate the fact that teachers might know their limitations in what concerns the educational plan.

Having these numbers connected, in our view it is rather obvious that even though teachers feel they can be innovative and they have seen changes to occur within the last 10-20 years, the biggest change barrier until now is still the bureaucratic and formal one.

This doesn't mean that the educational plan should be disregarded. On the contrary, we believe that these results show that the educational plan, which now has a unitary aspect, determining a uniform preparation of all institutions in terms of education, should be somehow adapted to the needs and specificity of each one.

However, as this is a higher level of management and would imply a real reform of education and a powerful decentralization, we shall leave the result only as a question, as a mentioned barrier. Otherwise, aspects that are to be treated would transform the result into a highly important aspect which cannot be debated within the limited space of the present paper.

Coming back to frequency of change perceived by the people that work in this system, we thought that it would be interesting to see if the results are similar for the teachers who have less experience than for those who have more experience (Table 4). We thus tried to emphasize a sort of "generation gap" in terms of what is thought about change in the educational system.

The highest value was obtained by the teachers with more than 10 years of experience in education. On average, they agreed with the affirmation that changes occurred more frequently within the last 10 years, in terms of teaching methods. The mean was 4.17.

The difference between this result and the perception of younger teachers is not that significant, as on average, teachers with less experience almost agree with the affirmation, the mean of 3.52 being closer to the acceptance value than of the neither agreement nor disagreement value.

This perception for younger teachers can be influenced by the experience and events happened while they were outside the system, as well as by the fact that every career, in its beginning, faces much more difficulty.

The difference in answers can also lie in the different understanding of the change. For some, change might mean partial novelty, variety, a glimpse of difference, whereas for others it might be seen as complete removal, substitution, undergoing a complete restoration.

Table 4. Descriptive statistics (perception of change)

Difference of Perception Depending on Experience	N	Mean	Std. deviation
<10 years experience	29	3.52	1.056
>10 years experience	71	4.17	0.761

In this light, a projector as a means of transmitting information can represent a change in teaching methods, for part of the generation, whereas for the other, it is only a logical technological advancement and change would consist also in the way this resource is used.

However, what is actually important to be remembered is that people within the system seem to recognize the fact that things started to move at another pace, which is a very good beginning for finding supporters in the change management process.

Table 5 shows the difference between what it is wanted to be done and what it is actually done. No matter the perceived barriers to change, we wanted to analyze how professors are driven to make some changes, mostly regarding the motivation driven by the students or by their inner self.

Therefore, numbers show that the highest value of 4.30 was obtained for the question "For you, adjusting the methods of teaching is mainly driven by the interests of the students", which means that on average, teachers almost completely agree with this affirmation. This result is as much logic as hoped for, because the main objective of a teacher should be to represent the students' interests.

However, interestingly enough, the lowest value was obtained by the question "You adjust your methods of teaching according to the types of students in a class", meaning that regardless of the personality types in a class and the different needs of the students, the teaching methods remain unchanged on average.

These results are rather surprising, mostly because of we connect them with another variable, "You adjust your methods of teaching during a semester, depending on the results your students have", where on average teachers agrees with it, obtaining a value of 4.19, we can reach contradictory conclusions.

On the one side, there is the desire of the teachers to respect and fulfill the interests of the students, the adaptation of their methods according to the results the students obtain, but on the other side, there is no flexibility regarding the types and different personalities in class.

3. RESULTS

The results of the analysis are presented and commented upon in this section of the paper.

Table 5. Descriptive statistics (applied change)

Variable	N	Min.	Max.	Mean	Std. deviation
You adjust your methods of teaching according to the types of students in a class.	100.00	1.00	5	2.88	1.249
You adjust your methods of teaching during a semester, depending on the feedback and the results your students have.	100.00	1.00	5	4.19	0.778
For you, adjusting the methods of teaching is mainly driven by the interests of the students.	100.00	1.00	5	4.30	0.541
For you, change in teaching methods is mainly driven by your need for research.	100.00	1.00	5	3.78	0.852
For you, change in teaching methods is mainly driven by the change of the school/university strategy.	100.00	1.00	5	3.27	1.127
Valid N (listwise)	100.00				

3.1. Hypothesis Testing

In order to use this method, we selected some of the variables which are more related to change and the factors that drive it. For these variables, the purpose was to determine if the mean of the sample of the respondents is statistically different to 5, which is the highest level of acceptance, or complete approval as a field of the questionnaire. Thus, using this method, the conclusion drawn wants to show if change and its main driver: interest of the students, is statistically viable for the sample in Table 6.

The values show that in the case of the variables chosen, the mean is significantly different to 5, which reveals that the teachers who participated to this research do not think as we assumed by the null hypothesis, meaning they are not fully convinced of the fact that change has made its way within the last 10 years.

Moreover, they are not in complete acceptance of the fact that they adjust themselves and their teaching methods according to the feedback and the results of the students.

We believe that even the result is statistically different, the mean obtained is rather satisfying so as to catch a glimpse of the fact that things are in indeed changing. I also think that the reason for which the mean was not 5 regarding the two variables "You adjust your methods of teaching during a semester, depending on the feedback and the results your students have" and "For you, adjusting the methods of teaching is mainly driven by the interests of the students" is based on the fact that Romanian students haven't learned yet how to take feedback.

There is no formal way to do it, it is not perceived and educated to be a positive and natural thing and furthermore, feedback is considered by most people criticism. Thus, in our view allowing the teachers to receive open feedback from their students, as well as creating the open environment to do so is essential.

Thus, we think that in order to reach a complete level of acceptance within the group of professors that feedback should be an important driver for change a culture of feedback should be created in schools and universities.

In what concerns interest of the students, we do think that professors are interested in them and do their best to represent them. The bias that keeps the mean to reach five could be

Table 6. One sample t-test

One-Sample t-Test						
	Test Value = 5					
	t	df	Sig. (2-tailed)	Mean Difference	95% Confidence Interval of the Difference	
					Lower limit	Upper limit
You adjust your methods of teaching during a semester, depending on the feedback and the results your students have.	-10.331	98	.000	-0.808	4.04	4.35
For you, adjusting the methods of teaching is mainly driven by the interests of the students.	-12.934	99	.000	-1.700	4.19	4.41
Within the last 10 years, you feel that the changes concerning teaching methods are more frequent.	-13.175	98	.000	-1.162	3.66	4.01

for sure the fact that drivers regarding interest of the students act together with the inners drivers of the teachers, their own willingness to change, their own desire to adapt etc.

3.2. Teaching Methods Analysis

We have structured our teaching methods analysis on two pillars:

- Teachers with an education experience lower than 5 years;
- Teachers with an education experience of 5-20 years, or even more.

In this way, we wanted to see what are the main teaching methods used by the new generation of teachers, that have just entered the system and are eager to make their way through, as well as the teaching methods used now by the professors with a different seniority.

Our attempt is to see if there are any differences between these two generations and also to emphasize the change in time of the teaching methods applied by the teacher with greater experience. Moreover, we want to analyze if the cycle of education has any influence or reveals any difference regarding adaptability of the teachers and the range of used teaching methods.

Firstly, our analysis revealed that from a list of 27 teaching methods, the most used on, no matter the experience in the educational system or the educational cycle, was "Questions and answers", which involves a free flow discussion and the involvement of students.

The teaching method that was almost never used according to this study is "Dictation". The results show right from the beginning a difference compared to 20 years ago (Figure 2).

This sample consists of 29 respondents, out of which 12 are primary/secondary school and high school teachers, whereas the rest of 17 are college/university professors.

The teaching methods were divided into whole class activities and clustered activities, mostly taking into account the way information is transmitted or tested.

Data shows that within the group of professors with little experience, the most used teaching methods for the entire class are blackboard activities and demonstrations. Also an often used method is free flowing class discussion, which is a counter part of questions and answers.

Figure 2. Whole class activities (experience of 1-5 years)

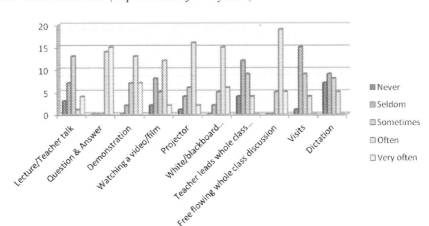

Within the less used teaching methods, one can observe visits and dictation, teacher leads whole class discussions and lecturing.

We believe that the conclusion drawn from these results is the fact the teaching has evolved from an authority centered activity to a one that involves the students actively in classes. This a very important change, as critical thinking is based on knowing how to take an argument for your standing and develop a way of communicating with others.

In our perspective, that's where free flowing discussion has a very important role. Demonstrations and blackboard activities are traditional teaching methods that have their purpose of understating the rational path of the things learned as well as to practice it within classes.

However, visits ranked the lowest in frequency, which shows the fact that teachers and professors don't perceive them as really important. However, even though visits were a custom in primary and secondary school, we think that there could be a great benefit to visits to plants for example, or manufacturing system for university. There are few better ways to learn about quality management than to see a standard applied in a manufacturing system or to learn about entrepreneurship and go visit a fresh-starter (Figure 3).

The most used teaching methods within this category proved to be case studies, exam-like questions as well as homework and private study. This appear to sustain the remark that teachers are now trying to turn towards the development of a much critical thinking, reason for which case studies and private study obtained such a high frequency.

The strengths of the case study approach is that it develops analytic problem solving skills, it allows exploration for solutions, contains experience which inspires and stimulates thinking to open discussion. Moreover, this teaching method is very useful for large groups and it develops team-working.

Within the less favored teaching methods, one can observe self-produced handouts, spokespersons and students' personal choice of assignments.

The personal choice of students is seldom selected as a method of teaching is due to the fact that grading it could be very difficult.

Th sample in Figure 4 consist of 71 respondents, out of which 3% are primary/secondary school teachers, 48% are high school teachers and 49% are university teachers.

Figure 3. Clustered activities (experience of 1-5 years)

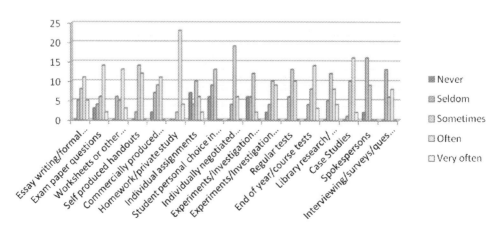

Figure 4. Whole class activities (experience of more than 5 years)

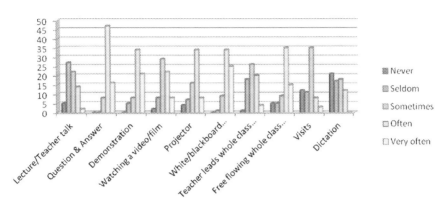

Within this group with seniority, among the most frequent methods used in the present, are questions and answers, white/blackboard activities, free flowing class discussion and projector. The similarity with the first group of professors is fairly obvious, the one difference consisting in the projector.

The most probable cause of the higher frequency of this method lies in the resources the schools and universities have at their disposal. As universities are more equipped and the cities of the respondents are Brasov and Bucuresti, one can draw the conclusion that this is the main leading aspect.

Within the less used teaching methods, data reveal lectures, dictation and visits. As mentioned beforehand, in our opinion the benefits that can be drawn from visits, in any educational cycle, seem to be oblivious now.

The analysis (Figure 5) in time regarding the preferred teaching methods shows considerable change within this category. As previously mentioned, it seems that education shifted its course from an authority centered one to a system that actively involves students. If in the past, some of the most used methods were lectures, teacher leading the whole class discussion and blackboard activities, now, even though some methods have kept

Figure 5. Change in whole class activities

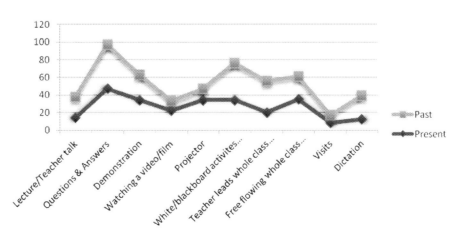

their importance, it can be seen a dramatic decrease of the professor centered activities in classrooms.

What strikes me as most emphasized is the questions and answers shift, that was and remains a main method of sharing and testing information within the selected sample of professors. In the same register are visits, which were and continue to be the less frequent method of teaching, especially for higher education cycles (Figure 6).

The most used teaching methods that fall within this category according to the analysis are case studies, exam-like questions, discovery based experiments, end of year tests and essays. These shows as a difference when comparing with the results obtained for the group of teachers with as experience of less than 5 years. Even though case studies are the link that connects the two, the teachers with more seniority seem to use also experiments and essays, with less emphasis on homework and private study.

The reasons of these findings may be of course the fact that higher educational cycles are structures in such a way so as to display a high tendency for end of year examinations,

which is why I shall leave this variable outside our observation.

However, discovery based experiments are not even close to the result of the previous group. This method is useful for both small and large groups and it introduces a problem situation, a means of exploration for solutions as well as the reaching of the "Aha principle" (a principle closely connected to Gestalt psychology, that refers to the moment of understanding something by re-organizing structures that the mind had understood before-it is actually understanding by reproductive thinking).

In what concerns essays, this is a widely known problem of Romanian students, as they seem to gather information from various sources without regard of the author or of their own opinion. From where we stand, essays are one of the most important methods that help the development of formal reasoning and of critical thinking. Essays can be a form of interaction if it is used for teams and also a means of diminishing superficiality when reading.

The less favored teaching methods revealed by the data are spokespersons, individual assignments and students' personal choice.

Figure 6. Clustered activities (experience of more than 5 years)

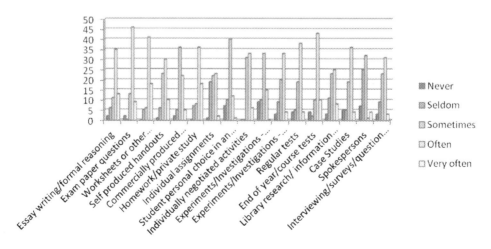

Some of the reasons for the lower frequency of the latter two were debated in the previous section.

However, the results once again show that spokespersons are not commonly used, not even ranking high at sometimes, which we believe to have a negative impact. The reasons could be many and could lie whether in the lack of availability of spokespersons, of the lack of resources for bringing guest speakers from abroad or even a lack of interest or awareness.

The analysis in time regarding the change of preferred methods is more dynamic than the one for the group of less than five years of experience. Data analysis reveals a powerful shift downwards for worksheets and individual work, private study, library research and regular tests. It is possible that some of these have been replaced with those variables that are now in preferred rankings, like essays and case studies.

No matter their replacement, in our opinion library research and any other method that could help improve the formal reasoning of students and work closely together with essays should be powerfully sustained.

Some of the teaching methods that were not preferred in the past nor are they preferred in the present are: students personal choice of assignments, individually negotiated assignments as well as spokespersons.

CONCLUSION

Communist era meant a total limitation for our educational system, which is supposed to have drawn Romania back with around 10 years from the rest of the European countries. Forbidden books, forbidden subjects and education by authority were the main character-

istics of this system. Unfortunately, many of their effect can be seen even today, whether in class management styles, in teaching methods or in the strategy of transmitting information without allowing student questions.

Without a qualitative education we cannot hope to reach the level of the developed countries, and for that matter, although in the last years some progresses were made, the gap between us and the rest of the EU countries is still very wide:

- **Inclusion Percentage:** In Romania, only 56.9% of the young people with ages between 15 and 24 years old are included in a form of education, percentage with which we rank under the European average of 59.7%, and under Hungary (64.5%), Poland (70.3%) or Czech Republic (61.6%). In the last 10 years, the inclusion percentage significantly increased, but the other countries have not been passive.
- **School Drop-Out:** The percentage of school drop-out in the elementary and secondary education system grew from 1.2% in school year 2001/2002, to 1.7% in school year 2008/2009. By residence environment, the school drop-out percentage was of 1.5% in the urban environment (constant value in the last years) and 1.9% in the rural environment, double value as compared to the one recorded 10 years before.

Today's political system, however, does not either seem to reach an equilibrium, which therefore translates in a lack of equilibrium for every institution that provides education, even though prospects now start to look better.

The purpose of this study was to give an empirical proof that things are now starting to shift to another direction and that our pace of reforms is now becoming faster.

It is however noteworthy that constant political reforms, which are now taking over our educational system are not the only barrier that prevents change. As validated in our research, management of schools and educational plans are still perceived to impede change, or at least that's what majority of the respondents of this study declared at the moment of being questioned.

Moreover, even though teachers do have initiatives and innovation is well perceived in our schools, the lack of resources and of fully equipped institutions prevents the teaching methods to rise to the expectations.

The finding of our paper is the slow but sure pace towards a change in our educational systems. This affirmation is supported by the fact the professors and teachers engaged within the system feel this change, see it within their peers and also perceive it in their own actions.

Results show that some of the teaching methods that were frequently used in the past, like dictation, are now seldom used and no longer part of the traditional way of teaching. Furthermore, teacher led whole class discussions as well as lecturing also seem to be revealed as becoming extinct within the sample of the hereby research. The very positive aspects are represented by the fact that these teaching methods are replaced with those that stimulate critical thinking, engage student to be actively involved in classes and participative, allows them to learn how to make a research and actually grants them the possibility of being highly qualified for a job market increasingly competitive, especially in today's spirit of globalization. As shown in the paper, the most frequently used teaching methods today seem to be case studies, questions and answers as well as involvement of the students in essays and individual study.

However, some teaching methods are not seen as highly important today and they could lead to significant improvements: spokespersons and library research.

In our opinion spokespersons brought to classes show involvement of the teacher who wants students to be aware of different perspectives of the same subject, shows initiative and moreover, offers the students a chance to learn more from an "authority in the field"; it also breaks the cycle of classes' linearity.

In what concerns library research and encouragement from the teachers, it would be helpful for the way students learn to gather information, to filter it and to form their own opinions by reading. Here we come back again to the development of critical thinking, which in our opinion is one of the weakest links of the Romanian students' abilities.

Though most teachers aspire to make critical thinking the main objective of their instruction, most of them do not realize that, to develop as thinkers, students must pass through stages of development in critical thinking. Thus, most teachers are unaware of the levels of intellectual development that people go through as they improve as thinkers. We believe that significant gains in the intellectual quality of student work will not be achieved except to the degree that teachers recognize that skilled critical thinking develops, only when properly cultivated, and only through predictable stages.

REFERENCES

Alexandersson, M. (1994). Focusing teacher consciousness: What do teachers direct their consciousness towards during their teaching? In I. Carlgren, G. Handal, & S. Vaage (Eds.), *Teachers' minds and actions: Research on teachers' thinking and practice*. Academic Press.

Biggs, J. (2003). *Teaching for quality learning in higher education* (2nd ed.). Open University Press.

Dall'Alba, G. (1991). Foreshadowing conceptions of teaching. *Research and Development in Higher Education, 13*.

Dewey, J. (1933). *How we think: A restatement of the relation of reflective thinking to the educative process*. San Francisco: New Lexington Press.

Entwistle, N. J. (1976). The verb 'to leam' takes the accusative. *The British Journal of Educational Psychology*.

Etzioni, A. E. (1964). *Modern organization*. Academic Press.

Handy, C. (2007). *The reading literacy of U.S. fourth-grade students in an international context: Results From the 2001 and 2006 progress in international reading literacy study (PIRLS)*. Academic Press.

Kember, D. (1997). A reconceptualisation of the research into university academics' conceptions of teaching. *Learning and Instruction, 7*, 255–275. doi:10.1016/S0959-4752(96)00028-X

Kember, D., & Gow, L. (1994). Orientations to teaching and their effect on the quality of student leaming. *The Journal of Higher Education, 65*.

Kember, D., & Kelly, M. (1993). *Improving teaching through action research (HERDSA Green Guide No 14)*. Jamison, ACT: HERDSA.

Kember, D., & Kwan, K. P. (2002). *Lecturers' approaches to teaching and their relation to conceptions of good teaching*. Academic Press.

Kember, D., & McKay, J. (1996). Action research into the quality of student learning: A paradigm for faculty development. *The Journal of Higher Education, 65*.

Kugel, P. (1993). How professors develop as teachers. *Studies in Higher Education, 18*.

Martin, E., & Balla, M. (1991). Conceptions of teaching and implications for learning. *Research and Development in Higher Education, 13*.

Martin, E., Prosser, M., Trigwell, K., Ramsden, P., & Benjamin, J. (2000). What university teachers teach and how they teach it. *Instructional Science, 28*.

McKenzie, A. (2003). *University of technology, variation and change in teachers' ways of experiencing teaching*. (PhD Dissertation).

Samuelowicz, K., & Bain, J. D. (1992). Conceptions of teaching held by academic teachers. *Higher Education*. doi:10.1007/BF00138620

Samuelowicz, K., & Bain, J. D. (2001). Revisiting academics' beliefs about teaching and learning. *Higher Education, 41*, 299–325. doi:10.1023/A:1004130031247

Chapter 10
Internal Communication in EU Project Management in Bucharest University of Economic Studies

Andra Florina Irinca
Bucharest University of Economic Studies, Romania

ABSTRACT

The present research underlines the importance of communication within an organization among its main stakeholders and its influence on the external market. It passes through explaining the communication in all fields and domains, creating an overview of the institutional communication, and why it is considered difficult to effectively propagate within a large institution. In addition, the internal communication and information and research so far conducted is analyzed with respect to the findings and lessons learned. In addition, it is important to know and understand how the internal communication evolved during years and which were the main approaches identified throughout the organizations. The case study aims to evaluate the level of information and the efficiency and effectiveness of the internal communication process within Bucharest University of Economic Studies with respect to its projects developed and financed through European funds in the last six years. The study is mainly run through the help of the questionnaire that was addressed to teachers and students within the faculty and has also the purpose to help improve the related communication in the foreseeable future based on the relevant findings.

1. INTRODUCTION

Every effective organization has a central process through which employees and members share information, create relationships, make sense of their organization and "construct" culture and values. This process combines people, messages, communication channels, diverse meanings, practices and purposes. Internal communication is the foundation of modern organizations and it has a very great impact on the effectiveness and efficiency of

DOI: 10.4018/978-1-4666-4325-3.ch010

its employees or internal stakeholders. Over the years, internal communication evolved drastically, and much research has been conducted in the field. Results showed that an effective communication motivates employees to do their work more effectively, to be more proactive, and to stay with the organization for more time. (Burton, 2006)

Communication is one of the most dominant and important activities in organizations because relationships grow out of communication, and organizations function and survive based on effective relationships among individuals and groups. Communication helps individuals and groups coordinate activities to achieve goals, make decisions, solve problems, share knowledge and manage change processes.

Internal communication also provides employees with important information about their jobs, organization, environment and each other. Effective communication can help motivate, build trust, create shared identity and spur engagement; it provides a way for individuals to express emotions, share hopes and ambitions and celebrate and remember accomplishments.

In addition, it has been discovered that a significant improvement in communication effectiveness in organizations was linked to 29.5 percent rise in market values, according to a study made by Watson Wyatt in 2004. A company can promote its services and products very much through its employees or internal stakeholders if they are well informed and involved in the company's strategy for growth and profit.

Taking all the above into consideration it can be said that internal communication is much important with respect to subjects out of date and of great interest on the market. For instance, we are now passing through a

programming period of an entire European Union development and the subject is very much debated into the country as many organizations and institutions are willing to run projects and get European funds for their institutional capacity building and development. This is also happening at the level of universities within the country which are very much encouraged to improve their educational programs, to ensure educational facilities for students, to get involved into research& development projects and to contribute to the overall sustainable development of humanity and other resources.

In this context, I consider that communication is a very important tool that can contribute to a fast growing of any organization. Thus, the purpose of this paper is to evaluate the internal communication process of BUES, one of the best universities of Romania, among its students and teachers, with respect to the opportunities it took so far for running projects financed through European funds in order to further improve its capacity and to improve the students and teachers development in their fields of interest. Results of the survey will not only help to draw some conclusions, but will also contribute to increasing the efficiency and effectiveness of the internal communication plan of the university in the foreseeable future. The study seeks to find the answers of some important questions like which are the university's main strengths and weaknesses in the field and how can it create a competitive advantage on the market, with respect to communication tools and European projects.

1.1 Communication: Definition

According to dictionary, the term communication is explained through notification, acknowledges, contact development within a group of people or a community, or opportunity that fosters the exchange of information. In the most general sense, communication is composed of four factors: the emitter, the receiver, the communication channel and the information transmitted. However, the dynamics of communication does not end with receiving or interpreting the information. The message can exert an effective influence upon opinions, ideas or receiver's behavior. Thus, the effect created may become another factor within the communication process. (Minulescu, 2004)

Therefore, many specialists define easily communication, as a process in which an emitter transmits the information to a receiver, through a communication channel, in order to produce certain effects.

A more complex and complete meaning underlines that communication is essential for any human community, regardless of its nature and extent. The continuous exchange of information and messages use to generate an image/vision and implicitly, a further action, by harmonizing the knowledge related to goals and the ways and means of achieving them. This happens as an effect of the promotion of information and skills needed through the relative homogeneity of groups in terms of affective and motivational aspects (opinions, interests, beliefs, attitudes) (Niculae& Gherghita, 2006).

1.2 The Importance of Communication

Lately, more and more scientists agree that communication is a key issue in any relation, organization, business or institution. In fact, it is highly important in any field and in any circumstance. Regarding organizational communication, many specialists argue that it is

one of the fastest growing disciplines. Also, its importance is one of the fastest growing academic disciplines. (Tourish, Hargie, 2004)

Pierre Fayard, a very famous professor of the Poitiers University, considers that information lives throughout communication. In the globalization context, where speed and pertinence make a difference, the physical frontiers and the highly dynamism constitute barriers of the strategic process of information. In order to keep the pace, to face the unknown and to anticipate the new trend and style of living in a more internationalized world, communication and information transfer became very important in any community or organization.

The knowledge communities model (*the Ba concept*) used in Japan shows to what extent the communication' practices around a project generate useful operational knowledge, both for the company and its partners and clients. Who else can notice better which are their needs, evolutions, losses, and the necessary improvements? An organization's performance is neither in vain, nor independent from others. Therefore, it deserves to be explicitly communicated and underlined in the relation between firm and its employees, clients or users. (Libaert, 2008) For instance, any improvement or loss at a university level affects directly or indirectly in the end, its teachers, students, partners – its stakeholders. This should be effectively communicated in order to duplicate or spread the success, more willingly, or to find measures of diminishing the negative impact.

Communication reflects a lot in the public media and messages that want to be transferred. In marketing and sales it represents the core activity. However, any field of interest cannot function without human resources or final users that in the end choose to buy the specific product or service. Any professional activity does have a result and a product in the end, even if it is tangible or not, and its credibility depends highly on the related communication. Effective communication became a competitive advantage and it should be much taken into consideration in such a competitive market. Brand's images increase the credibility and confidence and as a result, people prefer to pay more on a product if well-known. A created brand and image is nothing than an effective communication and a successful message transmitted, through the best means.

Organization communication should be conducted both internally and externally, in a proper manner, so it can help in achieving the desired objectives and results. However, this is not an easy job and this is why most firms and institutions do have a communication department.

1.3 Institutional Communication

In short, institutional communication represents "the speech" of institutions (public, private, associative) about themselves. Thus, it does not represent the discourse about its products or services offered which is in fact the role of the commercial communication. From a complementary perspective, the institutional communication refers to the nature of institution, legitimacy, principles and mission, organizational values, objectives, actions and performances. The information transmitted tries less to sell, but to inform, defend, increase the credibility and obtain endorsement. Regarding the targeted public, institutional communication does not target the market, but the public opinion – it does not target the client, but the social individual. However, this can create a positive reaction around the institution, so this might bring a lot of further benefits, even from the clients' territory, if there is one.

The institutional communication field extends itself from internal communication to the prestigious one, from the financial communication to the one related to its image, managerial team or organizational performance. The institutional communication has mainly the object of presenting the set of the organizational activities, its image and identity - these generally, accompanying the institutional policy.

The diversity of public institutions and of the relations established with the public, made the necessity of communication to be more important. If a public institution such as a university does also face the market competition, then a strategic communication is of utmost important.

Within this context, institutional communication becomes an efficient instrument used by organizations (public or private) for being successful in business, creating a pertinent public image, crossing a crisis, creating a favorite environment within the organization, changing the human behavior and perception toward its services/ products offered and defending/ challenging the competition in a legal framework. Specialists underline that institutional communication is very important in any organization because in this way the informational flow will be correctly perceived by the targeted public and this would lead to a major change of the organizational image, both in the business environment and in the eyes of any citizen.

According to scientists in the field, like Katz, Lazarsfeld, McCombs and Shaw, the basis of any communication is a mix of three important elements: information, attitude and behavior. Thus, communication becomes an art, even at the institutional level. Beside rules, techniques, and other theories, there is a creative, inventive, artistic side in any communication. Just like in any type of communication, it is import to create the image you want to be perceived for the organization. Therefore, the communicational zone is created and developed with respect to the public field specificity in which the organization runs its activity.

At the institutional level, the communication factors or components are the following: administration, message/information, public, communication channel and feedback received. The administration is composed of all institutional departments which work closely with the joint effort of calling a reaction from the interested groups or public opinion, regarding a debated issue. The message is compounded of all the information or formulated opinions which are framed in accordance to a set of specific rules related to the appropriate communication channel and the targeted public. From the communication point of view, the public is formed by individuals, governmental organizations, non-governmental organizations, private companies, social actors who have common interests. The public reaction follows from the communication perspective, the imposition of his personal opinions, in order to create the necessary environment for a social change. The channel of communication ensures the message transmission form the administration to the targeted public. They differ with respect to their type. In any public communication, mass-media plays a very important role. Last but not least, the feedback is essential as it emphasizes the level of perception and understanding of the message.

It is important to mention that any public communication is based on three communicational pillars: administration, mass-media and the public. Here, public doesn't refer to the targeted audience, but to the related groups who issue the organizational message. This public includes the organization's employees, clients, other stakeholders, competition, and governmental institutions with a regulatory role. These are usually referred to as the internal public, while the external one includes the community, government, international public and mostly mass-media. The external institutional communication targets both the direct and indirect public. The direct one refers mostly to the marketing one, and it addresses to clients, salesmen, distributors, providers and the competition. With respect to the indirect public, this includes the potential clients and investors, the financial community, government and the community oriented toward social responsibility such as environment protection. These three main pillars create the institutional image, as any organization does have an image on the market. The main issue here is if the wished image of the organization is projected on the market clearly and without any confusion, so the public can perceive it accordingly.

The communicational report realized among individual-institution-society is continuously changing. Its dynamism is not influenced only by the objectives' flexibility or by the communication methods and strategies used, but also by the psycho-social changes exhibited among social actors in contrast with the level of perception and problem solving of their daily activities. Thus, an effective institutional communication will lead to correct answers and favorable behaviors with respect to the message transmitted, from the receivers' side.

Years ago, Thomas Jefferson argued that whatever happens within a democratic society depends on the public consent. Thus, no matter the activity or field, an effective communication is necessary, so people/targeted audience can understand and perceive correctly what an institution/organization is operating/ looking to achieve. Only with their acceptance and maybe appreciation, the organization will have a chance to be successful in that specific field.

In addition, some specialists in the field argue that a good institutional communication must take into account the three institutional pillars: the regulator dimension of institutions, the normative one and the cognitive dimension. The first dimension is related to the coherence, level of perception and understanding of rules, norms and social actors. This side is characterized by a high level of formalization. The normative perspective includes both values and norms, that have to be taken into consideration whenever communicating within or outside the institution. This means integrity of an organization and gives the feeling of trust. While these two dimensions come from within the institution, the third one is more externalized and it relates to the modernism and dynamics of the modern human society. Today, the human action determines another communicational action which can be continuously adjusted, according to the level of knowledge and interpretation of an individual at a point in time. (Rogojanu, Crsitache, Tasnadi, 2004)

Institution communication can be considered an important part of public communication. The main channels of communication here are press articles, studies, books, printed or audio-visual public materials, radio or TV shows. However, at some point, these channels can be controllable or not. For instance, some press articles, rumors and discussions within employees or stakeholders cannot always be controllable. However, in order to reduce a negative impact or communication at this level, it is important to respect and take into consideration all things necessary for providing an effective and correct controllable communication.

1.4 Internal Communication

1.4.1 General Principles

Internal audience is at least as important as the external one – the employees of a company are its best ambassadors. This should be reflected in both internal communication and in foreign markets. One of the most serious errors in communication is that employees find out from press the changes within their organization. Where the distinction between the internal and external audience becomes faint, there is a need to change the organizational communication policy.

Internal communication starts with the business plan of the organization. The agreement and support of the management are fundamental elements in the internal communication program. It is essential to be established from the very beginning, which are the stages in which management gets involved and what would be the impact. (Boyd, 2007)

Any internal communication has specific objectives, which in large, can be divided into 4 general ones. First, the organization may want to support the project it runs by presenting its objectives and particularities. This global communication plan presents the organization choices and constraints and explains them to its employees. Secondly, management might need support, so he facilitates it through open dialogue and other instruments that allow them to increase the comprehensiveness and understanding of the organization's fundamental messages. In addition, sometimes there is a need for solidification of a group which is more and more disintegrated in time and space. Thus, the communication plan intends to reunite some strategic, operation and symbolic information, which further on expect to speed and unify and effectiveness of some groups, which are usually scattered.

Last but not least, there is a need of a punctual intervention on some specific policies, which must be the object of a wide distribution: a quality initiative, event, success, difficulties, crisis or launching a product. (Libaert, 2009) For instance, a good example here can be the context of European projects implemented within organizations, at this moment in Romania. Not only that the communication activity is imposed at the project level, but it is important for an organization to communicate its achievements, improvements and impact upon its employees, customers or even upon the general public. In the end this might brings only benefits. However, an internal communication plan must always establish more specific objectives and quantifiable one, so the evaluation and further improvement can be made possible.

Another important aspect in the internal communication is the validation of the internal messages with the external ones. Even if the internal and external messages are different, it is important that they do not contradict, but even support one another. However, the internal messages are far more discussed and analyzed. Employees or direct beneficiaries usually verify if what has been communicated was real and they usually ask for evidence in everything they are told. Thus, it is very important to transmit clear and correct messages to the targeted audience. With this respect, PR Specialists advice organizations to be careful in how they communicate, so they can reach entirely the internal public. It doesn't matter that a department is more involved than another in what wants to be communicated or that some are working more at the office, while the others are usually outside at the clients – it is important to communicate in such a way that all the internal audience can be reached. Otherwise, not only that the

people informed within the organization are fewer, but negative resentments and envy can appear among them. Every stakeholder wants to know more about the community in which he takes part or works for.

Nowadays, this communication issue is quite evolved and taken into consideration by many organizations, as many research showed lately how important it could be. Thus a one-direction or one-channel communication might be not enough, where there are so many there. Thus, a multi-directional communication should be planned to be run. But, no matter how efficient are the communication channels and instruments or how clear are the messages, communication becomes tough if the organization does not have an organized structure which should be responsible for the communication work. Usually, specialists advise to be done an audit preceding the communication strategy in order to highlight the effectiveness of the organizational structure. Whereas communication is a complex process, it is important to develop structures that allow and encourage continuous feedback.

With respect to the internal communication channels, many organizations prefer the intranet or e-mail as they are very fast, easy to use and costless. However, there are also other effective communication tools that can be used, such as meetings, conferences, internal journals, intern TVs, plasma screens, notice boards or newsletters.

1.4.2 Evolution of the Internal Communication

James Coleman, a specialist in the social science, had indentified from the historical points of view, the foundation of the big companies and he argued that these had changed their communicational practices through the help of two main interactions: communication within the big companies (B2B) and communication within big companies and individuals. The big organizations were relatively new in the early 20th century, beside government and army, and there have been developed some theories in order to explain how these organizations used to work and achieve their objectives. He described five theoretical approaches from the communication point of view, which evolved one by one in the last century: the classical approach, the interpersonal relation approach, the human relations approach, the system and the cultural approach.

Well-known scientists that supported the classical approach were: Frederick Taylor (1911), Henri Fayol (1949) and Max Weber (1947). Taylor concluded that work processes could be improved by applying scientific principles to the jobs and positions occupied by the employees, while Fayol considered that the operational efficiency could be improved through a better management practice. In this perspective, he defined five management elements: planning, organizing, authority, coordination, and control. He also argued that in order to reduce the misunderstandings, the internal communication must follow a hierarchical chain introduced by him, as well, called "The scalar chain". On the other hand, the German sociologist, Max Weber developed a bureaucracy theory in order to establish in a formally way the authority, the operational structures and the communication. Some key components of this approach included: a chain of command with centralized decision-making, clear delimitation of tasks and responsibilities, and information writing in order to avoid misunderstandings. The communicational characteristics here are targeting the avoidance of misunderstandings and communicational transfer from top management with respect to rules and decisions. The social aspect of communication is neglected, situation in which relationships among employees are based on information grapevine. (Berger, 2009)

The interpersonal relation approach is based on the Hawthorne studies that underlined the employees' work tasks and their needs. Studies have revealed the importance of groups and interpersonal relations at work. Thus, it was promoted the idea according to which a human could work more and be more productive if some aspects were analyzed and understood, such as: attitude toward work and management, insight motivation, professional satisfaction, attitude toward working groups, group integration, and everything related to the organizational climate. In addition, very important were considered the informal relations among employees, their active participation in the decision-making process of issues that involved themselves and their work, which was leading to a democratic or generic management, good communication and tight connections between subordinates and superiors, freedom of expression and equal treatment. In addition, it is considered that McGregor (1960) has best articulated the principles of human relations within an organization through the Theory X and Theory Y. These two perspectives based on two contradictory premises related to the authority of managers and their correspondence behavior. Thus, according to Theory X, managers believe that employees are not motivated, are resistant to change and indifferent to organizational goals. To combat this, managers must be strong and apply a forceful leadership in order to direct and control the employees. On the other hand, Theory Y argues that managers believe that their employees are highly motivated, creative and willing to meet their needs of achievement.

The role of managers in this case is to encourage these trends by involving employees in the decision-making process, management and problem solving within work teams. In this situation, the communication approach is designed by many face-to-face interactions/meetings, and recognition of the internal communication importance. Communication still dominates the top-down, but gather feedback to measure employee satisfaction. Managerial communications are less formal and social information is added to the entire process. (Popescu, 2010)

The human resources approach remind of the management grid developed by Blake and Mouton (1964) which was created in order to help train managers in leadership styles so they can stimulate the cognitive contribution of employees, in order to meet their needs and contribute to the organizational success. Other theoreticians argue that the best leadership style should vary from event to event, depending on the context. Fiedler (1967) stated that leaders should first determine the circumstances and then to define the most appropriate form of leadership. This theory recognizes that organizations and environment are constantly changing and so the environments need to be monitored, while information must be carefully analyzed before making decisions. Here communication becomes multi-direction and it is tightly connected with the existence relationships. Feedback is used for problem solving and ideas generating. Beside the social and work task information, innovation is a new element that appears in the communication process. Concepts related to employees' trust and commitment are important issues and organizations start to involve its employees in the decision-making process.

The general theory of systems states that any system is formed by groups of parties arranged in a complex way, and which interact among them through processes in order to achieve their goals. For instance, a pretty big company is formed by different departments in which individuals are working and team groups are set. Weick (1979) used the system theory in order to explain the organizational behavior and the sense creation. He argued that the key process of any organization is the internal communication. He explained that the information gathered as a conclusion of the production processes and behavioral patterns is very important for collecting knowledge with respect to systems and it may reduce the uncertainty of the environments in which it operates. The system communication approach starts from the premises that internal communication is vital for the exchange of information within the subsystems, and within systems by means of multi-directional communication channels. Feedback processes help the systems to adapt, change and maintain the control. Here, collective decision-making processes and shared responsibilities are prevalent.

The cultural approach emerged in 1970s in the context of increasing competition of the global market, due to the development of Japan and other nations. The idea of culture refers to the specific identity of an organization: the shared beliefs, values and behaviors of an organization that determines how it works and adapts to the external environment. As the performance of US companies began to decline, management specialists have begun to look for other explanations in favor of behavior and practices of companies that started to decline. Also, cultural approach was attractive because of its dynamic and the profound perspective it could provide. The cultural approach values communication which is perceives as a cultural process of information sharing, creating relationships and receiving training within the organization. Communication helps to create and develop the culture through formal and informal channels, stories, shared experience, and social activities.

These five approaches demonstrate how internal communication changed as organizations has evolved. Today, organizations use elements from all the five approaches described above as they have work rules, hierarchies, policies, training programs, work teams, job social rituals, human resource departments, customer focus and so on. (Berger, 2009)

As their role has evolved from simple propagators of information to strategic business partners, communication professional are required to a stronger bond between employers and employees and to provide them with the tools and skills necessary in order to communicate effectively, and also to ensure that the right messages reach their audience and have measurable results- all of which are real challenges. (Gay, Mahoney & Graves, 2005)

2. METHODOLOGY AND RESEARCH TOOLS

2.1 General Principles

No matter the organization type, the business it runs, segment of market it covers or field of operation, every organization has as main activity the internal communication which can or cannot bring an added value to the company. Not only the communication process, but all its other activities must at one point be evaluated so they can be further improved or radically changed. In this respect, there are IT audits, financial audits, communication, consumer's behavior, product, service, project evaluation, market research and so on.

Communication measurement helps organizations to quantify the value of effective internal communication, which is typically significant but often overlooked. It also helps internal communicators justify and gain adequate resource. Engagement and satisfaction surveys are typically carried out annually and can include some typical questions in order to provide insights into the effectiveness of the internal communication. If the goal is to estimate the impact of the internal communication, then it should be measured the stakeholder's attitude, awareness, and knowledge, before running a campaign or elaboration a communication plan. If the research wants to evaluate a specific communication or campaign, it is important to measure their impact at the program or initiative level. This should further allow to tailor the internal communication and to make sure that they are effective and are delivering quantifiable business value. In addition, the results can provide insights into the issues and challenges of the organization through feedback gathering.

Scientists and specialists in the field always encourage organizations to start making a development plan after relevant analysis in the field. Tom Peters, an American writer on business management practices stated within its book, *In search of Excellence* that *what gets measured gets managed.* In this perspective, the two main types of communication measurement are baseline and functional. The baseline communication measurement usually runs prior to the communication by gathering data related to knowledge, attitudes and behavior of employees. In addition, it determines the existing information available, how easily it can be find, the current communication channels available and other factors of influence with respect to attitudes and behaviors. On the other hand, the functional management measurement usually is taking place after a communication and campaign, when functional aspects of the communication have to be measured. Additional measures here can include the number and types of messages sent, timing of the messages, channel effectiveness and appeal, level of targeted public reached, audience satisfaction with the content and so on. As the objective of the internal communication is to change the behavior and attitudes of employees/ stakeholders – a well planned audit is very important.

With respect to data collection, there can be identified two types of data: primary and secondary. Primary data is collected for the first time with the help of marketing instruments and with a specific purpose. Secondary data is already collected for other purposes than those at hand. They both have advantages and disadvantages. While primary data is more efficient and costly, secondary data can be easily accessed but might be inaccurate. However, any study should include them both in order to have an effective research approach and relevant results. (Arnould& Price, 2004)

A good internal communication flourishes and creates an opened organizational climate that will foster the free flow of communication and information in all directions and in the external environment that may lead to the organization promotion into the market and thus, to a competitive advantage.

2.2 Research Process

Scientists agree that specific steps have to be followed in order to run a successful research. Naresh K. Malhotra divided the marketing research process into six steps, in his book, *Marketing Research* (2007). This marketing research process mainly refers to the external research. However, all the steps described next are to be followed for a successful internal research.

Step 1: Problem definition

As mentioned above, before starting to conduct a market research, it is important to establish what information is needed, so the purpose of the study or the existing problem to be defined.

Step 2: Development of an approach to the problem

Once the expectations are known, the marketers can decide which approach would be more effective for the research. It includes theoretical framework, analytical models, research questions and hypothesis.

Step 3: Research design formulation

This step details the procedures necessary for obtaining the required information. It implies secondary data analysis, qualitative research, methods of collecting quantitative data, questionnaire design, sampling process and size.

Step 4: Fieldwork or data collection

This has to do mainly with quantitative research and it involves field data collection in the case of personal interviewing, electronically or from an office by telephone.

Step 5: Data preparation and analysis

At this stage, marketers have to analyze the data, to verify it and to structure it accordingly. From data analysis, input and information for the marketing research problem are provided, so conclusions can be taken and decisions made.

Step 6: Report preparation and presentation

At this final step, the entire project should be documented in a written report and then presented in a form that answers to the initial problem and purpose. This can be done with the help of figures, graphs and tables, which clarify better the results.

2.3 Qualitative vs. Quantitative Research

Marketers recommend the use of both qualitative and quantitative methods for market research. In this way, much data is gathered and the study is more relevant. These two methods complement each other very well. While quantitative research involves many respondents who form a sample that can be generalized to the whole population; the qualitative method usually involves no more than ten persons and it collects mainly descriptive information and ideas sharing. However, when deciding which method is more applicable for the given situation, researchers have to take into consideration the purpose of the study and the types of data needed.

Qualitative research methods include depth interviews, focus groups, discussion guides, projective techniques and metaphor analysis. These are usually conducted by experts who appeal to emotions and psychological approaches, so respondents are stimulate to reveal their inner thoughts, beliefs and perceptions with concern to a specific product or service.

A depth interview takes place between a respondent and a highly trained interviewer, the latter having a more passive attitude. The respondent is encouraged to talk as much as possible and to share all his feelings and opinions with respect to a brand, product or service. Transcripts, audiotapes and videotapes are analyzed afterwards. Focus groups include

a moderator and up to ten respondents. The discussion is focused on lifestyles, motives, feelings and attitudes. Some marketers prefer focus group instead of depth interview because it lasts less, about two hours. On the other hand, respondents may feel intimidated by the other participants and information disclosed can be distorted. Discussion guides vary in the level of details and flexibility, they can focus on a single issue and thus they are more structured or they may have a more open form. Projective techniques consists of games and tests, such as incomplete sentences, untitled pictures or word-association tests that intend to reveal the unconscious motives of an individual, despite rationalization and conscious behavior. Last but not least, metaphor analysis is based on the principle that people don't think in words, but in images. Thus, they cannot express their feelings and ideas verbally, but through sounds, music, drawings or pictures. This tool enables consumers to express their emotions adequately. (Schiffman, 2007)

The qualitative research also includes data gathering from press articles, advertising, internet, social media or any other sources and pieces of information with respect to the subject that can give additional value to the research. For instance, in case of a communication audit, the impact upon the market can be perceived through the number of press releases with respect to the subject or other press articles that have spread the information given. A specific example is that any public event evaluates its impact upon the society thorough its communication channels by counting the articles in which it is mentioned in press, the day after the event. The number of people informed and the impact on the market may depend upon the importance of the event, its advertising or staff involvement. The latest implies that people do talk about their work and lives and they spread this type of information very fast within their acquaintances and connections.

Quantitative research represents a great interest, today, for all factors of decision in the field of market and marketing. The actual research of consumer behavior needs a deep knowledge of theoretical and practical aspects. One of the first problems in conducting a quantitative research is the sample size. Due to the fact that all data collected from the sample size must be generalized to the whole population, it has to be representative and chosen accordingly. Not only the size, but also the sample composition should be taken into consideration, so the results can be representative. Questionnaires are the central part of a quantitative research. Most firms that deal with marketing studies and quantitative research, have specialized teams for questionnaire elaboration, which are consistent with requirements and objectives established by research beneficiaries. (Catoiu, 2004)

The questionnaire design is not an easy job. Before developing it, all the information needed should be structured, so questions can be formulated accordingly. Secondly, the interview's procedure should be determined. It implies cost, time, place, and the position of respondents. Questions should be carefully prepared. It is important for respondents to understand and to be able to answer them. Before running a survey, few other persons should complete the questionnaire and give feedback. Usually, questionnaires include all types of questions, such as open, multiple-choice, binary or questions with pre-coded answers. Utility maximization, attractiveness of the questionnaire and the sequence of questions are other important steps over which should not be passed. A simple language, logic structure and a visual attractiveness through pictures and colors would make the questionnaire more effective and the respondent more willing to help. (Mitrut& Serban, 2003)

Marketers can choose from many data collection modes when distributing surveys. The four major methods are face-to-face, by telephone, on internet or a combination of these three. They all have advantages and disadvantages regarding time allocation, sincerity of respondents, the length of questionnaire and costs. However, the internet boom reoriented the industry to online surveys. These are very fast, easy and inexpensive. The questionnaires accommodate to all the standard question formats, and they are also flexible, including the ability to present pictures, diagrams or displays to respondents. Information is easily gathered and introduced in computer programs which organize and synthesize the results. (Burns, 2006)

3. INTERNAL COMMUNICATION OF EU PROJECT MANAGEMENT WITHIN BUCHAREST UNIVERSITY OF ECONOMIC STUDIES

3.1 European Funds in Romania

Currently, Romania is fully involved in a development program established and agreed at the EU level and thought as a multitude of active projects running all together, in all main sectors that have a major impact to the country's economy and its inhabitants. At the moment, all decision-makers and heads of ministries are hardly trying within their teams, to speed the processes and to give a helping hand, from top to bottom, in order to reach the objectives established at the national level and to meet the indicators of efficiency and effectiveness.

It is already history the moment when Romania joined EU in 2007 and became a member with full rights, being directly involved in the elaboration, adoption and implementation of EU policies. Getting aligned to the EU's main objective of transforming Europe into an attractive market for investments and labor, Romania joined the partnership between EU and the Member States in order to ensure the success of the new strategy. Thus, in 2007 it was developed the National Strategic Reference Network 2007-2013, the reference document for programming the structural instruments, ensuring conformity of these fund's intervention with community strategic guidelines regarding cohesion and national development priorities, together with the National Reform Plan. Within lines, it was very much insisted on research, knowledge promotion and innovation projects, these being considered the main tools for overcoming the long-time economical crisis.

Within this context, universities from all over the country were very much encouraged to access EU funds and to invest it into research& development projects, of whose finding might have had a great impact on the market. The funding at the university level is usually insufficient in Romania. Therefore, at the current moment, EU funds are a great opportunity to develop and finance projects with high perspectives and potential outcomes. The good part is that Universities from Romania did notice the opportunity and started to re-organize their activities and their staff, so they could take advantage of as many funds as possible and improve and develop their activities and make deeper research in their fields of study.

During these almost 7 years of projects' implementation, some of them succeeded to reach an impressive number of funds ac-cessed and considerable improvements made. However, they did not always run successfully the communication& information activity, as few Romanians do have a clue of what important results and developments have been done within the country, at all levels, including university& research. (Romanian Government, 2008)

With respect to communication, at the national level, Romania developed a National Communication Strategy for Structural Instruments (NCSSI), part of the European Funds, for all Operational Programs, approved by the Government, which is the basis of the communication plans sent to European Commission. As a result, it was founded the Information Center for Structural Instruments (ICSI) as it was necessary to exist a central coordinating system of the communication' activities for structural instruments which was about to ensure a coherent and balanced communication process, avoid duplication and conflicting information, and which was supposed to cover the communication gaps. Through the annual National Communication Strategy for Structural Instruments, ICSI was charged to be responsible to communicate on the general problem of Cohesion and Structural Funds and on the global fields connected with the management and national implementation of these funds, and the Management Authorities have to communicate specific problems with respect to the Operation Programs they are managing.

The requirements referred to communication and information of the cohesion policy 2007-2013, must be seen in the European Union as a renewed commitment for democracy context, transparency and increased efficiency. The Communication Plans have an important role in increasing the awareness of Romanian citizens and of beneficiaries regarding the role of European Commission during implementation of the Cohesion Policy 2007-2013, and the impact of structural instruments on the socio-economical development of the country.

The National Communication Strategy for Structural Instruments for the programming period 2007-2013 is based on a proactive approach which aims facilitating access to information in the field of European funds and structural instruments, together with ensuring a proper communication framework which should be efficient and facile to various public categories and targeted groups. In this context, all institutions and organizations that develop projects financed through EU funds are required to ensure transparency, to communicate effectively and inform the general public with respect to the project activities, people involved, results and indicators achieved. Thus, many companies took advantage of this and tried to promote their organizations by respecting the information and communication requirement of any project implementation through EU funds. (Romanian Government, 2008)

3.2 Presentation of the Study

The present study is quantitative research which aims to audit the internal communication within BUES concerning the projects it runs and are financed through European Funds. The other purpose was to identify the level of information of teachers and students with respect to these projects that develops the University and how do they have an impact toward them. It is important to measure their awareness, perception, opinion as they are a main asset of the university and any of its improvements has the ultimate goal of facilitating their studies or teaching activities. Also, an effective communication of the institution is very important both externally and internally, as students and teachers can assist with ideas, needs identification, willingness to help and contribute to the University's development, promote it and even take advantage of its best facilities if they are well informed. In this way they all can be better motivated in their usual activities like studying or teaching and the relationship between students and professors can be radically improved.

Based on the above assumptions, the qualitative analysis was conducted through a questionnaire that consisted of twenty questions. (as illustrated in Annex1) It was launched online, on the website www.isondaje.ro (as illustrated in Annex2) and it was drafted in Romanian language for the respondent's sake of being willingness to complete it. The survey included multiple, scalable, hierarchical and open-ended questions. Variables were measured through all four types of statistical scales: nominal, ordinal, interval and ratio. The nominal scale is characterized by using numerical symbols in order to represent the possible categories of variables. It is used mostly to identify rather than measure or evaluate quantities. Thus, it is appropriate for recording gender, marital status, occupation or profession. In the ordinal scale, numbers are hierarchies and express the place or the order in a series of data. Examples of variables suitable to be measured on the ordinal scale are the social class or behavioral attitudes. The interval scale allows the units to be grouped into classes, to establish an order and to identify distances between classes. It implies the existence of the measurement units, such as liters volume. Last but not least, the ratio scale implies in addition to the previous scales the existence of an original point, "zero". It is mostly used to emphasize physical characteristics, such as weight, height or the adrenaline level. (Serban, 2004)

All BUES students and teachers were eligible to complete it during more than one month, between 13th of April and 18th of May, 2013. The survey was published on more than twenty Yahoo groups of the faculties within the University, their Facebook's pages and also the Students Senate from BUES has distributed it on its forums and website. In the end, the questionnaire gathered 100 respondents, both students and teachers.

In addition, the BUES internal communication of its projects financed through European Funds can be measured indirectly, through external indicators. For instance, the number of BUES students who attended information seminars organized especially for students, at the Information Center of Structural Funds – the national official Center under Ministry of European Funds. Also, an internal effective communication of projects within BUES can be propagated outside it, externally and this can be measured through press and newspapers. As European funds is a very important, actual and debated subject throughout all the country, each day, there are news related with respect to legislation, public acquisitions, beneficiaries and projects under implementation. Thus, in addition, the current study also measures the number of times BUES appeared in press in the last three months in comparison with other universities from Romania that also are running projects financed through European funds.

In the end, all the results could help to draw conclusions and re-think the whole communication strategy of BUES with respect to its internal human resources, teachers and students.

3.3 External Communication of Universities including BUES

As it was already mentioned, the current study is a quantitative evaluation of the internal communication processes within BUES with respect to its projects financed through European funds. Data was gathered and analyzed from the students and teachers of the faculty with the help of an on-line survey. Throughout the questions and answers requested, it was measured the general level of information into the subject that could have been acknowledged both externally or internally. Thus, for a more complete analysis, external communication of BUES have been briefly analyzed in comparison to the other Romanian universities, based on three established indicators. These three indicators are strongly related to the activities within the Information Center of Structural Instruments, the official channel of communication with respect to Structural Instruments of Romania.

Thus, the first indicator represents the number of the university's appearance in press (newspapers) during three months time period, February-April, 2013 with respect to the projects implemented through European Funds. One of the activities run in the Information Center of Structural Instruments is the daily collection of all news related to the Structural Instruments in Romania from the main and related newspapers, both national and regional. Some of the main sources were: *Financiarul, Business Magazine, Jurnalul, Cotidianul, Curierul National, Agerpres, Adevarul, Ziarul Evenimentul* and many other online sources like *Mediafax* and *HotNews*. All this data is gathered daily from Monday to Friday and is distributed to the concerning personnel that is coordinating the Center and its activities, as an internal press review. As research& development and education fields are very important for Romania, eligible organizations such as universities are very much encouraged to apply and to develop this type of projects. Also, each project is obliged to run a communication activity in order to be as transparent as possible and to inform the general public with respect to what have been developed and evolved. In Table 1 it can be observed the universities from Romania that have appeared in press with concern to the subject. The information emphasizes the name and place of the concerning university, title of

the news that have appeared in press, source and date of the publication.

As it can be noticed, within three months period time, there have been eleven public appearances of the universities from Romania in press with respect to European funds. Out of these eleven articles, three are having a negative perspective and they are all connected with "Alexandru Ioan Cuza" University from Iasi. Most of the articles are regional, but they have the visibility at the national level. Many of the universities emphasized are in direct competition with BUES, especially Babes-Bolyai University from Cluj and Western University from Timisoara which

Table 1. Universities in press

Name of the University	Title of the News	Source	Date of Publication
"Alexandru Ioan Cuza" University from Iasi	*Beneficiaries from Cuza are in the verge of a revolt. They started a petition to the rector.*	Iasi Newspaper	1.04.2013
University of Craiova	*Traditional Romanian education system at the same level of EUs through the REGIO Program*	Ministry of Rural Development and Public Administration website	19.04.2013
"Vasile Goldis" Western University from Arad	*POSDRU Project at "Vlaicu"*	Arad online	25.04.2013
"Grigore. T. Popa" University of Medicine and Pharmacy from Iasi	*Unique center in Europe set up by MFU through a POSDRU project*	Iasi Newspaper	25.04.2013
University of Craiova	*15 millions university campus in Craiova, built with European Funds*	*Ziarul Financiar*	26.04.2013
Western University from Timisoara	*A European project has provided substantial grants for doctoral students at the Western University*	www.tion.ro – *News of Timis county*	05.03.2013
"Alexandru Ioan Cuza" University from Iasi	*Incredible! Further delays in grants from European funds at Cuza University*	www.bzi.ro – *Good day to Iasi*	06.03.2013
University of Medicine and Pharmacy from Craiova	*UMF Craiova – top of the European research projects*	www.gds.ro	13.03.2013
Western University from Timisoara	*Western University has courses for writing projects in order to access EU funds*	www.opiniatimisoarei.ro	13.03.2013
"Babes-Bolyai" University from Cluj	*Good news for doctoral students from Cluj: UBB is going to allocate this week the remaining scholarships*	*Adevarul Newspaper*	19.03.2013
"Alexandru Ioan Cuza" University from Iasi	*Unprecedented austerity measures at "Cuza" because of the reduced number of students*	www.ro.stiri.yahoo.com	20.03.2013

in the latest years attracted more and more students from the region while less fewer applied for the BUES University education, as it can be noticed. Publicity and media could have seriously influenced the previous choices. Unfortunately, BUES is not part of the list detailed above and none of the well-known universities from Bucharest which may be perceived from one side, having a poor communication in the field or not being involved at all. The negative consequence is the poor visibility on the market and a misleading impression consisting in lack of BUES improvements and educational development that are very important for the society at the current moment.

The second indicator is also a quantitative one and sums up the number of projects implemented by Universities and subscribed to the Information Center of Structural Instruments website of beneficiaries. The website is created especially for beneficiaries of EU funds in order to facilitate their interactions, to promote their projects and help them in the implementations' activities such as communication and public acquisitions. Taking

into account that the website was created only in 2012, at the end of the programming period, it has not been very successfully with respect to the number of beneficiaries subscribed and also willing to describe their projects. Thus, out of 52 projects published on the website, seven of them were run by universities and academic institutions. Being very active on the market and also in the field, "Babes-Bolyai" University from Cluj has subscribed six of the projects and "Alexandru Ioan Cuza" University from Iasi only one, as it can be noticed in Table 2. Projects have been detailed described, with their general and specific objectives, results, budget, activities and other relevant details. Unfortunately, BUES has not subscribed any of its projects so far, being again behind the competition from the informational and communication point of view, with respect to the concerning subject, projects financed through EU funds within universities.

The third indicator measures the interest of students from BUES with respect to the European funds and project implementation in comparison with students from other uni-

Table 2. Projects subscribed to the official website of Structural Instruments in Romania

Name of University	Project Title
"Babes-Bolyai" University from Cluj	*Improvement of undergraduate education teachers who teach Romanian language to national minorities*
"Babes-Bolyai" University from Cluj	*Application of a coherent and competent system at the same level with the European Masters Programs of economic analysis and evaluation of assets and businesses*
"Babes-Bolyai" University from Cluj	*Professional development of High school teachers who teach economic disciplines*
"Babes-Bolyai" University from Cluj	*Continuous professional development of teachers from schools with hearing deficiencies. Developing teaching skills by using Romanian sign language and ICT tools*
"Babes-Bolyai" University from Cluj	*Quality Assurance within the Internationalized Master Programs. Development of the national framework for ensuring compatibility with the European environment of the higher education*
"Babes-Bolyai" University from Cluj	*Increasing the quality of master programs in the field of public administration*
"Alexandru Ioan Cuza" University from Iasi	*Continuous education program for careers of managerial directors in public administration sector in order to develop the administrative capacity and enhance organizational effectiveness*

versities. Information Center of Structural Instruments has been organized periodical information sessions called "ABC of Structural Instruments" that had the objective to inform the current students, potential future beneficiaries about the Structural Instruments in Romania, legislative framework and show them examples of very good projects. The information sessions took place in Bucharest, at the office of Center of Structural Instruments starting from November 2012 until May 2013. Totally, there have been seven information sessions that limited the participation number of 30 persons per session. Interested students could have subscribed themselves online on the Center's official website or on Center's Facebook page. First 30 subscribers were selected to participate and this is how this part of the organizational point of view was set up. The total number of students that succeed to take part of the sessions was in the end 118. Out of this, the majority of 25% from students were from BUES, 19% from National School of Political and Administrative Studies from Bucharest and other 15% from University of Bucharest. The rest of participants came from University Politehnica from Bucharest, Tehnical University of Civil Engineering from Bucharest and other universities from Bucharest and even from other regions of the country. The data collected and centralized indicate that students from BUES are very much interested in the field and willing to be informed with respect to EU funds and related projects.

3.4 Questionnaire Based – Quantitative Analysis

The first part of the questionnaire goes for recording the general knowledge of the respondents with respect to the projects implemented within BUES by European funds mean. This part is compounded of three questions while the other twelve are focusing on the specific knowledge, information and communication related. Four more other questions are included in the third part as they aim to identify and group the respondents with respect to their general interest in European funds and their connection with BUES in terms of position and years. In the end, there is an open question that encourages to be recommended good practices of BUES in the concerning field.

1. **Distribution of the Answers for the First Question:** "From how long do you know about BUES's involvement in projects financed through EU funds?" is shown in Figure 1.

The term "*European projects*" from the title in Figure 1 relates in this study analysis to the projects of BUES that are financed through European funds.

The current programming period in which European funds could be accessed for national development started in 2007 which means more than six years ago. However, the funds could not be accessed at the very first moment as Romania was not ready in due time with all the corresponding legislation, procedures and regulations. Late in 2007 the set up at the national level was finalized and potential beneficiaries could apply to obtain funds and run projects within their organizations. BUES got financed only in 2008. The aim of the question was to identify the time period in which the student/teacher was aware of the University's development throughout projects financed thorough European funds.

The question is quantitative and numerical and it measures time throughout intervals.

According to the answers provided, a critical high number of 43% of the respondents have not heard of this type of projects within

Figure 1.

Awareness of the *European Projects* within BUES

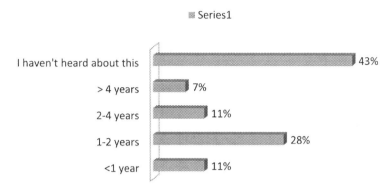

BUES until the time of the questionnaire was published. This is an alarming percentage as it's the highest and BUES has been already implemented projects financed through European funds for already more than five years. A percentage of 28% of the other respondents were aware of the subject from the last one to two years, an equal percentage of 11% have been notified less than a year ago or within the time period of the last two to four years, while the rest of 7% subscribed to being aware of the subject for more than four years ago.

As the respondents who answered negatively to the question above could not answer to the following ones which were more specific on the subject, they were directed to the end of the questionnaire, at question number 17.

2. **Distribution of the Answers for the Second Question:** "Did you feel that any of these projects did have an impact toward your study/teaching experience, so far? If so, please explain briefly" is emphasized in Figure 2 and Table 3.

Out of 57 respondents, 51% considered that these projects had no impact upon them within the University' activities; other 44%

answered "yes" which means that they realized and noticed specific impacts while other 5% did not want to answer to the question.

The question concealed two questions into one as it searched to measure the awareness of the projects' impact and how was that perceived. Thus, the question was an open-ended one where respondents who noticed an impact, could argue about how they felt it toward their study/teaching activities or upon

Figure 2.

European Projects' impact at the level of students and teachers

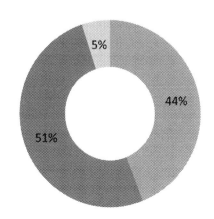

Table 3. Type of impact

Type of the Impact Mentioned	No. of Times	Positive/ Negative
Internship through POSDRU	13	P
Knowledge improvement	5	P
Establishing of the Business Risks Master Program	2	P
Library development	2	P
Much more bureaucracy	1	N
Less time for classes preparation and students' assistance	2	N
Increased earnings	1	P
More work	1	N
Personal development through participation in projects	3	P
Total	30	6 - P / 3 - N

ter Program establishment or the internships through POSDRU projects. POSDRU is one of the seven current Operational Programs in Romania which is dedicated to human resources and aims to improve their capacities and develop their professional skills. The most frequently types of impacts mentioned where the positive ones which are also underlined in Figure 3, as the top 3 impacts that have been considered. Thus, most of the respondents felt an impact through the opportunities for internships, secondly they mentioned the knowledge improvement, which is more a general impact and some more noticed a personal development through their active participation in these type of projects.

their personal development. Table 3 can be observed the types of impacts enumerated, how many respondents mentioned them and if they were perceived positively or negatively.

The 25 respondents who noticed an impact upon the University's services and their related activities mentioned six different types of positive impacts and other three negative ones, as can be observed above. The impact was not generally defined, but many were more specific such as the Business Risk Mas-

3. Distribution of projects financed through European funds that were perceived to have been run within BUES. The question is quantitative and numerical and it measures frequency throughout intervals (Figure 4).

As can be observed, 61% of the respondents did not have a clue regarding the number of projects that have been running in BUES so far. While 16% chose the interval 10-50, another 9% believed that have implemented

Figure 3.

Top 3 Positive Impacts

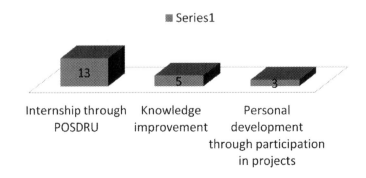

Figure 4.

No. of projects financed through European Funds within BUES

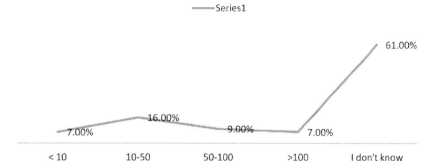

between 50 and 100 projects while an equal of 7% from the respondents, believed that more than 100 projects should have been run or less than 10. According to the BUES Guiding Office for Accessing Structural Funds, the University has completed 16 projects and is still running other 48. In conclusion, BUES succeeded to access funds for 64 projects that contribute to its development, which are now completed or and under implementation.

4. **Starting with Question Number 4:** The questionnaire aimed to record specific knowledge and perception of projects run within BUES. The question looked to identify positive aspects of BUES involvement in the projects financed by European funds. It is important to identify if students and teachers from the university are considering this activity as being beneficial for the university's future and encourage this. It is also important to understand their belief and considerations and to make the connections with their level of information, direct experience, and the main fields of development for which BUES have been accessing funds so far. As positive

outcomes can be many, the question limited the respondent to describe only the main three positive outcomes that they could think about, *"Please mention three positive outcomes (as of your knowledge) of AES involvement in running projects financed through EU funds"*. Besides description of the positive outcomes which were detailed by 77% of the respondents, 12% more didn't know any, other 9% didn't want to answer and a percentage of 2% which in fact identifies a single respondent didn't see any positive aspect. All these categories of answers and the respondent's choices can be observed in Table 4.

Table 4. Categories of answers to Q4

Respondent's Main Aswers	Percentage	No. of Respondents
Positive answers	77%	44
I don't know	12%	7
I don't want to answer	9%	5
I don't see any positive aspect	2%	1
Total	100%	57

The main's purpose of the question was to identify positive aspects in the perception of the respondents and their answers reached a number of 26 different positive aspects that are illustrated in Annex3. However, the three top positions of positive aspects mention in the first place both opportunities for students to get involved in projects and develop their professional experience and improved relations between students and teachers. Secondly most frequently mentioned positive outcomes were the increased popularity and visibility in the market and the academic development& improved quality educational services and knowledge sharing. Last but not least, on third level, were mentioned the in-ternational mobilities for students and the increased facilities of students' entry on the labor market. These three top positive aspects and their frequency can be observed in Figure 5.

5. Similarly with the previous question, the fifth open-ended one seek to identify the negative aspects perceived by teachers and students with respect to the BUES involvement in the projects financed by European funds. Distribution of the general categories of answers and the respondent's choices can be observed in Table 5.

Figure 5.

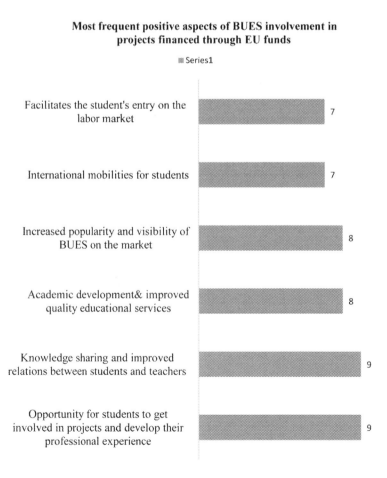

Most frequent positive aspects of BUES involvement in projects financed through EU funds

Table 5. Categories of answers to Q5

Respondent's Main Answers	Percentage	No. of Respondents
Detailed answers	68%	39
I don't know	14%	8
I don't want to answer	11%	6
I don't see any negative aspect	7%	4
Total	100%	57

As it can be noticed, 68% of the respondents were willing to give detailed answers, 14% didn't have any opinion, 11% didn't want to answer, and the rest of 7% didn't see any negative aspect with respect to the subject concerned. Out of the detailed answers, there could be grouped 27 types of negative elements that are listed in Annex4. The most negative frequent aspects mentioned are emphasized in Figure 6.

The top negative aspect mentioned was the poor communication, publicity, and promotion of the projects, according to the respondents' perception. Secondly they considered that there is a little involvement of students and also a high bureaucracy and the observance that teachers are more involved in the projects than in the teaching activity have been quoted in top three from the negative aspects of BUES involvement in the projects financed by European funds.

6. The distribution of the answers for the question, "In how many projects financed through EU funds have you been involved in the last 5 years with BUES?" is shown in Figure 7.

This is a quantitative and numerical question. Even though, it was drafted as an open-ended one. According to the records of the respondents, 54% have not been involved in any of the BUES projects, 25% had the chance to take part of one, while fewer respondents, 9%, stated that they were directly involved in two projects, only 7% were involved in three projects, and other 2% and 3% answered with four and respectively, five projects. These results shows that indeed, few teachers/students from BUES are directly involved in the university's this type of projects. However, on the other side, if taking into consideration that BUES has in total, yearly, thousands of students and hundreds of teachers, and only 64 projects financed through European funds

Figure 6.

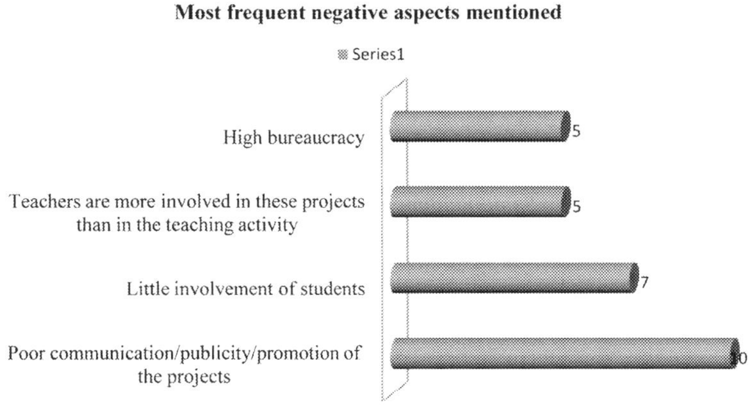

Most frequent negative aspects mentioned

Figure 7.

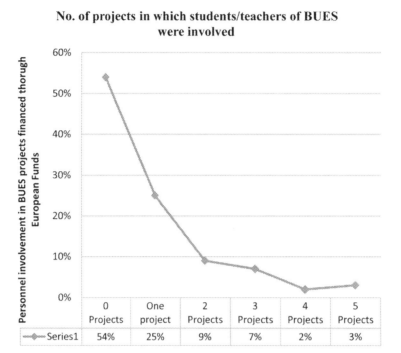

No. of projects in which students/teachers of BUES were involved

	0 Projects	One project	2 Projects	3 Projects	4 Projects	5 Projects
Series1	54%	25%	9%	7%	2%	3%

have been running till the current moment, it is remarkable to notice that some of the respondents had the chance to take part of more than 2 projects, so far.

7. The following question is also related to the respondents' involvement in this type of projects, but more generally as they were requested to mention the number of projects they've been part to, others than those within BUES. In this way, it can be noticed if internal stakeholders of BUES such as students and teachers are generally interested in this type of projects and they understand what they are about. According to the related answers, 63% of the respondents have not participated in any other projects, 16% did take part in one more, 2% have been involved in two more, 4% of them in three projects, 6% in four others, 4% in five others and

5% stated that they have been involved in more than five projects financed through EU funds, but with other organizations than BUES. The referent percentages and number of projects related can be observed in the graph in Figure 8.

8. In order to evaluate directly the information sources through which BUES is communicating the information related to its projects, the respondents were asked to mention three of the sources they use to access for reading, learning or accumulating knowledge with respect to the subject. The question was open-ended, quantitative and nominal. Being open-ended, not all respondents were willing to clearly answer. Thus, the main categories of answers were detailing examples with the information sources from 77% of the respondents, the standard "I don't know" answer given by 18% of the re-

Figure 8.

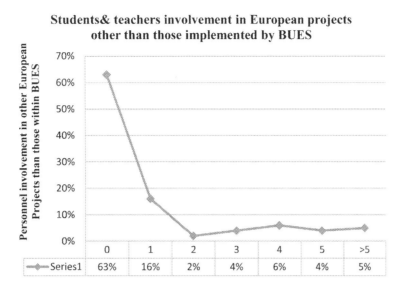

spondents and the third category in which the respondents are not interested so they don't get informed, answer related to 5% of the respondents. The distribution of the main three categories of answers can be observed in Figure 9.

However, from the 77% respondents who were willing to answer in details, there were collected 33 different information sources which are all illustrated in the table from An-

nex5. The answers were quite diversified, from specific sources of information such as full-name of websites (eg.: http://europa.eu/index_ro.htm) to more general ones that could identify only the type of source, such as brochures, internet, flyers and so on. However, the top 3 of the most frequently mentioned sources can be observed in Figure 10, where the website of BUES was mentioned 27th times as being considered the most relevant for searching related information, followed

Figure 9.

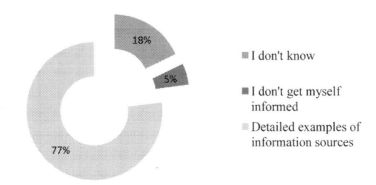

Figure 10.

Most frequently information sources mentioned

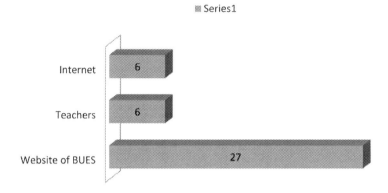

by other two sources such as internet and colleagues, the last two having a more general character.

9. The following question had the objective of finding out the frequency of accessing the mentioned sources on behalf of the respondents. The recordings are to emphasize the general interest of the internal stakeholders (teachers and students) within BUES in the subject and how often do they get informed. However, an effective communication is not measured by how many times a person access a specific source, but on how many times a specific communication/information reach the same person/audience/target people. In addition, an effective communication is two-sided, thus it is important to find out the willingness of one party to know, to get informed, to take part in. The recordings show that 23% of the respondents answered that they never access the information sources. If looking a bit into details, it can be noticed that this 23% are in fact the sum of the 18% who answered previously that they didn't know any information sources

with the 5% that answered previously that they were not getting informed in the field. Thus, from the relevant respondents, 21% stated that they are checking the information sources monthly and other 21% responded with "seldom". Another 18% of the respondents checked the "Every time I have the chance" answer which means that they are not truly interested as they don't go for information but at the same time, they are open with respect to the subject, if the information succeeded to reach them. Further 15% of the respondents stated that they access weekly the relevant information sources, while the last 2% are the most curios in the field and are getting updated, daily. Distribution of these frequencies can be observed in Figure 11.

The question was a quantitative one and measured the answers on a nominal scale.

10. In terms of the most efficient information source, the respondents were asked to choose only one answer out of seven choices and if none of them was considered the most efficient, they could select

Figure 11.

Frequency of accessing the mentioned sources

the option "other" and could further argue their answer. Here, the variables are qualitative and are measured on a nominal scale. The most relevant and efficient sources for communication/information were considered to be the newsletters, periodical magazines/brochures, an updated website, information sessions, conferences, and media. If the respondent was not interested in the subject and didn't have any opinion, he could also choose the "I don't feel the need to be informed" option (Table 6).

In addition, as it can be observed in Table 7, 5% of the respondents believed that other three sources are to be more relevant and efficient from the communication point of view, such as the BUES existing website, e-mails that can be received on Yahoo Groups from the Students' Senate and teachers from BUES that are supposed to be informed in the field and who should communicate to students more related information and relevant knowledge.

Table 6. The most efficient information sources in the field

Categories of Answers	Percentage	No.
Newsletters	21%	12
Periodical magazines/Brochures	2%	1
An updated and well structured website	**58%**	**33**
Information sessions	2%	1
Conferences	5%	3
Media	7%	4
I don't feel the need to be informed	**0**	**0**
Others	5%	3
Total	100%	57

Table 7. Other efficient sources mentioned by respondents with respect to the communication of the BUES projects financed through European funds

"Others" Efficient Sources	Total
BUES website	1
Mails received from the Students' Senate	1
Teachers should communicate more with students in this perspective	1

11. The question no.11 intended to find out the awareness of the respondents with respect to the existence of the BUES Guidance Office for Accessing EU Structural Funds and the assessment of its effectiveness. According to the recordings illustrated in Table 8, more than half of the respondents, 60%, haven't heard about the existence of the Office until present. An equal of 10% assessed its effectiveness as being very useful and pretty useful while other 9% chose the "so and so" and the "not very useful" options. In addition, only one respondent refused to answer to the question.

12. Further, a qualitative question is measured on an ordinal scale. For this, respondents have to scale from 1 to 10, the information sources with respect to the BUES's projects financed through European Funds that they have encountered so far, depending on their frequencies – where 1 is considered to be the most frequent and 10 is considered to be the less frequent information source encountered. In Table 9, the hierarchy shows the order of choices selected. The highest place is taken by the most voted option. The sum of points represents the total amount of all answers for the par-

Table 8 Utility of the Guidance and Accessing Office of EU Structural Funds within BUES

Options of Answer	Percentage	No.
Very useful	10%	6
Pretty useful	10%	6
So and so	9%	5
Not very useful	9%	5
I haven't heard about it before	**60%**	**34**
I don't want to answer	2%	1
Total	100%	57

Table 9. Frequency of the Top10 information sources encountered

Indicators - Information Sources Encountered	Hierarchy	Sum of Points
Students from BUES	1	247
Teachers from BUES	2	275
BUES's website	3	284
Newspapers	4	310
Conferences and other events within BUES	5	313
Acquaintances	6	329
Television	7	331
Internet (other websites and forums than those of BUES)	8	335
Media	9	365
Radio	10	401

ticular question. The most frequent response has the lowest number of points and vice versa. Therefore, it is easily notices that the top three places are assigned to students from BUES, teachers from BUES and BUES's website. These are considered the three most frequent indicators that have been encountered so far by respondents with respect to the present subject.

According to the recordings, the last three information sources that have been met are the internet that consists of other websites and forums than those of BUES, media and radio. The results shows that internal sources, teachers and students are those who mostly spread the information related to the subscribed projects, while external one are almost inexistent (Table 9).

13. The following question's objective was to measure the importance of an effective communication of BUES projects financed through European funds from

the point of view of the respondents. The result can be related to the level of interest of the respondents in the field and their willingness to get more involved. The graph below illustrates that from a scale from 1 to 5, the final results averages a 4.17 score on the level of importance. This underlines indeed, that respondents are curious and perceive the field as important and worthy of being effectively communicated (Figure 12).

14. Level of the respondents' interest and curiosity in the field can be measured also by their related interaction with other people. Thus, question no.14 requests the number of people to whom the respondent has been discussed with in the last month, on BUES's projects that are financed through European funds. Distribution of the answers can be observed in Figure 13.

Figure 12.

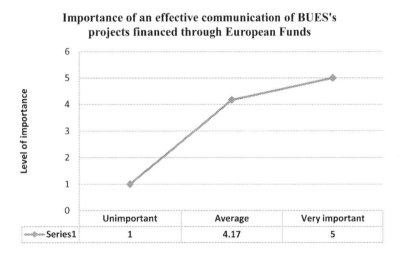

Importance of an effective communication of BUES's projects financed through European Funds

	Unimportant	Average	Very important
Series1	1	4.17	5

Figure 13.

No. of people discussed with about BUES's projects financed through European Funds in the last month

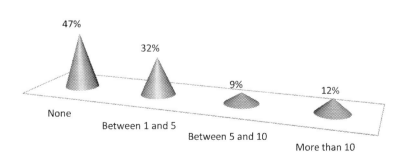

233

As it can be noticed, 47% of the respondents don't recall to have been talked to or discussed about the subject with some other persons in the last month. Another 32% stated that they did discuss with about one to five people, other 12% remember that they have talked to more than ten persons and the smaller percent of 9 chose the five to ten people category. Even if a very high number of the respondents don't use to talk upon the subject, more than a half, of 53% do talk and may also spread the information they have to some other people. The question is a quantitative one and measures its variables on an interval scale, which divides the respondents' choices in four classes. If going depth in the research, it is quite important to find out if those who use to discuss with others about the subject are selecting their conversational parties from the university environment or from different ones. Therefore, the next question completes the current one and seeks to identify the main environments in which the current subject is manly debated and of interest.

15. Distribution of the answers for the question "Which is the affiliation of the acquaintances" is illustrated in Figure 14.

As it can be noticed, most of the small talks and discussions in the field are held within the university, as 77% of the respondents selected the "within BUES" option. An equal percentage of 10 are having similar discussions in the NGOs and business environments while only 3% of the respondents stated that they used to talk also with some other universities with respect to the subject considered. It is also important to mention that a filter was inserted at the previous question, so only those 53% of the respondents who admitted that they use to talk with others in the field, could also complete the current question, as well. Variables of this question are qualitative and they are measured on a nominal scale.

Analysis of the result can conclude that as the main environment is BUES, internal stakeholders may be looking in finding more relevant information as they are interested in the field and maybe they are willing to improve

Figure 14.

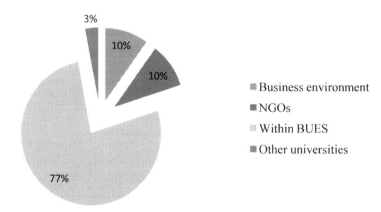

Environments in which discussions are held with concern to BUES's projects financed through European Funds

their knowledge and getting directly involved in this type of projects. The question had also the option of "other" where two respondents chose to be more specific and indicated that they use to discuss at work, which in Figure 14, it was affiliated with the business environment, and another one indicated two universities, such as University of Bucharest and Babes-Bolyai University. This last answer was also attributed to the option "other universities" from Figure 14.

16. From question number 16 onward starts the third part of the questionnaire that aims to find out some general information about the respondent with respect to his general interest of the European funds that are allocated to Romania for development projects and with respect to his long or short-term connection with BUES. Thus, the current question requests the frequency of reading articles concerning European funds and the distribution of answers can be observed in Figure 15.

According to Figure 15, 36% of the respondents are rarely reading European funds related articles, 22% have never done this, other 19% stated that they did it as many times they had the chance, 12% from the respondents mentioned that they were reading related articles weekly, 9% choose the "monthly" option and only 2% were daily readers in the field. It is also important to be mentioned that all 100 respondents have completed the current question and the following ones. The "as many times I have the chance" answer indicated that respondents may not be very interested in the subject, as they don't go and look for information. However, they are emphasizing their openness with respect to the subject, if the information succeeds to reach them. The question is a quantitative one and it measures its variables on a nominal scale. Another important aspect that can be noticed here is that 88% from the respondents are quite familiar with the European funds, however, as identified in the first question, 43% have not heard about this type of financing and the related projects within BUES.

Figure 15.

Frequency of reading articles concerning European Funds

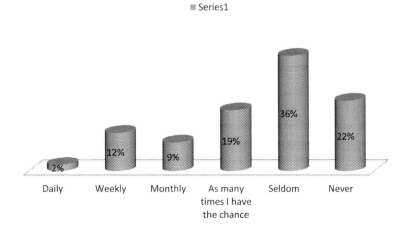

17. Distribution of the answers for the question "Do you know how many Operational Programs does Romania have in the current programming period?" is illustrated in Figure 16.

The question searches the level of general knowledge of respondents with respect to European funds and Operational Programs in Romania. According to recordings, 47% don't know how many Operational Programs are at the actual moment in Romania, 28% don't know what an Operational Program is, 13% do know that there are 7 which is also the correct answer. Other 12% of the respondents gave an incorrect answer, by selecting the 8, 6 or less than 6 Operational Programs. The result is pretty critical as taking into consideration that we are now in the 7th year of the current programming period, and the last one, almost one third of the respondents haven't heard about Operational Programs before and almost a half don't know how to answer. This is quite alarming if taking into consideration not only that BUES is running projects financed through European funds, but that the subject is actual and it is related to economi-cal issues, the central field of study within BUES. It is also interesting that if assuming that those 22% that responded to the previous question that they have never read articles with respect to European funds, there are also 6% who are seldom reading but they don't know what an Operational Program is which is a basic and general information with respect to the subject.

18. The further question is oriented toward the respondents' profile and their position within the University. Distribution of answers can be observed in Table 10.

As it can be noticed, 60% of the respondents are master students, 35% are bachelor students and only 5% are professors within the university. Even though the survey was published on websites, forums and Yahoo Groups of BUES, where usually, the professors are also subscribed, few teachers were willing to complete the questionnaire and most of the responses came from the students' side. From one point of view, this may emphasize a distant relationship between students and teachers. These two parties should be encouraged

Figure 16.

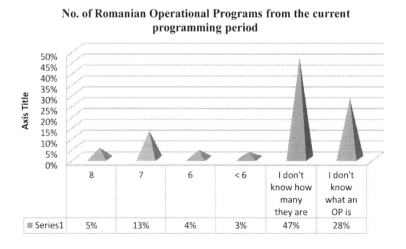

No. of Romanian Operational Programs from the current programming period

	8	7	6	< 6	I don't know how many they are	I don't know what an OP is
Series1	5%	13%	4%	3%	47%	28%

Table 10. Roles of respondents within BUES

Role within BUES	Percentage	No. of respondents
Bachelor student	35%	35
Master student	60%	60
PhD student	0	0
Teaching Assistant	1%	1
Assistant Professor	3%	3
University Lecturer	1%	1
University Professor	0%	0
Total	100%	100

to communicate more by social media too. On the other side, the low rate of responses may be argued by the time of year where many other surveys were conducted and they were also posted on more or less the same channels. This is sustained also by the fact that 100 respondents where gathered in more than a month which is a pretty long period of time for a 10 minutes-questionnaire.

19. The following question is also oriented toward the respondent's profile. It focuses on finding out how relevant are all the recordings from the questionnaire so far in relation to the long or short-term period in which the students or teachers have been studying or teaching within BUES. Thus, the distribution of answers can be observed in Figure 17.

The majority of the respondents, 37%, have been with the university for five years. Other 19% are part of the internal stakeholders for two years, 17% are also part of BUES for three years and 16% for four years. Only 9% from the respondents are with the university for one year and the smallest percent of 2 stated that they have more than five years experience within BUES. The question is a quantitative one that measures its variables by numerical means.

20. The last question is an open-ended one that looks for suggestions and recommendations related to the improvement of the communication of BUES projects financed through European funds. All 100 respondents, familiar or not with the situation were asked to complete the question. However, 77% of the respondents were willing to advice and

Figure 17.

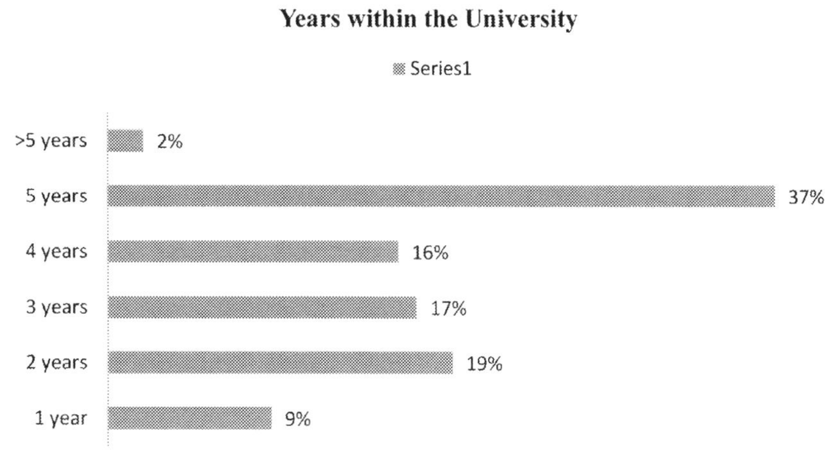

Years within the University

▨ Series1

>5 years	2%
5 years	37%
4 years	16%
3 years	17%
2 years	19%
1 year	9%

recommend while the other 23% didn't want to answer the question, as it can be noticed from Figure 18.

Totally, there could be grouped 24 different recommendations and suggestions that are illustrated in the table from Annex6. The top5 recommendations can be observed in Figure 19.

As it can be noticed, first recommendation is related to the level of information in the

Figure 18.

Answers to Q20

I don't know/want to answer

Answers detailed

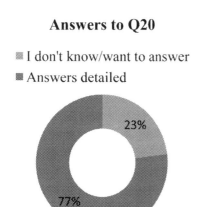

subject of professors and students. It is highly recommended that they should be better informed through posters, flyers or through online channels. Secondly, it is requested a better communication on publicity of the projects within the university and outside, as well. Many other stated that there should be encouraged periodical meetings, information sessions or more frequent conferences that can increase the awareness, informative level and may also promote the university's development, internally. Moreover, it is advised that teachers should communicate more on the subject with students, should transfer knowledge and even directly involved them so they can better understand and improve their capacities and skills. Also, in the top five, respondents suggested a more transparency of these funds and projects, their way of implementation, results and objectives reached. Besides these, others similar suggestions stated that students should be more involved in this type of projects and that BUES should better promote itself from this point of view.

Figure 19.

Top 5 Recommendations for BUES

Series1

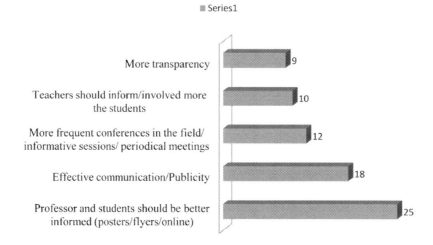

CONCLUSION AND RECOMMENDATIONS

General conclusions are easy to be taken as the entire questionnaire revealed that students and teachers within BUES are not very much informed and do not know pretty important and basic information with respect to European funds and projects related implemented by BUES. In addition, they are pretty much interested in the field and are willing to find out more and even get involved. They consider that communication of the subject is very important for them and also many mentioned that an effective communication can further promote the university and its improvements at the educational level. They are also requesting more transparency and effective distribution of related information, mainly through on-line means.

It is quite alarming the fact that BUES has been implementing many projects financed through European funds so far and almost half percent of the respondents, teachers and students, who are with the university for more than three years have not been noticed any improvement or could not identify any related project. Taking into consideration that all projects were required to ensure their visibility and properly communication on the market, it is very surprising that not even close related stakeholders are not very much informed in the field and do not know to answer some simple questions from the current questionnaire.

Results may indicate that the university's communication process and plan in the field was not very successful and efficient and there is still place for improvement and change. Main recommendations and problems identified so far with the help of the survey are connected with the university and projects transparency, lack of information sharing in the field and lack of active involvement of students and teachers, and poor internal communication and publicity.

Based on the relevant data gathered in the current study, both from questionnaire and other external sources and market analysis, it is recommended for the BUES to start to define its objective and goals in the field and ensure a better communication plan for the future programming period, as this might bring a lot of benefits for the university on the long term.

In order to increase the visibility of the university and to improve the communication and information distribution within the internal stakeholders like teachers and students, it is very important to design a communication plan and activities related, as they have the potential of a great positive impact toward university on the long-term. Therefore, the following activities and recommendations may be considered in order to ensure an effective promotion and internal communication of the Bucharest University of Economic Studies:

Recommendation 1: Realization of the Promotional Materials

Promotional materials ensure a good visibility upon the University and its ongoing projects not only directly, but also in an indirect way, making other people to promote it just through their usage.

The promotion materials to be realized are flyers, which meet the need of a synthetic material that describes the improved services of the faculties and the main objectives and results that are to be reached, related to the projects under implementation. These should be distributed within the University among students and teachers, with concern of their interest into the subject. In addition, there can be made maps for participants at related conferences and information sessions, banners, roll-up banners, pens, and block notes. Another attractive strategy may imply a distribution of pens, a block notes, flyers and other information materials that are accessible, such as brochures or magazines related to the subject. There can also be produced other additional promotional materials that can be also distributed to the participants at special events within projects, such as notebook bags, memory sticks, thermos cups, agendas for year 2014, calendars for year 2014 and even umbrellas for an increased visibility. It is important to mention that all these materials can be financed directly thorough the EU funds accessed for the projects, some being even a must in order to ensure visibility and transparency of projects.

Recommendation 2: Improving or Creating a New Website for the Projects

The website is one of the main communication channel through which BUES is offering information regarding its services and it is an indispensable element of the communication mix that engages many communication channels. At the moment, BUES's main website has a direct connection toward a page special created for BUES projects financed through European funds. It can be found in the *Research* category with the link *European projects*. The main tabs here are pretty well established and useful for any information seeker in the field: h*ome, useful documents, BUES projects, news* and *contact*. However, beside some legislation documents and responsibilities of the Guidance and accessing office of EU structural funds, no other information can be found. Not only that it is not constant updated, but it does not provide any information with respect to the European projects within BUES. First

of all, it is very important that the specific area designed for the European projects to be fulfilled with related information in an organized way, easy to follow. For this, the website can be developed in many ways. For instance, the graphical concept may be completely restored so that it becomes friendlier and the information to be better emphasized. In terms of organization of the information the menu can be restored so the information can be easily and faster accessed. From the technical point of view, the website can be optimized so it can be easily accessed through the search engines and it can also be better secured. Regarding the content of the website, the information already existing should be updated and the information not relevant anymore should be identified and erased. The information on the website should be both in a written format and audio-video.

My personal opinion is that it is better to design a special space for the European projects within BUES than creating a totally new one. In this way, projects are going to be correlated for sure with the university, which can help it very much in terms of advertising and visibility on the market. In addition, in this way, the website has a very good potential for growth. Another positive aspect is that it can become a reliable source of information by being presented within the official website of the university.

It is well known that the most visited websites are the "news" websites, that are able to create own editorial content. Thus, the projects part of website may contain, besides the information taken from the coordination and management of its internal projects and procedures, additional types of editorial content: news, editorial in the form of contributions required from experts in the field, interviews with leading personnel from public institutions, reports and important announcements.

All these can be illustrated with images that are to be bought on a contract basis. In addition, on the website can be posted in real time, recordings from relevant events. For this, it might be necessary to contract specialized firms in taking and processing the photo and audio-video content.

In addition, it can be a very good idea to develop an adjacent platform to the website, dedicated to the project managers that run the BUES related projects, where they can subscribe their projects, make public the acquisition announcements, communicate the results gained while implementing their projects, exchange best practices, discuss various aspects from the implementation period of the project and so on. The website can be a useful tool for the potential beneficiaries, as well, as the information provided and the successful examples can help them a lot. Thus, all projects subscribed in the database can be used in edited brochures, newsletter or other public materials, or events managed by BUES.

Recommendation 3: On-Line Communication

The result of a study made by European Commission showed that internet became one of the main and of most important communication channel with European citizens and best approach of various targeted groups. Internet allows an interactive relationship, different from messages or announcement made through press, which are unidirectional. This possibility of receiving feedback from the audience ensures a qualitative component of the process, in comparison with the standard means that imply mostly a quantitative approach of the targeted groups.

Therefore, an online banner campaign may be a good solution for promoting the European projects platform within BUES. The campaign should suppose development and posting of the banners on websites of the BUES partners and other related collaborators. They may increase the awareness on the market with respect to BUES development and activities and may create new partnerships, enforce the existing ones, and attract more students and teachers, both from within the country or international. On-line communication on the social networks should be also a must in this case. The website should be actively supported by social networks such as Facebook, Twitter and LinkedIn.

Recommendation 4: Information Sessions

As many of the respondents mentioned, there should also be organized within BUES, periodical information/promotion/debating events at which interests students and teachers may come to get updated and even involved in the related activities of European projects. This can also help the university to better define its strategic and operational plan on both long and short term. Specific work-shops and focus groups can be organized in the field in order to define problems, find innovative solutions and receive relevant feedbacks from the key interested parties in order to improve the further planning of the university's development and institutional capacity building.

Recommendation 5: Brochures and Informative Newsletters

Brochures and informative newsletters should be edited during the year, so it can be visible the active services and work done by the personnel responsible of the projects' implementation, but also to inform the existing students and teachers and also the potential ones toward the activities of development of the faculty, how can they do for being involved and to update them with the latest news in the field. For this, indicative topics may be the improvements made so far, interviews with managers of the projects and important partners involved or simply different experts in the field, at e high level from which many things can be learnt; news of new opportunities for different courses, postgraduate studies, calendar of events and conferences in the field, articles based on the Guidance and accessing office of EU structural funds experience that may contain the most frequent and interesting questions received from interested parties or main problems encountered; information related to the events organized within the project, recent legislative amendments, new opportunities for financing projects and many others subjects related. If necessary, all these may be translated into English. These materials can be distributed both electronically, which involves a low cost or in the printed format. Informative online newsletters may be very effective in this situation and does not imply any cost beside the human resource one. In order not to spam all the internal stakeholders, the website may be designed in such a way that all interested parties can subscribe to the university's related newsletters in the field. I definitely believe this is a good start for improving the communication and information

sharing in this field – very much debated and important nowadays.

Taking into consideration that the current research have been done during 2013, the sixth consecutive year in which BUES is involved and runs projects financed through European funds, results are quite important for future development and communication plan in the field. From 2014 until 2020 starts a new programming period with respect to European funds, thus opportunities for institution's and human's development are still opened and many can still take advantage of them. A university is looking for improving its services and educational programs, facilitating professional development of professors and attracting the best students. An institution with informed and active stakeholders has higher chances of a fast development that leads to higher competitiveness advantage on the market.

All the above recommendation activities, practices and outlines of a communication process can become a successfully implementation communication plan for the next years, as they are clear, concrete and they are based on the internal context analysis, problem identification in the field together with objectives and successful results that can be reached and propagated on long-term, all for the benefit of university.

REFERENCES

Arnould, E., & Price, L. (2004). *Consumers* (2nd ed.). Boston: McGraw-Hill Publishing House.

Berger, B. (2009, March 4). *Internal organizational communication*. Retrieved from http// www.pr-romania.ro/articole/comunicare-interna/142-comunicarea-organizationala-interna.html?start=4

Boyd, T. (2007, June 12). *Basic elements of internal communication*. Retrieved from http://www.pr-romania.ro/articole/comunicare-interna/45-elemente-de-baza-in-comunicarea-interna.html

Bratianu, C., & Vasilache, S. (2008). *Drafting, editing and delivering undergraduate and master's work*. Bucharest, Romania: Bucharest University Publishing House.

Burns, A. C. (2006). *Marketing research* (5th ed.). Upper Saddle River, NJ: Pearson Publishing House.

Cătoiu, I. (2004). *Consumer behavior* (2nd ed.). Bucharest, Romania: Uranius Publishing House.

Gay, C., Mahoney, M., & Graves, J. (2005). *Best practices of employee communication*. San Francisco: International Association of Business Communicators Publishing House.

Libaert, T. (2009). *The communication plan* (3rd ed.). Bucharest, Romania: Polirom Publishing House.

Malhotra, N. K. (2007). *Marketing research: An applied orientation* (5th ed.). Upper Saddle River, NJ: Pearson Publishing House.

Ministry of European Funds. (2013a). *Internal press review of information center of structural instruments*. Bucharest, Romania: Ministry of European Funds Publishing House.

Ministry of European Funds. (2013b, May 15). *Projects*. Retrieved from http://b.fonduri-ue.ro/proiecte

Ministry of European Funds. (2013c). *Centralization of the present sheets of the event ABC of structural instruments*. Bucharest, Romania: Ministry of European Funds Publishing House.

Minulescu, M. (2004). *Organizational communication*. Retrieved from http://www.slideshare.net/Elida82/comunicare-organizationala-m-minulescu

Mitruţ, C., & Serban, D. (2003). *Statistics for business administration*. Bucharest, Romania: BUES Publishing House.

Mucchielli, A. (2008). *Communication in institutions and organizations*. Bucharest, Romania: Polirom Publishing House.

Niculae, T., & Gherghita, D. I. (2006). *Organizational communication and crisis management*. Bucharest, Romania: Ministry of Administration and Interior Publishing House.

Popescu, D. I. (2010). *Organizational behavior*. Bucharest, Romania: BUES Publishing House.

Rabinowitz, P. (2012). *Promoting internal communication*. Retrieved from http://www.snapcomms.com/solutions/measuring-internal-communications-effectiveness.aspx

Rogojanu, A., Hristache, D. A., & Tasnadi, A. (2004). *Institutional communication*. Bucharest, Romania: BUES Publishing House.

Romanian Government. (2007). *National communication strategy for structural instruments of romania 2007-2013*. Bucharest, Romania: Romanian Government Publishing House.

Romanian Government. (n.d.). *National strategic reference framework of Romania 2007-2013 (NSRF)*. Bucharest, Romania: Romanian Government Publishing House.

Schiffman, L. G. (2007). *Consumer behavior* (9th ed.). Upper Saddle River, NJ: Pearson Publishing House.

Serban, D. (2004). *Statistics for marketing and business administration*. Bucharest, Romania: BUES Publishing House.

Tourish, D., & Hargie, O. (2004). *Key issues in organizational communication*. Oxford, UK: Routledge Publishing House.

Related References

To continue our tradition of advancing research in medicine, healthcare, and the life sciences, we have compiled a list of recommended IGI Global readings. These references will provide additional information and guidance to further enrich your knowledge, and assist you with your own research and future publications.

Abu-Faraj, Z. O. (2012). Bioengineering/biomedical engineering education. In Z. Abu-Faraj (Ed.), *Handbook of research on biomedical engineering education and advanced bioengineering learning: Interdisciplinary concepts* (pp. 1–59). Hershey, PA: Medical Information Science Reference. doi:10.4018/978-1-4666-0122-2.ch001

Achehboune, A., & Driouchi, A. (2014). Potential skilled labor migration, internationalization of education with focus on medical education: The case of Arab countries. In A. Driouchi (Ed.), *Labor and health economics in the Mediterranean region: Migration and mobility of medical doctors* (pp. 83–122). Hershey, PA: Medical Information Science Reference.

Adomi, E. E., Egbaivwie, E., & Ogugua, J. C. (2013). Use of the internet by medical practitioners in private hospitals in Warri, Delta State, Nigeria. In A. Cartelli (Ed.), *Fostering 21st century digital literacy and technical competency* (pp. 213–221). Hershey, PA: Information Science Reference.

Afolabi, M. O., Babalola, O. O., & Ola-Olorun, O. J. (2012). Counselling in pharmacy practice: Exploring the use of online counselling interactions to improve medicine use among people living with HIV/AIDS (PLWHA). In B. Popoola, & O. Adebowale (Eds.), *Online guidance and counseling: Toward effectively applying technology* (pp. 91–103). Hershey, PA: Information Science Reference. doi:10.4018/978-1-61350-204-4.ch007

Ahmad, Y. J., Raghavan, V. V., & Martz, W. B., Jr. (2011). Adoption of electronic health records. In I. Management Association (Ed.), Clinical technologies: Concepts, methodologies, tools and applications (pp. 132-146). Hershey, PA: Medical Information Science Reference. doi: doi:10.4018/978-1-60960-561-2.ch109

Al-Dossary, S., Al-Dulaijan, N., Al-Mansour, S., Al-Zahrani, S., Al-Fridan, M., & Househ, M. (2013). Organ donation and transplantation: Processes, registries, consent, and restrictions in Saudi Arabia. In M. Cruz-Cunha, I. Miranda, & P. Gonçalves (Eds.), *Handbook of research on ICTs for human-centered healthcare and social care services* (pp. 511–528). Hershey, PA: Medical Information Science Reference. doi:10.4018/978-1-4666-3986-7.ch027

Al-Khudairy, S. (2014). Caring for our aging population: Using CPOE and telehomecare systems as a response to health policy concerns. In C. El Morr (Ed.), *Research perspectives on the role of informatics in health policy and management* (pp. 153–166). Hershey, PA: Medical Information Science Reference.

Albert, A., Serrano, A. J., Soria, E., & Jiménez, N. V. (2010). Clinical decision support system to prevent toxicity in patients treated with Digoxin. In A. Shukla, & R. Tiwari (Eds.), *Intelligent medical technologies and biomedical engineering: Tools and applications* (pp. 1–21). Hershey, PA: Medical Information Science Reference. doi:10.4018/978-1-61520-977-4.ch001

Alexandrou, D. A., & Pardalis, K. V. (2014). SEMantic PATHways: Modeling, executing, and monitoring intra-organizational healthcare business processes towards personalized treatment. In I. Management Association (Ed.), Software design and development: Concepts, methodologies, tools, and applications (pp. 1036-1062). Hershey, PA: Information Science Reference. doi: doi:10.4018/978-1-4666-4301-7.ch050

Alhaqbani, B., & Fidge, C. (2013). A medical data trustworthiness assessment model. In I. Management Association (Ed.), User-driven healthcare: Concepts, methodologies, tools, and applications (pp. 1425-1445). Hershey, PA: Medical Information Science Reference. doi: doi:10.4018/978-1-4666-2770-3.ch071

Ali, S., Abbadeni, N., & Batouche, M. (2012). *Multidisciplinary computational intelligence techniques: Applications in business, engineering, and medicine* (pp. 1–365). Hershey, PA: IGI Global. doi:10.4018/978-1-4666-1830-5

Alonso, J. M., Castiello, C., Lucarelli, M., & Mencar, C. (2013). Modeling interpretable fuzzy rule-based classifiers for medical decision support. In I. Association (Ed.), *Data mining: Concepts, methodologies, tools, and applications* (pp. 1064–1081). Hershey, PA: Information Science Reference.

Alonso-Barba, J. I., Nielsen, J. D., de la Ossa, L., & Puerta, J. M. (2012). Learning probabilistic graphical models: A review of techniques and applications in medicine. In R. Magdalena-Benedito, E. Soria-Olivas, J. Martínez, J. Gómez-Sanchis, & A. Serrano-López (Eds.), *Medical applications of intelligent data analysis: Research advancements* (pp. 223–236). Hershey, PA: Information Science Reference. doi:10.4018/978-1-4666-1803-9.ch015

Anderson, J. G. (2010). Improving patient safety with information technology. In K. Khoumbati, Y. Dwivedi, A. Srivastava, & B. Lal (Eds.), *Handbook of research on advances in health informatics and electronic healthcare applications: Global adoption and impact of information communication technologies* (pp. 144–152). Hershey, PA: Medical Information Science Reference.

Anderson, J. G. (2011). Regional patient safety initiatives. In I. Management Association (Ed.), Clinical technologies: Concepts, methodologies, tools and applications (pp. 1491-1503). Hershey, PA: Medical Information Science Reference. doi: doi:10.4018/978-1-60960-561-2.ch506

Andonegui, J., Serrano, L., & Eguzkiza, A. (2010). E-health applications in ophthalmic diseases: Ongoing developments. In M. Cruz-Cunha, A. Tavares, & R. Simoes (Eds.), *Handbook of research on developments in e-health and telemedicine: Technological and social perspectives* (pp. 1088–1115). Hershey, PA: Medical Information Science Reference.

Andrés, A. R. (2014). Understanding the migration of medical doctors in the context of Europe. In A. Driouchi (Ed.), *Labor and health economics in the Mediterranean region: Migration and mobility of medical doctors* (pp. 139–157). Hershey, PA: Medical Information Science Reference.

Ann, O. C., & Theng, L. B. (2014). A facial expression mediated natural user interface communication model for children with motor impairments. In G. Kouroupetroglou (Ed.), *Assistive technologies and computer access for motor disabilities* (pp. 254–284). Hershey, PA: Medical Information Science Reference.

Anselma, L., Bottrighi, A., Molino, G., Montani, S., Terenziani, P., & Torchio, M. (2011). Supporting knowledge-based decision making in the medical context: The GLARE approach. [IJKBO]. *International Journal of Knowledge-Based Organizations*, *1*(1), 42–60. doi:10.4018/ijkbo.2011010103

Apostolakis, I., Valsamos, P., & Varlamis, I. (2011). Quality assurance in evidence-based medicine. In A. Moumtzoglou, & A. Kastania (Eds.), *E-health systems quality and reliability: Models and standards* (pp. 86–99). Hershey, PA: Medical Information Science Reference.

Archibald, D., MacDonald, C. J., Hogue, R., & Mercer, J. (2013). Accessing knowledge from the bedside: Introducing the tablet computer to clinical teaching. In C. Rückemann (Ed.), *Integrated information and computing systems for natural, spatial, and social sciences* (pp. 96–109). Hershey, PA: Information Science Reference.

Aspradaki, A. A. (2013). Deliberative democracy and nanotechnologies in health. [IJT]. *International Journal of Technoethics*, *4*(2), 1–14. doi:10.4018/jte.2013070101

Assis-Hassid, S., Reychav, I., Pliskin, J. S., & Heart, T. H. (2013). The effects of electronic medical record (EMR) use in primary care on the physician-patient relationship. In M. Cruz-Cunha, I. Miranda, & P. Gonçalves (Eds.), *Handbook of research on ICTs for human-centered healthcare and social care services* (pp. 130–150). Hershey, PA: Medical Information Science Reference. doi:10.4018/978-1-4666-3986-7.ch007

Atanasov, A. (2011). Quality and reliability aspects in evidence based e-medicine. In A. Moumtzoglou, & A. Kastania (Eds.), *E-health systems quality and reliability: Models and standards* (pp. 100–117). Hershey, PA: Medical Information Science Reference. doi:10.4018/978-1-60960-561-2.ch112

Attalla, D. S. (2011). Health hazards of mobile information communication technologies. In A. Abdel-Wahab, & A. El-Masry (Eds.), *Mobile information communication technologies adoption in developing countries: Effects and implications* (pp. 237–251). Hershey, PA: Information Science Reference.

Au, S., & Gupta, A. (2011). Gastrointestinal motility online educational endeavor. In A. Moumtzoglou, & A. Kastania (Eds.), *E-health systems quality and reliability: Models and standards* (pp. 163–182). Hershey, PA: Medical Information Science Reference.

Azar, A. T. (2013). Overview of biomedical engineering. In I. Management Association (Ed.), Bioinformatics: Concepts, methodologies, tools, and applications (pp. 1-28). Hershey, PA: Medical Information Science Reference. doi: doi:10.4018/978-1-4666-3604-0.ch001

Azar, A. T., & Eljamel, M. S. (2014). Medical robotics. In I. Management Association (Ed.), Robotics: Concepts, methodologies, tools, and applications (pp. 1116-1147). Hershey, PA: Information Science Reference. doi: doi:10.4018/978-1-4666-4607-0.ch054

Bagheri, F. B. (2013). eSelf or computerized self network: A tool for individual empowerment & implementation of optimal healthcare. [IJUDH]. *International Journal of User-Driven Healthcare*, *3*(2), 20–32. doi:10.4018/ijudh.2013040103

Baharadwaj, N., Wadhwa, S., Goel, P., Sethi, I., Arora, C. S., & Goel, A. et al. (2014). De-noising, clustering, classification, and representation of microarray data for disease diagnostics. In R. Srivastava, S. Singh, & K. Shukla (Eds.), *Research developments in computer vision and image processing: Methodologies and applications* (pp. 149–174). Hershey, PA: Information Science Reference.

Baijou, A. (2014). A descriptive overview of the emigration of medical doctors from MENA to EU. In A. Driouchi (Ed.), *Labor and health economics in the Mediterranean region: Migration and mobility of medical doctors* (pp. 192–218). Hershey, PA: Medical Information Science Reference.

Bauer, K. (2010). Healthcare ethics in the information age. In J. Rodrigues (Ed.), *Health information systems: Concepts, methodologies, tools, and applications* (pp. 1761–1776). Hershey, PA: Medical Information Science Reference.

Bauer, K. A. (2013). Caught in the web: The internet and the demise of medical privacy. In I. Management Association (Ed.), User-driven healthcare: Concepts, methodologies, tools, and applications (pp. 1252-1272). Hershey, PA: Medical Information Science Reference. doi: doi:10.4018/978-1-4666-2770-3.ch063

Bayona, S., Espadero, J. M., Fernández, J. M., Pastor, L., & Rodríguez, Á. (2011). Implementing virtual reality in the healthcare sector. In N. Rao (Ed.), *Virtual technologies for business and industrial applications: Innovative and synergistic approaches* (pp. 138–163). Hershey, PA: Business Science Reference.

Begg, M., Dewhurst, D., & Ross, M. (2010). Game informed virtual patients: Catalysts for online learning communities and professional development of medical teachers. In J. Lindberg, & A. Olofsson (Eds.), *Online learning communities and teacher professional development: Methods for improved education delivery* (pp. 190–208). Hershey, PA: Information Science Reference. doi:10.4018/978-1-61520-869-2.ch020

Bennett, E. E., Blanchard, R. D., & Fernandez, G. L. (2012). Knowledge sharing in academic medical centers: Examining the nexus of higher education and workforce development. In V. Wang (Ed.), *Encyclopedia of e-leadership, counseling and training* (pp. 212–232). Hershey, PA: Information Science Reference.

Bera, T. K., & Nagaraju, J. (2014). Electrical impedance tomography (EIT): A harmless medical imaging modality. In R. Srivastava, S. Singh, & K. Shukla (Eds.), *Research developments in computer vision and image processing: Methodologies and applications* (pp. 235–273). Hershey, PA: Information Science Reference.

Berler, A., & Apostolakis, I. (2014). Normalizing cross-border healthcare in europe via new e-prescription paradigms. In C. El Morr (Ed.), *Research perspectives on the role of informatics in health policy and management* (pp. 168–208). Hershey, PA: Medical Information Science Reference.

Beswetherick, J. (2012). Health care information systems and the risk of privacy issues for the disabled. In I. Management Association (Ed.), Cyber crime: Concepts, methodologies, tools and applications (pp. 870-890). Hershey, PA: Information Science Reference. doi: doi:10.4018/978-1-61350-323-2.ch411

Bhattacharya, P., Asanga, A. P., & Biswas, R. (2011). Stomodeum to proctodeum: Email narratives on clinical problem solving in gastroenterology. In R. Biswas, & C. Martin (Eds.), *User-driven healthcare and narrative medicine: Utilizing collaborative social networks and technologies* (pp. 34–53). Hershey, PA: Medical Information Science Reference.

Biswas, R., & Martin, C. M. (2011). *User-driven healthcare and narrative medicine: Utilizing collaborative social networks and technologies.* Hershey, PA: IGI Global.

Biswas, R., Martin, C. M., Sturmberg, J., Mukherji, K., Lee, E. W., & Umakanth, S. (2011). Social cognitive ontology and user driven healthcare. In I. Management Association (Ed.), Clinical technologies: Concepts, methodologies, tools and applications (pp. 1996-2012). Hershey, PA: Medical Information Science Reference. doi: doi:10.4018/978-1-60960-561-2.ch710

Biswas, R., Sturmberg, J., Martin, C. M., Ganesh, A. U., Umakanth, S., & Lee, E. W. (2011). Persistent clinical encounters in user driven e-health care. In I. Management Association (Ed.), Clinical technologies: Concepts, methodologies, tools and applications (pp. 1030-1046). Hershey, PA: Medical Information Science Reference. doi: doi:10.4018/978-1-60960-561-2.ch403

Black, N. P., Fromme, H. B., Maniscalco, J., Ferrell, C., Myers, J., & Augustine, E. . . . Blankenburg, R. (2013). Innovation in patient care and medical resident education: Using blended instruction to transform nighttime patient care from a service model into an educational model. In A. Ritzhaupt, & S. Kumar (Eds.) Cases on educational technology implementation for facilitating learning (pp. 161-176). Hershey, PA: Information Science Reference. doi: doi:10.4018/978-1-4666-3676-7. ch010

Blatt, A. J. (2013). Geospatial applications in disease surveillance: Solutions for the future. [IJAGR]. *International Journal of Applied Geospatial Research*, *4*(2), 1–8. doi:10.4018/jagr.2013040101

Boaduo, N. A., & Boaduo, N. K. (2012). ICTs for enhanced use of indigenous medicinal plants by the Ashante speaking people of Ghana. In R. Lekoko, & L. Semali (Eds.), *Cases on developing countries and ICT integration: Rural community development* (pp. 16–24). Hershey, PA: Information Science Reference.

Boboc, C., & Titan, E. (2014). Inputs from the new economics of migration of medical doctors in eastern and central Europe. In A. Driouchi (Ed.), *Labor and health economics in the Mediterranean region: Migration and mobility of medical doctors* (pp. 241–266). Hershey, PA: Medical Information Science Reference.

Boboc, C., & Ţiţan, E. (2014). Migration of medical doctors, health, medical education, and employment in eastern and central Europe. In A. Driouchi (Ed.), *Labor and health economics in the Mediterranean region: Migration and mobility of medical doctors* (pp. 158–191). Hershey, PA: Medical Information Science Reference.

Bolsin, S., & Colson, M. (2010). IT benefits in healthcare performance and safety. In J. Rodrigues (Ed.), *Health information systems: Concepts, methodologies, tools, and applications* (pp. 71–88). Hershey, PA: Medical Information Science Reference.

Bongers, B., & Smith, S. (2014). Interactivating rehabilitation through active multimodal feedback and guidance. In I. Association (Ed.), *Assistive technologies: Concepts, methodologies, tools, and applications* (pp. 1650–1674). Hershey, PA: Information Science Reference.

Borges, A. P., & Laranjeira, E. (2013). Why and how did health economics appear? Who were the main authors? What is the role of ITCs in its development? In M. Cruz-Cunha, I. Miranda, & P. Gonçalves (Eds.), *Handbook of research on ICTs and management systems for improving efficiency in healthcare and social care* (pp. 971–987). Hershey, PA: Medical Information Science Reference. doi:10.4018/978-1-4666-3990-4.ch051

Bourgeois, S., & Yaylacicegi, U. (2012). Electronic health records: Improving patient safety and quality of care in Texas acute care hospitals. In J. Tan (Ed.), *Advancing technologies and intelligence in healthcare and clinical environments breakthroughs* (pp. 18–32). Hershey, PA: Medical Information Science Reference. doi:10.4018/978-1-4666-1755-1.ch002

Brandt, R., & Rice, R. (2012). Dermatological telemedicine diagnoses and andragogical training using web 2.0 mobile medicine video conferencing. In V. Dennen, & J. Myers (Eds.), *Virtual professional development and informal learning via social networks* (pp. 276–293). Hershey, PA: Information Science Reference. doi:10.4018/978-1-4666-1815-2.ch016

Brzezinski, J., Kosiedowski, M., Mazurek, C., Slowinski, K., Slowinski, R., Stroinski, M., & Weglarz, J. (2013). Towards telemedical centers: Digitization of inter-professional communication in healthcare. In M. Cruz-Cunha, I. Miranda, & P. Gonçalves (Eds.), *Handbook of research on ICTs and management systems for improving efficiency in healthcare and social care* (pp. 805–829). Hershey, PA: Medical Information Science Reference. doi:10.4018/978-1-4666-3990-4.ch042

Carlén, U., & Lindström, B. (2012). Informed design of educational activities in online learning communities. In A. Olofsson, & J. Lindberg (Eds.), *Informed design of educational technologies in higher education: Enhanced learning and teaching* (pp. 118–134). Hershey, PA: Information Science Reference.

Carrigan, E., Ugaz, A., Moberly, H. K., Page, J., Alpi, K. M., & Vreeland, C. (2013). Veterinary medicine: All collections great and small. In S. Holder (Ed.), *Library collection development for professional programs: Trends and best practices* (pp. 248–268). Hershey, PA: Information Science Reference.

Caruana, C. J. (2012). The ongoing crisis in medical device education for healthcare professionals: Breaking the vicious circle through online learning. [IJRQEH]. *International Journal of Reliable and Quality E-Healthcare*, *1*(2), 29–40. doi:10.4018/ijrqeh.2012040103

Catapano, G., & Verkerke, G. J. (2012). Artificial organs. In Z. Abu-Faraj (Ed.), *Handbook of research on biomedical engineering education and advanced bioengineering learning: Interdisciplinary concepts* (pp. 60–95). Hershey, PA: Medical Information Science Reference. doi:10.4018/978-1-4666-0122-2.ch002

Chandra, S., Shah, N. K., & Sriganesh, V. (2011). The cochrane students journal club and creating a secondary learning resource for gathering and appraising evidence: An example of rational use of medicines to prevent malaria relapse. [IJUDH]. *International Journal of User-Driven Healthcare*, *1*(4), 31–41. doi:10.4018/ijudh.2011100103

Chang, A. Y., Littman-Quinn, R., Ketshogileng, D., Chandra, A., Rijken, T., & Ghose, S. et al. (2012). Smartphone-based mobile learning with physician trainees in Botswana. [IJMBL]. *International Journal of Mobile and Blended Learning*, *4*(2), 1–14. doi:10.4018/jmbl.2012040101

Charissis, G., Melas, C., Moustakis, V., & Zampetakis, L. (2010). Organizational implementation of healthcare information systems. In M. Cruz-Cunha, A. Tavares, & R. Simoes (Eds.), *Handbook of research on developments in e-health and telemedicine: Technological and social perspectives* (pp. 419–450). Hershey, PA: Medical Information Science Reference.

Chaudhuri, A., Young, J., Martin, C. M., Sturmberg, J. P., & Biswas, R. (2011). Hematology: The river within. In R. Biswas, & C. Martin (Eds.), *User-driven healthcare and narrative medicine: Utilizing collaborative social networks and technologies* (pp. 16–33). Hershey, PA: Medical Information Science Reference.

Chen, J. Y., Xu, H., Shi, P., Culbertson, A., & Meslin, E. M. (2013). Ethics and privacy considerations for systems biology applications in predictive and personalized medicine. In I. Management Association (Ed.), Bioinformatics: Concepts, methodologies, tools, and applications (pp. 1378-1404). Hershey, PA: Medical Information Science Reference. doi: doi:10.4018/978-1-4666-3604-0.ch071

Cherian, E. J., & Ryan, T. W. (2014). Incongruent needs: Why differences in the iron-triangle of priorities make health information technology adoption and use difficult. In C. El Morr (Ed.), *Research perspectives on the role of informatics in health policy and management* (pp. 209–221). Hershey, PA: Medical Information Science Reference.

Chetioui, Y. (2014). Perception by Moroccan physicians of factors affecting their migration decisions. In A. Driouchi (Ed.), *Labor and health economics in the mediterranean region: Migration and mobility of medical doctors* (pp. 337–375). Hershey, PA: Medical Information Science Reference.

Chorbev, I., & Joksimoski, B. (2011). An integrated system for e-medicine (e-health, telemedicine and medical expert systems). In I. Management Association (Ed.), Clinical technologies: Concepts, methodologies, tools and applications (pp. 486-507). Hershey, PA: Medical Information Science Reference. doi: doi:10.4018/978-1-60960-561-2.ch218

Ciufudean, C., Ciufudean, O., & Filote, C. (2013). New models for ICT-based medical diagnosis. In M. Cruz-Cunha, I. Miranda, & P. Gonçalves (Eds.), *Handbook of research on ICTs and management systems for improving efficiency in healthcare and social care* (pp. 892–911). Hershey, PA: Medical Information Science Reference. doi:10.4018/978-1-4666-3990-4.ch046

Clark, J. M. (2014). Implementation of electronic records in a medical practice setting. In J. Krueger (Ed.), *Cases on electronic records and resource management implementation in diverse environments* (pp. 211–225). Hershey, PA: Information Science Reference.

Clark, T. (2011). Health and health care grid services and delivery integrating eHealth and telemedicine. In E. Kldiashvili (Ed.), *Grid technologies for e-health: Applications for telemedicine services and delivery* (pp. 36–64). Hershey, PA: Medical Information Science Reference.

Claster, W., Ghotbi, N., & Shanmuganathan, S. (2010). Data-mining techniques for an analysis of non-conventional methodologies: Deciphering of alternative medicine. In W. Pease, M. Cooper, & R. Gururajan (Eds.), *Biomedical knowledge management: Infrastructures and processes for e-health systems* (pp. 82–91). Hershey, PA: Medical Information Science Reference. doi:10.4018/978-1-60566-266-4.ch006

Condaris, C. (2012). Scales to scalpels: Doctors who practice the healing arts of music and medicine. [IJUDH]. *International Journal of User-Driven Healthcare, 2*(3), 84–84. doi: doi:10.4018/ijudh.2012070109

Corrigan, D., Hederman, L., Khan, H., Taweel, A., Kostopoulou, O., & Delaney, B. (2013). An ontology-driven approach to clinical evidence modelling implementing clinical prediction rules. In A. Moumtzoglou, & A. Kastania (Eds.), *E-health technologies and improving patient safety: Exploring organizational factors* (pp. 257–284). Hershey, PA: Medical Information Science Reference.

Crisóstomo-Acevedo, M. J., & Aurelio Medina-Garrido, J. (2010). Difficulties in accepting telemedicine. In J. Rodrigues (Ed.), *Health information systems: Concepts, methodologies, tools, and applications* (pp. 1628–1639). Hershey, PA: Medical Information Science Reference.

Danforth, D. R. (2010). Development of an interactive virtual 3-D model of the human testis using the second life platform. [IJVPLE]. *International Journal of Virtual and Personal Learning Environments, 1*(2), 45–58. doi:10.4018/jvple.2010040104

Daniel, V. M. (2011). Genomics and genetic engineering: Playing god? In S. Hongladarom (Ed.), *Genomics and bioethics: Interdisciplinary perspectives, technologies and advancements* (pp. 111–129). Hershey, PA: Medical Information Science Reference.

Daskalaki, A. (2010). *Informatics in oral medicine: Advanced techniques in clinical and diagnostic technologies*. Hershey, PA: IGI Global. doi:10.4018/978-1-60566-733-1

Davis, S. A. (2013). Global telemedicine and eHealth: Advances for future healthcare – Using a systems approach to integrate healthcare functions. In V. Gulla, A. Mori, F. Gabbrielli, & P. Lanzafame (Eds.), *Telehealth networks for hospital services: New methodologies* (pp. 15–32). Hershey, PA: Medical Information Science Reference. doi:10.4018/978-1-4666-2979-0.ch002

de Leeuw, E. (2012). The politics of medical curriculum accreditation: Thoughts, not facts? [IJUDH]. *International Journal of User-Driven Healthcare, 2*(1), 53–69. doi:10.4018/ijudh.2012010108

De Luca, S., & Memo, E. (2010). Better knowledge for better health services: Discovering guideline compliance. In J. Rodrigues (Ed.), *Health information systems: Concepts, methodologies, tools, and applications* (pp. 233–255). Hershey, PA: Medical Information Science Reference.

DeSimio, T., & Chrisagis, X. (2012). Medical e-reference: A benchmark for e-reference publishing in other disciplines. In S. Polanka (Ed.), *E-reference context and discoverability in libraries: Issues and concepts* (pp. 116–125). Hershey, PA: Information Science Reference.

Dhakal, B., & Ross, S. D. (2011). Medical student perspectives: Journey through different worlds. In R. Biswas, & C. Martin (Eds.), *User-driven healthcare and narrative medicine: Utilizing collaborative social networks and technologies* (pp. 125–133). Hershey, PA: Medical Information Science Reference.

Dong, Y., Lu, H., Gajic, O., & Pickering, B. (2012). Intensive care unit operational modeling and analysis. In A. Kolker, & P. Story (Eds.), *Management engineering for effective healthcare delivery: Principles and applications* (pp. 132–147). Hershey, PA: Medical Information Science Reference.

Doyle, D. (2011). E-medical education: An overview. In A. Shukla, & R. Tiwari (Eds.), *Biomedical engineering and information systems: Technologies, tools and applications* (pp. 219–238). Hershey, PA: Medical Information Science Reference.

Driouchi, A. (2014). Introduction to labor and health economics: Mobility of medical doctors in the Mediterranean region. In A. Driouchi (Ed.), *Labor and health economics in the Mediterranean region: Migration and mobility of medical doctors* (pp. 1–22). Hershey, PA: Medical Information Science Reference.

Driouchi, A. (2014). Medical knowledge, north-south cooperation, and mobility of medical doctors. In A. Driouchi (Ed.), *Labor and health economics in the Mediterranean region: Migration and mobility of medical doctors* (pp. 376–395). Hershey, PA: Medical Information Science Reference.

Duan, X., Wang, X., & Huang, Q. (2014). Medical manipulators for surgical applications. In I. Management Association (Ed.), Robotics: Concepts, methodologies, tools, and applications (pp. 608-618). Hershey, PA: Information Science Reference. doi: doi:10.4018/978-1-4666-4607-0.ch030

Dyro, J. F. (2012). Clinical engineering. In Z. Abu-Faraj (Ed.), *Handbook of research on biomedical engineering education and advanced bioengineering learning: Interdisciplinary concepts* (pp. 521–576). Hershey, PA: Medical Information Science Reference. doi:10.4018/978-1-4666-0122-2.ch012

El Morr, C., & Subercaze, J. (2010). Knowledge management in healthcare. In M. Cruz-Cunha, A. Tavares, & R. Simoes (Eds.), *Handbook of research on developments in e-health and telemedicine: Technological and social perspectives* (pp. 490–510). Hershey, PA: Medical Information Science Reference.

Eleni, A., & Maglogiannis, I. (2010). Adoption of wearable systems in modern patient telemonitoring systems. In M. Cruz-Cunha, A. Tavares, & R. Simoes (Eds.), *Handbook of research on developments in e-health and telemedicine: Technological and social perspectives* (pp. 1004–1023). Hershey, PA: Medical Information Science Reference.

Epstein, J. H., Goldberg, A., Krol, M., & Levine, A. (2013). Virtual tools in medical education. In Y. Kats (Ed.), *Learning management systems and instructional design: Best practices in online education* (pp. 364–380). Hershey, PA: Information Science Reference. doi:10.4018/978-1-4666-3930-0.ch019

Eskeland, S., & Oleshchuk, V. (2010). Information security and privacy in medical application scenario. In K. Khoumbati, Y. Dwivedi, A. Srivastava, & B. Lal (Eds.), *Handbook of research on advances in health informatics and electronic healthcare applications: Global adoption and impact of information communication technologies* (pp. 274–287). Hershey, PA: Medical Information Science Reference.

Esposito, A. (2013). The impact of social media on scholarly practices in higher education: Online engagement and ICTs appropriation in senior, young, and doctoral researchers. In B. Pătruţ, M. Pătruţ, & C. Cmeciu (Eds.), *Social media and the new academic environment: Pedagogical challenges* (pp. 342–367). Hershey, PA: Information Science Reference. doi:10.4018/978-1-4666-2851-9.ch017

Facelli, J. C., Hurdle, J. F., & Mitchell, J. A. (2012). Medical informatics and bioinformatics. In Z. Abu-Faraj (Ed.), *Handbook of research on biomedical engineering education and advanced bioengineering learning: Interdisciplinary concepts* (pp. 577–604). Hershey, PA: Medical Information Science Reference. doi:10.4018/978-1-4666-0122-2.ch013

Fairchild, K. D., & Moorman, J. R. (2012). Heart rate characteristics monitoring in the NICU: A new tool for clinical care and research. In W. Chen, S. Oetomo, & L. Feijs (Eds.), *Neonatal monitoring technologies: Design for integrated solutions* (pp. 175–200). Hershey, PA: Medical Information Science Reference. doi:10.4018/978-1-4666-0975-4.ch008

Fakhar, A. (2014). Beyond brain drain: A case study of the benefits of cooperation on medical immigration. In A. Driouchi (Ed.), *Labor and health economics in the Mediterranean region: Migration and mobility of medical doctors* (pp. 294–313). Hershey, PA: Medical Information Science Reference.

Farrell, M. (2011). Use of handheld computers in nursing education. In I. Management Association (Ed.), Clinical technologies: Concepts, methodologies, tools and applications (pp. 1504-1517). Hershey, PA: Medical Information Science Reference. doi: doi:10.4018/978-1-60960-561-2.ch507

Ferrer-Roca, O. (2011). Standards in telemedicine. In A. Moumtzoglou, & A. Kastania (Eds.), *E-health systems quality and reliability: Models and standards* (pp. 220–243). Hershey, PA: Medical Information Science Reference.

Fiaidhi, J., Mohammed, S., & Wei, Y. (2010). Implications of web 2.0 technology on healthcare: A biomedical semantic blog case study. In S. Kabene (Ed.), *Healthcare and the effect of technology: Developments, challenges and advancements* (pp. 269–289). Hershey, PA: Medical Information Science Reference. doi:10.4018/978-1-61520-733-6.ch016

Fialho, A. S., Cismondi, F., Vieira, S. M., Reti, S. R., Sousa, J. M., & Finkelstein, S. N. (2013). Challenges and opportunities of soft computing tools in health care delivery. In M. Cruz-Cunha, I. Miranda, & P. Gonçalves (Eds.), *Handbook of research on ICTs and management systems for improving efficiency in healthcare and social care* (pp. 321–340). Hershey, PA: Medical Information Science Reference. doi:10.4018/978-1-4666-3990-4.ch016

Freitas, A., Brazdil, P., & Costa-Pereira, A. (2012). Cost-sensitive learning in medicine. In I. Management Association (Ed.), Machine learning: Concepts, methodologies, tools and applications (pp. 1625-1641). Hershey, PA: Information Science Reference. doi: doi:10.4018/978-1-60960-818-7.ch607

Freitas, A., & Costa-Pereira, A. (2010). Learning cost-sensitive decision trees to support medical diagnosis. In T. Nguyen (Ed.), *Complex data warehousing and knowledge discovery for advanced retrieval development: Innovative methods and applications* (pp. 287–307). Hershey, PA: Information Science Reference.

Freitas, L., Pereira, R. T., Pereira, H. G., Martini, R., Mozzaquatro, B. A., Kasper, J., & Librelotto, G. (2013). Ontological representation and an architecture for homecare pervasive systems. In R. Martinho, R. Rijo, M. Cruz-Cunha, & J. Varajão (Eds.), *Information systems and technologies for enhancing health and social care* (pp. 215–234). Hershey, PA: Medical Information Science Reference. doi:10.4018/978-1-4666-3667-5.ch015

Frigo, C. A., & Pavan, E. E. (2014). Prosthetic and orthotic devices. In I. Association (Ed.), *Assistive technologies: Concepts, methodologies, tools, and applications* (pp. 549–613). Hershey, PA: Information Science Reference.

Frunza, O., & Inkpen, D. (2012). Natural language processing and machine learning techniques help achieve a better medical practice. In R. Magdalena-Benedito, E. Soria-Olivas, J. Martínez, J. Gómez-Sanchis, & A. Serrano-López (Eds.), *Medical applications of intelligent data analysis: Research advancements* (pp. 237–254). Hershey, PA: Information Science Reference. doi:10.4018/978-1-4666-1803-9.ch016

Fung-Kee-Fung, M., Morash, R., & Goubanova, E. (2011). Evaluating CoPs in cancer surgery. In O. Hernáez, & E. Bueno Campos (Eds.), *Handbook of research on communities of practice for organizational management and networking: Methodologies for competitive advantage* (pp. 456–466). Hershey, PA: Information Science Reference. doi:10.4018/978-1-60566-802-4.ch025

Gabbrielli, F. (2013). Telemedicine R&D influencing incoming strategies and organization models. In V. Gulla, A. Mori, F. Gabbrielli, & P. Lanzafame (Eds.), *Telehealth networks for hospital services: New methodologies* (pp. 250–264). Hershey, PA: Medical Information Science Reference. doi:10.4018/978-1-4666-2979-0.ch017

Ganz, A., Schafer, J., Yu, X., Lord, G., Burstein, J., & Ciottone, G. R. (2013). Real-time scalable resource tracking framework (DIORAMA) for mass casualty incidents. [IJEHMC]. *International Journal of E-Health and Medical Communications*, *4*(2), 34–49. doi:10.4018/jehmc.2013040103

Gao, X. W., Loomes, M., & Comley, R. (2012). Bridging the abridged: The diffusion of telemedicine in Europe and China. In J. Rodrigues, I. de la Torre Díez, & B. Sainz de Abajo (Eds.), *Telemedicine and e-health services, policies, and applications: Advancements and developments* (pp. 451–495). Hershey, PA: Medical Information Science Reference. doi:10.4018/978-1-4666-0888-7.ch017

Gavgani, V. Z. (2011). Ubiquitous information therapy service through social networking libraries: An operational web 2.0 service model. In R. Biswas, & C. Martin (Eds.), *User-driven healthcare and narrative medicine: Utilizing collaborative social networks and technologies* (pp. 446–461). Hershey, PA: Medical Information Science Reference.

Germaine-McDaniel, N. S. (2013). The emerging hispanic use of online health information in the United States: Cultural convergence or dissociation? In I. Management Association (Ed.), User-driven healthcare: Concepts, methodologies, tools, and applications (pp. 1607-1621). Hershey, PA: Medical Information Science Reference. doi:doi:10.4018/978-1-4666-2770-3.ch079

Ghalib, N. (2014). The design and implementation of paperless medical system (PMS) for offshore operating company: A structured approach. In I. Management Association (Ed.), Software design and development: Concepts, methodologies, tools, and applications (pp. 1064-1072). Hershey, PA: Information Science Reference. doi:doi:10.4018/978-1-4666-4301-7.ch051

Gill, S., & Paranjape, R. (2010). A review of recent contribution in agent-based health care modeling. In J. Rodrigues (Ed.), *Health information systems: Concepts, methodologies, tools, and applications* (pp. 356–373). Hershey, PA: Medical Information Science Reference.

Gilligan, J., & Smith, P. (2014). A formal representation system for modelling assistive technology systems. In G. Kouroupetroglou (Ed.), *Disability informatics and web accessibility for motor limitations* (pp. 1–42). Hershey, PA: Medical Information Science Reference.

Goldberg, E. M. (2014). Business continuity and disaster recovery considerations for healthcare technology. In I. Management Association (Ed.), Crisis management: Concepts, methodologies, tools and applications (pp. 1455-1462). Hershey, PA: Information Science Reference. doi: doi:10.4018/978-1-4666-4707-7.ch073

Gonçalves, F., & David, G. (2013). Definition of a retrospective health information policy based on (re)use study. In M. Cruz-Cunha, I. Miranda, & P. Gonçalves (Eds.), *Handbook of research on ICTs and management systems for improving efficiency in healthcare and social care* (pp. 1130–1155). Hershey, PA: Medical Information Science Reference. doi:10.4018/978-1-4666-3990-4.ch059

Gopalakrishnan, R., & Mugler, D. H. (2010). The evolution of hermite transform in biomedical applications. In A. Shukla, & R. Tiwari (Eds.), *Intelligent medical technologies and biomedical engineering: Tools and applications* (pp. 260–278). Hershey, PA: Medical Information Science Reference. doi:10.4018/978-1-61520-977-4.ch013

Goyal, R. K., O'Neill, M., Agostinelli, N., & Wyer, P. (2011). Critical illness and the emergency room. In R. Biswas, & C. Martin (Eds.), *User-driven healthcare and narrative medicine: Utilizing collaborative social networks and technologies* (pp. 63–74). Hershey, PA: Medical Information Science Reference.

Graham, I. W. (2011). The nature of nursing work. In A. Cashin, & R. Cook (Eds.), *Evidence-based practice in nursing informatics: Concepts and applications* (pp. 51–63). Hershey, PA: Medical Information Science Reference.

Greenshields, I., & El-Sayed, G. (2012). Aspects of visualization and the grid in a biomedical context. In I. Management Association (Ed.), Grid and cloud computing: Concepts, methodologies, tools and applications (pp. 1686-1701). Hershey, PA: Information Science Reference. doi: doi:10.4018/978-1-4666-0879-5.ch710

Grimnes, S., & Høgetveit, J. O. (2012). Biomedical sensors. In Z. Abu-Faraj (Ed.), *Handbook of research on biomedical engineering education and advanced bioengineering learning: Interdisciplinary concepts* (pp. 356–436). Hershey, PA: Medical Information Science Reference. doi:10.4018/978-1-4666-0122-2.ch009

Guedouar, R., & Zarrad, B. (2012). Forward projection for use with iterative reconstruction. In A. Malik, T. Choi, & H. Nisar (Eds.), *Depth map and 3D imaging applications: Algorithms and technologies* (pp. 27–55). Hershey, PA: Information Science Reference.

Gullà, V. (2013). Leading the technological innovation in healthcare systems: The telematic medicine approach. In V. Gulla, A. Mori, F. Gabbrielli, & P. Lanzafame (Eds.), *Telehealth networks for hospital services: New methodologies* (pp. 134–153). Hershey, PA: Medical Information Science Reference. doi:10.4018/978-1-4666-2979-0.ch009

Guo, R., Wang, Y., Yan, H., Li, F., Yan, J., & Xu, Z. (2011). Pulse wave analysis of traditional chinese medicine based on hemodynamics principles. In L. Liu, D. Wei, & Y. Li (Eds.), *Interdisciplinary research and applications in bioinformatics, computational biology, and environmental sciences* (pp. 194–203). Hershey, PA: Medical Information Science Reference.

Gupta, A., Goyal, R. K., Joiner, K. A., & Saini, S. (2010). Outsourcing in the healthcare industry: Information technology, intellectual property, and allied aspects. In M. Khosrow-Pour (Ed.), *Global, social, and organizational implications of emerging information resources management: Concepts and applications* (pp. 18–44). Hershey, PA: Information Science Reference. doi:10.4018/978-1-61520-965-1.ch715

Gupta, S., Mukherjee, S., & Roy, S. S. (2013). Modernization of healthcare and medical diagnosis system using multi agent system (MAS): A comparative study. In S. Bhattacharyya, & P. Dutta (Eds.), *Handbook of research on computational intelligence for engineering, science, and business* (pp. 592–622). Hershey, PA: Information Science Reference.

Ha, S. H. (2011). Medical domain knowledge and associative classification rules in diagnosis. [IJKDB]. *International Journal of Knowledge Discovery in Bioinformatics*, 2(1), 60–73. doi:10.4018/jkdb.2011010104

Haheim, L. L., & Morland, B. (2010). Health technology assessment: Development and future. In J. Rodrigues (Ed.), *Health information systems: Concepts, methodologies, tools, and applications* (pp. 26–41). Hershey, PA: Medical Information Science Reference.

Hai-Jew, S. (2010). An elusive formula: The IT role in behavior change in public health. In T. Yuzer, & G. Kurubacak (Eds.), *Transformative learning and online education: Aesthetics, dimensions and concepts* (pp. 347–373). Hershey, PA: Information Science Reference. doi:10.4018/978-1-61520-985-9.ch022

Haida, M. (2013). Implications of NIRS brain signals. In J. Wu (Ed.), *Biomedical engineering and cognitive neuroscience for healthcare: Interdisciplinary applications* (pp. 120–128). Hershey, PA: Medical Information Science Reference.

Haidegger, T. (2012). Surgical robots: System development, assessment, and clearance. In T. Sobh, & X. Xiong (Eds.), *Prototyping of robotic systems: Applications of design and implementation* (pp. 288–326). Hershey, PA: Information Science Reference. doi:10.4018/978-1-4666-0176-5.ch010

Hajiheydari, N., Khakbaz, S. B., & Farhadi, H. (2013). Proposing a business model in healthcare industry: E-diagnosis. [IJHISI]. *International Journal of Healthcare Information Systems and Informatics*, 8(2), 41–57. doi:10.4018/jhisi.2013040104

Hanada, E. (2013). Effective use of RFID in medicine and general healthcare. In T. Issa, P. Isaías, & P. Kommers (Eds.), *Information systems and technology for organizations in a networked society* (pp. 335–352). Hershey, PA: Business Science Reference. doi:10.4018/978-1-4666-4062-7.ch018

Hara, H. (2013). Women and health in Japan: The rise and obstacles of gender and sex-specific medicine. In M. Merviö (Ed.), *Healthcare management and economics: Perspectives on public and private administration* (pp. 203–207). Hershey, PA: Medical Information Science Reference. doi:10.4018/978-1-4666-3982-9.ch016

Harnett, B. (2013). Patient centered medicine and technology adaptation. In I. Management Association (Ed.), User-driven healthcare: Concepts, methodologies, tools, and applications (pp. 77-98). Hershey, PA: Medical Information Science Reference. doi: doi:10.4018/978-1-4666-2770-3.ch005

Hatton, J. D., Schmidt, T. M., & Jelen, J. (2013). Adoption of electronic health care records: Physician heuristics and hesitancy. In R. Martinho, R. Rijo, M. Cruz-Cunha, & J. Varajão (Eds.), *Information systems and technologies for enhancing health and social care* (pp. 148–165). Hershey, PA: Medical Information Science Reference. doi:10.4018/978-1-4666-3667-5.ch010

Heaberg, G. (2011). Case study: Research matchmaker, an advanced nursing practice informatics application. In A. Cashin, & R. Cook (Eds.), *Evidence-based practice in nursing informatics: Concepts and applications* (pp. 217–236). Hershey, PA: Medical Information Science Reference.

Hegde, B. (2011). Learning medicine: A personal view. In R. Biswas, & C. Martin (Eds.), *User-driven healthcare and narrative medicine: Utilizing collaborative social networks and technologies* (pp. 184–190). Hershey, PA: Medical Information Science Reference.

Heilman, J. (2012). Creating awareness for using a wiki to promote collaborative health professional education. [IJUDH]. *International Journal of User-Driven Healthcare*, 2(1), 86–87. doi:10.4018/ijudh.2012010113

Heinzel, A., Fechete, R., Söllner, J., Perco, P., Heinze, G., & Oberbauer, R. et al. (2012). Data graphs for linking clinical phenotype and molecular feature space. [IJSBBT]. *International Journal of Systems Biology and Biomedical Technologies*, 1(1), 11–25. doi:10.4018/ijsbbt.2012010102

Hernández-Chan, G. S., Rodríguez-González, A., & Colomo-Palacios, R. (2013). Using social networks to obtain medical diagnosis. In M. Cruz-Cunha, I. Miranda, & P. Gonçalves (Eds.), *Handbook of research on ICTs and management systems for improving efficiency in healthcare and social care* (pp. 306–320). Hershey, PA: Medical Information Science Reference. doi:10.4018/978-1-4666-3990-4.ch015

Hine, M. J., Farion, K. J., Michalowski, W., & Wilk, S. (2011). Decision making by emergency room physicians and residents: Implications for the design of clinical decision support systems. In J. Tan (Ed.), *New technologies for advancing healthcare and clinical practices* (pp. 131–148). Hershey, PA: Medical Information Science Reference. doi:10.4018/978-1-60960-780-7.ch008

Hoonakker, P., McGuire, K., & Carayon, P. (2011). Sociotechnical issues of tele-ICU technology. In D. Haftor, & A. Mirijamdotter (Eds.), *Information and communication technologies, society and human beings: Theory and framework (festschrift in honor of Gunilla Bradley)* (pp. 225–240). Hershey, PA: Information Science Reference.

Hopper, K. B., & Johns, C. L. (2012). Educational technology in the medical industry. In I. Management Association (Ed.), Wireless technologies: Concepts, methodologies, tools and applications (pp. 1306-1322). Hershey, PA: Information Science Reference. doi: doi:10.4018/978-1-61350-101-6.ch511

Hsu, P., Tsai, W., & Tsai, C. (2013). Patient safety concerns among emergency medical staff and patients. [IJPHIM]. *International Journal of Privacy and Health Information Management, 1*(1), 29–52. doi:10.4018/ijphim.2013010103

Huang, K., Geller, J., Halper, M., Elhanan, G., & Perl, Y. (2011). Scalability of piecewise synonym identification in integration of SNOMED into the UMLS. [IJCMAM]. *International Journal of Computational Models and Algorithms in Medicine, 2*(3), 26–45. doi:10.4018/jcmam.2011070103

Hughes, B. (2012). Managing e-health in the age of web 2.0: The impact on e-health evaluation. In I. Management Association (Ed.), E-marketing: Concepts, methodologies, tools, and applications (pp. 1268-1288). Hershey, PA: Business Science Reference. doi: doi:10.4018/978-1-4666-1598-4.ch074

Hyde, A., Nee, J., Butler, M., Drennan, J., & Howlett, E. (2011). Preferred types of menopause service delivery: A qualitative study of menopausal women's perceptions. [IJHDRI]. *International Journal of Healthcare Delivery Reform Initiatives, 3*(1), 1–12. doi:10.4018/jhdri.2011010101

Ilie, V., Van Slyke, C., Courtney, J. F., & Styne, P. (2011). Challenges associated with physicians' usage of electronic medical records. In J. Tan (Ed.), *New technologies for advancing healthcare and clinical practices* (pp. 234–251). Hershey, PA: Medical Information Science Reference. doi:10.4018/978-1-60960-780-7.ch014

Inomata, C., & Nitta, S. (2013). Nursing in integrative medicine and nurses' engagement in caring-healing: A discussion based on the practice and study of music therapy and nursing care for patients with neurodegenerative disorders. In J. Wu (Ed.), *Technological advancements in biomedicine for healthcare applications* (pp. 235–239). Hershey, PA: Medical Information Science Reference.

Inthiran, A., Alhashmi, S. M., & Ahmed, P. K. (2012). Medical information retrieval strategies: An exploratory study on the information retrieval behaviors of non-medical professionals. [IJHISI]. *International Journal of Healthcare Information Systems and Informatics, 7*(1), 31–45. doi:10.4018/jhisi.2012010103

Isern, D., & Moreno, A. (2010). HeCaSe2: A multi-agent system that automates the application of clinical guidelines. In R. Paranjape, & A. Sadanand (Eds.), *Multi-agent systems for healthcare simulation and modeling: Applications for system improvement* (pp. 113–136). Hershey, PA: Medical Information Science Reference.

Ishaq, G. M., Hussain, P. T., Iqbal, M. J., & Mushtaq, M. B. (2013). Risk-benefit analysis of combination vs. unopposed HRT in post-menopausal women. In I. Management Association (Ed.), Bioinformatics: Concepts, methodologies, tools, and applications (pp. 1424-1440). Hershey, PA: Medical Information Science Reference. doi: doi:10.4018/978-1-4666-3604-0.ch073

Iwaki, S. (2013). Multimodal neuroimaging to visualize human visual processing. In J. Wu (Ed.), *Biomedical engineering and cognitive neuroscience for healthcare: Interdisciplinary applications* (pp. 274–282). Hershey, PA: Medical Information Science Reference.

James, R. (2011). Practical pointers in medicine over seven decades: Reflections of an individual physician. In R. Biswas, & C. Martin (Eds.), *User-driven healthcare and narrative medicine: Utilizing collaborative social networks and technologies* (pp. 173–183). Hershey, PA: Medical Information Science Reference.

Janczewski, M. (2010). Healthcare transformation in a net-centric environment. In S. Ghosh (Ed.), *Net centricity and technological interoperability in organizations: Perspectives and strategies* (pp. 99–114). Hershey, PA: Information Science Reference.

Jesus, Â., & Gomes, M. J. (2013). Web 2.0 tools in biomedical education: Limitations and possibilities. In Y. Kats (Ed.), *Learning management systems and instructional design: Best practices in online education* (pp. 208–231). Hershey, PA: Information Science Reference. doi:10.4018/978-1-4666-3930-0.ch011

Ji, Z., Sugi, T., Goto, S., Wang, X., & Nakamura, M. (2013). Multi-channel template extraction for automatic EEG spike detection. In J. Wu (Ed.), *Biomedical engineering and cognitive neuroscience for healthcare: Interdisciplinary applications* (pp. 255–265). Hershey, PA: Medical Information Science Reference.

Jifa, G., Wuqi, S., Zhengxiang, Z., Rui, G., & Yijun, L. (2012). Expert mining and traditional Chinese medicine knowledge. In W. Lee (Ed.), *Systems approaches to knowledge management, transfer, and resource development* (pp. 239–251). Hershey, PA: Information Science Reference. doi:10.4018/978-1-4666-1782-7.ch016

Johnson, D. E. (2012). Electronic medical records (EMR): Issues and implementation perspectives. In A. Kolker, & P. Story (Eds.), *Management engineering for effective healthcare delivery: Principles and applications* (pp. 333–351). Hershey, PA: Medical Information Science Reference.

Johnson, K., & Tashiro, J. (2013). Interprofessional care and health care complexity: Factors shaping human resources effectiveness in health information management. In I. Management Association (Ed.), User-driven healthcare: Concepts, methodologies, tools, and applications (pp. 1273-1302). Hershey, PA: Medical Information Science Reference. doi: doi:10.4018/978-1-4666-2770-3.ch064

Jose, J. (2012). Pharmacovigilance: Basic concepts and applications of pharmacoinformatics. In T. Gasmelseid (Ed.), *Pharmacoinformatics and drug discovery technologies: Theories and applications* (pp. 322–343). Hershey, PA: Medical Information Science Reference. doi:10.4018/978-1-4666-0309-7.ch020

Juzoji, H. (2012). Legal bases for medical supervision via mobile telecommunications in Japan. [IJEHMC]. *International Journal of E-Health and Medical Communications*, 3(1), 33–45. doi:10.4018/jehmc.2012010103

Juzwishin, D. W. (2010). Enabling technologies and challenges for the future of ubiquitous health the interoperability framework. In S. Mohammed, & J. Fiaidhi (Eds.), *Ubiquitous health and medical informatics: The ubiquity 2.0 trend and beyond* (pp. 596–622). Hershey, PA: Medical Information Science Reference. doi:10.4018/978-1-61520-777-0.ch028

Kabene, S., & Wolfe, M. (2011). Risks and benefits of technology in health care. In I. Management Association (Ed.), Clinical technologies: Concepts, methodologies, tools and applications (pp. 13-24). Hershey, PA: Medical Information Science Reference. doi: doi:10.4018/978-1-60960-561-2.ch102

Kabene, S. M. King, Lisa, & Gibson, C. J. (2010). Technology and human resources management in health care. In S. Mohammed, & J. Fiaidhi (Eds.) Ubiquitous health and medical informatics: The ubiquity 2.0 trend and beyond (pp. 574-595). Hershey, PA: Medical Information Science Reference. doi: doi:10.4018/978-1-61520-777-0.ch027

Kabene, S. M., Wolfe, M., & Leduc, R. (2012). Recruitment and retention of healthcare professionals for the changing demographics, culture, and access in Canada. In I. Management Association (Ed.), Human resources management: Concepts, methodologies, tools, and applications (pp. 276-290). Hershey, PA: Business Science Reference. doi: doi:10.4018/978-1-4666-1601-1.ch017

Kadiri, M., & Zouag, N. (2014). The new economics of skilled labor migration: The case of medical doctors in MENA. In A. Driouchi (Ed.), *Labor and health economics in the Mediterranean region: Migration and mobility of medical doctors* (pp. 267–292). Hershey, PA: Medical Information Science Reference.

Kalantri, S. P. (2012). On being a patient. [IJUDH]. *International Journal of User-Driven Healthcare*, 2(4), 1–4. doi:10.4018/ijudh.2012100101

Kaldoudi, E., Konstantinidis, S., & Bamidis, P. D. (2010). Web 2.0 approaches for active, collaborative learning in medicine and health. In S. Mohammed, & J. Fiaidhi (Eds.), *Ubiquitous health and medical informatics: The ubiquity 2.0 trend and beyond* (pp. 127–149). Hershey, PA: Medical Information Science Reference. doi:10.4018/978-1-61520-777-0.ch007

Kannry, J. L. (2011). Operationalizing the science. In I. Management Association (Ed.), Clinical technologies: Concepts, methodologies, tools and applications (pp. 1600-1622). Hershey, PA: Medical Information Science Reference. doi: doi:10.4018/978-1-60960-561-2.ch601

Karayanni, D. (2010). A cluster analysis of physician's values, prescribing behaviour and attitudes towards firms' marketing communications. [IJCRMM]. *International Journal of Customer Relationship Marketing and Management*, 1(4), 62–79. doi:10.4018/jcrmm.2010100104

Kastania, A., & Moumtzoglou, A. (2012). Quality implications of the medical applications for 4G mobile phones. [IJRQEH]. *International Journal of Reliable and Quality E-Healthcare*, 1(1), 58–67. doi:10.4018/ijrqeh.2012010106

Kastania, A. N. (2013). Evaluation considerations for e-health systems. In I. Management Association (Ed.), User-driven healthcare: Concepts, methodologies, tools, and applications (pp. 1126-1140). Hershey, PA: Medical Information Science Reference. doi: doi:10.4018/978-1-4666-2770-3.ch057

Kaufman, D. (2010). Simulation in health professional education. In D. Kaufman, & L. Sauvé (Eds.), *Educational gameplay and simulation environments: Case studies and lessons learned* (pp. 51–67). Hershey, PA: Information Science Reference. doi:10.4018/978-1-61520-731-2.ch003

Kazandjian, V. A. (2013). Learning to accept uncertainty as a quality of care dimension. In A. Moumtzoglou, & A. Kastania (Eds.), *E-health technologies and improving patient safety: Exploring organizational factors* (pp. 1–12). Hershey, PA: Medical Information Science Reference.

Kearns, W. D., Fozard, J. L., & Lamm, R. S. (2011). How knowing who, where and when can change health care delivery. In C. Röcker, & M. Ziefle (Eds.), *E-health, assistive technologies and applications for assisted living: Challenges and solutions* (pp. 139–160). Hershey, PA: Medical Information Science Reference. doi:10.4018/978-1-60960-469-1.ch007

Khan, T. (2013). Transformation of a reluctant patient to a proactive health advocate. [IJUDH]. *International Journal of User-Driven Healthcare, 3*(1), 71–74. doi:10.4018/ijudh.2013010109

Khetarpal, A., & Singh, S. (2012). Disability studies in medical education. [IJUDH]. *International Journal of User-Driven Healthcare, 2*(2), 44–51. doi:10.4018/ijudh.2012040105

Kim, J. (2011). The development and implementation of patient safety information systems (PSIS). In I. Management Association (Ed.), Clinical technologies: Concepts, methodologies, tools and applications (pp. 2054-2072). Hershey, PA: Medical Information Science Reference. doi: doi:10.4018/978-1-60960-561-2.ch804

Kldiashvili, E. (2011). The application of virtual organization technology for eHealth. In E. Kldiashvili (Ed.), *Grid technologies for e-health: Applications for telemedicine services and delivery* (pp. 1–17). Hershey, PA: Medical Information Science Reference.

Kldiashvili, E. (2012). The cloud computing as the tool for implementation of virtual organization technology for eHealth. [JITR]. *Journal of Information Technology Research, 5*(1), 18–34. doi:10.4018/jitr.2012010102

Kldiashvili, E. (2013). Implementation of telecytology in Georgia. In V. Gulla, A. Mori, F. Gabbrielli, & P. Lanzafame (Eds.), *Telehealth networks for hospital services: New methodologies* (pp. 341–361). Hershey, PA: Medical Information Science Reference. doi:10.4018/978-1-4666-2979-0.ch022

Klemer, D. P. (2010). Advances in biosensors for in vitro diagnostics. In A. Lazakidou (Ed.), *Biocomputation and biomedical informatics: Case studies and applications* (pp. 178–186). Hershey, PA: Medical Information Science Reference.

Kotwani, A. (2013). Transparency and accountability in public procurement of essential medicines in developing countries. In I. Association (Ed.), *Supply chain management: Concepts, methodologies, tools, and applications* (pp. 1437–1452). Hershey, PA: Business Science Reference.

Kuehler, M., Schimke, N., & Hale, J. (2012). Privacy considerations for electronic health records. In G. Yee (Ed.), *Privacy protection measures and technologies in business organizations: Aspects and standards* (pp. 210–226). Hershey, PA: Information Science Reference.

Kukar, M., Kononenko, I., & Grošelj, C. (2013). Automated diagnostics of coronary artery disease: Long-term results and recent advancements. In I. Association (Ed.), *Data mining: Concepts, methodologies, tools, and applications* (pp. 1043–1063). Hershey, PA: Information Science Reference.

Kumalasari, C. D., Caplow, J. A., & Fearing, N. (2013). Simulation followed by a reflection and feedback session in medical education. In L. Tomei (Ed.), *Learning tools and teaching approaches through ICT advancements* (pp. 68–81). Hershey, PA: Information Science Reference.

Kumar, R., & Srivastava, R. (2014). Detection of cancer from microscopic biopsy images using image processing tools. In R. Srivastava, S. Singh, & K. Shukla (Eds.), *Research developments in computer vision and image processing: Methodologies and applications* (pp. 175–194). Hershey, PA: Information Science Reference.

Kuruvilla, A., & Alexander, S. M. (2010). Predicting ambulance diverson. [IJISSS]. *International Journal of Information Systems in the Service Sector, 2*(1), 1–10. doi:10.4018/jisss.2010093001

Kyriazis, D., Menychtas, A., Tserpes, K., Athanaileas, T., & Varvarigou, T. (2010). High performance computing in biomedicine. In A. Lazakidou (Ed.), *Biocomputation and biomedical informatics: Case studies and applications* (pp. 106–118). Hershey, PA: Medical Information Science Reference.

LaBrunda, M., & LaBrunda, A. (2010). Fuzzy logic in medicine. In M. Khosrow-Pour (Ed.), *Breakthrough discoveries in information technology research: Advancing trends* (pp. 218–224). Hershey, PA: Information Science Reference.

Lagares-Lemos, Á. M., Lagares-Lemos, M., Colomo-Palacios, R., García-Crespo, Á., & Gómez-Berbís, J. M. (2011). DISMON. In I. Management Association (Ed.), Clinical technologies: Concepts, methodologies, tools and applications (pp. 995-1007). Hershey, PA: Medical Information Science Reference. doi: doi:10.4018/978-1-60960-561-2.ch324

Lagares-Lemos, Á. M., Lagares-Lemos, M., Colomo-Palacios, R., García-Crespo, Á., & Gómez-Berbís, J. M. (2013). DISMON: Using social web and semantic technologies to monitor diseases in limited environments. In M. Khosrow-Pour (Ed.), *Interdisciplinary advances in information technology research* (pp. 48–59). Hershey, PA: Information Science Reference. doi:10.4018/978-1-4666-3625-5.ch004

Lappas, K. (2014). Functional assessment of persons with motor limitations: Methods and tools. In G. Kouroupetroglou (Ed.), *Disability informatics and web accessibility for motor limitations* (pp. 43–74). Hershey, PA: Medical Information Science Reference.

Lazakidou, A., & Daskalaki, A. (2012). *Quality assurance in healthcare service delivery, nursing and personalized medicine: Technologies and processes*. Hershey, PA: IGI Global.

Leal, S., Suarez, C., Framinan, J. M., Parra, C. L., & Gómez, T. (2010). Virtual reality for supporting surgical planning. In M. Cruz-Cunha, A. Tavares, & R. Simoes (Eds.), *Handbook of research on developments in e-health and tele-medicine: Technological and social perspectives* (pp. 614–635). Hershey, PA: Medical Information Science Reference.

Lemma, F., Denko, M. K., Tan, J. K., & Kassegne, S. K. (2011). Envisioning a national e-medicine network architecture in a developing country: A case study. In J. Tan (Ed.), *Developments in healthcare information systems and technologies: Models and methods* (pp. 35–53). Hershey, PA: Medical Information Science Reference.

Li, G., You, M., Xu, L., & Huang, S. (2012). Personalized experience sharing of Cai's TCM gynecology. In A. Lazakidou, & A. Daskalaki (Eds.), *Quality assurance in healthcare service delivery, nursing and personalized medicine: Technologies and processes* (pp. 26–47). Hershey, PA: Medical Information Science Reference.

Lim, V. K. (2012). The process of medical curriculum development in Malaysia. [IJUDH]. *International Journal of User-Driven Healthcare*, 2(1), 33–39. doi:10.4018/ijudh.2012010105

Lin, H. (2013). Cultivating chan as proactive therapy for social wellness. In M. Cruz-Cunha, I. Miranda, & P. Gonçalves (Eds.), *Handbook of research on ICTs for human-centered healthcare and social care services* (pp. 151–170). Hershey, PA: Medical Information Science Reference. doi:10.4018/978-1-4666-3986-7.ch008

Liu, Q., Poon, C. C., & Zhang, Y. T. (2012). Wearable technologies for neonatal monitoring. In W. Chen, S. Oetomo, & L. Feijs (Eds.), *Neonatal monitoring technologies: Design for integrated solutions* (pp. 12–40). Hershey, PA: Medical Information Science Reference. doi:10.4018/978-1-4666-0975-4.ch002

Llobet, H., Llobet, P., & LaBrunda, M. (2011). Imaging advances of the cardiopulmonary system. In I. Management Association (Ed.), Clinical technologies: Concepts, methodologies, tools and applications (pp. 2183-2190). Hershey, PA: Medical Information Science Reference. doi: doi:10.4018/978-1-60960-561-2.ch812

Logeswaran, R. (2010). Neural networks in medicine: improving difficult automated detection of cancer in the bile ducts. In R. Chiong (Ed.), *Nature-inspired informatics for intelligent applications and knowledge discovery: Implications in business, science, and engineering* (pp. 144–165). Hershey, PA: Information Science Reference.

Logeswaran, R. (2011). Neural networks in medicine. In I. Management Association (Ed.), Clinical technologies: Concepts, methodologies, tools and applications (pp. 744-765). Hershey, PA: Medical Information Science Reference. doi: doi:10.4018/978-1-60960-561-2.ch308

Long, L. R., Antani, S., Thoma, G. R., & Deserno, T. M. (2011). Content-based image retrieval for advancing medical diagnostics, treatment and education. In J. Tan (Ed.), *New technologies for advancing healthcare and clinical practices* (pp. 1–17). Hershey, PA: Medical Information Science Reference. doi:10.4018/978-1-60960-780-7.ch001

Lueth, T. C., D'Angelo, L. T., & Czabke, A. (2010). TUM-AgeTech: A new framework for pervasive medical devices. In A. Coronato, & G. De Pietro (Eds.), *Pervasive and smart technologies for healthcare: Ubiquitous methodologies and tools* (pp. 295–321). Hershey, PA: Medical Information Science Reference. doi:10.4018/978-1-61520-765-7.ch014

Lui, K. (2013). The health informatics professional. In I. Management Association (Ed.), User-driven healthcare: Concepts, methodologies, tools, and applications(pp. 120-141). Hershey, PA: Medical Information Science Reference. doi: doi:10.4018/978-1-4666-2770-3.ch007

Lui, T., & Goel, L. (2012). A framework for conceptualizing the current role and future trends of information systems in medical training. [IJHISI]. *International Journal of Healthcare Information Systems and Informatics, 7*(1), 1–12. doi:10.4018/jhisi.2012010101

MacDonald, C. J., McKeen, M., Leith-Gudbranson, D., Montpetit, M., Archibald, D., & Rivet, C. … Hirsh, M. (2013). University of Ottawa department of family medicine faculty development curriculum framework. In K. Patel, & S. Vij (Eds.) Enterprise resource planning models for the education sector: Applications and methodologies (pp. 197-215). Hershey, PA: Information Science Reference. doi: doi:10.4018/978-1-4666-2193-0.ch014

MacGregor, R. C., Hyland, P. N., & Harvie, C. (2010). Associations between driving forces to adopt ICT and benefits derived from that adoption in medical practices in Australia. In M. Cruz-Cunha, A. Tavares, & R. Simoes (Eds.), *Handbook of research on developments in e-health and telemedicine: Technological and social perspectives* (pp. 652–668). Hershey, PA: Medical Information Science Reference.

Mackert, M., Whitten, P., & Holtz, B. (2010). Health infonomics: Intelligent applications of information technology. In J. Rodrigues (Ed.), *Health information systems: Concepts, methodologies, tools, and applications* (pp. 117–132). Hershey, PA: Medical Information Science Reference.

Malik, A. S., & Malik, R. H. (2012). Adolescent medicine curriculum at faculty of medicine, Universiti Teknologi MARA, Malaysia. [IJUDH]. *International Journal of User-Driven Healthcare, 2*(1), 40–48. doi:10.4018/ijudh.2012010106

Martin, C. M., Biswas, R., Sturmberg, J. P., Topps, D., Ellaway, R., & Smith, K. (2011). Patient journey record systems (PaJR) for preventing ambulatory care sensitive conditions: A developmental framework. In R. Biswas, & C. Martin (Eds.), *User-driven healthcare and narrative medicine: Utilizing collaborative social networks and technologies* (pp. 93–112). Hershey, PA: Medical Information Science Reference.

Masayuki, K., Eiji, K., Tetsuo, T., & Nozomu, M. (2013). Evaluation of olfactory impairment in Parkinson's disease using near-infrared spectroscopy. In J. Wu (Ed.), *Biomedical engineering and cognitive neuroscience for healthcare: Interdisciplinary applications* (pp. 293–302). Hershey, PA: Medical Information Science Reference.

Mazzanti, I., Maolo, A., & Antonicelli, R. (2014). E-health and telemedicine in the elderly: State of the art. In I. Association (Ed.), *Assistive technologies: Concepts, methodologies, tools, and applications* (pp. 693–704). Hershey, PA: Information Science Reference.

Medhekar, A., Wong, H. Y., & Hall, J. (2014). Innovation in medical tourism service marketing: A case of India. In A. Goyal (Ed.), *Innovations in services marketing and management: Strategies for emerging economies* (pp. 49–66). Hershey, PA: Business Science Reference.

Medhekar, A., Wong, H. Y., & Hall, J. (2014). Medical tourism: A conceptual framework for an innovation in global healthcare provision. In A. Goyal (Ed.), *Innovations in services marketing and management: Strategies for emerging economies* (pp. 148–169). Hershey, PA: Business Science Reference.

Memmola, M., Palumbo, G., & Rossini, M. (2010). Web & RFID technology: New frontiers in costing and process management for rehabilitation medicine. In J. Symonds (Ed.), *Ubiquitous and pervasive computing: Concepts, methodologies, tools, and applications* (pp. 623–647). Hershey, PA: Information Science Reference.

Menciassi, A., & Laschi, C. (2014). Biorobotics. In I. Management Association (Ed.), *Robotics: Concepts, methodologies, tools, and applications* (pp. 1613-1643). Hershey, PA: Information Science Reference. doi: doi:10.4018/978-1-4666-4607-0.ch079

Mika, K. (2010). Cybermedicine, telemedicine, and data protection in the United States. In J. Rodrigues (Ed.), *Health information systems: Concepts, methodologies, tools, and applications* (pp. 274–296). Hershey, PA: Medical Information Science Reference.

Mirbagheri, A., Baniasad, M. A., Farahmand, F., Behzadipour, S., & Ahmadian, A. (2013). Medical robotics: State-of-the-art applications and research challenges. [IJHISI]. *International Journal of Healthcare Information Systems and Informatics*, 8(2), 1–14. doi:10.4018/jhisi.2013040101

Miscione, G. (2013). Telemedicine and development: Situating information technologies in the Amazon. In J. Abdelnour-Nocera (Ed.), *Knowledge and technological development effects on organizational and social structures* (pp. 132–145). Hershey, PA: Information Science Reference.

Mobasheri, A. (2013). Regeneration of articular cartilage: Opportunities, challenges, and perspectives. In A. Daskalaki (Ed.), *Medical advancements in aging and regenerative technologies: Clinical tools and applications* (pp. 137–168). Hershey, PA: Medical Information Science Reference.

Monzon, J. E. (2012). Bioethics. In Z. Abu-Faraj (Ed.), *Handbook of research on biomedical engineering education and advanced bioengineering learning: Interdisciplinary concepts* (pp. 198–237). Hershey, PA: Medical Information Science Reference. doi:10.4018/978-1-4666-0122-2.ch005

Morais da Costa, G. J., Araújo da Silva Nuno, M., & Alves da Silva Nuno, S. (2010). The human centred approach to bionanotechnology in telemedicine: Ethical considerations. In M. Cruz-Cunha, A. Tavares, & R. Simoes (Eds.), *Handbook of research on developments in e-health and telemedicine: Technological and social perspectives* (pp. 311–335). Hershey, PA: Medical Information Science Reference.

Morgade, A. T., Martínez-Romero, M., Vázquez-Naya, J. M., Loureiro, M. P., Albo, Á. G., & Loureiro, J. P. (2011). Development of a knowledge based system for an intensive care environment using ontologies. [JITR]. *Journal of Information Technology Research*, 4(1), 21–33. doi:10.4018/jitr.2011010102

Morita, A. (2013). The quantitative EEG change in Parkinson's disease. In J. Wu (Ed.), *Biomedical engineering and cognitive neuroscience for healthcare: Interdisciplinary applications* (pp. 225–234). Hershey, PA: Medical Information Science Reference.

Moumtzoglou, A. (2011). E-health as the realm of healthcare quality: A mental image of the future. In A. Moumtzoglou, & A. Kastania (Eds.), *E-health systems quality and reliability: Models and standards* (pp. 291–310). Hershey, PA: Medical Information Science Reference.

Moumtzoglou, A. (2011). E-health as the realm of healthcare quality. In I. Management Association (Ed.), Clinical technologies: Concepts, methodologies, tools and applications (pp. 73-92). Hershey, PA: Medical Information Science Reference. doi: doi:10.4018/978-1-60960-561-2.ch105

Moumtzoglou, A. (2011). E-health: A bridge to people-centered health care. In A. Moumtzoglou, & A. Kastania (Eds.), *E-health systems quality and reliability: Models and standards* (pp. 47–63). Hershey, PA: Medical Information Science Reference.

Moumtzoglou, A. (2013). Health 2.0 and medicine 2.0: Safety, ownership and privacy issues. In I. Management Association (Ed.), User-driven healthcare: Concepts, methodologies, tools, and applications (pp. 1508-1522). Hershey, PA: Medical Information Science Reference. doi: doi:10.4018/978-1-4666-2770-3.ch075

Moumtzoglou, A. (2013). Risk perception as a patient safety dimension. In A. Moumtzoglou, & A. Kastania (Eds.), *E-health technologies and improving patient safety: Exploring organizational factors* (pp. 285–299). Hershey, PA: Medical Information Science Reference.

Mourtzikou, A., Stamouli, M., & Athanasiadi, E. (2013). Improvement of clinical laboratory services through quality. [IJRQEH]. *International Journal of Reliable and Quality E-Healthcare*, 2(2), 38–46. doi:10.4018/ijrqeh.2013040103

Muriithi, M. K., & Mwabu, G. (2014). Demand for health care in Kenya: The effects of information about quality. In P. Schaeffer, & E. Kouassi (Eds.), *Econometric methods for analyzing economic development* (pp. 102–110). Hershey, PA: Business Science Reference.

Murugan, B. O., & Sornam, S. A. (2013). Internet and online medical journal access skills of the medical practitioners of Tamilnadu: A study. In S. Thanuskodi (Ed.), *Challenges of academic library management in developing countries* (pp. 75–82). Hershey, PA: Information Science Reference.

Nadathur, S. G. (2010). Bayesian networks in the health domain. In A. Ali, & Y. Xiang (Eds.), *Dynamic and advanced data mining for progressing technological development: Innovations and systemic approaches* (pp. 342–376). Hershey, PA: Information Science Reference.

Naidoo, V., & Naidoo, Y. (2014). Home telecare, medical implant, and mobile technology: Evolutions in geriatric care. In C. El Morr (Ed.), *Research Perspectives on the role of informatics in health policy and management* (pp. 222–237). Hershey, PA: Medical Information Science Reference.

Najarian, S., & Afshari, E. (2010). Applications of robots in surgery. In A. Shukla, & R. Tiwari (Eds.), *Intelligent medical technologies and biomedical engineering: Tools and applications* (pp. 241–259). Hershey, PA: Medical Information Science Reference. doi:10.4018/978-1-61520-977-4.ch012

Nakajima, I. (2012). Cross-border medical care and telemedicine. [IJEHMC]. *International Journal of E-Health and Medical Communications*, 3(1), 46–61. doi:10.4018/jehmc.2012010104

Nakayasu, K., & Sato, C. (2012). Liability for telemedicine. [IJEHMC]. *International Journal of E-Health and Medical Communications*, 3(1), 1–21. doi:10.4018/jehmc.2012010101

Narasimhalu, D. (2010). Redefining medical tourism. In S. Becker, & R. Niebuhr (Eds.), *Cases on technology innovation: Entrepreneurial successes and pitfalls* (pp. 267–285). Hershey, PA: Business Science Reference. doi:10.4018/978-1-61520-609-4.ch014

Naulaers, G., Caicedo, A., & Van Huffel, S. (2012). Use of near-infrared spectroscopy in the neonatal intensive care unit. In W. Chen, S. Oetomo, & L. Feijs (Eds.), *Neonatal monitoring technologies: Design for integrated solutions* (pp. 56–83). Hershey, PA: Medical Information Science Reference. doi:10.4018/978-1-4666-0975-4.ch004

Nokata, M. (2014). Small medical robot. In I. Management Association (Ed.),Robotics: Concepts, methodologies, tools, and applications (pp. 638-646). Hershey, PA: Information Science Reference. doi: doi:10.4018/978-1-4666-4607-0.ch032

Noteboom, C. (2013). Physician interaction with EHR: The importance of stakeholder identification and change management. In S. Sarnikar, D. Bennett, & M. Gaynor (Eds.), *Cases on healthcare information technology for patient care management* (pp. 95–112). Hershey, PA: Medical Information Science Reference.

Noury, N., Bourquard, K., Bergognon, D., & Schroeder, J. (2013). Regulations initiatives in France for the interoperability of communicating medical devices. [IJEHMC]. *International Journal of E-Health and Medical Communications*, 4(2), 50–64. doi:10.4018/jehmc.2013040104

O'Hanlon, S. (2013). Avoiding adverse consequences of e-health. In A. Moumtzoglou, & A. Kastania (Eds.), *E-health technologies and improving patient safety: Exploring organizational factors* (pp. 13–26). Hershey, PA: Medical Information Science Reference.

O'Leary, D. E. (2012). An activity theory analysis of RFID in hospitals. In Z. Luo (Ed.), *Innovations in logistics and supply chain management technologies for dynamic economies* (pp. 148–166). Hershey, PA: Business Science Reference. doi:10.4018/978-1-4666-0267-0.ch010

O'Neill, L., Talbert, J., & Klepack, W. (2010). Physician characteristics associated with early adoption of electronic medical records in smaller group practices. In J. Rodrigues (Ed.), *Health information systems: Concepts, methodologies, tools, and applications* (pp. 1503–1512). Hershey, PA: Medical Information Science Reference.

Ogawa, T., Ikeda, M., Suzuki, M., & Araki, K. (2014). Medical practical knowledge circulation based on purpose-oriented service modeling. In M. Kosaka, & K. Shirahada (Eds.), *Progressive trends in knowledge and system-based science for service innovation* (pp. 400–424). Hershey, PA: Business Science Reference.

Oliveira, T. C., Oliveira, M. D., & Peña, T. (2013). Towards a post-implementation evaluation framework of outpatient electronic drug prescribing. In M. Cruz-Cunha, I. Miranda, & P. Gonçalves (Eds.), *Handbook of research on ICTs and management systems for improving efficiency in healthcare and social care* (pp. 133–155). Hershey, PA: Medical Information Science Reference. doi:10.4018/978-1-4666-3990-4.ch007

Orizio, G., & Gelatti, U. (2012). Human behaviors in online pharmacies. In Z. Yan (Ed.), *Encyclopedia of cyber behavior* (pp. 661–670). Hershey, PA: Information Science Reference. doi:10.4018/978-1-4666-0315-8.ch056

Otero, A., Félix, P., & Barro, S. (2010). Current state of critical patient monitoring and outstanding challenges. In M. Cruz-Cunha, A. Tavares, & R. Simoes (Eds.), *Handbook of research on developments in e-health and telemedicine: Technological and social perspectives* (pp. 981–1003). Hershey, PA: Medical Information Science Reference.

Ozturk, Y., & Sharma, J. (2013). mVITAL: A standards compliant vital sign monitor. In I. Management Association (Ed.), IT policy and ethics: Concepts, methodologies, tools, and applications (pp. 515-538). Hershey, PA: Information Science Reference. doi: doi:10.4018/978-1-4666-2919-6.ch024

Pal, K., Ghosh, G., & Bhattacharya, M. (2014). Biomedical watermarking: An emerging and secure tool for data security and better tele-diagnosis in modern health care system. In R. Srivastava, S. Singh, & K. Shukla (Eds.), *Research developments in computer vision and image processing: Methodologies and applications* (pp. 208–234). Hershey, PA: Information Science Reference.

Paolucci, F., Ergas, H., Hannan, T., & Aarts, J. (2011). The effectiveness of health informatics. In I. Management Association (Ed.), Clinical technologies: Concepts, methodologies, tools and applications (pp. 25-49). Hershey, PA: Medical Information Science Reference. doi: doi:10.4018/978-1-60960-561-2.ch103

Parasher, A., Goldschmidt-Clermont, P. J., & Tien, J. M. (2012). Healthcare delivery as a service system: Barriers to co-production and implications of healthcare reform. In A. Kolker, & P. Story (Eds.), *Management engineering for effective healthcare delivery: Principles and applications* (pp. 191–214). Hershey, PA: Medical Information Science Reference.

Parry, D. (2010). Coding and messaging systems for women's health informatics. In J. Rodrigues (Ed.), *Health information systems: Concepts, methodologies, tools, and applications* (pp. 2192–2205). Hershey, PA: Medical Information Science Reference.

Parry, D. (2012). Computerised decision support for women's health informatics. In I. Management Association (Ed.), Machine learning: Concepts, methodologies, tools and applications (pp. 1404-1416). Hershey, PA: Information Science Reference. doi: doi:10.4018/978-1-60960-818-7.ch513

Payne, G. W. (2011). The role of blended learning in 21st century medical education: Current trends and future directions. In A. Kitchenham (Ed.), *Blended learning across disciplines: Models for implementation* (pp. 132–146). Hershey, PA: Information Science Reference. doi:10.4018/978-1-60960-479-0.ch008

Penchovsky, R. (2013). Engineering gene control circuits with allosteric ribozymes in human cells as a medicine of the future. In I. Management Association (Ed.), Bioinformatics: Concepts, methodologies, tools, and applications (pp. 860-883). Hershey, PA: Medical Information Science Reference. doi: doi:10.4018/978-1-4666-3604-0.ch047

Pestana, O. (2014). Information value and quality for the health sector: A case study of search strategies for optimal information retrieval. In G. Jamil, A. Malheiro, & F. Ribeiro (Eds.), *Rethinking the conceptual base for new practical applications in information value and quality* (pp. 116–133). Hershey, PA: Information Science Reference.

Peterson, C., & Willis, E. (2011). Social construction of chronic disease: Narratives on the experience of chronic illness. In R. Biswas, & C. Martin (Eds.), *User-driven healthcare and narrative medicine: Utilizing collaborative social networks and technologies* (pp. 395–409). Hershey, PA: Medical Information Science Reference.

Petoukhov, S., & He, M. (2010). Biological evolution of dialects of the genetic code. In S. Petoukhov, & M. He (Eds.), *Symmetrical analysis techniques for genetic systems and bioinformatics: Advanced patterns and applications* (pp. 50–64). Hershey, PA: Medical Information Science Reference.

Petty, G. C., & Joyner, D. H. (2012). The efficacy of continuing education technology for public health physicians practicing in remote areas. In V. Wang (Ed.), *Encyclopedia of e-leadership, counseling and training* (pp. 453–467). Hershey, PA: Information Science Reference.

Phua, C., Roy, P. C., Aloulou, H., Biswas, J., Tolstikov, A., & Foo, V. S. … Xu, D. (2014). State-of-the-art assistive technology for people with dementia. In I. Association (Ed.), Assistive technologies: Concepts, methodologies, tools, and applications (pp. 1606-1625). Hershey, PA: Information Science Reference. doi: doi:10.4018/978-1-4666-4422-9.ch085

Portela, F., Cabral, A., Abelha, A., Salazar, M., Quintas, C., & Machado, J. … Santos, M. F. (2013). Knowledge acquisition process for intelligent decision support in critical health care. In R. Martinho, R. Rijo, M. Cruz-Cunha, & J. Varajão (Eds.) Information systems and technologies for enhancing health and social care (pp. 55-68). Hershey, PA: Medical Information Science Reference. doi: doi:10.4018/978-1-4666-3667-5.ch004

Postolache, O., Girão, P., & Postolache, G. (2013). Seismocardiogram and ballistocardiogram sensing. In A. Lay-Ekuakille (Ed.), *Advanced instrument engineering: Measurement, calibration, and design* (pp. 223–246). Hershey, PA: Engineering Science Reference. doi:10.4018/978-1-4666-4165-5.ch017

Premkumar, K. (2011). Mobile learning in medicine. In A. Kitchenham (Ed.), *Models for interdisciplinary mobile learning: Delivering information to students* (pp. 137–153). Hershey, PA: Information Science Reference. doi:10.4018/978-1-60960-511-7.ch008

Price, M. (2011). A bio-psycho-social review of usability methods and their applications in healthcare. In I. Management Association (Ed.), Clinical technologies: Concepts, methodologies, tools and applications (pp. 1874-1899). Hershey, PA: Medical Information Science Reference. doi: doi:10.4018/978-1-60960-561-2.ch704

Prigione, A. (2012). Stem cell-based personalized medicine: From disease modeling to clinical applications. In I. Management Association (Ed.), Computer engineering: Concepts, methodologies, tools and applications (pp. 1855-1866). Hershey, PA: Engineering Science Reference. doi: doi:10.4018/978-1-61350-456-7.ch803

Quinaz, F., Fazendeiro, P., Castelo-Branco, M., & Araújo, P. (2013). Soft methods for automatic drug infusion in medical care environment. In M. Cruz-Cunha, I. Miranda, & P. Gonçalves (Eds.), *Handbook of research on ICTs and management systems for improving efficiency in healthcare and social care* (pp. 830–854). Hershey, PA: Medical Information Science Reference. doi:10.4018/978-1-4666-3990-4.ch043

Quoniam, L., & Lima de Magalhães, J. (2014). Perception of the information value for public health: A case study for neglected diseases. In G. Jamil, A. Malheiro, & F. Ribeiro (Eds.), *Rethinking the conceptual base for new practical applications in information value and quality* (pp. 211–232). Hershey, PA: Information Science Reference.

Raghupathi, W. (2010). Designing clinical decision support systems in health care: A systemic view. In M. Hunter (Ed.), *Strategic information systems: Concepts, methodologies, tools, and applications* (pp. 652–661). Hershey, PA: Information Science Reference.

Raghupathi, W., & Nerur, S. (2012). The intellectual structure of health and medical informatics. In J. Tan (Ed.), *Advancing technologies and intelligence in healthcare and clinical environments breakthroughs* (pp. 1–16). Hershey, PA: Medical Information Science Reference. doi:10.4018/978-1-4666-1755-1.ch001

Räisänen, T., Oinas-Kukkonen, H., Leiviskä, K., Seppänen, M., & Kallio, M. (2010). Managing mobile healthcare knowledge: Physicians' perceptions on knowledge creation and reuse. In J. Rodrigues (Ed.), *Health information systems: Concepts, methodologies, tools, and applications* (pp. 733–749). Hershey, PA: Medical Information Science Reference.

Raval, M. S. (2011). Data hiding in digitized medical images: From concepts to applications. In A. Daskalaki (Ed.), *Digital forensics for the health sciences: Applications in practice and research* (pp. 29–47). Hershey, PA: Medical Information Science Reference. doi:10.4018/978-1-60960-483-7.ch003

Ravka, N. (2014). Informatics and health services: The potential benefits and challenges of electronic health records and personal electronic health records in patient care, cost control, and health research – An overview. In C. El Morr (Ed.), *Research perspectives on the role of informatics in health policy and management* (pp. 89–114). Hershey, PA: Medical Information Science Reference.

Reyes Álamo, J. M., Yang, H., Babbitt, R., & Wong, J. (2010). Support for medication safety and compliance in smart home environments. In J. Rodrigues (Ed.), *Health information systems: Concepts, methodologies, tools, and applications* (pp. 2091–2110). Hershey, PA: Medical Information Science Reference.

Ribeiro, C., Monteiro, M., Corredoura, S., Candeias, F., & Pereira, J. (2013). Games in higher education: Opportunities, expectations, challenges, and results in medical education. In S. de Freitas, M. Ott, M. Popescu, & I. Stanescu (Eds.), *New pedagogical approaches in game enhanced learning: Curriculum integration* (pp. 228–247). Hershey, PA: Information Science Reference. doi:10.4018/978-1-4666-3950-8.ch012

Rocci, L. (2010). Biomedical technoethics. In R. Luppicini (Ed.), *Technoethics and the evolving knowledge society: Ethical issues in technological design, research, development, and innovation* (pp. 128–145). Hershey, PA: Information Science Reference. doi:10.4018/978-1-60566-952-6.ch007

Rockland, R., Kimmel, H., Carpinelli, J., Hirsch, L. S., & Burr-Alexander, L. (2014). Medical robotics in k-12 education. In I. Management Association (Ed.), Robotics: Concepts, methodologies, tools, and applications (pp. 1096-1115). Hershey, PA: Information Science Reference. doi: doi:10.4018/978-1-4666-4607-0.ch053

Rodrigues, J. J. (2012). *Emerging communication technologies for e-health and medicine*. Hershey, PA: IGI Global. doi:10.4018/978-1-4666-0909-9

Rodrigues, J. J. (2013). *Digital advances in medicine, e-health, and communication technologies*. Hershey, PA: IGI Global. doi:10.4018/978-1-4666-2794-9

Rodrigues, J. J. (2014). *Advancing medical practice through technology: Applications for healthcare delivery, management, and quality*. Hershey, PA: IGI Global.

Rodríguez-González, A., García-Crespo, Á., Colomo-Palacios, R., Gómez-Berbís, J. M., & Jiménez-Domingo, E. (2013). Using ontologies in drug prescription: The SemMed approach. In J. Wang (Ed.), *Intelligence methods and systems advancements for knowledge-based business* (pp. 247–261). Hershey, PA: Information Science Reference.

Rojo, M. G., & Daniel, C. (2011). Digital pathology and virtual microscopy integration in e-health records. In I. Management Association (Ed.), Clinical technologies: Concepts, methodologies, tools and applications (pp. 1235-1262). Hershey, PA: Medical Information Science Reference. doi:doi:10.4018/978-1-60960-561-2.ch415

Rompas, A., Tsirmpas, C., Anastasiou, A., Iliopoulou, D., & Koutsouris, D. (2013). Statistical power and sample size in personalized medicine. [IJSBBT]. *International Journal of Systems Biology and Biomedical Technologies*, 2(2), 72–88. doi:10.4018/ijsbbt.2013040105

Rosiek, A. B., & Leksowski, K. (2011). Quality assurance and evaluation of healthcare reform initiatives: Strategy for improving the quality of health care services in public health care units, management model that allows the providing of high quality health care and efficient brand-building. [IJHDRI]. *International Journal of Healthcare Delivery Reform Initiatives*, 3(3), 42–53. doi:10.4018/jhdri.2011070104

Ross, S. (2011). A lexicon for user driven healthcare. [IJUDH]. *International Journal of User-Driven Healthcare*, 1(1), 50–54. doi:10.4018/ijudh.2011010107

Ross, S. D. (2011). Multiple paths in health care. In R. Biswas, & C. Martin (Eds.), *User-driven healthcare and narrative medicine: Utilizing collaborative social networks and technologies* (pp. 113–124). Hershey, PA: Medical Information Science Reference.

Rosu, S. M., & Dragoi, G. (2014). E-health sites development using open source software and OMT methodology as support for family doctors' activities: A Romanian case study. In M. Cruz-Cunha, F. Moreira, & J. Varajão (Eds.), *Handbook of research on enterprise 2.0: Technological, social, and organizational dimensions* (pp. 72–88). Hershey, PA: Business Science Reference.

Ruiz-Fernandez, D., & Soriano-Paya, A. (2011). A distributed approach of a clinical decision support system based on cooperation. In I. Management Association (Ed.), Clinical technologies: Concepts, methodologies, tools and applications (pp. 1782-1799). Hershey, PA: Medical Information Science Reference. doi: doi:10.4018/978-1-60960-561-2.ch612

Ryan, P. (2012). Paying for performance: Key design features and the bigger picture. [IJPPHME]. *International Journal of Public and Private Healthcare Management and Economics, 2*(2), 1–16. doi:10.4018/ijpphme.2012040101

Sainz de Abajo, B., & Ballestero, A. L. (2012). Overview of the most important open source software: Analysis of the benefits of OpenMRS, Open-EMR, and VistA. In J. Rodrigues, I. de la Torre Díez, & B. Sainz de Abajo (Eds.), *Telemedicine and e-health services, policies, and applications: Advancements and developments* (pp. 315–346). Hershey, PA: Medical Information Science Reference. doi:10.4018/978-1-4666-0888-7.ch012

Salcido, G. J., & Delgado, E. C. (2013). Intelligent agent to identify rheumatic diseases. In M. Cruz-Cunha, I. Miranda, & P. Gonçalves (Eds.), *Handbook of research on ICTs and management systems for improving efficiency in healthcare and social care* (pp. 451–473). Hershey, PA: Medical Information Science Reference. doi:10.4018/978-1-4666-3990-4.ch023

Schallenberg, S., Petzold, C., Riewaldt, J., & Kretschmer, K. (2013). Regulatory T cell-based immunotherapy: Prospects of antigen-specific tolerance induction. In A. Daskalaki (Ed.), *Medical advancements in aging and regenerative technologies: Clinical tools and applications* (pp. 112–136). Hershey, PA: Medical Information Science Reference.

Scheepers-Hoeks, A., Klijn, F., van der Linden, C., Grouls, R., Ackerman, E., & Minderman, N. … Korsten, E. (2013). Clinical decision support systems for 'making it easy to do it right. In I. Association (Ed.), Data mining: Concepts, methodologies, tools, and applications (pp. 1461-1471). Hershey, PA: Information Science Reference. doi: doi:10.4018/978-1-4666-2455-9.ch076

Seçkin, G. (2012). Cyber behaviors of self health care management. In Z. Yan (Ed.), *Encyclopedia of cyber behavior* (pp. 722–734). Hershey, PA: Information Science Reference. doi:10.4018/978-1-4666-0315-8.ch061

Serrano, M., Elmisery, A., Foghlú, M. Ó., Donnelly, W., Storni, C., & Fernström, M. (2013). Pervasive computing support in the transition towards personalised health systems. In J. Rodrigues (Ed.), *Digital advances in medicine, e-health, and communication technologies* (pp. 49–64). Hershey, PA: Medical Information Science Reference. doi:10.4018/978-1-4666-2794-9.ch003

Shachak, A., & Reis, S. (2010). The computer-assisted patient consultation: Promises and challenges. In S. Kabene (Ed.), *Healthcare and the effect of technology: Developments, challenges and advancements* (pp. 72–83). Hershey, PA: Medical Information Science Reference. doi:10.4018/978-1-61520-733-6.ch005

Shachak, A., & Reis, S. (2011). The computer-assisted patient consultation. In I. Management Association (Ed.), Clinical technologies: Concepts, methodologies, tools and applications (pp. 160-171). Hershey, PA: Medical Information Science Reference. doi: doi:10.4018/978-1-60960-561-2.ch111

Shankar, P. R. (2011). Medical Humanities. In R. Biswas, & C. Martin (Eds.), *User-driven healthcare and narrative medicine: Utilizing collaborative social networks and technologies* (pp. 210–227). Hershey, PA: Medical Information Science Reference.

Shanmuganathan, S. (2010). A stroke information system (SIS): Critical issues and solutions. In W. Pease, M. Cooper, & R. Gururajan (Eds.), *Biomedical knowledge management: Infrastructures and processes for e-health systems* (pp. 177–191). Hershey, PA: Medical Information Science Reference. doi:10.4018/978-1-60566-266-4.ch012

Shegog, R. (2010). Application of behavioral theory in computer game design for health behavior change. In J. Cannon-Bowers, & C. Bowers (Eds.), *Serious game design and development: Technologies for training and learning* (pp. 196–232). Hershey, PA: Information Science Reference. doi:10.4018/978-1-61520-739-8.ch011

Shendge, S., Deka, B., & Kotwani, A. (2012). A cross-sectional evaluation of illness perception about asthma among asthma patients at a referral tertiary care public chest hospital in Delhi, India. [IJUDH]. *International Journal of User-Driven Healthcare*, 2(3), 32–43. doi: doi:10.4018/ijudh.2012070104

Shimoyama, I., Shimada, H., & Ninchoji, T. (2013). Kanji perception and brain function. In J. Wu (Ed.), *Biomedical engineering and cognitive neuroscience for healthcare: Interdisciplinary applications* (pp. 266–273). Hershey, PA: Medical Information Science Reference.

Shrestha, S. (2013). Clinical decision support system for diabetes prevention: An illustrative case. In S. Sarnikar, D. Bennett, & M. Gaynor (Eds.), *Cases on healthcare information technology for patient care management* (pp. 308–329). Hershey, PA: Medical Information Science Reference.

Shukla, A., Tiwari, R., & Rathore, C. P. (2011). Intelligent biometric system using soft computing tools. In A. Shukla, & R. Tiwari (Eds.), *Biomedical engineering and information systems: Technologies, tools and applications* (pp. 259–276). Hershey, PA: Medical Information Science Reference.

Sibinga, C. T., & Oladejo, M. A. (2013). Bridging the knowledge gap in management and operations of transfusion medicine: Planning, policy and leadership issues. [JCIT]. *Journal of Cases on Information Technology*, 15(1), 69–82. doi:10.4018/jcit.2013010105

Slavens, B., & Harris, G. F. (2012). Biomechanics. In Z. Abu-Faraj (Ed.), *Handbook of research on biomedical engineering education and advanced bioengineering learning: Interdisciplinary concepts* (pp. 284–338). Hershey, PA: Medical Information Science Reference. doi:10.4018/978-1-4666-0122-2.ch007

Sliedrecht, S., & Kotzé, E. (2013). Patients with a spinal cord injury inform and co-construct services at a spinal cord rehabilitation unit. In I. Management Association (Ed.), User-driven healthcare: Concepts, methodologies, tools, and applications (pp. 1054-1072). Hershey, PA: Medical Information Science Reference. doi: doi:10.4018/978-1-4666-2770-3.ch053

Sood, R., & Ananthakrishnan, N. (2012). Reforming medical curriculum in India in recent years: Conflicts of political, regulator, educationist and professional natures and strategies for their resolution. [IJUDH]. *International Journal of User-Driven Healthcare*, 2(1), 1–13. doi:10.4018/ijudh.2012010101

Springer, J. A., Beever, J., Morar, N., Sprague, J. E., & Kane, M. D. (2011). Ethics, Privacy, and the future of genetic information in healthcare information assurance and security. In M. Dark (Ed.), *Information assurance and security ethics in complex systems: Interdisciplinary perspectives* (pp. 186–205). Hershey, PA: Information Science Reference.

Srivastava, S. (2011). Medical transcription a pioneer in the healthcare informatics. In A. Shukla, & R. Tiwari (Eds.), *Biomedical engineering and information systems: Technologies, tools and applications* (pp. 239–258). Hershey, PA: Medical Information Science Reference.

Srivastava, S., Sharma, N., & Singh, S. (2014). Image analysis and understanding techniques for breast cancer detection from digital mammograms. In R. Srivastava, S. Singh, & K. Shukla (Eds.), *Research developments in computer vision and image processing: Methodologies and applications* (pp. 123–148). Hershey, PA: Information Science Reference.

Stanescu, L., & Burdescu, D. D. (2010). Medical hybrid learning tools. In F. Wang, J. Fong, & R. Kwan (Eds.), *Handbook of research on hybrid learning models: Advanced tools, technologies, and applications* (pp. 355–370). Hershey, PA: Information Science Reference.

Staudinger, B., Ostermann, H., & Staudinger, R. (2011). IT-based virtual medical centres and structures. In I. Management Association (Ed.), Clinical technologies: Concepts, methodologies, tools and applications (pp. 2035-2046). Hershey, PA: Medical Information Science Reference. doi: doi:10.4018/978-1-60960-561-2.ch802

Stefaniak, J. E. (2013). Resuscitating team roles within Wayburn health system. In A. Ritzhaupt, & S. Kumar (Eds.), *Cases on educational technology implementation for facilitating learning* (pp. 130–145). Hershey, PA: Information Science Reference. doi:10.4018/978-1-4666-3676-7.ch008

Stein, R. A. (2012). Direct-to-consumer genetic testing: Interdisciplinary crossroads. [JITR]. *Journal of Information Technology Research, 5*(1), 35–67. doi:10.4018/jitr.2012010103

Stergachis, A., Keene, D., & Somani, S. (2013). Informatics for medicines management systems in resource-limited settings. In I. Association (Ed.), *Supply chain management: Concepts, methodologies, tools, and applications* (pp. 634–645). Hershey, PA: Business Science Reference.

Stevens, D., & Kitchenham, A. (2011). An analysis of mobile learning in education, business, and medicine. In A. Kitchenham (Ed.), *Models for interdisciplinary mobile learning: Delivering information to students* (pp. 1–25). Hershey, PA: Information Science Reference. doi:10.4018/978-1-60960-511-7.ch001

Stolba, N., Nguyen, T. M., & Tjoa, A. M. (2010). Data warehouse facilitating evidence-based medicine. In T. Nguyen (Ed.), *Complex data warehousing and knowledge discovery for advanced retrieval development: Innovative methods and applications* (pp. 174–207). Hershey, PA: Information Science Reference.

Sugaretty, D. (2014). Risk management in a pandemic crisis at a global non profit health care organization. In I. Management Association (Ed.), Crisis management: Concepts, methodologies, tools and applications (pp. 1253-1270). Hershey, PA: Information Science Reference. doi: doi:10.4018/978-1-4666-4707-7.ch063

Sugi, T., Goto, K., Goto, S., Goto, Y., Yamasaki, T., & Tobimatsu, S. (2013). Topography estimation of visual evoked potentials using a combination of mathematical models. In J. Wu (Ed.), *Biomedical engineering and cognitive neuroscience for healthcare: Interdisciplinary applications* (pp. 129–141). Hershey, PA: Medical Information Science Reference.

Sujan, H., Borrero, S., & Cranage, D. (2014). Good treats: Eating out not just for joy but also for well-being. In A. Goyal (Ed.), *Innovations in services marketing and management: Strategies for emerging economies* (pp. 118–135). Hershey, PA: Business Science Reference.

Swennen, M. H. (2011). The gap between what is knowable and what we do in clinical practice. In R. Biswas, & C. Martin (Eds.), *User-driven healthcare and narrative medicine: Utilizing collaborative social networks and technologies* (pp. 335–356). Hershey, PA: Medical Information Science Reference. doi:10.4018/978-1-60960-561-2.ch705

Szewczak, E. J., & Snodgrass, C. R. (2011). Business associates in the national health information network: Implications for medical information privacy. In I. Lee (Ed.), *E-business applications for product development and competitive growth: Emerging technologies* (pp. 186–198). Hershey, PA: Business Science Reference.

Tabrizi, N. T., Torabi, Z., Bastani, P., Mokhtarkhani, M., Madani, N., Parnian, N., & Hajebrahimi, S. (2013). Assessing the perception of pain and distress of female patients undergoing routine urethral catheterization in cesarean delivery. [IJUDH]. *International Journal of User-Driven Healthcare, 3*(2), 78–84. doi:10.4018/ijudh.2013040109

Tanaka, H., & Furutani, M. (2013). Sleep management promotes healthy lifestyle, mental health, QOL, and a healthy brain. In J. Wu (Ed.), *Biomedical engineering and cognitive neuroscience for healthcare: Interdisciplinary applications* (pp. 211–224). Hershey, PA: Medical Information Science Reference.

Tang, X., Gao, Y., Yang, W., Zhang, M., & Wu, J. (2013). Audiovisual integration of natural auditory and visual stimuli in the real-world situation. In J. Wu (Ed.), *Biomedical engineering and cognitive neuroscience for healthcare: Interdisciplinary applications* (pp. 337–344). Hershey, PA: Medical Information Science Reference.

Tashiro, M., Okamura, N., Watanuki, S., Furumoto, S., Furukawa, K., & Funaki, Y. … Yanai, K. (2011). Quantitative analysis of amyloid ß deposition in patients with Alzheimer's disease using positron emission tomography. In J. Wu (Ed.), Early detection and rehabilitation technologies for dementia: Neuroscience and biomedical applications (pp. 220-230). Hershey, PA: Medical Information Science Reference. doi: doi:10.4018/978-1-60960-559-9.ch029

Taylor, B. W. (2014). Decision-making and decision support in acute care. In C. El Morr (Ed.), *Research perspectives on the role of informatics in health policy and management* (pp. 1–18). Hershey, PA: Medical Information Science Reference.

Thatcher, B. (2012). Intercultural rhetorical dimensions of health literacy and medicine. In *Intercultural rhetoric and professional communication: Technological advances and organizational behavior* (pp. 247–282). Hershey, PA: Information Science Reference.

Tiwari, S., & Srivastava, R. (2014). Research and developments in medical image reconstruction methods and its applications. In R. Srivastava, S. Singh, & K. Shukla (Eds.), *Research developments in computer vision and image processing: Methodologies and applications* (pp. 274–312). Hershey, PA: Information Science Reference.

Toro-Troconis, M., & Partridge, M. R. (2010). Designing game-based learning activities in virtual worlds: Experiences from undergraduate medicine. In Y. Baek (Ed.), *Gaming for classroom-based learning: Digital role playing as a motivator of study* (pp. 270–280). Hershey, PA: Information Science Reference. doi:10.4018/978-1-61520-713-8.ch016

Trojer, T., Katt, B., Breu, R., Schabetsberger, T., & Mair, R. (2012). Managing privacy and effectiveness of patient-administered authorization policies. [IJCMAM]. *International Journal of Computational Models and Algorithms in Medicine*, *3*(2), 43–62. doi:10.4018/jcmam.2012040103

Übeyli, E. D. (2010). Medical informatics: Preventive medicine applications via telemedicine. In M. Cruz-Cunha, A. Tavares, & R. Simoes (Eds.), *Handbook of research on developments in e-health and telemedicine: Technological and social perspectives* (pp. 475–489). Hershey, PA: Medical Information Science Reference.

Übeyli, E. D. (2011). Telemedicine and biotelemetry for e-health systems. In I. Management Association (Ed.), Clinical technologies: Concepts, methodologies, tools and applications (pp. 676-692). Hershey, PA: Medical Information Science Reference. doi: doi:10.4018/978-1-60960-561-2.ch304

Vahe, M., Zain-Ul-Abdin, K., & Türel, Y. K. (2012). Social media as a learning tool in medical education: A situation analysis. In V. Dennen, & J. Myers (Eds.), *Virtual professional development and informal learning via social networks* (pp. 168–183). Hershey, PA: Information Science Reference. doi:10.4018/978-1-4666-1815-2.ch010

Vivekananda-Schmidt, P. (2013). Ethics in the design of serious games for healthcare and medicine. In S. Arnab, I. Dunwell, & K. Debattista (Eds.), *Serious games for healthcare: Applications and implications* (pp. 91–106). Hershey, PA: Medical Information Science Reference.

von Lubitz, D. (2010). Healthcare among the people: Teams of leaders concept (ToL) and the world of technology-oriented global healthcare. In S. Kabene (Ed.), *Healthcare and the effect of technology: Developments, challenges and advancements* (pp. 145–177). Hershey, PA: Medical Information Science Reference. doi:10.4018/978-1-61520-733-6.ch010

von Lubitz, D. (2011). The teams of leaders (Tol) concept: The grid, the mesh, and the people in the world of information and knowledge-based global healthcare. In E. Kldiashvili (Ed.), *Grid technologies for e-health: Applications for telemedicine services and delivery* (pp. 65–104). Hershey, PA: Medical Information Science Reference.

Vouyioukas, D., & Maglogiannis, I. (2010). Communication issues in pervasive healthcare systems and applications. In A. Coronato, & G. De Pietro (Eds.), *Pervasive and smart technologies for healthcare: Ubiquitous methodologies and tools* (pp. 197–227). Hershey, PA: Medical Information Science Reference. doi:10.4018/978-1-61520-765-7.ch010

Walczak, S., Brimhall, B. B., & Lefkowitz, J. B. (2010). Nonparametric decision support systems in medical diagnosis: Modeling pulmonary embolism. In M. Hunter (Ed.), *Strategic information systems: Concepts, methodologies, tools, and applications* (pp. 1483–1500). Hershey, PA: Information Science Reference.

Walczak, S., Brimhall, B. B., & Lefkowitz, J. B. (2011). Diagnostic cost reduction using artificial neural networks. In I. Management Association (Ed.), Clinical technologies: Concepts, methodologies, tools and applications (pp. 1812-1830). Hershey, PA: Medical Information Science Reference. doi: doi:10.4018/978-1-60960-561-2.ch614

Wang, G., Cong, A., Gao, H., Zhang, J., Weir, V. J., Xu, X., & Bennett, J. (2012). Medical imaging. In Z. Abu-Faraj (Ed.), *Handbook of research on biomedical engineering education and advanced bioengineering learning: Interdisciplinary concepts* (pp. 634–712). Hershey, PA: Medical Information Science Reference. doi:10.4018/978-1-4666-0122-2.ch015

Watanabe, Y., Tanaka, H., & Hirata, K. (2013). Evaluation of cognitive function in migraine patients: A study using event-related potentials. In J. Wu (Ed.), *Biomedical engineering and cognitive neuroscience for healthcare: Interdisciplinary applications* (pp. 303–310). Hershey, PA: Medical Information Science Reference.

Watfa, M. K., Majeed, H., & Salahuddin, T. (2012). Healthcare applications for clinicians. In M. Watfa (Ed.), *E-healthcare systems and wireless communications: Current and future challenges* (pp. 49–69). Hershey, PA: Medical Information Science Reference.

Weigel, F. K., Rainer, R. K., Hazen, B. T., Cegielski, C. G., & Ford, F. N. (2012). Use of diffusion of innovations theory in medical informatics research. [IJHISI]. *International Journal of Healthcare Information Systems and Informatics*, 7(3), 44–56. doi:10.4018/jhisi.2012070104

Whitaker, R. (2013). Securing health-effective medicine in practice: A critical perspective on user-driven healthcare. In R. Biswas (Ed.), *Clinical solutions and medical progress through user-driven healthcare* (pp. 35–50). Hershey, PA: Medical Information Science Reference.

Wilkowska, W., & Ziefle, M. (2011). User diversity as a challenge for the integration of medical technology into future smart home environments. In M. Ziefle, & C. Röcker (Eds.), *Human-centered design of e-health technologies: Concepts, methods and applications* (pp. 95–126). Hershey, PA: Medical Information Science Reference.

Xuan, X., & Xiaowei, Z. (2012). The dilemma and resolution: The patentability of traditional Chinese medicine. [IJABIM]. *International Journal of Asian Business and Information Management*, 3(3), 1–8. doi:10.4018/jabim.2012070101

Yamamoto, S. (2010). IT applications for medical services in Japan. In W. Pease, M. Cooper, & R. Gururajan (Eds.), *Biomedical knowledge management: Infrastructures and processes for e-health systems* (pp. 327–336). Hershey, PA: Medical Information Science Reference. doi:10.4018/978-1-60566-266-4.ch024

Yan, B., Lei, Y., Tong, L., & Chen, K. (2013). Functional neuroimaging of acupuncture: A systematic review. In J. Wu (Ed.), *Biomedical engineering and cognitive neuroscience for healthcare: Interdisciplinary applications* (pp. 142–155). Hershey, PA: Medical Information Science Reference.

Yang, J. (2014). Towards healthy public policy: GIS and food systems analysis. In C. El Morr (Ed.), *Research perspectives on the role of informatics in health policy and management* (pp. 135–152). Hershey, PA: Medical Information Science Reference.

Yang, W., Gao, Y., & Wu, J. (2013). Effects of selective and divided attention on audiovisual interaction. In J. Wu (Ed.), *Biomedical engineering and cognitive neuroscience for healthcare: Interdisciplinary applications* (pp. 311–319). Hershey, PA: Medical Information Science Reference.

Yap, K. Y. (2013). The evolving role of pharmacoinformatics in targeting drug-related problems in clinical oncology practice. In I. Management Association (Ed.), User-driven healthcare: Concepts, methodologies, tools, and applications (pp. 1541-1588). Hershey, PA: Medical Information Science Reference. doi: doi:10.4018/978-1-4666-2770-3.ch077

Young, J. W., Thapaliya, P., & Sapkota, S. (2013). Caught in the middle: The divide between conventional and alternative medicine. In R. Biswas (Ed.), *Clinical solutions and medical progress through user-driven healthcare* (pp. 26–34). Hershey, PA: Medical Information Science Reference.

Yu, J., Guo, C., & Kim, M. (2010). Developing a user centered model for ubiquitous healthcare system implementation: An empirical study. In J. Rodrigues (Ed.), *Health information systems: Concepts, methodologies, tools, and applications* (pp. 1243–1259). Hershey, PA: Medical Information Science Reference.

Yu, J., Guo, C., & Kim, M. (2011). Towards a conceptual framework of adopting ubiquitous technology in chronic health care. In J. Tan (Ed.), *Developments in healthcare information systems and technologies: Models and methods* (pp. 214–231). Hershey, PA: Medical Information Science Reference.

Zaheer, S. (2014). Implementation of evidence-based practice and the PARIHS framework. In C. El Morr (Ed.), *Research perspectives on the role of informatics in health policy and management* (pp. 19–36). Hershey, PA: Medical Information Science Reference.

Zhang, H. H., Meyer, R. R., Shi, L., & D'Souza, W. D. (2012). Machine learning applications in radiation therapy. In S. Kulkarni (Ed.), *Machine learning algorithms for problem solving in computational applications: Intelligent techniques* (pp. 59–84). Hershey, PA: Information Science Reference. doi:10.4018/978-1-4666-1833-6.ch005

Zhang, W. (2011). YinYang bipolar quantum bioeconomics for equilibrium-based biosystem simulation and regulation. In *YinYang bipolar relativity: A unifying theory of nature, agents and causality with applications in quantum computing, cognitive informatics and life sciences* (pp. 266–297). Hershey, PA: Information Science Reference. doi:10.4018/978-1-60960-525-4.ch009

Zhang, Z., Gao, B., Liao, G., Mu, L., & Wei, W. (2011). The study of transesophageal oxygen saturation monitoring. In I. Management Association (Ed.), Clinical technologies: Concepts, methodologies, tools and applications (pp. 2191-2200). Hershey, PA: Medical Information Science Reference. doi: doi:10.4018/978-1-60960-561-2.ch813

Zhao, B., Zhang, D. S., & Zhao, Y. Z. (2013). Construction competitiveness evaluation system of regional BioPharma industry and case study: Taking Shijiazhuang as an example. In T. Gao (Ed.), *Global applications of pervasive and ubiquitous computing* (pp. 80–88). Hershey, PA: Information Science Reference.

Zheng, K., Padman, R., Johnson, M. P., & Hasan, S. (2010). Guideline representation ontologies for evidence-based medicine practice. In K. Khoumbati, Y. Dwivedi, A. Srivastava, & B. Lal (Eds.), *Handbook of research on advances in health informatics and electronic healthcare applications: Global adoption and impact of information communication technologies* (pp. 234–254). Hershey, PA: Medical Information Science Reference.

Zhou, F., Yan, J., Wang, Y., Li, F., Xia, C., Guo, R., & Yan, H. (2011). Digital auscultation system of traditional Chinese medicine and its signals acquisition: Analysis methods. In L. Liu, D. Wei, & Y. Li (Eds.), *Interdisciplinary research and applications in bioinformatics, computational biology, and environmental sciences* (pp. 183–193). Hershey, PA: Medical Information Science Reference.

Zijlstra, W., Becker, C., & Pfeiffer, K. (2011). Wearable systems for monitoring mobility related activities: From technology to application for healthcare services. In C. Röcker, & M. Ziefle (Eds.), *E-Health, assistive technologies and applications for assisted living: Challenges and solutions* (pp. 244–267). Hershey, PA: Medical Information Science Reference. doi:10.4018/978-1-60960-469-1.ch011

Zimmer, J., Degenkolbe, E., Wildemann, B., & Seemann, P. (2013). BMP signaling in regenerative medicine. In I. Management Association (Ed.), Bioinformatics: Concepts, methodologies, tools, and applications (pp. 1252-1281). Hershey, PA: Medical Information Science Reference. doi: doi:10.4018/978-1-4666-3604-0.ch064

Zouag, N. (2014). Patterns of migration of medical doctors from MENA and ECE to EU economies with descriptive analysis of relatives wages. In A. Driouchi (Ed.), *Labor and health economics in the Mediterranean region: Migration and mobility of medical doctors* (pp. 124–138). Hershey, PA: Medical Information Science Reference.

Zouag, N., & Driouchi, A. (2014). Trends and prospects of the moroccan health system: 2010-2030. In A. Driouchi (Ed.), *Labor and health economics in the Mediterranean region: Migration and mobility of medical doctors* (pp. 314–336). Hershey, PA: Medical Information Science Reference.

Zybeck, K. L. (2013). A question of degrees: Collecting in support of the allied health professions. In S. Holder (Ed.), *Library collection development for professional programs: Trends and best practices* (pp. 145–163). Hershey, PA: Information Science Reference.

Compilation of References

Abramo, G., D'angelo, C., Di Costa, F., & Solazzi, M. (2009). University-industry collaboration in Italy: A bibliometric examination. *Technovation*, *29*(6/7), 498–507. doi:10.1016/j.technovation.2008.11.003

Abramo, G., D'Angelo, C., & Di Costa, F. (2010). Citations versus journal impact factor as proxy of quality: Could the latter ever be preferable? *Scientometrics*, *84*(3), 821–833. doi:10.1007/s11192-010-0200-1

Aghion, P., Dewatripont, M., Hoxby, C., Mas-Colell, A., & Sapir, A. (2008). *Higher aspirations: An agenda for reforming European universities*. Brussels: Bruegel Blueprint Series.

Agoston, S., & Dima, A. (2012). Trends and strategies within the process of academic internationalization. *Management & Marketing*, *7*(1), 43–57.

Ahire, S. L., Golhar, D. Y., & Waller, M. A. (1996). Development and validation of TQM implementation constructs. *Decision Sciences*, *27*, 23–56. doi:10.1111/j.1540-5915.1996.tb00842.x

Ahire, S. L., & O'Shaughnessy, K. C. (1998). The role of top management commitment in quality management: An empirical analysis of the auto parts industry. *International Journal of Quality Science*, *31*, 5–37. doi:10.1108/13598539810196868

Albert, S., & Whetten, D. A. (2004). Organizational identity. In M. J. Hatch, & M. Schultz (Eds.), *Organisational identity: A reader*. Oxford, UK: Oxford University Press.

Alexandersson, M. (1994). Focusing teacher consciousness: What do teachers direct their consciousness towards during their teaching? In I. Carlgren, G. Handal, & S. Vaage (Eds.), *Teachers' minds and actions: Research on teachers' thinking and practice*. Academic Press.

Altbach, P. G., Reisberg, L., & Rumbley, L. E. (2009). *Trends in global higher education: Tracking an academic revolution*. Paris: UNESCO.

Alvesson, M. (1990). Organisation: From substance to image. *Organization Studies*, *11*, 373–394. doi:10.1177/017084069001100303

Alvesson, M. (2002). *Postmodernism and social research*. Buckingham: Open University Press.

Alvesson, M., & Willmott, H. (2004). Identity regulations as organisational control producing the appropriate individual. In M. J. Hatch, & M. Schultz (Eds.), *Organisational identity: A reader*. Oxford, UK: Oxford University Press.

Arango, J. B. (1998). *Helping non-profits become more effective*. Retrieved from http://www.algodonesassociates.com

Argentin, G., & Triventi, M. (2010). Social inequalities and labour market in a period of institutional reforms: Italy 1992-2007. *Higher Education*, *61*(3), 309–323. doi:10.1007/s10734-010-9379-6

Argyris, C. (1999). *On organizational learning* (2nd ed.). Oxford, UK: Oxford University Press.

Arnould, E., & Price, L. (2004). *Consumers* (2nd ed.). Boston: McGraw-Hill Publishing House.

Aronowitz, S. (2000). *The knowledge factory: Dismantling the corporate university and creating true higher learning*. Boston: Beacon Press.

Ashforth, B. E., & Mael, F. (2004). Social identification theory and the organisation. In M. J. Hatch, & M. Schultz (Eds.), *Organisational identity: A reader*. Oxford, UK: Oxford University Press.

Ashkanasy, N. M., Wilderom, C. P., & Peterson, M. F. (Eds.). (2000). *Handbook of organizational culture and climate*. Thousand Oaks, CA: Sage Publications.

Astor, A., Akhtar, T., Matallana, M. A., Muthuswamy, V., Olowu, F. A., Tallo, V., & Lie, R. K. (2005). Physician migration: Views from professionals in Colombia, Nigeria, India, Pakistan and the Philippines. *Social Science & Medicine*, *61*(12), 2492–2500. doi:10.1016/j.socscimed.2005.05.003 PMID:15953667

Auranen, O., & Nieminen, M. (2010). University research funding and publication performance—An international comparison. *Research Policy*, *39*, 822–834. doi:10.1016/j.respol.2010.03.003

Baggs, J. G., & Schmitt, M. H. (1997). Nurses' and resident physicians' perceptions of the process of collaboration in an MICU. *Research in Nursing & Health*, *20*, 71–80. doi:10.1002/(SICI)1098-240X(199702)20:1<71::AID-NUR8>3.0.CO;2-R PMID:9024479

Baker, D. P., Beaubien, J. M., & Holtzman, A. K. (2003). *Medical team training programs: An independent case study analysis*. Washington, DC: American Institutes for Research.

Baker, D. P., Gustafson, S., Beaubien, J. M., Salas, E., & Barach, P. (2003). *Medical teamwork and patient safety: The evidence-based relation*. Washington, DC: American Institutes for Research.

Baldridge, J. V., Julius, D. J., & Pfeffer, J. (2000). Power failure in administrative environments. *Academic Leadership, 11*(1).

Barksdale, H. C., Johnson, J. T., & Suh, M. (1997). A relationship maintenance model: A comparison between managed health care and traditional-free for service. *Serv. Journal of Business Research*, *40*, 237–247. doi:10.1016/S0148-2963(96)00240-8

Barone, C., & Ortiz, L. (2010). *Over-education among European university graduates* (DEMO-SOC Working Paper 2010/33). Departament of Political Science & Sociology, University of Pompeu Fabra.

Bartell, M. (2003). Internationalization of universities: A university culture-based framework. *Higher Education*, *45*, 43–70. doi:10.1023/A:1021225514599

Bass, B. M. (1985). *Leadership and performance beyond expectations*. New York: Free Press.

Bass, B. M., & Avolio, B. J. (1994). *Improving organizational effectiveness through transformational leadership*. Newbury Park, CA: Sage.

Bate, P. (1984). The impact of organisational culture on approaches to organisational problem solving. *Organization Studies*, 5.

Baumol, W. J., & William, G. B. (1966). *Performing arts: The economic dilemma*. New York: The Twentieth Century Fund.

Bausinger, H. (1983). Sensless identity. In *Identity: Personal and socio-cultural: A symposium*. Łódź: Wydawnictwo Uniwersytetu Łódzkiego.

Becher, T., & Trowler, P. (2001). *Academic tribes and territories*. Buckingham, UK: Open University Press.

Belbin, M. (1985). *Management teams: Why they succeed or fail*. London: Heinemann.

Berger, B. (2009, March 4). *Internal organizational communication*. Retrieved from http//www.pr-romania.ro/articole/comunicare-interna/142-comunicarea-organizationala-interna.html?start=4

Biggs, J. (2003). *Teaching for quality learning in higher education* (2nd ed.). Open University Press.

Birnbaum, R. (1988). *How colleges work: The cybernetics of academic organization and leadership*. San Francisco, CA: Jossey-Bass.

Bishop, P. B., & Wing, P. C. (2006). Knowledge transfer in family physicians managing patients with acute low back pain: A prospective randomized control trial. *The Spine Journal*, *6*(3), 282–288. doi:10.1016/j.spinee.2005.10.008 PMID:16651222

Blau, P. M. (1974). *On the nature of organizations*. New York: John Wiley & Sons.

Bogalska-Martin, E. (2007). Wprowadzenie do teorii kulturowych uwarunkowań rozwoju gospodarczego. In R. Piasecki (Ed.), *Ekonomia rozwoju*. Warszawa: PWE.

Bontin-Foster, C., Foster, J. C., & Konopasek, L. (2008). Physician, know thyself: The professional culture of medicine as a framework for teaching cultural competence. *Academic Medicine*, *83*(1), 106–111. doi:10.1097/ACM.0b013e31815c6753 PMID:18162762

Bornstein, D. (2011). A way to pay for college, with dividends. *New York Times Opininator.* Retrieved from http://opinionator.blogs.nytimes.com/2011/06/02/a-way-to-pay-for-college-with-dividends

Bossuyt, P., & Kortenray, J. (Eds.). (2001). *Evidence-based medicine in practice*. Amsterdam: Uitgeverij Boom.

Bosua, R., & Scheepers, R. (2007). Towards a model to explain knowledge sharing in complex organizational environments. *Knowledge Management Research and Practice*, *5*(2), 93–109. doi:10.1057/palgrave.kmrp.8500131

Bourdieu, P., & Johnson, R. (1993). *The field of cultural production: Essays on art and literature*. New York: Columbia University Press.

Boyd, T. (2007, June 12). *Basic elements of internal communication.* Retrieved from http://www.pr-romania.ro/articole/comunicare-interna/45-elemente-de-baza-in-comunicarea-interna.html

Boyer, L., Francois, P., Doutre, E., Weil, G., & Labarere, J. (2006). Perception and use of the result of patient satisfaction surveys by care providers in a French teaching hospital. *International Journal for Quality in Health Care*, *18*(5), 356–364. doi:10.1093/intqhc/mzl029

Bratianu, C. (2010). A critical analysis of the Nonaka's model of knowledge dynamics. In *Proceedings of the 2nd European Conference on Intellectual Capital*. Lisbon, Portugal: ISCTE Lisbon University Institute.

Bratianu, C., & Andriessen, D. (2008). Knowledge as energy: A metaphorical analysis. In *Proceedings of the 9th European Conference on Knowledge Management*, (pp.75-82). Reading, MA: Academic Publishing.

Bratianu, C., & Orzea, I. (2010). Tacit knowledge sharing in organizational knowledge dynamics. In *Proceedings of the 2nd European Conference on Intellectual Capital*, (pp. 107-114). Reading, MA: Academic Publishing.

Brătianu, C., Jianu, I., & Vasilache, S. (2007). Integratori pentru capitalul intelectual al unei organizaţii (I). *Revista de Management şi Inginerie Economică*, *6* (2), 11-23.

Bratianu, C. (2009). The frontier of linearity in the intellectual capital metaphor. *Electronic Journal of Knowledge Management*, *7*(4), 415–424.

Bratianu, C., Jianu, I., & Vasilache, S. (2011). Integrators for organizational intellectual capital. *International Journal of Learning and Intellectual Capital*, *8*(1), 5–17. doi:10.1504/IJLIC.2011.037355

Bratianu, C., & Vasilache, S. (2008). *Drafting, editing and delivering undergraduate and master's work*. Bucharest, Romania: Bucharest University Publishing House.

Bratianu, C., & Vasilache, S. (2012). Knowledge transfer in medical education from a teamwork perspective. *Management & Marketing*, *7*(3), 381–392.

Bratnicki, M., Kryś, R., & Stachowicz, J. (1988). *Kultura organizacyjna przedsiębiorstw: Studium kształtowania procesu zmian zarządzania.* Wrocław: Ossolineum, PAN.

Brilman, J. (2002). *Nowoczesne koncepcje i metody zarządzania.* Warszawa: PWE.

Brittan, A. (1977). *The privatized world.* London: Routledge and Kegan Paul.

Brown, A. D. (1997). Narcissism, identity and legitymacy. *Academy of Management Review, 22.*

Bruke-Miller, J. K., Cook, I. A., Cohen, M. H., Hessol, N. A., Wilson, T. E., & Richardson, L. et al. (2006). Longitudinal relationship between use of highly active antiretroviral therapy and satisfaction with care among women living with HIV/AIDS. *American Journal of Public Health, 96*(6), 1044–1051. doi:10.2105/AJPH.2005.061929 PMID:16670232

Brunsson, N., & Sahlin-Andersson, K. (2000). Constructing organizations: The example of public sector reform. *Organization Studies, 21*(4), 721–746. doi:10.1177/0170840600214003

Building Capacities of East-Central Europe National Agencies to Promote Higher Education outside the EU: Project Overview. (2008), Retrieved from http://www.highereducationpromotion.eu/web/overview.html

Burford, B. (2012). Group processes in medical education: Learning from social identity theory. *Medical Education, 46,* 143–152. doi:10.1111/j.1365-2923.2011.04099.x PMID:22239328

Burke, P. (2009). *Identity theory.* New York: Academic Press. doi:10.1093/acprof:oso/9780195388275.001.0001

Burns, A. C. (2006). *Marketing research* (5th ed.). Upper Saddle River, NJ: Pearson Publishing House.

Burns, C. (2005). *Leadership.* University of Strathclyde.

Burroughs, T. E., Waterman, A. R., Cira, J., & Dunagan, W. C. (1999). Understanding patient willingness to recommend and return: A strategy for prioritizing improvement opportunities. *Joint Commission of Quality Improvement, 25*(6), 271–287. PMID:10367265

Cătoiu, I. (2004). *Consumer behavior* (2nd ed.). Bucharest, Romania: Uranius Publishing House.

Cheney, G., & Christensen, L. T. (2004). Organisational identity: Linkages between internal and external communication. In M. J. Hatch, & M. Schultz (Eds.), *Organisational identity: A reader.* Oxford, UK: Oxford University Press.

Chet, K., & McCluskey, P. (2004). Public versus private patient priorities and satisfaction in cataract surgery. *Clinical & Experimental Ophthalmology, 32,* 482. doi:10.1111/j.1442-9071.2004.00868.x PMID:15498059

Choi, T. Y., & Behling, O. C. (1997). Top managers and TQM success: One more look after all these years. *The Academy of Management Executive, 11*(1), 37–47.

Clark, B. R. (1998). Creating entrepreneurial universities: Organizational pathways of transformation. *Higher Education, 38*(3), 373–374.

Clegg, S., & Steel, J. (2002). The emperor's new clothes: Globalisation and e-learning. *British Journal of Sociology of Education, 24*(1), 39–53. doi:10.1080/01425690301914

CMU. (n.d.). Retrieved from www.cmu.ro

Code de la Sante Publique. (1996). Ordonance no 96 – 346 du 24 avril 1996 portant reforme de l'hospitalization publique et privee. *Journal Officiele de la Republique Francaise,* 6324-6336.

Cohen, A. M. (Ed.). (1973). *Toward a professional faculty.* San Francisco: Jossey-Bass.

Connerley, M. L., & Pedersen, P. (2005). *Leadership in a diverse and multicultural environment: Developing awareness, knowledge, and skills.* Thousand Oaks, CA: Sage Publications.

Cooke, R. A., & Rousseau, D. M. (1988). Behavioral norms and expectations: A quantitative approach to the assessment of organizational culture. *Group & Organization Studies*, *13*(3), 245–273. doi:10.1177/105960118801300302

Council of Europe. (n.d.). *European convention for the prevention of torture and inhuman or degrading treatment or punishment*. Brussels: Council of Europe.

Cunningham, L. (1991). *The quality connection in health care: Integrating patient satisfaction and risk management*. San Francisco, CA: Jossey-Bass.

Curran, V. R., Sharpe, D., & Forristall, J. (2007). Attitudes of health sciences faculty members towards interprofessional teamwork and education. *Medical Education*, *41*, 892–896. doi:10.1111/j.1365-2923.2007.02823.x PMID:17696982

Czarniawska-Joerges, B. (2004). Narratives of individual and organisational identities. In M. J. Hatch, & M. Schultz (Eds.), *Organisational identity: A reader*. Oxford, UK: Oxford University Press.

Daaleman, T. P., & Mueller, J. (2004). Chatting behavior and patient satisfaction in the outpatient encounter. *Journal of the National Medical Association*, *96*(5), 666–670. PMID:15160982

Dall'Alba, G. (1991). Foreshadowing conceptions of teaching. *Research and Development in Higher Education, 13*.

Davies, J. L. (2001). The emergence of entrepreneurial cultures in European universities. *Higher Education Management*, *12*, 25–43.

Dawes, P., & Davison, P. (1994). Informed consent: What do patients want to know? *Journal of the Royal Society of Medicine*, *87*, 149–152. PMID:8158593

de Rudder, H. (2010). Mission accomplished? Which mission? The Bologna process – A view from Germany. *Higher Education*, *43*(1), 3–20.

de Wit, B., & Meyer, R. (2007). *Synteza strategii*. Warszawa: PWE.

De Wit, H. (2010). *Internationalization of higher education in Europe and its assessment, trends and issues*. Den Haag, The Netherlands: Academic Press.

Deal, T. E., & Kennedy, A. A. (1982). *Corporate cultures: The rites and rituals of corporate life*. Boston. Cambridge: Perseus Publishing.

Del Rey, E., & Recionero, M. (2010). Financing schemes for higher education. *European Journal of Political Economy*, *26*, 104–113. doi:10.1016/j.ejpoleco.2009.09.002

Deshapande, R., & Parasurman, R. (1987). Linking corporate culture to strategie planning. *Organizacja i Kierownictwo, 6*.

D'Este, P., & Patel, P. (2007). University-industry linkages in the UK: What are the factors determining the variety of interactions with industry? *Research Policy*, *36*(9), 1295–1313. doi:10.1016/j.respol.2007.05.002

Dewey, J. (1933). *How we think: A restatement of the relation of reflective thinking to the educative process*. San Francisco: New Lexington Press.

Dima, A., & Agoston, S. (2011). Internationalization of universities, reflections on the past and future perspectives. In *Proceedings of the 6th International Conference Business Excellence*, (vol. 1, pp. 177-182). Academic Press.

Dixon, M. (2006). Globalisation and international higher education: Contested positioning. *Journal of Studies in International Education*, *10*(4), 319–333. doi:10.1177/1028315306287789

Dobrzyński, M. (1977). Klimat organizacyjny jako wyznacznik stylu zarządzania. *Przegląd Organizacji*, *1*, 54–64.

Dodds, E. R. (1951). *The Greeks and the irrational*. Berkeley, CA: University of California Press.

Dutton, J., & Dukerich, J. (1991). Keeping eye on the mirror: Image and identity in organisational adaptation. *Academy of Management Journal*, *34*, 517–554. doi:10.2307/256405

Educaţiei, M. Cercetării, Tineretului şi Sportului. (2011). *Metodologia de scolarizare a cetăţenilor de origine etnică română din Republica Moldova, din alte state învecinate şi a etnicilor români cu domiciliul stabil în străinătate în învăţământul din România, în anul şcolar/universitar 2011 – 2012.* Retrieved from http://www.edu.ro/index.php/articles/proiecte_acte_norm/15217

Elder, M. J., & Suter, A. (2004). What patients want to know before they have cataract surgery. *The British Journal of Ophthalmology, 88,* 331–332. doi:10.1136/bjo/2003.020453 PMID:14977762

Enders, J. (2004). Higher education, internationalization, and the nation-state: Recent developments and challenges to governance theory. *Higher Education, 47,* 361–382. doi:10.1023/B:HIGH.0000016461.98676.30

Entwistle, N. J. (1976). The verb 'to learn' takes the accusative. *The British Journal of Educational Psychology.*

Estermann, T., & Pruvot, B. E. (2011). *Financially sustainable universities II – European universities diversifying income streams.* EUA Publications. Retrieved from http://www.eua.be/Pubs/Financially_Sustainable_Universities_II.pdf

Etzioni, A. E. (1964). *Modern organization.* Academic Press.

European Commission. (2001). *Abschlussbericht der kommission uber die umsetzung des programms sokrates 1995-1999.* Retrieved from http://ec.europa.eu/dgs/education_culture/evalreports/education/2001/sociexpost/soc1xp-COM_de.pdf

European Commission. (2012). *ERASMUS statistics Romania.* Retrieved from http://ec.europa.eu/education/erasmus/doc/stat/0910/countries/romania_en.pdf

European Commission. (2012). *Outgoing and incoming ERASMUS student mobility for studies in 2009/2010.* Retrieved from http://ec.europa.eu/education/erasmus/doc/stat/0910/students.pdf

European Quality Award (EQA). (1994). *TI Europe excellence.* Retrieved from http://www.ti.com/europe/docs/busex/winner.html

Eurydice. (2007). *Key data on higher education in Europe.* Brussels: Eurydice.

Ferraro, G. (2010). *The cultural dimension of international business.* Upper Saddle River, NJ: Prentice Hall.

Fingleton, B., & López-Bazo, G. (2006). Empirical growth models with spatial effects. *Papers in Regional Science, 85*(2), 177–198. doi:10.1111/j.1435-5957.2006.00074.x

Flin, R., Fletcher, G., & McGeorge, P. et al. (2003). Anaesthetists' attitudes to teamwork and safety. *Anaesthesia, 58,* 233–242. doi:10.1046/j.1365-2044.2003.03039.x PMID:12603453

Flin, R., & Maran, N. (2004). Identifying and training non-technical skills for teams in acute medicine. *Quality & Safety in Health Care, 13*(Suppl. 1), i80–i84. doi:10.1136/qshc.2004.009993 PMID:15465960

Florea, S., & Wells, P. J. (2012). *Higher education in Romania.* Bucharest, Romania: Cepes.

Forest, J. F. J. (2002). *Higher education in the United States: an encyclopedia.* ABC-CLIO Publishers.

Foss, N. J. (1997). *Resources, firms and strategy: A reader in the resource-based perspective.* Oxford, UK: Oxford University Press.

Francken, D. A., & Van Raaij, W. F. (1981). Satisfaction with leisure time activities. *Journal of Leisure Research, 13,* 337–352.

François, F. (1980). Identité et hétérogénite de l'espase discursif. In P. Tap (Ed.), *Identités collectives et changements sociaux.* Toulouse: Privat.

Friesner, D., Neufelder, D., Raisor, J., & Bozman, S. C. (2009). How to improve patient satisfaction when patients are already satisfied: A continuous process-improvement approach. *Hospital Topics, 87*(1), 24–40. doi:10.3200/HTPS.87.1.24-40 PMID:19103585

Frolich, N., Schmidt, E. K., & Rosa, M. J. (2010). Funding systems for higher education and their impacts on institutional strategies and academia. *International Journal of Educational Management*, *24*(1), 7–21. doi:10.1108/09513541011013015

Frost, P. J., Moore, L. F., & Louis, M. R. (1991). *Reframing organizational culture*. Thousand Oaks, CA: Sage.

Fukuyama, F. (2001). Culture and economic development. In N. J. Smesler, & P. B. Baltes (Eds.), *International encyclopedia of the social and behavioral sciences*. Oxford: Pergamon. doi:10.1016/B0-08-043076-7/04584-8

Gaba, D. M., Howard, S. K., Fish, K. J., Smith, B. E., & Sowb, Y. A. (2001). Simulation-based training in anesthesia crisis resource management (ACRM): A decade of experience. *Simulation & Gaming*, *32*, 175–193. doi:10.1177/104687810103200206

Gaba, D. M., Howard, S. K., Flanagan, B., Smith, B. E., Fish, K. J., & Botney, R. (1998). Assessment of clinical performance during simulated crises using both technical and behavioral ratings. *Anesthesiology*, *89*, 8–18. doi:10.1097/00000542-199807000-00005 PMID:9667288

Garden, A. L., Merry, A. F., Holland, R. L., & Petrie, K. J. (1996). Anaesthesia information – What patients want to know about anaesthesia. *Anaesthesia and Intensive Care*, *24*, 594–598. PMID:8909673

Gauthier, N., Ellis, K., Bol, N., & Stolee, P. (2005). Beyond knowledge transfer: A model of knowledge integration in a clinical setting. *Healthcare Management Forum*, *18*(4), 33. doi:10.1016/S0840-4704(10)60067-1 PMID:16509279

Gay, C., Mahoney, M., & Graves, J. (2005). *Best practices of employee communication*. San Francisco: International Association of Business Communicators Publishing House.

Geertz, C. (1973). *The interpretation of cultures*. New York: Basic Books.

Geisler, E., & Wickramasinghe, N. (2009). *Principles of knowledge management: Theory, practice, and cases*. New York: M.E.Sharpe.

Geneva Convention. (1949, August 12). *Convention (III) relative to the treatment of prisoners of war*. Geneva, Switzerland: Geneva Convention.

Gherghina, R., Nicolae, F., & Mocanu, M. (2010). Comparative research on the correlation of the quantum to public funding for the public institutions of higher education and the institution's performance within the European Union member states. *Management & Marketing Challenges for Knowledge Society*, *5*(3), 103–118.

Gillespie, B. M., Chabover, W., Longbottom, P., & Wallis, M. (2010). The impact of organizational and individual factors on team communication in surgery: A qualitative study.[PubMed doi:10.1016/j.ijnurstu.2009.11.001]. *International Journal of Nursing Studies*, *47*(6), 732–741.

Gioia, D. A., Schultz, M., & Corley, K. (2004). Organisational Identity, image and adaptive instability. In M. J. Hatch, & M. Schultz (Eds.), *Organisational identity: A reader*. Oxford, UK: Oxford University Press.

Goffee, R., & Jones, G. (1996, November-December). What holds the modern company together? *Harvard Business Review*.

Goffee, R., & Jones, G. (1998). *The character of a corporation*. New York: Harper Collins Publishers.

Goffman, E. (1981). *Człowiek w teatrze życia codziennego*. Warszawa: PIW.

Gupta, K. S. (2008). A comparative analysis of knowledge sharing climate. *Knowledge and Process Management*, *15*(3), 186–195. doi:10.1002/kpm.309

Hagopian, A., Thompson, M. J., Fordyce, M., Johnson, K. E., & Hart, L. G. (2004). The migration of physicians from sub-Saharan Africa to the United States of America: Measures of the African brain drain. *Human Resources for Health*, *2*, 2–17. doi:10.1186/1478-4491-2-17 PMID:15078577

Hall, E. T. (1984). *Poza kulturą*. Warszawa: PWN.

Hampden-Turner, C., & Trompenaars, A. (1998). *Siedem kultur kapitalizmu: USA, Japonia, Niemcy, Wielka Brytania, Szwecja, Holandia*. Warsaw: Dom Wydawniczy ABC.

Handy, C. (1995). *Gods of management: The changing work of organizations*. Academic Press.

Handy, C. (2007). *The reading literacy of U.S. fourth-grade students in an international context: Results From the 2001 and 2006 progress in international reading literacy study (PIRLS)*. Academic Press.

Hanson, L. (2010). Global citizenship, global health, and the internationalization of curriculum: A study of transformative potential. *Journal of Studies in International Education, 14*(1), 70–88. doi:10.1177/1028315308323207

Harrison, R. (1972). Understanding your organization's character. *Harvard Business Review, 5*(3), 119–128.

Harvard Business Essentials. (2005). *Time management*. Cambridge, MA: Harvard Business School Publishing Corporations.

Hatch, M. J. (2002). *Teoria organizacji*. Warszawa: PWN.

Hatch, M. J., & Schultz, M. S. (2000). Scaling the tower of Babel: Relational differences between identity, image and culture in organizations. In M. S. Schultz, M. J. Hatch, & M. H. Larsen (Eds.), *The expressive organisation: Linking identity, reputation and the corporate brand*. Oxford, UK: Oxford University Press.

Hatch, M. J., & Schultz, M. S. (2004). The dynamics of organisational identity. In M. J. Hatch, & M. Schultz (Eds.), *Organisational identity: A reader*. Oxford, UK: Oxford University Press.

Healey, A. N., Undre, S., & Vincent, C. A. (2004). Developing observational measures of performance in surgical teams. *Quality & Safety in Health Care, 13*, i33–i40. doi:10.1136/qshc.2004.009936 PMID:15465953

Hemphill, J. K., & Coons, A. E. (1957). Development of the leader behavior description questionnaire. In *Leader behavior: Its description and measurement*. Columbus, OH: Bureau of Business Research of The Ohio State University.

Hicks, D. (2012). Performance-based university research funding systems. *Research Policy, 41*, 251–261. doi:10.1016/j.respol.2011.09.007

Hofstede, G. (1984). *Culture's consequences*. Beverly Hills, CA: Sage Publications.

Hofstede, G., & Hofstede, G. J. (2007). *Kultury i organizacje*. Warszawa: PWE.

Holzman, R. S., Cooper, J. B., Gaba, D. M., Philip, J. H., Small, S. D., & Feinstein, D. (1995). Anesthesia crisis resource management: Real-life simulation training in operating room crises. *Journal of Clinical Anesthesia, 7*, 675–687. doi:10.1016/0952-8180(95)00146-8 PMID:8747567

Hoppers, C. (2009). Education, culture and society in a globalizing world: Implications for comparative and international education. *Compare: A Journal of Comparative Education, 39*(5), 601–614. doi:10.1080/03057920903125628

Horner, M. (1997). Leadership theory: Past, present and future. *Team Performance Management, 3*(4), 270–287. doi:10.1108/13527599710195402

House, R. J., Hanges, P. J., & Javidan, M. et al. (2004). *Culture, leadership, and organizations: The GLOBE study of 62 societies*. Thousand Oaks, CA: Sage.

House, R. J., Hanges, P., & Ruiz-Quintanilla, A. (1997). GLOBE: The global leadership and organizational behavior: Effectiveness: Research program. *Polish Psychological Bulletin, 28*(3), 215–254.

House, R. J., Javidan, M., & Hanges, P. et al. (2002). Understanding cultures and implicit leadership theories across the globe: An introduction to project GLOBE. *Journal of World Business, 37*(1), 3. doi:10.1016/S1090-9516(01)00069-4

Howard, S. K., Gaba, D. M., Fish, K. J., Yang, G., & Sarnquist, F. H. (1992). Anesthesia crisis resource management training: Teaching anesthesiologists to handle critical incidents. *Aviation, Space, and Environmental Medicine, 63*, 763–770. PMID:1524531

Huggins, R., & Izushi, H. (2008). *UK competitiveness index 2008*. Centre for International.

Hunter, M. (2005). *Guide to managerial communication*. Upper Saddle River, NJ: Prentice Hall.

Ichijo, K., & Nonaka, I. (2007). *Knowledge creation and management: New challenges for managers*. Oxford, UK: Oxford University Press.

Informationszentrum Bukarest, D. A. A. D. (2010). *Deutschsprachige studiengänge an hochschulen in Rumänien*. Bucharest, Romania: DAAD.

Inglehart, R. (1997). *Modernization and postmodernization: Cultutal, economic and political change in 43 societies*. Princeton, NJ: Princeton University Press.

Isern, J., & Pung, C. (2007). Driving radical change. *The McKinsey Quarterly, 4*(24).

Jacques, E. (1952). *The changing culture of a factory*. New York: Fryden Press.

Jansen, L. (2008). Collaborative and interdisciplinary health care teams: Ready or not? *Journal of Professional Nursing, 24*(4), 218–227. doi:10.1016/j.profnurs.2007.06.013 PMID:18662657

Jenkins, R. (1996). *Social identity*. London: Routledge.

Johnson, M. (2011). *The diversity code*. AMA Printer House.

Johnstone, D. B. (2009). An international perspective on the financial fragility of higher education institutions and systems. In *Turnaround: Leading stressed colleges and universities to excellence*. Baltimore: The Johns Hopkins University Press.

Jongbloed, B. (2008). *Funding higher education: A view from Europe*. Paper presented at the seminar Funding Higher Education: A Comparative Overview. Retrieved from http://www.utwente.nl/mb/cheps/summer_school/Literature/Brazil%20funding%20vs2.pdf

Kain, Z. N., Wang, S. M., Caramico, L. A., Hofstadter, M., & Mayes, L. C. (1997). Parental desire for perioperative information and informed consent: A two-phase study. *Anesthesia and Analgesia, 84*, 299–306. PMID:9024018

Kaiser, F., Vossensteyn, H., & Koelman, J. (2001). *Public funding of higher education: A comparative study of funding mechanisms in ten countries*. Enschede, The Netherlands: Center for Higher Education Policy Studies.

Kalisch, B. J., & Begeny, S. (2005). *Improving patient care in hospitals, creating team behavior*. Organizational Engineering Institute. Retrieved from http://www.oeinstitute.org/articles/improving-patient-care.html

Kanji, G. K. (1998). Measurement of business excellence. *Total Quality Management, 9*, 633–643. doi:10.1080/0954412988325

Kaplan, R. S., & Norton, D. P. (1996, January-February). Using the balance scorecard as a strategic management system. *Harvard Business Review*, , 11.

Kehm, B., & Teichler, U. (2007). Research on internationalization in higher education. *Journal of Studies in International Education, 11*(4), 260–273. doi:10.1177/1028315307303534

Kember, D. (1997). A reconceptualisation of the research into university academics' conceptions of teaching. *Learning and Instruction, 7*, 255–275. doi:10.1016/S0959-4752(96)00028-X

Kember, D., & Gow, L. (1994). Orientations to teaching and their effect on the quality of student learning. *The Journal of Higher Education, 65*.

Kember, D., & Kelly, M. (1993). *Improving teaching through action research (HERDSA Green Guide No 14)*. Jamison, ACT: HERDSA.

Kember, D., & Kwan, K. P. (2002). *Lecturers' approaches to teaching and their relation to conceptions of good teaching*. Academic Press.

Kember, D., & McKay, J. (1996). Action research into the quality of student learning: A paradigm for faculty development. *The Journal of Higher Education*, 65.

Kerner, J. F. (2006). Knowledge translation versus knowledge integration: A funder's perspective. *The Journal of Continuing Education in the Health Professions*, 26, 72–80. doi:10.1002/chp.53 PMID:16557513

Klingle, R. S., Burgoon, M., Afifi, W., & Callister, M. (1995). Rethinking how to measure organizational culture in the hospital setting. *Evaluation & the Health Professions*, 18(2), 166–186. doi:10.1177/016327879501800205 PMID:10143010

Knight, J. (1999). *Internationalization of higher education in OECD, quality and internationalization in higher education*. Paris: OECD.

Knight, J. (2004). Internationalization remodeled: Definition, approaches, and rationales. *Journal of Studies in International Education*, 8(1), 5–31. doi:10.1177/1028315303260832

Knight, J. (2008). *Higher education in turmoil: The changing world of internationalization*. Rotterdam, The Netherlands: Sense Publishers.

Knox, G. E., & Simpson, K. R. (2004). Teamwork: The fundamental building block of high-reliability organizations and patient safety. In *Patient safety handbook*. Boston: Jones and Bartlett.

Kobi, J.-M., & Wüthrich, H. (1991). *Culture d'entreprise: Modes d'action: Diagnostic et intervention*. Paris: Nathan.

Kohn, L. T., Corrigan, J. M., & Donaldson, M. S. (1999). *To err is human*. Washington, DC: National Academy Press.

Konecki, K. (1999). Transformacja tożsamości organizacyjnej. *Master of Business Administration, 4.*

Korka, M. (2009). *Bologna process: Report Romania 2008*. Retrieved from http://bologna.ro/a/upfolders/National_Report_Romania_2009.pdf

Kostera, M. (1996). *Postmodernizm w zarządzaniu*. Warszawa: PWE.

Kotler, P., Roberto, N., & Lee, N. (2002). *Social marketing: Improving the quality of life*. Thousand Oaks, CA: Sage.

Kroeber, A. L., & Kluckhon, C. (1952). Culture: A critical review of concepts and definitions. *Peabode Museum of American Antropology and Ethnology Papers*, 47(1).

Krücken, G. (2006). Innovationsmythen in Politik und Gesselschaft. In *Kluges entscheiden: Disziplinäre grundlagen und interdisziplinäre verknüpfungen*. Tübingen: Mohr Siebeck.

Kugel, P. (1993). How professors develop as teachers. *Studies in Higher Education*, 18.

Kunda, G. (1992). *Engineering culture: Control and commitment in a high-tech corporation*. Philadelphia: Temple University Press.

Kwiek, M. (2006). *Academic entrepreneurship and private education in Europe*. Retrieved from www.cpp.amu.edu.pl/pdf/Kwiek_Entrepreneurialism_PHE.pdf

Kwiek, M. (2006). The European integration of higher education and the role of private higher education. In S. Slantcheva, & D. C. Levy (Eds.), *Private higher education in post-communist Europe: In search of legitimacy*. New York: Palgrave.

Kyndt, E., Dochy, F., & Nijs, H. (2009). Learning conditions for non-formal and informal workplace learning. *Journal of Workplace Learning*, 21(5), 369–383. doi:10.1108/13665620910966785

Labarere, J., & Francois, P. (1999). Evaluation de la satisfaction des patients par les etablissements de soins: Revue de la literature. *Revue d'Epidemiologie et de Sante Publique*, 47, 175–184. PMID:10367304

Labrere, J., Francois, P., & Auquier, P. et al. (2001). Development of a French impatient satisfaction questionnaire. *International Journal for Quality in Health Care*, *13*, 99–108. doi:10.1093/intqhc/13.2.99 PMID:11430670

Landes, D. S. (2000). *Bogactwo i nędza narodów: Dlaczego jedni są tak bogaci, a inni tak ubodzy*. Warsaw: Muza.

Landry, R., Saihi, M., Amara, N., & Ouimet, M. (2010). Evidence on how academics manage their portfolio of knowledge transfer activities. *Research Policy*, *39*(10), 1387–1403. doi:10.1016/j.respol.2010.08.003

Lasch, K. (2011). *Teorii ale identitatii, natiunii si ale nationalismului. Referat stiintific in cadrul cercetarii doctorale Problema identitatii nationale a moldovenilor din Basarabia la inceputul secolului al XX-lea*. Universitatea Babes-Bolyai, Cluj Napoca.

Lee, K. J. (2005). A practical method of predicting client revisit intention in a hospital setting. *Health Care Management Review*, *31*(3), 157–167. doi:10.1097/00004010-200504000-00009 PMID:15923917

Legare, F., Ratte, S., Gravel, K., & Graham, I. D. (2008). Barriers and facilitators to implementing shared decision-making in clinical practice: Update of a systematic review of health professionals' perceptions. *Patient Education and Counseling*, *73*(3), 526–535. doi:10.1016/j.pec.2008.07.018 PMID:18752915

Lencioni, P. (2002). *The five dysfunctions of a team*. San Francisco: Jossey-Bass.

Leonard, M., Graham, S., & Bonacum, D. (2004). The human factor: The critical importance of effective teamwork and communication in providing safe care. *Quality & Safety in Health Care*, *13*(Suppl. 1), i85–i90. doi:10.1136/qshc.2004.010033 PMID:15465961

Leuthesser, L., & Kohli, C. (1997). Corporate identity: The role of mission statements. *Business Horizons*. doi:10.1016/S0007-6813(97)90053-7

Levine, A. S., Plume, S. K., & Nelson, E. C. (1997). Transforming patient feedback into strategic actions plan. *Quality Management Care*, *5*, 28–40.

Levy, D. (2006). Private-public interfaces in higher education development: Two sectors in sync? In *Proceedings of the 2007 World Bank Regional Seminar on Development Economics*. Retrieved from siteresources.worldbank.org/INTABCDE-2007BEI/Resources/DanielLevy.PDF

Lewis, D. R. (2006). *When cultures collide*. WS. Bookwell Printing House.

Libaert, T. (2009). *The communication plan* (3rd ed.). Bucharest, Romania: Polirom Publishing House.

Lin, C., Tan, B., & Chang, S. (2008). An exploratory model of knowledge flow barriers within healthcare organizations. *Information & Management*, *45*(5), 331–339. doi:10.1016/j.im.2008.03.003

Lingard, L., Regehr, G., & Orser, B. et al. (2008). Evaluation of a preoperative checklist and team briefing among surgeons, nurses, and anesthesiologists to reduce failures in communication. *Archives of Surgery (Chicago, Ill.)*, *143*, 12–17. doi:10.1001/archsurg.2007.21 PMID:18209148

Liveng, A. (2010). Learning and recognition in health and care work: An inter-subjective perspective. *Journal of Workplace Learning*, *22*(1/2), 41–52. doi:10.1108/13665621011012843

Lonsdale, N., & Hutchison, G. L. (1991). Patients' desire for information about anaesthesia. *Anaesthesia*, *46*, 410–412. doi:10.1111/j.1365-2044.1991.tb09560.x PMID:2035796

Lukes, S. (1973). *Individualism*. Oxford, UK: Oxford University Press.

Lunn, J. (2008). Global perspectives in higher education: Taking the agenda forward in the United Kingdom. *Journal of Studies in International Education*, *12*(3), 231–254. doi:10.1177/1028315307308332

Lyotard, J.-F. (2004). Anamnesis: Of the visible. *Theory, Culture & Society*, *21*(1), 107–119. doi:10.1177/0263276404040483

Macdonald, M. (2003). Knowledge management in healthcare: What does it involve? How is it measured? *Healthcare Management Forum*, *16*(3), 7–11. doi:10.1016/S0840-4704(10)60225-6 PMID:14618826

Mahrous, A., & Ahmed, A. (2010). A cross-cultural investigation of students' perceptions of the effectiveness of pedagogical tools the Middle East, the United Kingdom, and the United States. *Journal of Studies in International Education*, *14*(3), 289–386. doi:10.1177/1028315309334738

Makary, M. A., Sexton, J. B., & Freischlag, J. A. et al. (2006). Operating room teamwork among physicians and nurses: Teamwork in the eye of the beholder. *Journal of the American College of Surgeons*, *202*, 746–752. doi:10.1016/j.jamcollsurg.2006.01.017 PMID:16648014

Malcolm Baldrige National Quality Award (MBNQA). (1997). *The Malcolm Baldrige criteria for performance excellence*. Author.

Malhotra, N. K. (2007). *Marketing research: An applied orientation* (5th ed.). Upper Saddle River, NJ: Pearson Publishing House.

Mandruleanu, A., & Ivanovici, M. (2008). Knowledge management implications. *Management & Marketing*, *3*(2), 105–116.

Marginson, S., & van der Wende, M. (2009). The new global landscape of nations and institutions. In Higher education to 2030, vol. 2: Globalisation. Paris: OECD.

Maringe, F., Foskett, N., & Roberts, D. (2009). I can survive on jam sandwiches for the next three year: The impact of the new fees regime on students' attitudes to HE and debt. *International Journal of Educational Management*, *23*(2), 145–160. doi:10.1108/09513540910933503

Martin, E., & Balla, M. (1991). Conceptions of teaching and implications for learning. *Research and Development in Higher Education, 13*.

Martin, E., Prosser, M., Trigwell, K., Ramsden, P., & Benjamin, J. (2000). What university teachers teach and how they teach it. *Instructional Science*, 28.

Martin, G. P., & Learmonth, M. (2012). A critical account of the rise and spread of 'leadership': The case of UK healthcare. *Social Science & Medicine*, *74*(3), 281–288. doi:10.1016/j.socscimed.2010.12.002 PMID:21247682

Martin, J. (2002). *Organizational culture: Mapping the terrain*. London: Sage.

Mayer, R. E. (2010). Applying the science of learning to medical education. *Medical Education*, *44*, 543–549. doi:10.1111/j.1365-2923.2010.03624.x PMID:20604850

Mazzocco, K., Petitti, D. B., & Fong, K. T. et al. (2009). Surgical team behaviors and patient outcomes. *American Journal of Surgery*, *197*, 678–685. doi:10.1016/j.amjsurg.2008.03.002 PMID:18789425

McAlearney, A. S. (2008, September/October). Using leadership development programs to improve quality and efficiency in healthcare. *Journal of Healthcare Management*. PMID:18856137

McDermott, R. P., & Church, J. (1976). Making sense and feeling good: The etnography of communication and identity work. In L. Thyayer (Ed.), *Communication and identity*. Author.

McKenzie, A. (2003). *University of technology, variation and change in teachers' ways of experiencing teaching*. (PhD Dissertation).

Mead, G. H. (1975). *Umysł, osobowość, społeczeństwo*. Warszawa: PWN.

Medcenter . (n.d.). Retrieved from www.medcenter.ro

Mediafax. (n.d.). *Romania private healthcare market seen up 13 this year*. Retrieved from http://www.mediafax.ro/english/romania-private-healthcare-market-seen-up-13-this-year-to-eur420m-report-5767473/

Medicover. (n.d.). Retrieved from www.medicover.ro

Medlife . (n.d.). Retrieved from www.medlife.ro

Mennin, S. (2010). Self-organisation, integration and curriculum in the complex world of medical education. *Medical Education, 44*, 20–30. doi:10.1111/j.1365-2923.2009.03548.x PMID:20078753

Meyer, A. D. (1982). Adapting to environmental jolts. *Administrative Science Quarterly, 27*(4), 515–537. doi:10.2307/2392528 PMID:10257768

Miller, M. R., Elixhauser, A., & Zhan, C. et al. (2001). Patient safety indicators: Using administrative data to identify potential patient-safety concerns. *Health Services Research, 36*, 110–132. PMID:16148964

Miller, R. L., & Cangemi, J. P. (1993). Why total quality management fails: Perspective from top management. *Journal of Management Development, 12*(7), 40–50. doi:10.1108/02621719310044956

Mills, P., Neily, J., & Dunn, E. (2008). Teamwork and communication in surgical teams: Implications for patient safety. *Journal of the American College of Surgeons, 206*, 107–112. doi:10.1016/j.jamcollsurg.2007.06.281 PMID:18155575

Ministerul Afacerilor Externe. (2011). *Burse oferite cetăţenilor străini de statul român prin MAE*. Retrieved from http://www.mae.ro/node/1794

Ministry of European Funds. (2013). *Internal press review of information center of structural instruments*. Bucharest, Romania: Ministry of European Funds Publishing House.

Ministry of European Funds. (2013, May 15). *Projects*. Retrieved from http://b.fonduri-ue.ro/proiecte

Ministry of European Funds. (2013). *Centralization of the present sheets of the event ABC of structural instruments*. Bucharest, Romania: Ministry of European Funds Publishing House.

Mintzberg, H. (1979). *The structuring of organizations: A synthesis of the research*. Englewood Cliffs, NJ: Prentice-Hall.

Mintzberg, H. (1983). *Structures in five: Designing effective organizations*. Englewood Cliffs, NJ: Prentice-Hall.

Minulescu, M. (2004). *Organizational communication*. Retrieved from http://www.slideshare.net/Elida82/comunicare-organizationala-m-minulescu

Miroiu, A., & Aligica, P. D. (2002). *Public higher education financing: A comparison of the historical and formula-based mechanism*. Academic Press.

Mitruţ, C., & Serban, D. (2003). *Statistics for business administration*. Bucharest, Romania: BUES Publishing House.

Mohr, J., Batalden, P., & Barach, P. (2004). The clinical microsystem and patient safety. *Quality & Safety in Health Care, 13*, 34–38. doi:10.1136/qshc.2003.009571 PMID:15576690

Monin, N. (2004). *Management theory: A critical and reflective reading*. London: Routledge. doi:10.4324/9780203356814

Montaglione, C. J. (1999). The physician-patient relationship: Cornerstone of patient trust, satisfaction, and loyalty. *Managed Care Quarterly, 7*(3), 5–21. PMID:10620959

Moorman, C., Zeltman, G., & Deshpande, R. (1992). Relationship between providers and users of marketing research: The dynamic of trust within and between organization. *JMR, Journal of Marketing Research, 29*, 314–329. doi:10.2307/3172742

Morey, J. C., Simon, R., Jay, G. D., Wears, R., Salisbury, M., Dukes, K. A., & Berns, S. D. (2002). Error reduction and performance improvement in the emergency department through formal teamwork training: Evaluation results of the MedTeams project. *Health Services Research, 37*, 1553–1581. doi:10.1111/1475-6773.01104 PMID:12546286

Morgan, L., Doyle, M.E., & Albers, J.A. (2005). Knowledge continuity management in healthcare. *Journal of Knowledge Management Practice, 6.*

Morgan, L. W., & Schwab, I. R. (1986). Informed consent in senile cataract extraction. *Archives of Ophthalmology, 104,* 42–45. doi:10.1001/archopht.1986.01050130052018 PMID:3942543

Mucchielli, A. (2008). *Communication in institutions and organizations.* Bucharest, Romania: Polirom Publishing House.

Naidoo, V. (2009). Transnational higher education: A stock take of current activity. *Journal of Studies in International Education, 13*(3), 310–330. doi:10.1177/1028315308317938

Nawrocka, A. (2008). *Etos w zawodach medycznych.* WAM.

Neave, G. (2002). Anything goes: Or: How the accommodation of Europe's universities to European integration integrates an inspiring number of contradictions. *Tertiary Education and Management, 8*(3), 178–191. doi:10.1080/13583883.2002.9967078

Newton-Howes, P. A., Bedford, N. D., Dobbs, B. R., & Frizelle, F. A. (1998). Informed consent: What do patients want to know? *The New Zealand Medical Journal, 111,* 340–342. PMID:9785548

Nicolescu, L., Pricopie, R., & Popescu, A. (2009). Country differences in the internationalization of higher education – How can countries lagging behind diminish the gap. *Review of International Comparative Management, 10*(5), 976–989.

Niculae, T., & Gherghita, D. I. (2006). *Organizational communication and crisis management.* Bucharest, Romania: Ministry of Administration and Interior Publishing House.

Nisselle, P. (1993). Informed consent. *The New Zealand Medical Journal, 106,* 331–332. PMID:8341472

Nissen, M. E. (2006). *Harnessing knowledge dynamics: Principled organizational knowing & learning.* Hershey, PA: IGI Global.

Nixon, I., Smith, K., Stafford, R., & Camm, S. (2006). *Work-based learning: Illuminating the higher education landscape.* York, UK: Higher Education Academy.

Nonaka, I. (1994). A dynamic theory of organizational knowledge creation. *Organization Science, 5*(1), 14–37. doi:10.1287/orsc.5.1.14

Nonaka, I., & Takeuchi, H. (1995). *The knowledge creating company: How Japanese companies create the dynamics of innovation.* Oxford, UK: Oxford University Press.

NPC. (2000). *Prime minister's quality award: Regulation and application procedure.* Kuala Lumpur: Jabatan Percetakan Negara.

O'Donovan, G. (2006). *The corporate culture handbook: How to plan, implement and measure a successful culture change programme.* Dublin, Ireland: The liffey Press.

O'Reilly, C., Clatman, J., & Caldwell, D. (1991). People and organizational culture: A Q-sort approach to assessing fit. *Academy of Management Journal, 34,* 487–516. doi:10.2307/256404

OECD. (2007). *Education at a glance 2007.* Paris: OECD.

Ouchi, W. (1980). Markets, beaucracies and clans. *Administrative Science Quarterly, 25.*

Ouschan, R., Sweeney, J., & Lester, J. (2006). Customer empowerment and relationship outcomes in healthcare consultations. *European Journal of Marketing, 40*(9/10), 1068–1086. doi:10.1108/03090560610681014

Pattison, S., & Pill, R. (2004). *Values in professional practice: Lessons for health, social care and other professionals.* Oxford, UK: Radcliffe Medical Press.

Pawlowsky, P. (2001). The treatment of organizational learning in management science. In *Handbook of organizational learning & knowledge*. Oxford, UK: Oxford University Press.

Payne, A. (1993). *The essence of services marketing*. Hemel Hempstead, UK: Prentice Hall.

Peel, M. (2005). Human rights and medical ethics. *Journal of the Royal Society of Medicine, 98*, 171–173. doi:10.1258/jrsm.98.4.171 PMID:15805563

Perrow, C. (1967). A framework for comparative organizational analisis. *American Sociological Review, 32*(2). doi:10.2307/2091811

Peters, T. J., & Waterman, R. H. (2000). *Poszukiwanie doskonałości w biznesie*. Warsaw: Medium.

Popescu, D. I. (2010). *Organizational behavior*. Bucharest, Romania: BUES Publishing House.

Porter, M. E. (1981). *Competitive strategy: Techniques for analysing industries and competition*. New York: Free Press.

Porter, M. E., & Teisberg, E. (2007). *Redefining health care: Creating value-based competition on results*. Cambridge, MA: Harvard Business School Publishing.

Power, M. (2000). The audit society - Second thoughts. *International Journal of Auditing, 4*(1), 111–119. doi:10.1111/1099-1123.00306

Pratt, M. G., & Rafaeli, A. (2004). Organizational dress as a symbol of multilayered social identities. In M. J. Hatch, & M. Schultz (Eds.), *Organisational identity: A reader*. Oxford, UK: Oxford University Press.

Prugsamatz, R. (2010). Factors that influence organization learning sustainability in non-profit organizations. *The Learning Organization, 17*(3), 243–267. doi:10.1108/09696471011034937

Prusak, L., & Weiss, L. (2007). Knowledge in organizational settings: how organizations generate, disseminate, and use knowledge for their competitive advantage. In *Knowledge creation and management: New challenges for managers*. Oxford, UK: Oxford University Press.

Quinn, R. E. (1988). *Beyond rational management: Mastering the paradoxes and competing demands of high performance*. San Francisco: Jossey-Bass.

Quinn, R. E., & Rohrbbaug, J. (1983). A spatial model of effectiveness criteria: Towards a competing values approach to organizational analysis. *Management Science, 29*(3). doi:10.1287/mnsc.29.3.363

Rabinowitz, P. (2012). *Promoting internal communication*. Retrieved from http://www.snapcomms.com/solutions/measuring-internal-communications-effectiveness.aspx

Ratto, M., Propper, C., & Burgess, S. (2002). Using financial incentives to promote teamwork in health care. *Journal of Health Services Research & Policy, 7*(2), 69–70. doi:10.1258/1355819021927683 PMID:11934370

Readings, B. (1996). *The university in ruins*. Cambridge, MA: Harvard University Press.

Reddy, M. C., & Jansen, B. J. (2008). A model for understanding collaborative information behavior in context: A study of two healthcare teams. *Information Processing & Management, 44*(1), 256–273. doi:10.1016/j.ipm.2006.12.010

Reichert, S. (2009). *Institutional diversity in European higher education: Tensions and challenges for policy-makers and institutional leaders*. Brussels: EUA.

Roberts, K. H. (1990). Managing high reliability organizations. *California Management Review*, 101–113.

Rodriguez-Tomé, H., & Bariaud, F. (1980). La structure de l'identité à l'adolescence. In P. Tap (Ed.), *Identités collectives et changements sociaux*. Toulouse: Privat.

Rogojanu, A., Hristache, D. A., & Tasnadi, A. (2004). *Institutional communication*. Bucharest, Romania: BUES Publishing House.

Romanian Government. (2007). *National communication strategy for structural instruments of romania 2007-2013*. Bucharest, Romania: Romanian Government Publishing House.

Romanian Government. (2009). *Government decision nr. 51 regarding the structure and function of the ministry of education, research and innovation*. Retrieved from http://www.edu.ro/index.php/articles/12645

Romanian Government. (n.d.). *National strategic reference framework of Romania 2007-2013 (NSRF)*. Bucharest, Romania: Romanian Government Publishing House.

Romaniei, P. (2011). *Legea educatiei nationale (Monitorul Oficial Nr.18/2011)*. Author.

Roos, G., Pike, S., & Fernström, L. (2005). *Managing intellectual capital in practice*. Amsterdam: Elsevier.

Rowe, A. J. (Ed.). (1990). *Strategic management: A methodological approach*. Reading, MA: Addison-Wesley Pub. Co.

Rue, L. W., & Holland, P. G. (1989). *Strategic management. Concepts and experiences*. New York: McGraw-Hill.

Rutka, R., & Czerska, M. (2002). Wpływ kultury organizacyjnej na metody i narzędzia pełnienia ról kierowniczych. In J. Stankiewicz (Ed.), *Nowoczesne zarządzanie przedsiębiorstwem*. Zielona Góra: Redakcja Wydawnictw Matematyczno-Ekonomicznych.

Ryu, H. (2003). *Modeling cyclic interaction: An account of goal-elimination process*. Paper presented at the CHI 2003. Ft. Lauderdale, FL.

Salas, E., Dickinson, T. L., & Converse, S. A. (1992). Toward an understanding of team performance and training. In *Teams: Their training and performance*. Norwood, NJ: Ablex.

Samuelowicz, K., & Bain, J. D. (1992). Conceptions of teaching held by academic teachers. *Higher Education*. doi:10.1007/BF00138620

Samuelowicz, K., & Bain, J. D. (2001). Revisiting academics' beliefs about teaching and learning. *Higher Education*, *41*, 299–325. doi:10.1023/A:1004130031247

Samuelson, P. A. (1954). The pure theory of public expenditure. *The Review of Economics and Statistics*, *36*, 387–389. doi:10.2307/1925895

Sanador. (n.d.). Retrieved from www.sanador.ro

Schein, E. H. (1983). The role of the founder in creating organizational culture. *Organizational Dynamics*, 13–28. doi:10.1016/0090-2616(83)90023-2

Schein, E. H. (1984). Coming to a new awareness of organizational culture. *Sloan Management Review*, 3–16.

Schein, E. H. (1985). How culture forms, develops and changes. In R. H. Kilmann (Ed.), *Gaining control of the corporate culture* (pp. 17–43). Academic Press.

Schein, E. H. (2010). *Organizational culture and leadership: A dynamic view*. San Francisco: Jossey-Bass.

Schenplein, H. (1988). Kultura przedsiębiorstwa i jej rozwój. *Organizacja i Kierowanie, 7/8*.

Schultz, D. I., Stanley, I., Tannenbaum, I., & Lauterborn, R. (1993). *Integrated marketing communication: Putting it together & making it work*. NTC Publishing Group.

Schurr, P. H., & Ozanne, J. L. (1985). Influences on exchange processes: Buyer's preconception of a seller's trustworthiness and bargaining toughness. *The Journal of Consumer Research*, *11*, 939–953. doi:10.1086/209028

Schwartz, S. H. (1994). Are there universal aspects in the structure and contents of human values? *The Journal of Social Issues*, *50*, 19–45. doi:10.1111/j.1540-4560.1994.tb01196.x

Schwartz, S. H. (1996). Value priorities and behavior: Applying a theory of integrated value systems. In *The psychology of values: The Ontario symposium*. Mahwah, NJ: Lawrence Erlbaum Associates.

Schwartz, S. H. (2005). *Human values*. Brussels: European Social Survey Education Net.

Schwartz, S. H. (2005). Robustness and fruitfulness of a theory of universals in individual human values. In *Valores e trabalho*. Brasilia: Editora Universidade de Brasilia.

Scott, J. C. (2006). The mission of the university: Medieval to postmodern transformations. *The Journal of Higher Education, 77*(1), 1–39. doi:10.1353/jhe.2006.0007

Serban, D. (2004). *Statistics for marketing and business administration*. Bucharest, Romania: BUES Publishing House.

Sheffield, J. (2008). Inquiry in health knowledge management. *Journal of Knowledge Management, 12*(4), 160–172. doi:10.1108/13673270810884327

Shortell, S. M., Casalino, L. P., & Fisher, E. S. (2010, July). How the center for medicare and medicaid innovation should test accountable care organizations. *Health Affairs*. doi:10.1377/hlthaff.2010.0453 PMID:20606176

Sikorski, C. (1999). *Zachowania ludzi w organizacji: Społeczno-kulturowe skutki zachowań*. Warszawa: PWN.

Sikorski, C. (2002). *Kultura organizacyjna*. Warszawa: C.H. Beck.

Sitzia, J., & Wood, N. (1997). Patient satisfaction: A review of issues and concepts. *Social Science & Medicine, 45*(12), 1828–1843. doi:10.1016/S0277-9536(97)00128-7 PMID:9447632

Smircich, L. (1983). Organizations as shared meaning. In *Organization symbolism*. Greenwich, CT: JAI Press.

Smircich, L. (1983). Studing organisations as cultures. In G. Morgan (Ed.), *Beyond method: Strategies for social research*. Thousand Oaks, CA: Sage.

Smith-Jentsch, K. A., Salas, E., & Baker, D. P. (1996). Training team performance-related assertiveness. *Personnel Psychology, 49*, 909–936. doi:10.1111/j.1744-6570.1996.tb02454.x

Smith, P. B., Peterson, M. F., & Schwartz, S. H. (2002). Cultural values, sources of guidance, and their relevance to managerial behavior: A 47-nation study. *Journal of Cross-Cultural Psychology, 33*(2), 188–208. doi:10.1177/0022022102033002005

Stiglitz, J. E. (1988). *Economics of the public sector*. New York: Norton.

Strategor. (1997). *Zarządzanie firm: Strategie, struktury, decyzje, tożsamość*. Warszawa: PWE.

Strober, M. (2006). Habits of the mind: Challenges for multidisciplinary engagement. *Social Epistemology, 20*(3/4), 315–331. doi:10.1080/02691720600847324

Subhash, C. J. (1999). *Marketing planning and strategy* (6th ed.). South-Western Publishing Co.

Sułkowski, Ł. (2006). Tożsamość organizacyjna a kultura organizacyjna – Problemy metodologiczne. In T. Listwan (Eds.), Sukces w zarządzaniu kadrami: Kapitał ludzki w organizacjach międzynarodowych. Wrocław: Wydawnictwo Akademii Ekonomicznej im. Oskara Langego.

Sułkowski, Ł. (2009). Interpretative approach in management sciences. *Argumenta Oeconomica, 2*.

Sułkowski, Ł. (2002). *Kulturowa zmienność organizacji*. Warszawa: PWE.

Sułkowski, L. (2005). *Epistemologia w naukach o zarządzaniu*. Warszawa: PWE.

Sulzer-Azaroff, B., & Austin, J. (2000). Does BBS work? Behavior-based safety and injury reduction: A survey of evidence. *Professional Safety*, *45*, 19–24.

Surgical Checklist, W. H. O. (2010). UK pilot experience. *BMJ (Clinical Research Ed.)*, *340*, 133–135.

Tajfel, H., & Turner, J. (1979). An integrative theory of intergroup conflict. In W. G. Austin, & S. Worchel (Eds.), *The social psychology of intergroup relations*. Oxford, UK: Oxford University Press.

Teece, D. J. (2009). *Dynamic capabilities & strategic management: Organizing for innovation and growth*. Oxford, UK: Oxford University Press.

Teichler, U. (1996). Comparative higher education: Potentials and limits. *Higher Education*, *32*(4), 431–465. doi:10.1007/BF00133257

Teichler, U. (2004). The changing debate on internationalization of higher education. *Higher Education*, *48*, 5–26. doi:10.1023/B:HIGH.0000033771.69078.41

Teichler, U. (2009). Internationalization of higher education: European experiences. *Asia Pacific Education Review*, *10*(1), 93–106. doi:10.1007/s12564-009-9002-7

Teichler, U. (2010). Internationalization as a challenge for higher education. *Europe Tertiary Education and Management*, *5*(1), 5–23. doi:10.1080/13583883.1999.9966978

Thistlethwaite, J. (2012). Interprofessional education: A review of context, learning and the research agenda. *Medical Education*, *46*, 58–70. doi:10.1111/j.1365-2923.2011.04143.x PMID:22150197

Thomas, E. J., Sexton, J. B., & Helmreich, R. L. (2004). Translating teamwork behaviors from aviation to healthcare: Development of behavioral markers for neonatal resuscitation. *Quality & Safety in Health Care*, *13*, i57–i64. doi:10.1136/qshc.2004.009811 PMID:15465957

Thompson, K. R., & Luthans, F. (1990). Organisational culture: A behavioural perspective. In B. Schneider (Ed.), *Organisational climate and culture*. Oxford, UK: Jossey-Bass.

Tomusk, V. (2004). *The open world and closed societies: Essays in higher education policies in transition*. New York: Palgrave. doi:10.1057/9781403979476

Tourish, D., & Hargie, O. (2004). *Key issues in organizational communication*. Oxford, UK: Routledge Publishing House.

Tucker, A. L., & Edmondson, A. C. (2002). Managing routine exceptions: A model of nurse problem solving behavior. *Advances in Health Care Management*, *3*, 87–113. doi:10.1016/S1474-8231(02)03007-0

Turner, J. (1990). Emile Durkheim's theory of social organization. *Social Forces*, *68*, 1089–1103.

Undre, S., Sevdalis, N., & Healey, A. N. et al. (2006). Teamwork in the operating theatre: Cohesion or confusion? *Journal of Evaluation in Clinical Practice*, *12*, 182–189. doi:10.1111/j.1365-2753.2006.00614.x PMID:16579827

UNESCO Institute for Statistics. (2009). *Global education digest- Comparing education statistics across the world*. Paris: UNESCO.

UNESCO Institute for Statistics. (2012). *Global education digest data base*. Retrieved from www.uis.unesco.org/education

UNESCO. (2006). *UNESCO guidelines on intercultural education*. Paris: UNESCO.

United Nations. (n.d.a). *International covenant on civil and political rights*. New York: UN.

United Nations. (n.d.b). *International covenant on economic, social and cultural rights*. New York: UN.

United Nations. (n.d.c). *Universal declaration of human rights*. New York: UN.

Van der Wende, M. (2010). Internationalization of higher education. In *International encyclopedia of education* (Vol. 4, pp. 540–545). Oxford, UK: Elsevier. doi:10.1016/B978-0-08-044894-7.00836-8

Vandenberghe, C. (1999). Organizational culture, person-culture fit, and turnover. *Journal of Organizational Behavior*, *20*, 175–184. doi:10.1002/(SICI)1099-1379(199903)20:2<175::AID-JOB882>3.0.CO;2-E

Vandenberghe, V., & Debande, D. (2008). Refinancing Europe's higher education through deferred and income-contingent fees: An empirical assessment using Belgian, German & UK data. *European Journal of Political Economy*, *24*, 364–386. doi:10.1016/j.ejpoleco.2007.09.005

Vikis, E. A., Mihalynuk, T. V., Pratt, D. D., & Sidhu, R. S. (2008). Teaching and learning in the operating room is a two-way street: Resident perceptions. *American Journal of Surgery*, *195*(5), 594–598. doi:10.1016/j.amjsurg.2008.01.004 PMID:18367140

Volpe, C. E., Cannon-Bowers, J. A., Salas, E., & Spector, P. E. (1996). The impact of cross training on team functioning: An empirical investigation. *Human Factors*, *38*, 87–100. doi:10.1518/001872096778940741 PMID:8682521

Wailoo, A., Roberts, J., Brazier, J., & McCabe, C. (2004). Efficiency, equity, and NICE clinical guidelines. *British Medical Journal*, *328*, 536–537. doi:10.1136/bmj.328.7439.536 PMID:15001481

Waldman, D. A. (1994). Designing performance measurement systems for total quality implementation. *Journal of Organizational Change Management*, *7*(2), 31–44. doi:10.1108/09534819410056113

Wang, S., & Noe, R. A. (2010). Knowledge sharing: A review and directions for future research. *Human Resource Management Review*, *20*(2), 115–131. doi:10.1016/j.hrmr.2009.10.001

Wang, Z. T. (2004). *Knowledge system engineering*. Beijing, China: Science Press.

Warren, K. (2008). *Strategic management dynamics*. Chichester, UK: John Wiley & Sons.

Webb, D. A. (2000). E-marketplace best practices. *Industrial Distribution*, *89*(9), 122.

Weber, M. (2002). *Gospodarka i społeczeństwo: Zarys socjologii rozumiejącej*. Warszawa: PWN.

Westbrook, R. A. (1981). Sources of satisfaction with retail outlets. *J Retail*, 68-85.

Whalen, D. J. (2007). *The professional communication toolkit*. Thousand Oaks, CA: Sage Publications.

Wilkinson, T. J. (2002). Teaching teamwork to medical students: Goals, roles and power. *Medical Education*, *36*, 1089–1090. doi:10.1046/j.1365-2923.2002.13385.x PMID:12406275

Willem, A., & Scarbrough, H. (2006). Social capital and political bias in knowledge sharing: An exploratory study. *Human Relations*, *59*(10), 1343–1371. doi:10.1177/0018726706071527

Wilson, K. A., Burke, C. S., Priest, H., & Salas, E. (2005). Promoting health care safety through training high reliability teams. *Quality & Safety in Health Care*, *14*, 303–309. doi:10.1136/qshc.2004.010090 PMID:16076797

Winston, W. J. (1985). *How to write a marketing plan for health care organizations* (Vol. 2). Haworth Press, Inc.

World Medical Association. (n.d.). *Declaration of Tokyo. Author.*

Young, G., Materko, M., & Desai, K. (2000). Patient satisfaction with hospital care: Effects of demographic and institutional characteristics. *Medical Care, 38,* 325–334. doi:10.1097/00005650-200003000-00009 PMID:10718357

Yukl, G. (2006). *Leadership in organizations* (6th ed.). Upper Saddle River, NJ: Prentice Hall.

Yule, S., Flin, R., & Paterson-Brown, S. et al. (2006). Non-technical skills for surgeons in the operating room: A review of the literature. *Surgery, 139,* 140–149. doi:10.1016/j.surg.2005.06.017 PMID:16455321

Zairi, M. (1994). *Measuring performance for business result.* London: Chapman & Hall. doi:10.1007/978-94-011-1302-1

Zandbelt, L. C., Smets, E., Oort, J., Godfried, H., & de Haes, H. (2007). Medical specialists' patient-centered communication and patient reported outcomes. *Medical Care, 45*(4), 330–339. doi:10.1097/01.mlr.0000250482.07970.5f PMID:17496717

Zarębska, A. (2009). *Identyfikacja tożsamości organizacyjnej w zarządzaniu przedsiębiorstwem.* Warszawa: Difin.

Zbiegień-Maciąg, L. (1999). *Kultura w organizacji: Identyfikacja kultur znanych firm.* Warszawa: PWN.

Zeigler, K. (2008). *Getting organized at work.* New York: McGraw-Hill Printing House.

About the Contributors

Simona Vasilache, PhD, is Associate Professor of Cross-Cultural Management and Organizational Behavior at the UNESCO Department for Business Administration, Bucharest University of Economic Studies. Her research interests include: Knowledge Management, Organizational Culture, Organizational Intelligence. She has published over 10 books, 20 chapters in books, and 100 research articles nationally and internationally.

* * *

Simona Agoston is a lecturer at the Academy of Economic Studies of Bucharest, Faculty for Business Administration (German and English Department). She holds a PhD in the field of Business Administration since 2011. Her scientific interests include: social entrepreneurship, cross-cultural management, intellectual capital, European business environment. Besides international academic experience (e.g. Germany, Spain) Simona Agoston proves engagement in various other projects, especially in the field of adult education conducted in collaboration with national and international organizations.

Ramona Cantaragiu, Assistant Professor at the UNESCO Department for Business Administration, Bucharest University of Economic Studies, is completing a PhD in Business Administration and a PhD in Sociology. Her research interests include General Management, Entrepreneurship, European Business Environment.

Alina Mihaela Dima, PhD, is Professor of International Business, Head of the UNESCO Department for Business Administration, Bucharest University of Economic Studies. Her research interests include: Competition Policy, International Commercial Law, Organizational Culture. She is editor-in-chief of the *Management & Marketing* journal, editor for academic titles and co-author of over 20 books. She has co-authored over 200 chapters, articles, conference papers and reports.

Andra Florina Irinca is 24 years old and she has graduated both bachelor and master programs in Business Administration at Bucharest University of Economic Studies. At the moment she is working as a Management Consultant on projects in the public sector, having already 1 year and a half experience in European projects. So far, Florina published few articles related to Structural Instruments in Romania, within brochures and newsletters that appeared in 2013 under Ministry of European Funds. Further on, she is interested in evaluating the economic growth of Romanian regions in the period 2007-2013 and the population awareness regarding the next EU programming period.

Katja Lasch is the director of the Information Centre of German Academic Exchange Service (DAAD) in Bucharest. She finished her PhD in 2013 in the field of modern history and has completed postgraduate courses in management. Her current research interests include: higher education marketing, educational policies and entrepreneurship.

Krzysztof Leksowski (Professor DSc MD) graduated from Military Medical Academy of Lodz, Faculty of Medicine. At present the Head of the Department of General, Thoracic and Vascular Surgery Military Hospital in Bydgoszcz, and Chair of Public Health Collegium Medicum in Bydgoszcz, Nicolas Copernicus in Toruń. Experience in practical application of non-invasive surgery gained during courses, seminaries and workshops in Poland and abroad. Member of national and international science associations and editorial boards of medical journals. Author of many scientific works on the subject of the use of non-invasive techniques in various branches of surgery.

Anna Rosiek's scientific work is closely related to the author's interest in health issues and a broad range of issues aimed at improving the functioning of medical institutions. Since 2002 author worked for both the medical community and the business community. Opportunity to exchange experience in the medical and business fields with countries such as Switzerland, the United States and United Kingdom has contributed to the start of author's research in the field of Public Health. A degree of doctor of health sciences received in 2012 at the Nicolas Copernicus University in Toruń, Collegium Medicum in Bydgoszcz. Since 2012 I am a member of Society for the Promotion of Quality of Health Care in Poland.

Dina Rusnac has completed a master thesis within the Bucharest University of Economic Studies, based on an intensive research on the regime of private healthcare providers. Her insights have linked marketing and strategy studies, as well as organizational behavior aspects.

Joanna Sulkowska is a medical doctor specializing in hospital management issues. She works as an assistant professor in University of Social Sciences and the Clinical Hospital of the Medical University of Lodz. She published over 30 articles on marketing and managing medical units in Poland. Currently she is doing research on the social aspects of management problems in Polish hospitals.

Lukasz Sulkowski is a professor of economics specializing in management sciences. He works as a head of department in Institute of Public Affairs of the Jagiellonian University and director of the Academic Development Center and the Clark University in University of Social Sciences. He is a member of academic societies: Academy of Management (PM), Reseau Pays du Groupe de Vysegrad (PGV), and Polish Accreditation Committee (PAC Presidium). He published more than 300 publications on: cognitive and methodological problems of management and marketing, management, family businesses, corporate culture and human capital and management in the medical sector. He is the author of seven monographs including "Evolution in management sciences. Managers Darwin "(PWE, 2010) and" Family businesses - how to succeed in the relay generations "(Poltext, 2009). Lukasz Sulkowski is a promoter of eight doctoral dissertations defended on several institutions of higher education in Poland. He is the editor of the "Journal of Intercultural Management", as well as leading international conferences: "Congress of Intercultural Management. Intercultural Management" and "Family Business". He serves on the scientific boards and serves as a reviewer in several, well-known Polish and foreign scientific journals. He participates in the work of the scientific committees of several conferences, including: "Human Resource Management" (University of Wroclaw, Wroclaw University of Economics), "Current trends of research in the sciences Management" (Jagiellonian University), "Strategic Management practice and theory" (Wroclaw University of Economics). He has participated in several international research projects funded by the EU, State Committee for Scientific Research (KBN) and Ministry of Science and Higher Education (MNiSW). He currently directs projects: "Cultural Determinants of organizational changes in Polish hospitals" and "Integrated reporting - new communication model of performance and social responsibility as a challenge for polish companies" (National Science Centre).

Index